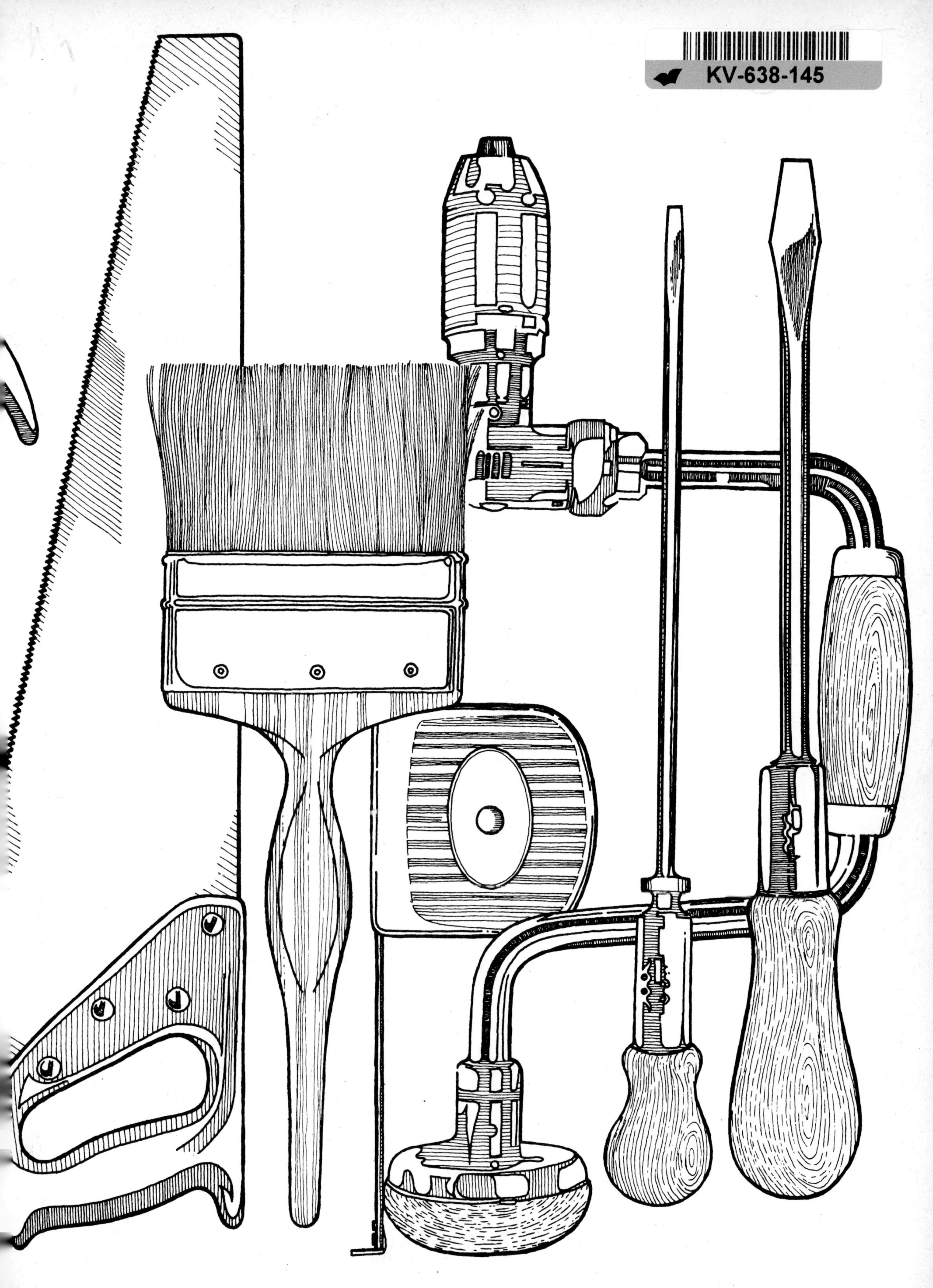

DO-IT-YOURSELF FURNITURE

edited by
HARRY BUTLER

Marshall Cavendish
London and New York

Published by Marshall Cavendish Publications Limited,
58 Old Compton Street, London W1V 5PA

This material was first published
by Marshall Cavendish Limited in *Golden Homes*
This volume first published 1975
Printed in Gt. Britain by Ben Johnson & Co Ltd

ISBN 0 85685 114 0
This volume is not to be sold in
the USA, Canada or the Philippines.

Introduction

If you want to give your home extra sparkle and style – the inexpensive way – this book has been designed with you specially in mind. There are over thirty exciting ideas for making bright new furniture which could be a handsome and practical addition to any home.

The types of furniture range from small to large – from a handy telephone table to an imposing four-poster bed. For the very ambitious, there are challenging projects including an ultra-efficient kitchen unit with oven and hob and a luxurious modern sofa/bed. For the beginner, there are easier projects – a versatile storage stool and a compact corner cupboard. Or, if you are looking for something a bit different, there's an elegant Victorian butler's tray or a project on how to install a hi-fi in a chimney breast.

The detailed instructions give full information on what materials and tools to buy and how you can best utilize them for building. Hundreds of clear and colourful diagrams also make the step-by-step instructions clear and easy to follow.

Don't miss the opportunity of sprucing up your home without spending a fortune. Try your hand at constructing any (or all!) of the appealing and attractive items in this valuable book.

Left. A modern sofa/bed, instructions on page 83.

Overleaf. An easy to build hall stand/storage unit, instructions on page 61.

Contents

A versatile storage stool

Many problems of storage involve small items which are often irritatingly difficult to fit into the general storage scheme of your home. A child's coin or stamp collection, for example, and other items, are likely to get lost in a large cupboard. This storage stool provides a safe place for them.

The stool is also perfect for many of the range of small modern pianos that are on the market. If you wish to use it as a piano stool, make it in the same timber that is used to veneer the piano—in this case sapele is used.

General construction

The construction of the storage stool is quite simple. It consists of four sides, or rails, housed together in a box shape. Legs are fixed to the two short sides, or rails, of the box. The base of the box is a ½in. or 13mm plywood panel. The lifting lid of the stool consists of two plywood panels. One panel is covered with foam and upholstered and then screwed to the other, lower, panel. This panel is hinged to the back rail with concealed cabinet hinges.

The frame

The frame of the storage stool consists of four sides, or rails—a front and back rail and two side rails. The front and back rails have a housing cut in them to take the side rails. The legs of the stool are glued and screwed to the ends of the side rails and in the finished construction the outer wide surface of the legs is set back ⅛in (3mm) from the ends of the front and back rails. The tops of the side rails and legs are covered with strips of timber, referred to as handles.

The first step is to make the legs. Cut the timber for the legs a little overlength and place all four pieces together in a vice. Mark the exact length of the legs—17in. (432mm)—on the timbers and square lines through these points with a try square. Take the legs out of the vice and continue the squared lines right round the timbers.

Now cut the timber for the front and back rails overlength, put them in a vice and mark out the finished length of 21¾in. (546mm). From these lines, down towards the centre of the timber, mark a distance of 1in. (25mm). Then mark inwards a further ¾in. (19mm), or the exact thickness of the timber you are using for the side rails. This marks the position of the housings shown in Fig.3.

Left. This beautiful stool provides safe storage for small items—such as a child's stamp collection—that are likely to get lost in a large storage unit.

Take the front and back rails out of the vice and square lines right round the timber at the points which mark the finished length of these pieces. Square a line through the points which mark the position of the housings, on the inner wide surface of the rails only. With a marking gauge set to $\frac{1}{16}$in. (4.7mm), mark the depth of the housings on the narrow edge of the timber, within the area of the lines marking the housing.

With the two short rails held together in a vice, mark them to a length of 12⅝in. (321mm). Take them from the vice and continue the lines right round the timber. Mark out the handles in the same way.

Now cut the side rails, the front and back rails, the legs and the handles to length. Use a tenon saw for this, cutting down the marked lines. With a saw and chisel, cut out the housings in the front and back rails. Further details on this process can be obtained from a do-it-yourself manual.

Polishing the components

The outer surfaces of the components are polished before they are glued together with a woodworking adhesive. Polishing the components before you glue them means that you don't have to deal with awkward corners. It also enables you to lift surplus glue off the surface of the timber when the glue has dried. Removing dried excess glue from bare timber without damaging the surface is almost impossible.

To finish the components, first plane all the pieces to a smooth finish with a finely set smoothing plane. If the grain of the timber is rather wild and tears easily, a cabinet scraper will produce a smooth finish. Trail assemble the components and flush off the top and bottom edges of the box construction.

Smooth all the components with fine glasspaper. Then mark the contact surfaces clearly—these are the surfaces that will be coated with adhesive later. Make sure that these surfaces remain free from polish or you won't be able to make a good glued joint between the components.

Coat all the outer surfaces—not the contact surfaces—with a cellulose sanding sealer. Alternatively, apply a thin coating of polyurethane varnish, mixed 50/50 with turpentine substitute. Glasspaper the surfaces when the coating has dried and wax polish them.

Assembly

With a woodworking adhesive, glue the handles onto the side rails (see Fig.4) and cramp them. Let the adhesive dry. Glue and screw the legs to the side rails, as shown in Fig.4. Make sure that the distances X and Y, marked on the diagram, are the same. Check that the $\frac{3}{16}$in. (4.7mm) overlap where the side rail projects into the housing, is even all the way down the rail. Fig.3 shows this. Let the glue jointing the side rails to the legs dry.

Next, trail assemble the side rail, legs and handle and the front and back rail. Check that they fit together well. Take the components apart, apply adhesive and re-assemble them. Cramp the assembly and measure the diagonals to check that the assembly is square.

When the adhesive has dried, plane off any slight overlap at the ends of the side rails or on the handles. Be careful when planing end grain as you can easily damage the corners of the timber. A good DIY manual can provide you with different methods for planing and ending grain. Polish the end grain.

The lid

The lid of the storage stool consists of a plywood panel, hinged to the stool frame. Sapele edging strip is glued to the edges of this panel. A second plywood panel is covered with foam and fabric or leather. This is then screwed to the first panel, through its bottom surface.

Cut the two panels that make the lid to size. Take the lower panel and square the edges. Glue a length of ¼in. (6mm) sapele edging strip to the short sides of the panel. When the adhesive dries, trim the edging to the required size. Then apply edging strip to the two long edges. The sizes of the edging strips used are shown in Fig.2. Clean up and polish the edging strip when the glue has dried.

The next step is to fit concealed cabinet hinges to the bottom panel of the lid and to the back of the stool. The hinges used are 'Woodfit' hinges, shown in Fig.1. You will need a 35mm 'Shaper Craft' boring bit to fit these hinges. Full instructions on fitting these hinges are supplied by the manufacturer.

The top panel of the lid can now be upholstered—it was cut to size earlier. A rebate is cut round this panel into the bottom surface to take the turn-in of the material under the seat. Cut the rebate ⅝in. (16mm) deep with a rebate

Fig.1. The lid of the stool is fixed to the back rail of the stool with concealed cabinet hinges. You will need a 'Shaper Craft' boring bit to fit these hinges.

Fig. 2

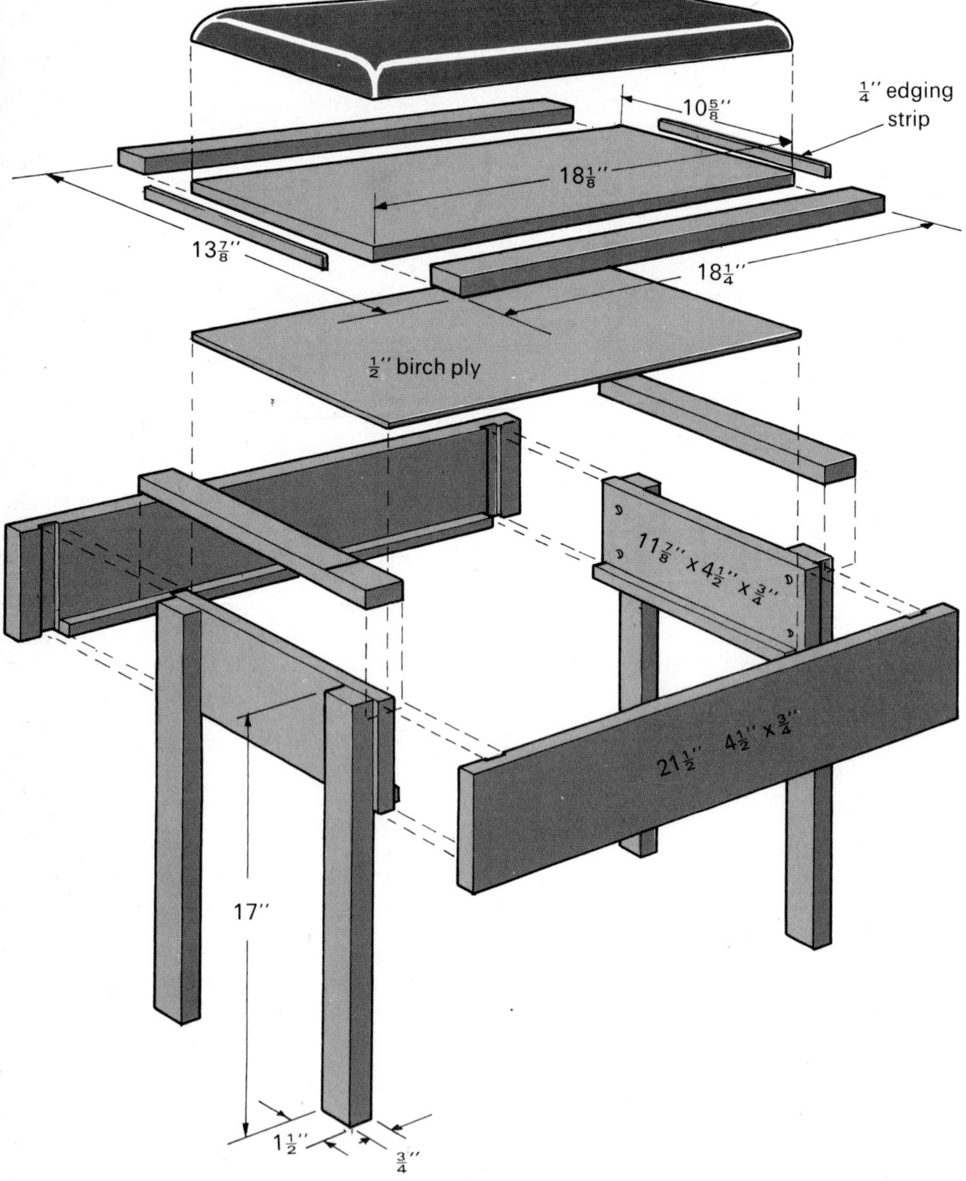

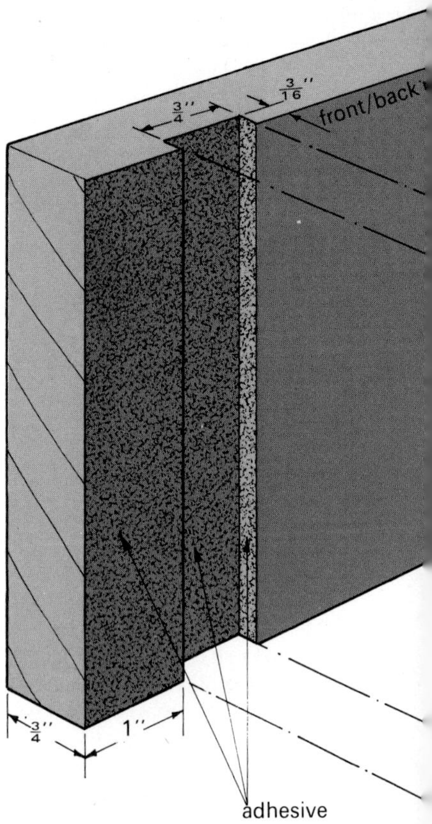

TRI-ART

plane, fitted with a ⅛in. (3mm) blade.

The panel is covered with a 1in. or 25mm layer of reconstituted foam—this gives a fairly firm finish. The foam is then covered with material of your choice. Leather, as shown on the stool in the photograph, gives an opulent look but any other hardwearing material will do. The material is laid over the foam, pleated at the corners and turned under, where it is tacked with ⅜ in. (9·5mm) upholsterers' tacks. It is important to tack the covering material securely as it will undergo a good deal of stress.

Drill holes through the lower panel near the corners for ¾in. (19mm) No.6 countersunk screws. Drill holes in the underside of the upholstered panel also. Screw the upholstered panel to the lower panel.

The next step is to cover the underside of the lid with a material that matches the top. It can be the same material as the top or a cheaper sort—this surface does not incur wear. Fix the material with gimp pins.

The base of the stool

The final step in making the stool is to fit a base panel near the bottom edges of the four rails. To do this, screw lengths of ½in. x ½in. (13mm x 13mm) timber to the inner surface of the rails. Position them so that one edge is flush with the bottom edge of the rails. The plywood panel, the dimensions of which are shown in Fig.2., is simply pinned to these supports. Then cover the panel with a material that matches that used on the lid.

Polish the stool with wax polish and fit metal domes of silence to the leg ends. You now have an attractive piece of furniture that gives you a safe place to store treasured possessions.

Fig.2. *An exploded view of the storage stool showing all the necessary dimensions.*
Fig.3. *A housing is cut into the back and front long rails of the storage stool to accommodate the ends of the short rails.*
Fig.4. *The arrangement of the short rails, the legs and the handles of the storage stool. Use a woodworking adhesive to glue these pieces together. Ensure that the distances marked X and Y are equal so that the legs are perfectly parallel.*
Fig.5. *The lid of the storage stool. The top diagram shows the sapele edging strip and the two plywood panels that make up the lid. The panels are screwed together after the top panel has been upholstered. The lower diagram shows a corner detail of the upholstered lid with the material covering the foam layer turned under and pinned to the lower panel.*

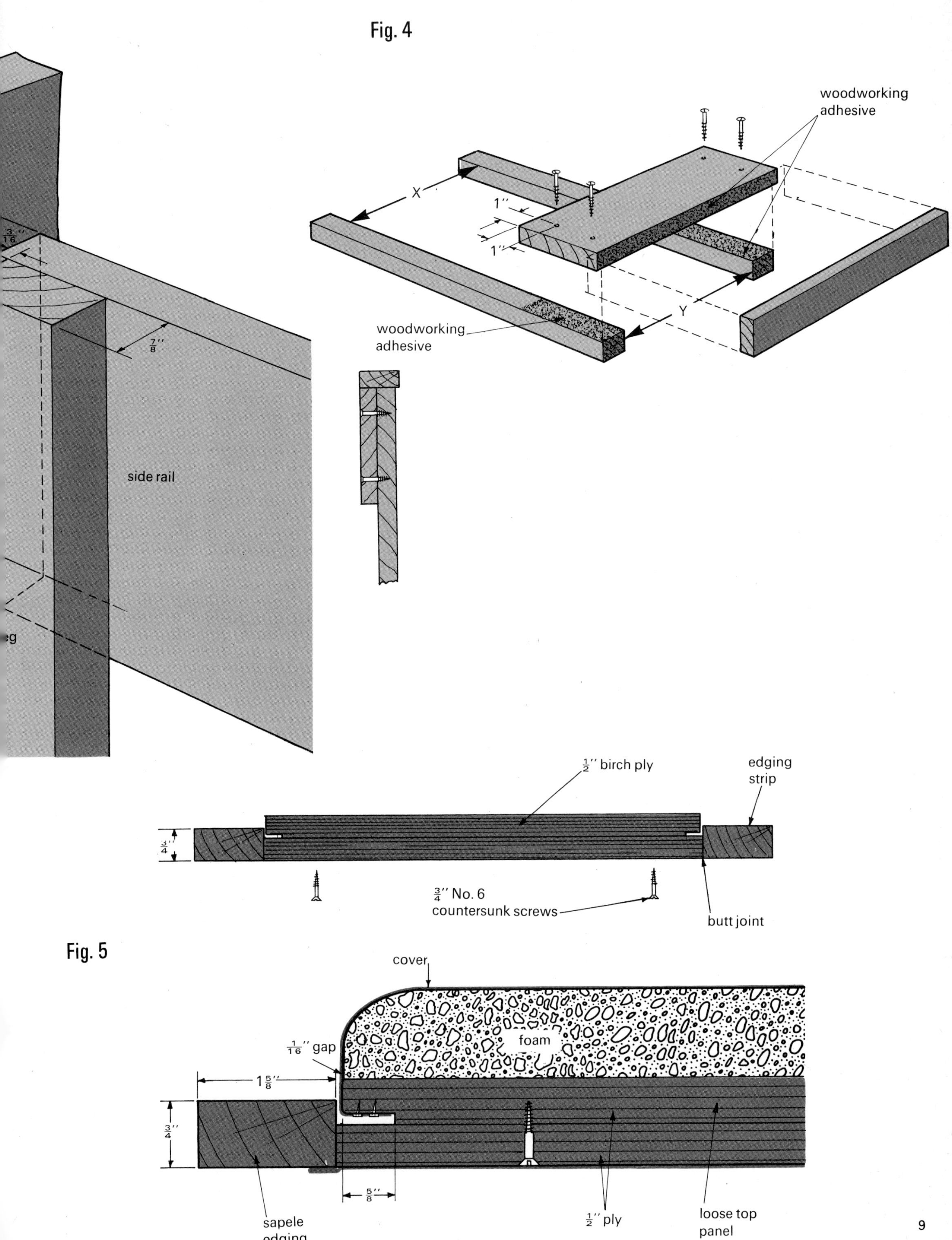

Fig. 4
woodworking
adhesive
X
1″
1″
Y
woodworking
adhesive
3/16″
7/8″
side rail
eg
½″ birch ply
edging
strip
¾″
¾″ No. 6
countersunk screws
butt joint
Fig. 5
cover
foam
1/16″ gap
1⅝″
¾″
⅝″
sapele
edging
strip
½″ ply
loose top
panel

Go anywhere storage boxes

Today's living has created the need for a wide range of storage units, particularly units which have other uses as well and which are decorative as well as functional. Here is a modular system built on the use of boxes of a standard size which can be assembled in various combinations, positions and colours.

The system is based on a single unit with exterior measurements 15½in. x 15½in. x 11½in. (394mm x 394mm x 292mm). The top, bottom and sides are constructed of ½in. (13mm) plywood and the back of ⅛in. (3mm) hardboard.

The principle of the design is based on the grouping of these boxes into various combinations and designs, as wall units, wall dividers, island pieces and so on. They can be used in any room in the house, or in the workshop or garage. Also, they have a wide number of commercial uses—as office equipment, retail store shelving and counters, wall storage units, archives, window displays, exhibition fixtures, etc.

In the home they can be used to house books, magazines, games, toys, ornaments, radio, TV and hi-fi units and speakers, wine bottles, and so on. The combinations are limitless—or limited only by your own ingenuity and artistic sense.

Of course, as illustrated here, you are not limited by the size of the unit as long as you stick to multiples of the overall dimensions of the basic box. In other words, you could make a double unit by doubling the height. The only standard dimensions you must stay with is the front-to-rear depth. The main point to remember when you construct a double unit is that it is the *outside* measurements which count, so that they will fit in exactly with the dimensions of the other units with which it is grouped.

Just think what you could do with this very neat range of boxes, as shelves and drawers and cabinets for putting things into, as drawers fixed to walls making shelves in bathrooms and kitchens; they really do have a thousand uses around the house. Here are some suggestions:

Bedside table

A neat and functional bedside table can be made simply by joining two units together. One could have shelves for books, medicines, etc., and one could have sliding doors. A reading lamp could stand on its surface.

Filing cabinet

Three boxes attached, with shelves or divisions according to your requirements. This would be ideal in the office or study for housing account books, correspondence files, stationery, confidential documents. The beauty about these units is that they can be extended to suit your needs, e.g., four boxes as upright cabinet, eight boxes as four-tiered double unit; a complete wall of boxes for papers and books.

Coffee table

Four boxes grouped in a tight rectangle beside a divan in the corner of the room, a tasteful reading lamp standing in the centre of the unit, with ashtrays and cigarette box or ornament. The shelves in the two boxes facing outwards can hold books and magazines.

Wall divider

A grouping of double and single units can make an attractive division separating the dining and living areas of a large room. The blank areas on one side of the divider indicate that functional recesses can be used on the other side. For instance, shelf areas on the living room side can be used for books, radio, hi-fi, or ornaments, while those on the dining room side can be used as a china cabinet, wine-bottle storage etc. Double boxes could have glass sliding doors. Boxes could be left out of the wall to give an attractive see-through effect to the wall divider.

Desk

Made of four boxes, two on each side, with shelves and sliding doors; a table-top of ⅝in. (16mm) plywood or chipboard (with veneer edge trim) rests on top of the two top boxes. All units are joined by screws or simply glued.

Divan and storage unit

In this case five double-sized weight-holding boxes are made of heavier material, such as ¾in. (19mm) ply. The exterior dimensions of these boxes is identical with those of the standard units. Two standard boxes are used for paperbacks and books, radio, etc. A covered foam-rubber mattress is placed on top of the heavier boxes, which are double the front-to-rear depth of the standard boxes.

Construction

To make the single basic unit, without doors or shelves, cut the two end members 15½in. x 11½in. x ½in. (394mm x 292mm x 13mm) and the top and bottom members 15¼in. x 11½in. x ½in. (388mm x 292mm x 13mm) from ½in. (13mm) thick birch plywood.

Plywood is a particularly good choice because

***Right.** This picture shows two of the small standard modular units with one double-unit with sliding doors, assembled as an attractive table storage unit for books, knick-knacks and personal belongings.*

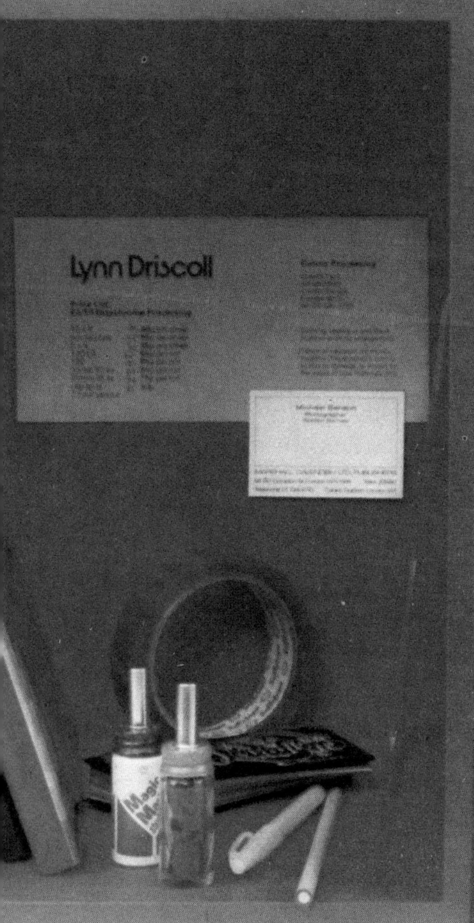
Lynn Driscoll

it is a precision-made factory-produced product and you can rely on the accuracy of its thickness. Birch ply is a good choice. It has a plain light-coloured surface that will take a good polish and will give a good flat finish when painted.

Take care to check that the sheet you buy is flat, that the edges (or at least two adjacent ones) are sound, that the veneers of ply which make up the sheet are firmly stuck together and that no knots have fallen out. Remember that plywood should be stored flat and not on edge, otherwise it will twist and the edge may be damaged.

Because each unit must be identical with the others in every detail, it might be as well to set up a jig arrangement on your bench to ensure that all lengths of top and bottom members are identical, and that all lengths of side members are identical.

Rebate the ends of both end members across the narrow width $\frac{1}{2}$in. x $\frac{3}{8}$in. (13mm x 10mm) to take the top and bottom members. Since the top and bottom members are $\frac{1}{4}$in. (6mm) shorter than the side members, the $\frac{1}{8}$in. (3mm) added at each end makes the four sides of the box identical.

Again, it could be a good idea to set up a jig to ensure that the rebates are executed with precision accuracy. Rebates may be cut with a router (see photo), circular saw or hand tenon saw.

Now rebate the long rear edge of all plywood members $\frac{1}{8}$in. x $\frac{3}{8}$in. (3mm x 10mm) to take the hardboard panel. Cut the panel of $\frac{1}{8}$in. hardboard 15$\frac{1}{4}$in. x 15$\frac{1}{4}$in. x $\frac{1}{8}$in. (388mm x 388mm x 3mm).

To assemble the unit, pin and glue the top and bottom members to the end members, fitting the top and bottom members into the rebates. Use 1$\frac{1}{2}$in. (38mm) panel pins. See Fig.2.

Fit the hardboard panel into the all round rebate of the end and top and bottom panel rear edges. Pin and glue into position, using $\frac{3}{4}$in. (19mm) panel pins. Punch all nails and fill the holes with plastic wood. Glasspaper to a fine finish and paint or polish according to your requirements.

Bear in mind that you should decide on the specific use of each unit before you complete its assembly. One important reason for this is that if, for instance, sliding doors are to be fitted, it will be necessary to check the size of available plastic sliding track and to rebate the top and bottom edges accordingly (see Fig.3 and drawing).

The sliding channel is placed in position after the main assembly has been carried out. Also

Fig.2. *Rebating rear edges of panels may be done with an electric router.*
Fig.3. *Assemble unit by nailing with 1$\frac{1}{2}$in. panel pins and glueing top and bottom members to end member with contact adhesive.*

Fig.4. *Pin and glue hardboard back in position, recessed into the rebates all round.*
Fig.5. *Push doors into the top track then the lower before dropping into position; note that the top track is deeper than the bottom.*

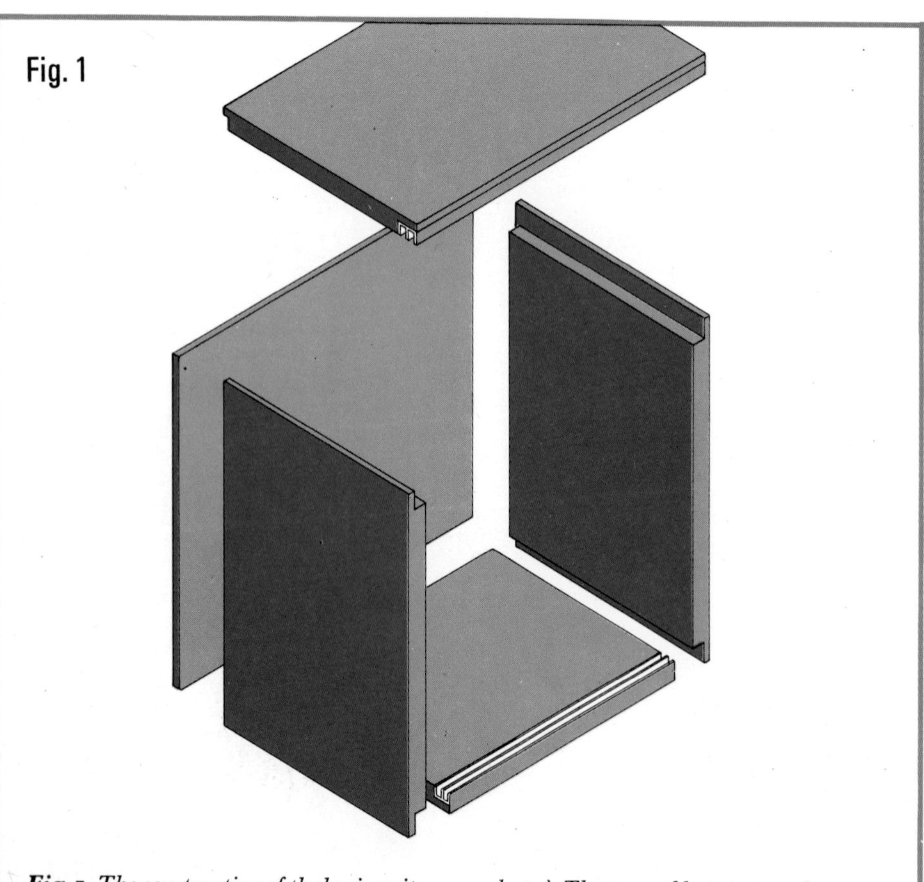

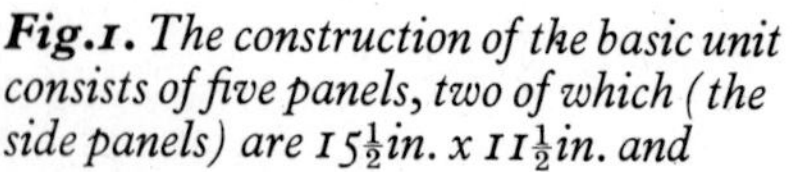

Fig.1. *The construction of the basic unit consists of five panels, two of which (the side panels) are 15$\frac{1}{2}$in. x 11$\frac{1}{2}$in. and rebated. The top and bottom panels are 15$\frac{1}{4}$in. x 11$\frac{1}{2}$in. and are rebated to take the back panels and sliding channel.*

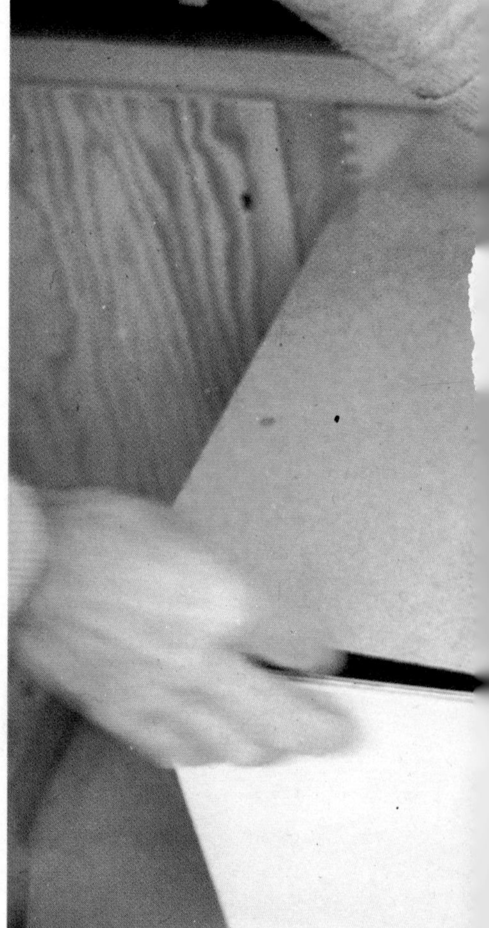

2

3

4

5

HARRY BUTLER

remember that doors must be cut to suit available plastic track.

Double unit

For the double unit, cut the two end members $15\frac{1}{2}$in. x $11\frac{1}{2}$in. x $\frac{1}{2}$in. (394mm x 292mm x 13mm) and the top and bottom members $30\frac{3}{4}$in. x $11\frac{1}{2}$in. x $\frac{1}{2}$in. (780mm x 292mm x 13mm). Rebate the ends of both end members across the narrow width $\frac{1}{2}$in. x $\frac{3}{8}$in. (13mm x 10mm) to take the top and bottom members. Now rebate the long rear edges of all plywood members $\frac{1}{8}$in. x $\frac{3}{8}$in. (3mm x 10mm) to take the hardboard panel. Cut the panel of $\frac{1}{8}$in. (3mm) hardboard $30\frac{3}{4}$in. x $15\frac{1}{4}$in. x $\frac{1}{8}$in. (780mm x 388mm x 3mm).

To assemble the unit, pin and glue the top and bottom members to the end members, fitting the top and bottom members into the rebates. Use $1\frac{1}{2}$in. (38mm) panel pins.

Fit the hardboard panel into the all round rebate of the end of top and bottom panel rear edges. Pin and glue into position, using $\frac{3}{4}$in. (19mm) panel pins. Punch all nails and fill the holes with plastic wood. Glasspaper to a fine finish and paint or polish according to your requirements.

The above instructions are for a standard basic unit without drawers, shelves or sliding doors. Should you decide to fit sliding doors to this double unit (as illustrated), it will be necessary to check the size and availability of plastic sliding track and to rebate the top and bottom edges before assembly.

Cut the rebates to fit the track along the top and bottom members.

In this particular example the doors have been cut from $\frac{1}{8}$in. (3mm) hardboard $14\frac{7}{8}$in. x $15\frac{1}{4}$in. x $\frac{1}{8}$in. (379mm x 388mm x 3mm). Assemble the basic unit, then glue the plastic sliding channel into position. The top track is deeper than the bottom. This allows the door to be pushed up intó the top track and then over the lower before being dropped into position (see Fig.5).

Shelves

Shelves should be constructed of the same material as the top, bottom and side members. Cut all shelves and partitions $14\frac{1}{2}$in. x $11\frac{3}{8}$in. x $\frac{1}{2}$in. (368mm x 289mm x 13mm) but check dimensions physically before cutting. Mark positions carefully. Glasspaper to obtain a good accurate fit without forcing, as forcing will bow out the side and throw the unit's sides out of alignment. Note the four standard designs in Fig.6—

a) box without shelves;

b) box with one division; note that it can be used as a shelf or division;

c) box with two divisions or shelves;

d) box with five divisions or shelves.

Note that where sliding doors are to be used, the divisions would be $\frac{1}{2}$in. (13mm) narrower, or more, according to the width of the plastic track.

Fig.6. The principle of the design is based on the grouping of the boxes into various combinations and designs, as wall units, wall dividers, and so on. Also, they have a wide number of commercial uses, as shown below.

Cutting list Single unit

Material	Imperial	Metric
Plywood		
2 panels	$15\frac{1}{2}$ x $11\frac{1}{2}$ x $\frac{1}{2}$	394 x 292 x 13
2 panels	$15\frac{1}{4}$ x $11\frac{1}{2}$ x $\frac{1}{2}$	388 x 292 x 13
Hardboard		
1 panel	$15\frac{1}{4}$ x $15\frac{1}{4}$ x $\frac{1}{8}$	388 x 388 x 3

Cutting list Double unit

Material	Imperial	Metric
2 panels	$15\frac{1}{2}$ x $11\frac{1}{2}$ x $\frac{1}{2}$	394 x 292 x 13
2 panels	$30\frac{3}{4}$ x $11\frac{1}{2}$ x $\frac{1}{2}$	780 x 292 x 13
Hardboard		
1 panel	$30\frac{3}{4}$ x $15\frac{1}{4}$ x $\frac{1}{8}$	780 x 388 x 3
2 panels	$14\frac{7}{8}$ x $15\frac{1}{4}$ x $\frac{1}{8}$	379 x 388 x 3
Plastic door track		
Top track	$30\frac{3}{4}$	780
Bottom track	$30\frac{3}{4}$	780

You will also need:
$1\frac{1}{2}$in. (38mm) panel pins; $\frac{3}{4}$in. (19mm) panel pins; woodworking adhesive; glasspaper, paint, plastic wood.

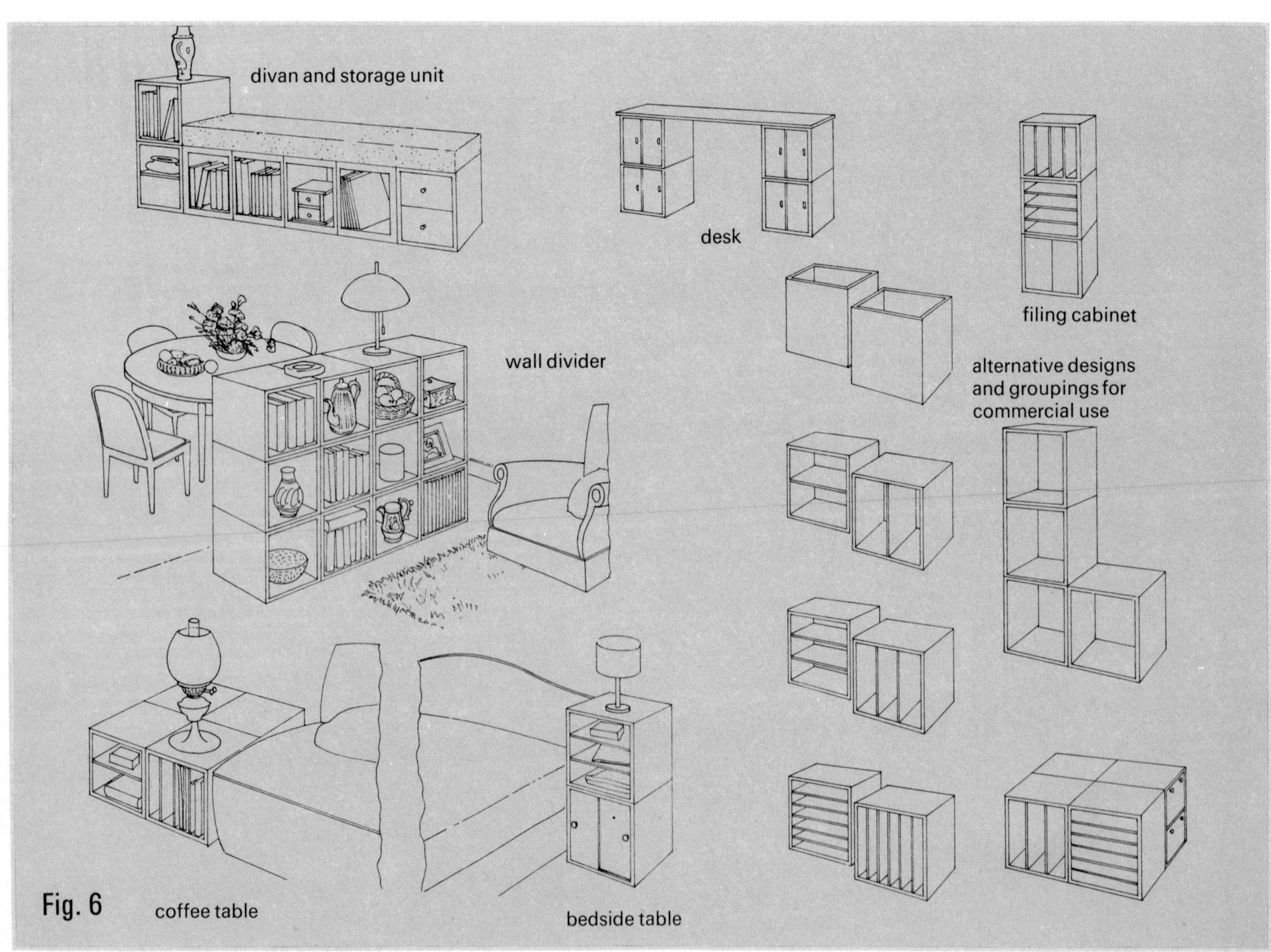

Fig. 6

A slot-together armchair

How to make a slot-together armchair

Four things make this chair a really attractive piece of furniture. The design is stylishly modern, it can be built in a day by even a comparatively inexperienced carpenter and, above all, it is supremely comfortable. Apart from these features it can be taken apart when not in use—a real asset in a home where space is at a premium.

A continuing trend in modern furniture design has been the sacrificing of comfort for economy and space. While agreeing that those huge Victorian armchairs were really luxurious, designers today would argue that they would be very much out of place in a modern house, as well as being inordinately expensive. So, designers concentrate on producing chairs which can easily be mass produced and which fit contemporary tastes. Unfortunately of course, the result of such thinking is that most chairs manufactured now tend to merely ornament a room without being very comfortable.

Perhaps the greatest limitation on furniture design is the smallness of modern houses. To be comfortable, a chair must not only be well designed, constructed and padded, but also it must be fairly large. As few people can afford the space for a large suite of furniture, armchairs become increasingly smaller.

One answer to the problem, which has been developed over the last few years, is furniture which can easily and quickly be stowed away when not in use. Nowadays it is possible to buy inflatable chairs, and more conventional chairs which can be assembled or dismantled in a matter of seconds. It is on this latter principle that the knock-down chair has been designed.

This chair has a very simple construction. It consists simply of four panels which slot together to give a stable assembly. Despite its simplicity, its lines are as stylish as any manufactured chair and will complement any living room.

Materials

Wood is used for the basic frame. Pine or some other softwood is suitable, but a satisfactory (and cheaper) alternative is $\frac{5}{8}$in. (16mm) plywood. As with most manufactured materials, there are different grades of plywood and you should choose a high quality type, such as Finnish birch, which takes a very good painted finish on both surfaces.

It is possible to have cushions made up for you by professionals, but they are easy to make yourself from foam rubber and the covering of your choice.

Cutting out

Cut out all the pieces to the sizes given in the cutting list, taking care that the two side panels match exactly. These pieces now have to be cut to the patterns in Fig.1 and, as this work represents the major part of the construction processes, great care should be taken.

First take the two side panels and cut out the angled rear edge. To do this accurately, mark a line 1in. (25mm) from the rear edge, then draw a line diagonally from opposite corners. Provided your two side panels match exactly in size, you can clamp them together and cut along the diagonal line to give a matching pair.

NIGEL MESSETT

Now cut the slots in the side panels. There are two on each : one houses the back panel and the other houses the seat panel. Make the slot for the seat panel first. This slot, which is $\frac{5}{8}$in. (16mm) wide, runs at an angle, from a point about halfway down the front edge, to a point 14$\frac{1}{2}$in. (368mm) from the front edge. Fig.1 shows the exact location and size of this slot. To mark it in exactly, first draw a point on the front, short edge, 10$\frac{1}{2}$in. (267mm) from the top long edge. With a protractor set at 86° mark in the angle at which the seat panel meets the front edge of the side panel, as shown in Fig.1. Then use the two marked points to draw in a line extending 14$\frac{1}{2}$in. (368mm) from the front short edge of the side panel. This line marks the proposed location of the upper surface of the seat panel. To mark out the correct width of the slot, draw another point $\frac{5}{8}$in. (16mm) from that already marked on the front short edge of the side panel and, with the aid of a protractor, draw another line parallel to the first and $\frac{5}{8}$in. (16mm) from it.

Use a tenon saw to cut the slot, following the rules on correct sawing techniques given in most DIY manuals. If you cut exactly to the marked lines, you will make the slot slightly too wide. Instead, position the saw so that one face is just inside and parallel to the line. When you have cut down the lines, cut out the short edge of the slot with a jig saw or chisel.

Provided both side panels have been cut to exactly the same size, there is no reason why you should not clamp them together with all edges flush and cut out paired slots at the same time.

Now mark and cut out the slots which house the back panel. These are 6$\frac{1}{2}$in. (165mm) long, $\frac{5}{8}$in. (13mm) wide, and run at an angle of 82° to the top edges of the side panels, as shown in Fig.1. Use the methods detailed above to mark and cut them accurately.

The seat panel has two slots cut in it, corresponding to those cut in the front edge of the side panels. Each slot is located 2$\frac{1}{2}$in. (64mm) from, and parallel to the short sides, and is

Left. *Big enough to curl up on, this very comfortable chair can be taken apart in a few moments and stored in a small space.*

14½in. (368mm) in length.

Two slots corresponding to those cut in the top edges of the side panels are made in the back panel. They are the same length—6½in. (165mm) and are located 2½in. (64mm) from, and parallel to, the short sides.

Finishing and assembly

Before assembling or sanding the panels, round off the corners of the top edges of the back and side panels and the front edge of the seat panel with a jig saw. If desired, you can round off all the edges (except the bottom edges of the side panels) with a spokeshave. Or you can simply remove the sharp edges with glasspaper.

Smooth all the panels, using coarse then fine glasspaper, taking particular care to ensure that no irregularities are left on the surfaces of the slots. Once you have achieved a smooth, plane finish, trial assemble the chair, having first lubricated the slots by rubbing candle grease in them. If you have cut out the slots correctly, all the panels should fit together easily to give a stable unit. If any slot has been cut undersize, do not force the panel home, but dismantle it and trim the offending slot to size.

Before painting the chair, first apply strips of gummed paper ⅝in. (16mm) wide on a line extending from each slot. This helps prevent the panels sticking when the chair has been painted. Apply a good quality undercoat, followed by two coats of hard wearing polyurethane gloss in the colour of your choice. When the paint has dried, assemble the chair.

The cushions

Nowadays, with the wide range of foam rubber paddings available, it is a simple job to make your own cushions. You can either buy foam in varying hardnesses and densities, or you can cut up an old, unwanted foam mattress. Polyether foam with a minimum density of 1.5 lb per cu ft is most suitable, and is available in different textures. The ideal thickness for a chair of this type is between 4in.-6in. (100mm-150mm).

Cut out two foam bases to the sizes given in the cutting list, using a fine-toothed hacksaw, a sharp cook's knife or an electric carving knife.

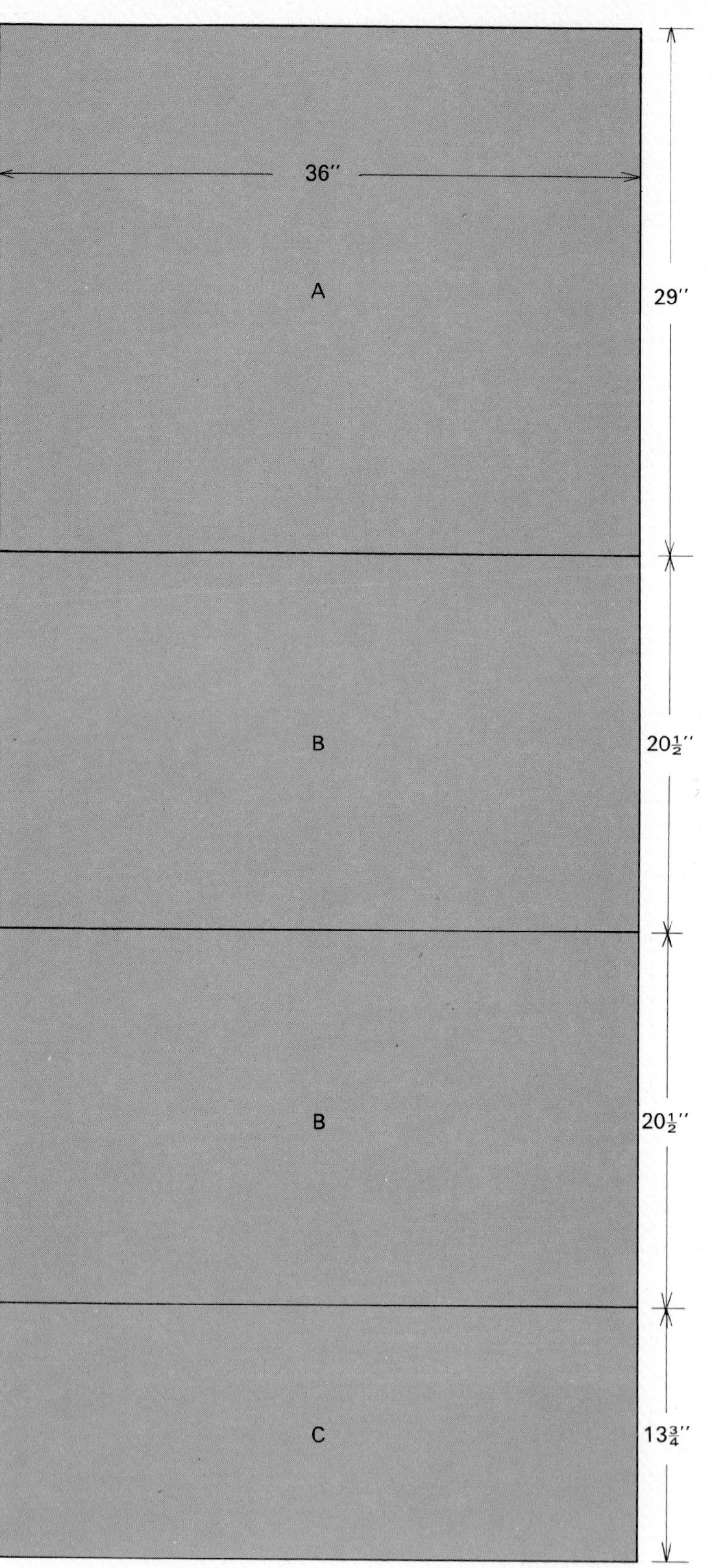

Fig.1. *All the panels can be cut from a single sheet of birch plywood, as shown on the left. The slot system is a simple but effective method of construction.*

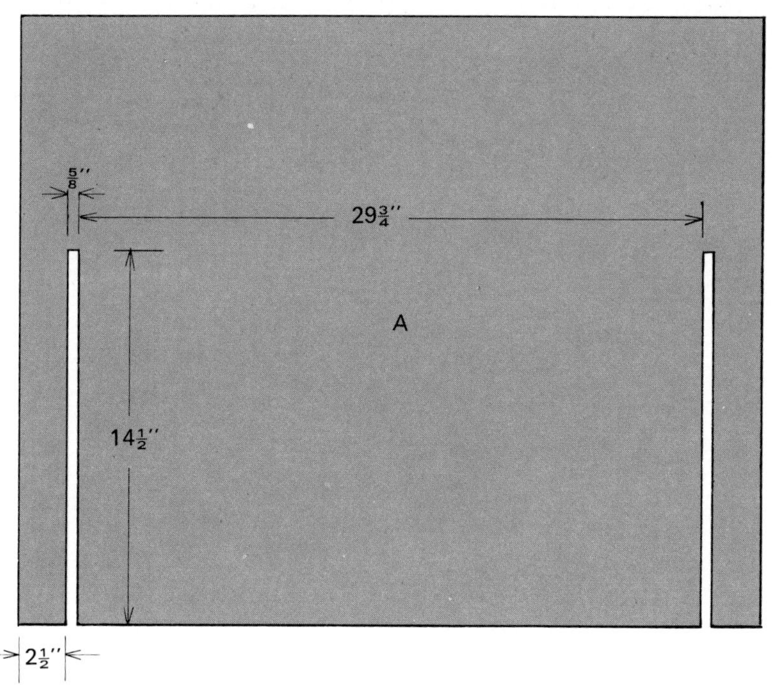

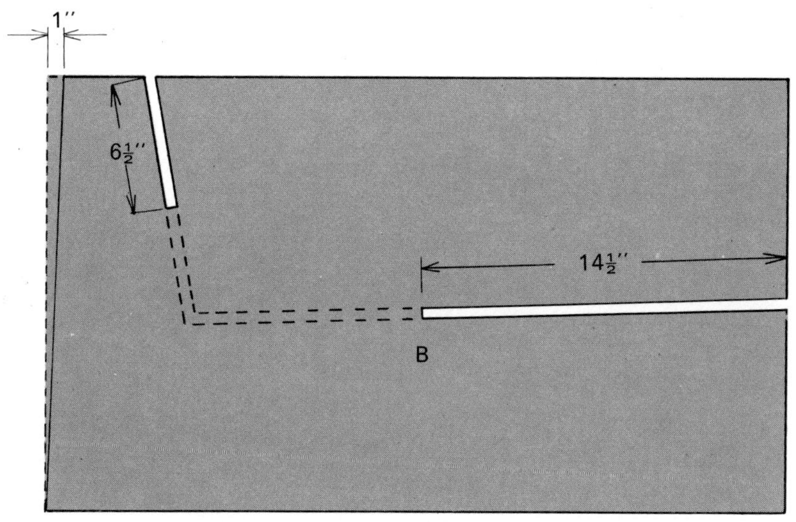

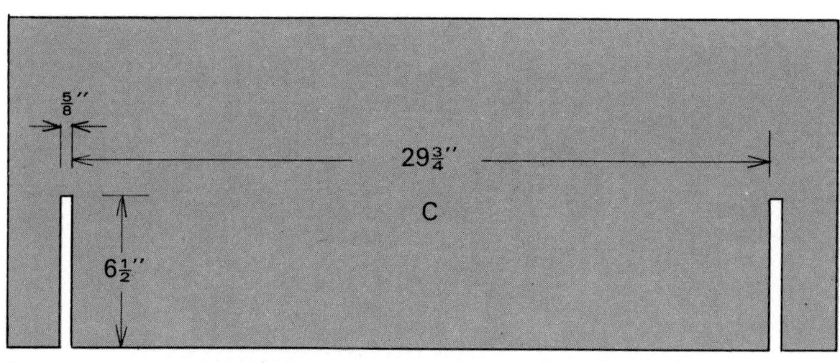

You can cover them with a washable material to match both the colour of the frame and your overall decor.

If the foam base is latex rather than polyether, it is advisable to make a non-removable inner cover from calico. This will act as a barrier for any fragments that, inevitably with this material, break loose. Cut both the inner and outer coverings slightly undersize, so that when they are fitted they compress the foam slightly and so prevent any wrinkles forming.

There are several different methods of making up covers and if you decide to tackle one of them, a good upholstery or sewing magazine should be consulted.

Once you have made up the cushions and experienced how comfortable the chair is, you might consider making a matched suite to the same design. You can easily adapt the design to produce a couch which can double as a bed for the unexpected guest. The only structural modification required to make such a couch would be the addition of some form of full length batten to support the length of the seat panel. A whole suite made to this design would not only be inexpensive and easy to make, it would also suit perfectly a rather low room, which can look cramped when fitted with conventional furniture. You would have little difficulty in finding matching furniture, such as casual tables, and the resulting decor would strike a bold contemporary note while being very comfortable.

CUTTING LIST

Finnish Birch Plywood	imperial	metric
2 side panels	36 x 20½ x ⅝	914 x 521 x 16
1 seat panel	36 x 29 x ⅝	914 x 736 x 16
1 back panel	36 x 13¾ x ⅝	914 x 349 x 16
You will also need:		
1 seat cushion	30 x 28½ x 4	762 x 724 x 102
1 back cushion	30 x 11 x 4	762 x 279 x 102

Material to cover. Tenon saw. Keyhole saw. ⅝in. (16mm) chisel. Jigsaw. Spokeshave. Sandpaper. Gummed paper. Undercoat. Polyurethane gloss.

All imperial measurements in inches, all metric measurements in millimetres.

A space-saving folding table

Foldaway tables have long been a favourite carpentry exercise for the average home handyman: with their particular combination of compact utility and simplicity of construction, it is not difficult to understand why. The kitchen, the children's bedrooms, and the den are all candidates for the installation of a foldaway table or desk—in fact, any room that needs an extra working surface, perhaps only from time to time, may be nicely complemented by the addition of one.

By scaling the design up or down you can adapt the foldaway to your specific situation and requirements. Within the limits of the materials and construction techniques used, you do have quite a good deal of scope to change not only the size but also the concept of the finished article. Various suggestions in this respect are included in a later section of this chapter.

Materials and accessories

The foldaway essentially consists of three rectangular pieces of plywood, joined together with piano hinges and a drop flap stay. The piece fixed to the wall is further provided with stripping, which can be made from off-cuts of the plywood, so that the whole table will fold back into a compact, visually neat wall hanging.

You will also need four 2in. (50mm) Number 6 screws and a selection of small nails. The former are to fix the back piece to the wall, but if you have some other method of fixing in mind you will not require them. The nails are for attaching the stripping (see Fig.2) to the sides of the wall piece—remember that (if you think there is any danger of splitting the plywood as you drive them through the stripping) slightly blunted nails may be called for.

The drop flap stay, as shown in Fig.1, should have an arm length of around 3½in. (88mm). It is quite possible that the stay, as supplied, will be made so that the screw attachments at either end are facing in opposite directions, which is not suitable here. In this case, you simply take out the rivet at one end and turn the attachment to face in the same direction as the other.

The catch at the top that holds the folded table in can be made in many ways—the pattern showed in Fig.2 is a very simple type, but is just as effective as a more elaborate hook-and-eye clasp, or something along the lines of a spring-loaded catch fitted to the top stripping.

The foldaway can be finished in paint, varnish, or even covered with a fabric that will harmonize with the room it is built for. Since the leg flap is going to be visible whenever the table is in the folded position, it is obviously this surface that should receive the most attention when the decorative angle is considered. The finish naturally depends on how the end product is to be used—for example, if it is to go in a youngster's room, a dart board, perhaps backed by a corkboard sheeting as a protection for the wood, could be screwed into the leg flap. Alternatively, a thin blackboard surface can be fixed to this flap, to serve either as a daily bulletin board if the table is, say, used as an ironing board/general extra kitchen working surface, or just for doodling if it is in a child's room. Another idea that might appeal is to inlay (or paint) a chess board on the table flap.

Construction and cutting

A piece of standard ⅜in. (9mm) plywood, measuring 3ft x 8ft (0.9m x 2.4m), is a suitable size for the type of table described here, but clearly this depends on the size of table you have in mind. A foldaway ironing board will, for example, be narrower and longer, whereas a foldaway kitchen table will probably need to be about the same length but a little wider. Within reason, the dimensions can be quite drastically changed around, the main point to watch out for being the relative sizes of the pieces—that is, allowing just the right amount of clearance between the pieces when they are folded up. Too little will either result in pressure at the top catch or even make it impossible to close the table up properly, while too much will be unsightly.

With this in mind, therefore, the following pieces can be cut:

wall—24in. x 31½in. or 600mm x 778mm
desk top—23¾in. x 30¾in. or 594mm x 769mm
leg (support) flap—23¾in. x 30in. or 594mm x 750mm.

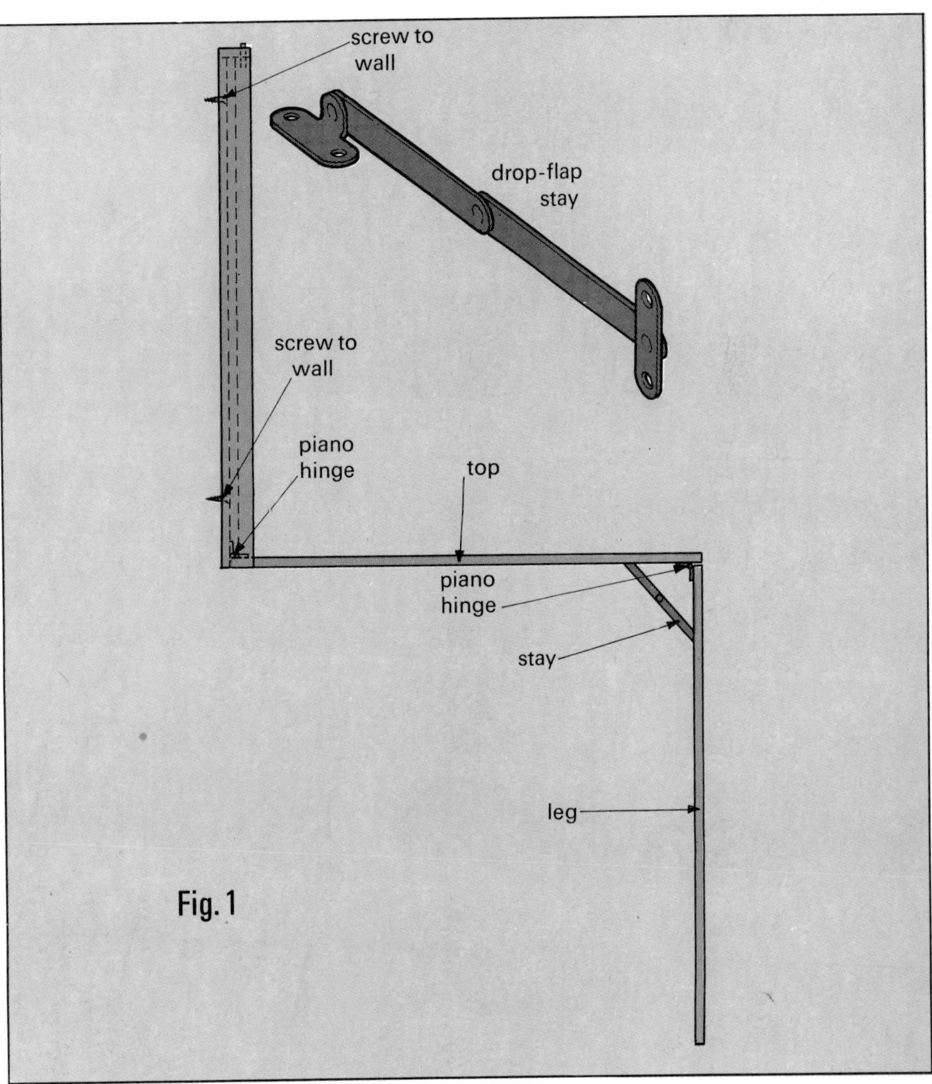

(Opposite). *The complete unit. It need not be a desk; it could be designed as an occasional working surface or dinette table in the kitchen. Or an ironing board—in fact anything that requires an occasional surface.* ***Fig.1.*** *Side view of the desk unit. Although only one stay is shown, there should be one on each side for maximum rigidity.*

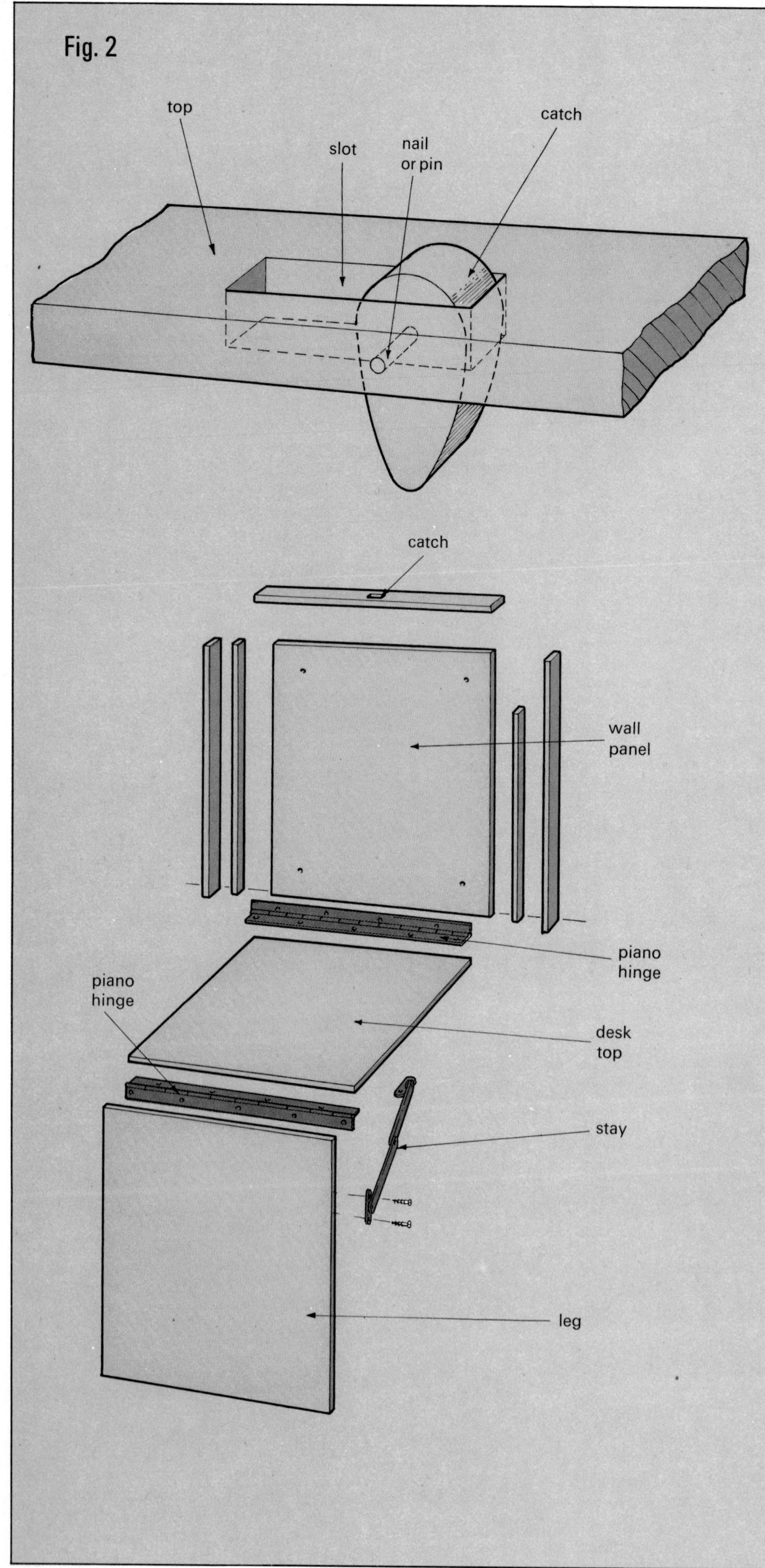

Three lengths of stripping, 1¾in. (44mm) wide, are then cut from the plywood board. Two of them should be long enough to fit flush with the two vertical sides of the wall piece, with the other cut to meet these two at the top corners in whatever joint you decide on. In the table shown on page 20, no joint has been used at the corners, and if the finished product is to be more functional than decorative this might appeal to you also. A box or comb joint – described in most comprehensive do-it-yourself manuals – is the most suitable of the worked joints for this type and size of wood. You may, of course, decide on simply running the ends of the stripping together, and then glue and pin them, using dovetailed nailing.

The back edges of the stripping are fitted flush to the back of the wall piece and tacked into place with ⅝in. (16mm) panel or moulding pins. The vertical sides of the wall piece must be fitted with additional stripping (see Fig.2), around ¾in. (19mm) wide, to take the main stripping out clear of the folding pieces. Remember that this subsidiary stripping must be cut short on the side where the drop flap stay is fitted, and be sure to fix the stay so that it folds up neatly along the side of the two flaps it connects.

A detail of the top piece of stripping with its clasp for the folded flaps is shown in Fig.2. The idea and its execution are both elementary, and yet provided the carpentry has been done carefully and the folded flaps are not under any abnormal pressure to pop out, it is quite effective.

Once the three main pieces have been measured and cut, they are joined with the piano hinges, which are themselves tailored to fit from end to end of the edges they join. With the flaps in the folded position, the stripping can now be added, but make sure there is adequate clearance before actually finishing the tacking on. It is probably safest to put the top stripping in loosely before making the slot and tongue catch, so that the slot can be positioned just in front of, or level with, the 'front' (i.e. the bottom, when in use) of the flap that serves as the table surface. The slot itself can either be gouged out with a handyman's knife, or drilled and then chiselled out. The tongue, which is just a small piece of wood (preferably with the ends rounded) must be cut to pivot around through 180°.

To fix the finished article to the wall, a masonry drill should be used to insert the fibre or plastic plugs that take the screws. This part of the job requires meticulous attention, since the stability of the table depends largely on the accuracy with which the wall piece has been positioned. After the screws have been securely fixed, the facing for the wall piece can be glued on. The wall piece of the table shown here has been fronted with corkboard, but this again is entirely up to you.

Fig. 2 *Exploded view of the complete construction. On the desk shown on page 20, the edge battening does not joint or butt. This is purely for decorative effect. If the unit is to be used a lot, it would be better to join the corners. Glueing and pinning is the most simple method, but for a really secure join make a box, or comb, joint.*

TRI-ART

A Victorian butler's tray

RICHARD SHARP

Above. *An elegant butler's tray is the ideal unit for holding television snacks or drinks. The tray lifts off the legs and the stand folds up when not in use, a real advantage over a conventional trolley.*

Evocative of a more gracious and leisured age, this fine reproduction of a Victorian butler's tray adds an elegant and useful touch to the most modern dining room. Genuine antique trays are both expensive and difficult to find and are an unusual item because they are scarce and costly. This chapter gives you the opportunity to make a butler's tray hardly distinguishable from the genuine antique, at a fraction of the cost.

First used in the eighteenth century, butler's trays were used as a sideboard for the butler. Later, in the Victorian and Edwardian eras, they acted as dumb waiters in the ritual of afternoon tea. Nowadays they are useful for holding everything from drinks to television snacks—the simple design and fold-away construction is readily adaptable to changing times.

The unit

The unit is in two parts, the tray, which has one short side cut away to allow easy access to glasses or plates, and a folding X-shaped stand on which the tray rests. To prevent the tray slipping off the stand, the bottom is covered in felt or baize; and two canvas webbing pieces attached between the tops of the frames hold the frames open.

Choosing a wood

Hardwood should be used because it does not stain as much as softwood. Traditionally, mahogany is used but there are attractive alternatives. Good quality utile possesses all the essential qualities and has an attractive finish. In this project the whole frame and the sides and tray edgings are constructed from this, while the tray base is made from ½in. plywood veneered with matching mahogany.

Cutting out and preliminaries

Cut out all the pieces to the sizes given in the cutting list. The two long sides are cut down at one end and handles cut in them. Figs.2 and 3 are templates which give the exact dimensions of these features. Use a jigsaw or a coping saw, for cutting them, but do not attempt to cut exactly to the mark; you will find it easier to leave a small margin which can be sanded down later.

The top edges of the tray sides and the outer edges of the edging strips are radiused with a spokeshave.

The joints used in the construction of the tray edge are mitre joints which are described in most DIY manuals. Cut these joints on the ends of the side pieces and edging strips, taking care they will butt together exactly.

At this stage, sand all the pieces, and if there are any irregularities on the joints they must be removed.

Assembling the tray

Begin by fixing the edging strips to the base of the tray with glue and veneer pins. The pins should be skew nailed and punched under the surface of the wood, and the holes filled with a filler to match the wood.

The sides of the tray are fitted to the base so that they overlap the edging to base joint by ⅛in. (3mm) all round. Fix by glueing and pinning initially, and to assist in keeping the mitre joints correctly aligned, clamp blocks of softwood to the internal corners of the tray.

Final fixing is done by screwing 1in. No. 4 c/s steel woodscrews through the base into the sides. Four screws to each side is sufficient and their heads must be recessed flush with the surface.

Assembling the stand

The stand is made up of two leg frames which are made separately. One leg frame is narrower then the other and fits closely inside it. Construct the wider outer frame first.

Housing joints ¾in. (19mm) wide are cut where the legs and cross members meet. Take two of the leg pieces and mark lines 6in. (152mm) and 6¾in. (171mm) from one end. On one of the longer cross members mark lines ¾in. (19mm) and 1½in. (38mm) from each end.

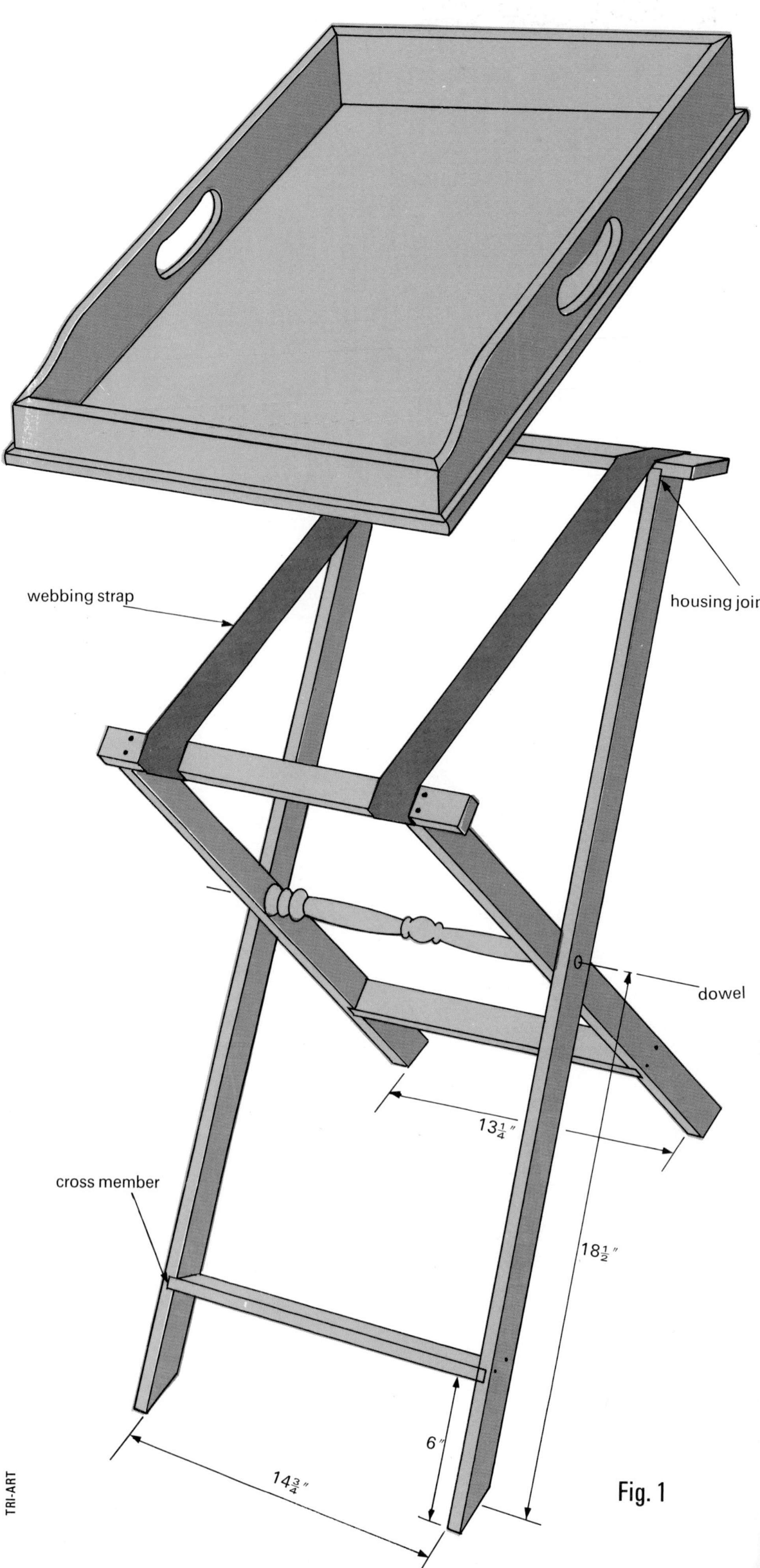

***Fig.1.** Assembly of the butler's tray is easy. The tray is built first and then the two separate frames for the stand. These frames are connected by the centre piece and canvas webbing attached across their tops. Finally, the unit is varnished and polished.*

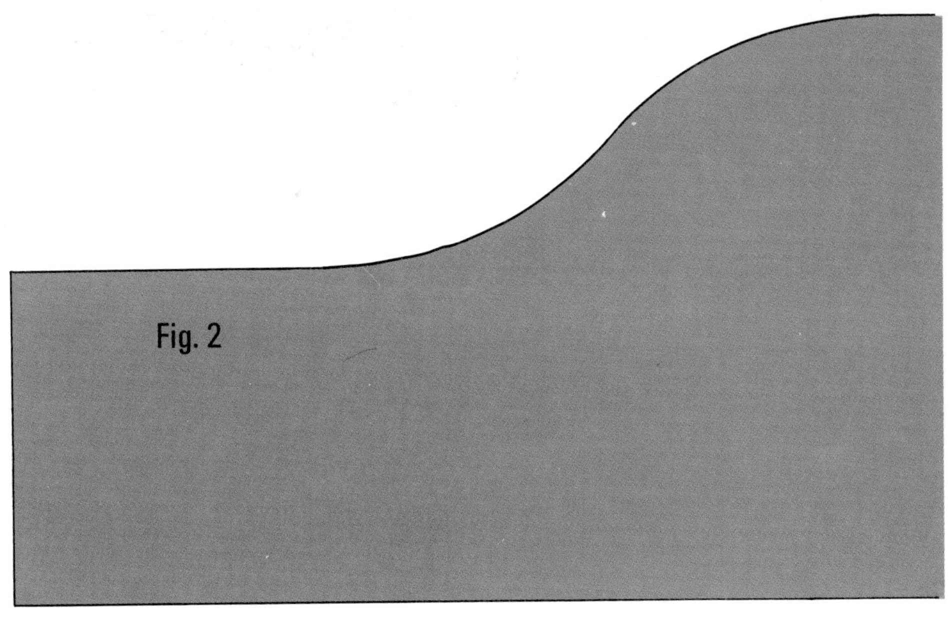

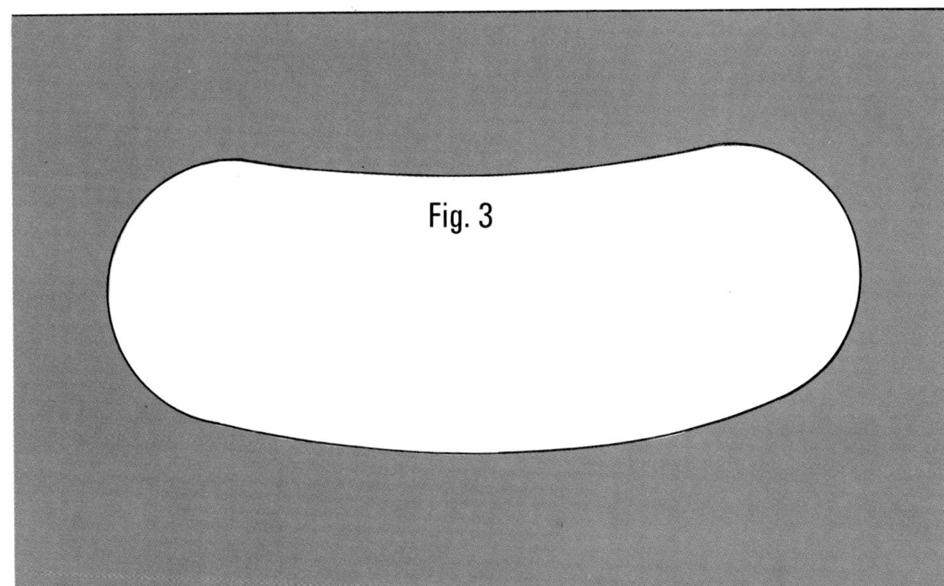

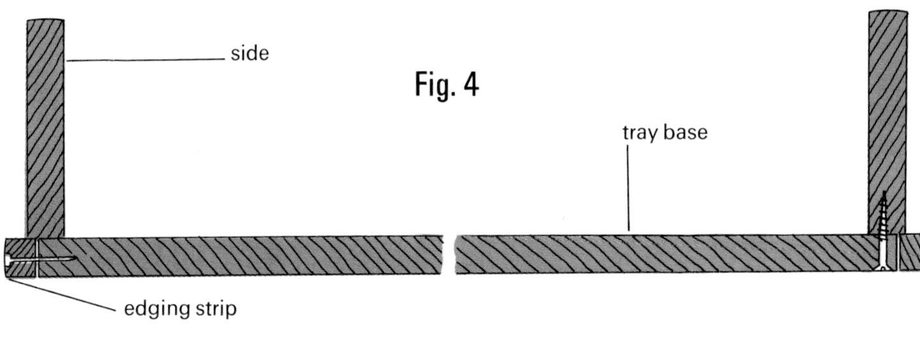

These lines are marked across one side and continue $\frac{1}{2}$in. (13mm) across each narrow edge. Cut the joints out with a tenon saw and remove any irregularities with a chisel. Assemble the frame with glue and fix with countersunk $1\frac{3}{4}$in. No. 6 twinfast steel screws with plastic wood heads.

The narrower frame is made in exactly the same way, but the housing joints in the top cross members are situated $1\frac{1}{2}$in. (38mm) from their ends to allow the finished frame to slip inside the larger frame.

Cutting list

Solid wood

PAR	imperial	metric
2 tray sides	$27 \times 3 \times \frac{1}{2}$	686 x 76 x 13
1 tray end	$20 \times 3 \times \frac{1}{2}$	508 x 76 x 13
1 tray end	$20 \times 1\frac{3}{4} \times \frac{1}{2}$	508 x 45 x 13
2 tray edge strips	$27\frac{3}{4} \times \frac{1}{2} \times \frac{1}{2}$	705 x 13 x 13
2 tray edge strips	$20\frac{3}{4} \times \frac{1}{2} \times \frac{1}{2}$	527 x 13 x 13
1 tray base	$26\frac{3}{4} \times 19\frac{3}{4} \times \frac{1}{2}$	680 x 502 x 13
4 stand legs	$37 \times 1\frac{3}{4} \times \frac{3}{4}$	940 x 45 x 19
2 stand top cross members	$18 \times 1\frac{3}{4} \times \frac{3}{4}$	457 x 45 x 19
1 stand lower cross member	$14\frac{1}{4} \times 1\frac{3}{4} \times \frac{3}{4}$	362 x 45 x 19
1 stand lower cross member	$15\frac{3}{4} \times 1\frac{3}{4} \times \frac{3}{4}$	400 x 45 x 19
1 turned centre cross member	$13\frac{3}{8} \times 2 \times 2$	340 x 51 x 51
or square centre cross member	$13\frac{3}{8} \times 1\frac{1}{2} \times 1\frac{1}{2}$	340 x 38 x 38
2 $\frac{3}{8}$in. leg pivot	$3\frac{1}{2}$	

You will also require:
40 veneer pins and punch. Wood adhesive. Panel pins. 16 1in. No. 4 c/s steel woodscrews. 20 $1\frac{3}{4}$in. x No. 6 twinfast steel screws with matching plastic wood heads. 2 canvas webbing straps 30in. x 2in. (762 x 51mm). 1 piece of baize or felt $26\frac{3}{4}$in. x $19\frac{3}{4}$in. (680 x 502mm). Tenon saw. Jigsaw. Spokeshave. Hammer, screwdriver, $\frac{1}{2}$in. chisel and mallet. Fine sandpaper. Clear matt polyurethane. Turpentine substitute. Grade '0' steel wool.

The centre cross member

If you possess a lathe this piece can be turned on the same pattern shown in Fig.1. Otherwise you can fit a $1\frac{1}{2}$in. (38mm) diameter piece of dowel without shaping it. Lathework is described in most DIY manuals.

A $\frac{3}{8}$in. (10mm) diameter hole is bored $2\frac{1}{4}$in. (58mm) deep into the centre cross member. A corresponding $\frac{3}{8}$in. (10mm) hole is bored right through the centre point of the inner leg frame and $\frac{1}{2}$in. (13mm) deep into the centre point of the inside of the outer frame member. Take two $3\frac{1}{2}$in. (89mm) hardwood dowels and drive them through the inner leg frame into the centre cross member. Slip the outer frame over

Fig.2. A full size template of the cut-away side of the tray.
Fig.3. Full size template of a handle cut in each tray side.
Fig.4. An edging strip surrounds the bottom of the tray and the tray sides are located over part of it. All the outside edges of the tray are rounded off with a spokeshave.

TRI-ART

the inner and locate it on the projecting dowels by 'springing' it into position. The frame will now move round the dowels which allows you to fold the stand when not in use.

Attaching the canvas straps

The stand when open should be fixed so that the angle at the centre between frame members is 60°. This is achieved by fitting canvas webbing strips between the top cross members. Take a 30in. (762mm) length of webbing and mark lines $4\frac{1}{4}$in. (108mm) from each end. Place the webbing across the two top cross members and open the stand so that $4\frac{1}{4}$in. (108mm) of webbing projects at both ends. Tack the webbing in position. The free ends of the strap are wrapped around 2in. x 1in. (51 x 26mm) hardboard plates which are then screwed underneath the leg frame top cross members. Repeat the procedure with the other strap and when both are firmly secured remove the tacks.

Levelling the legs

To give greater stability to the stand the legs must be levelled off so that their bases are level with the floor. This involves cutting a section off each leg. The easiest method of measuring and cutting the right amount is as follows.

Place the stand on a perfectly flat surface. If there is any wobble, caused by one leg being shorter than the others, place waste pieces of wood under the short leg until the frame stands level.

Now take a waste block of wood measuring

Fig.5. *The four sides of the tray, which are all of different dimensions.*
Fig.6. *Before the tray sides are fixed, an edging strip is located round the base of the tray and fixed with glue and panel pins.*
Fig.7. *The tray sides are fixed together by glueing and nailing. To assist in keeping the sides properly aligned, a square block of softwood is held in each corner.*
Fig.8. *When the tray sides have been assembled, they are located over the joint between the tray base and the edging strip. Initially they are held by glue and panel pins; final fixing being done with steel woodscrews. All the screws used in the construction are recessed below the surface, and on all visible surfaces are covered by stained filler.*

5

7

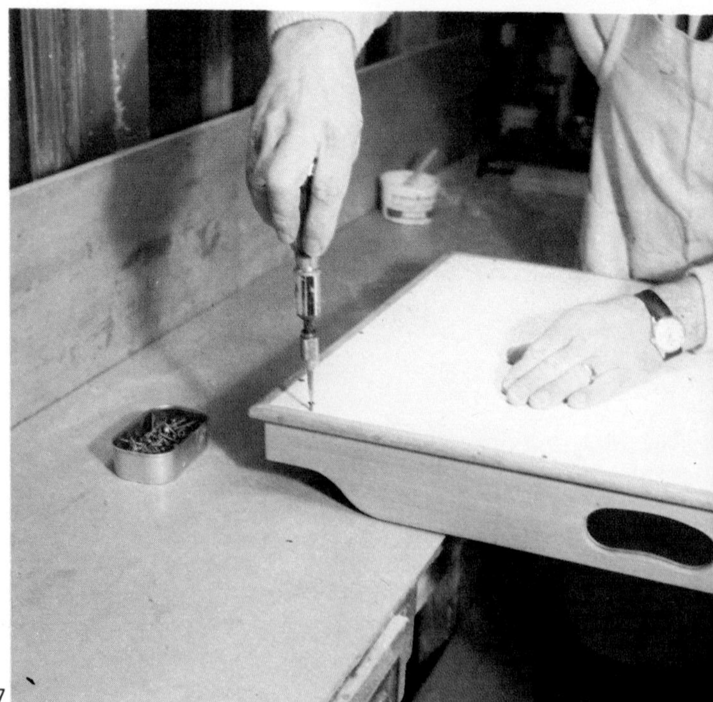

Fig.9. *The frame cross-pieces are housed in joints cut in the leg members and fixed with twinfast type screws with plastic wood heads.*
Fig.10. *The frame revolves round the centre cross member, which is held in place by dowels which are inserted through holes in the legs, into the cross member.*
Fig.11. *The outer leg frame is held in place by locating it over the projecting dowel and 'springing' it into place. The frame will now move round the dowels, allowing you to fold the frame when not in use.*
Fig.12. *Canvas webbing is attached across the top of the frame and is fixed to small wooden plates which are screwed under the top cross members. The length of webbing should allow the frame to open to the correct angle.*

about 4in. x 3in. x 1in. (102 x 76 x 25mm). Drill a hole slightly less than the diameter of a pencil, through the centre of the 3in. (76mm) edge. Push a pencil into this hole so that about 1in. (26mm) protrudes, then lay the waste block on the flat surface so that the pencil is parallel to the floor and 1½in. (38mm) above it. Carefully draw a line around the bottom of each leg and carefully cut through the legs around these lines.

Finishing and varnishing

Add the piece of baize or felt to the base of the tray and sand all the surfaces for a fine finish. With a soft cloth damped with turpentine substitute wipe all the surfaces so that the fine dust caused by sanding is picked up.

Using a good quality 2in. (50mm) brush, sparingly apply a varnish of clear matt polyurethane and turpentine substitute blended 50/50. When this coat has dried cut down with fine glasspaper, wipe the surface with the cloth again and recoat with the same mixture. Leave this coat to dry then finish with grade '0' steel wool. Clean the surface with neat turpentine substitute, leave overnight, then apply neat polyurethane as sparingly as possible.

After a few days the unit can be polished with a dry soft cloth to give the unit a deep, rich, lasting sheen.

With only a few hours of work you will have built a butler's tray that is a perfect reproduction of a valuable antique. The simple but strong construction ensures that it will give years of useful service.

9

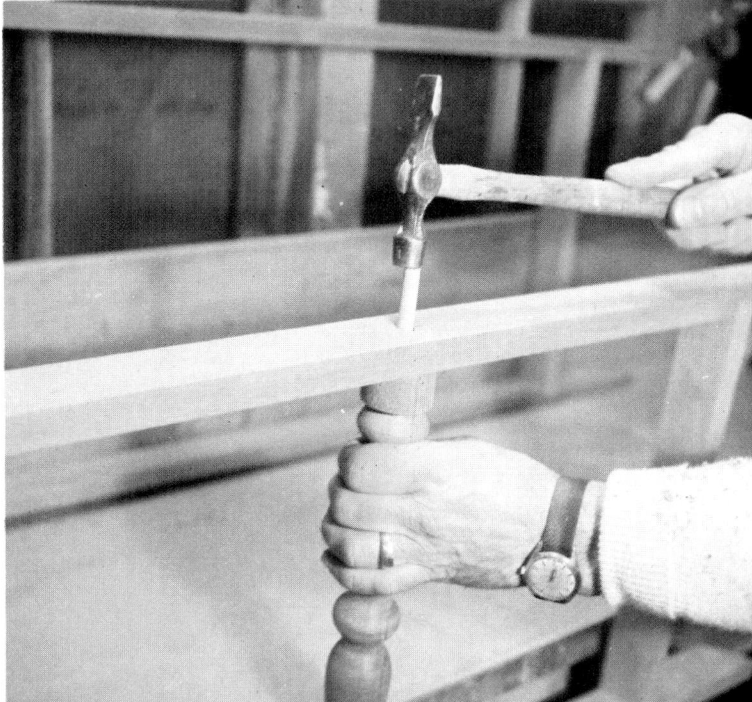

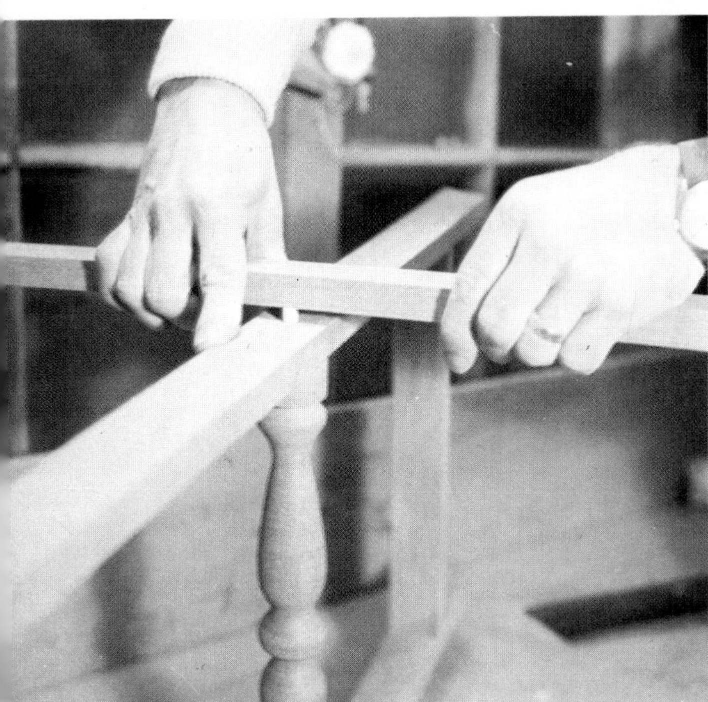
11

12

HARRY BUTLER

Penelope
AIRPORT
Arthur Hailey
COCINA MEXICANA

A useful storage unit

In these days when space is at a premium, a great deal of furniture is designed to fulfil more than one function, and multi-purpose units are particularly acceptable in bedsitters and small flats. This small unit, which occupies a minimum of floorspace, can double as a bedside table, writing desk, dining table for one person and a book case.

Before deciding on dimensions and materials, give some thought to the actual uses for such an item, for it could turn out to be an especially useful addition to your home.

Having been fitted with castors, the unit is easily moved from one location to another, one day to be used as a homework desk in one of the children's bedrooms, another to be used as a bedside table in the main bedroom, still another to be wheeled out into the annexe for use by someone who is convalescing.

With two flap-down panels instead of one, it could make a dining table for two in a bed-sitter. Situated against a wall, with a wall-light above it, it could make an especially cosy setting. The design of the flap gives adequate knee-room. In fact, with a few more inches of width, it could make an even larger and more functional dining table, as well as being used as a storage unit.

Having cleared up these points and decided on your dimensions, the next thing you have to decide before purchasing your materials relates to the appearance of the unit. You have to be sure that it will not clash with the room aesthetically. A room with traditional furniture, for instance, would probably call for a unit made of dark-stained timber.

The material used here is high-density veneered chipboard, which is available in a variety of timbers; and, of course, the unit could be stained or painted.

Chipboard is recommended as the ideal material for your purpose. It is easy to work and will give a professional finish. Having no grain direction, it can be cut without danger of splitting, and, being a mass-produced precision-made product it can be relied upon for the accuracy of its thickness and the flatness of its surfaces. It will not bend or warp under conditions of extreme heat.

Chipboard lends itself to the use of all hand-tools, saws, planes and chisels; while drills and power-tools may be used with confidence. The material is available in a variety of veneers and laminates, giving a wide range of tonings, including oak, teak, mahogany and white, to mention only a few.

The material used for the unit described in this article is pre-finished, plastic-veneered, teak-patterned chipboard $\frac{5}{8}$in. (16mm) thick.

This product—Conti-Plas is one example—is ideal for the purpose since it comes in standard widths, in this case 15in. This width, naturally, is used as the front to rear width of the carcass members, which are simply cross-cut from the panel.

The construction has been kept even more simple by the use of joining battens of standard $\frac{3}{4}$in. x $\frac{3}{4}$in. (19mm x 19mm) hardwood moulding, which eliminate the need for cut grooves. Thus the unit is an ideal do-it-yourself subject, for as long as you are careful to cut accurately, you will have a simple, strong, well-finished construction. It can be made with an absolute minimum of tools—panel saw, screw-driver, hammer, plus screw pins, glasspaper and woodworking adhesive.

Construction

For the two side panels and the back panel, cut three members 28in. x 15in. x $\frac{5}{8}$in. (710mm x 381mm x 16mm). Place the two side panels back edge to back edge and carefully rule the location of the shelf and base panel.

The top surface of the shelf is 9in. (229mm) below the top edge of the two side panels. The under-surface of the base panel is to be $1\frac{1}{4}$in. (31mm) from the bottom edge of the side panels.

From dressed hardwood moulding, cut two joint battens $12\frac{1}{2}$in. x $\frac{3}{4}$in. x $\frac{3}{4}$in. (318mm x 19mm x 19mm) for the fixing of the top panel.

To locate accurately, mark the positions of the battens flush with the top edges of the two side panels; in other words, rule a line $\frac{3}{4}$in. (19mm) from the top edges of the panels for the position of the bottom edge of the battens.

Note that these battens must be 1in. (25mm) in from the back edge. Using three screws per batten, screw and glue the two top battens into position on the side panels.

Cut a batten 10in. x $\frac{3}{4}$in. x $\frac{3}{4}$in. (254mm x 19mm x 19mm). Screw and glue it to the rear panel, fixing it centrally flush with the top edge of the panel.

Cut two panels 15in. x $13\frac{1}{2}$in. x $\frac{5}{8}$in. (381mm x 343mm x 16mm) for the shelf and the base member. Cut four battens 13in. x $\frac{3}{4}$in. x $\frac{3}{4}$in. (330mm x 19mm x 19mm). Mark the positions of the two shelf battens on the under-surface of the shelf panel, the rear ends flush with the rear edge of the panel. Screw and glue into position. Mark the positions of the two other battens on the under-surface of the base panel, the rear ends being flush with the rear edge of the panel. Screw and glue into position.

Cut two battens 10in. x $\frac{3}{4}$in. x $\frac{3}{4}$in. (254mm x 19mm x 19mm). Screw and glue to the under surface of the base panel, fixed centrally and flush with the front and rear edges.

Cut the top panel $17\frac{1}{2}$in. x 15in. x $\frac{5}{8}$in. (444mm x 381mm x 16mm). Cut the top flap section 12in. x 15in. x $\frac{5}{8}$in. (305mm x 381mm x 16mm). Shape each member ready for the hinged join by cutting or planing the lower jointing edges at a 45° angle (see detail in Fig.9).

Cut two drawer runners: 12in. x $\frac{3}{4}$in. x $\frac{3}{8}$in. (305mm x 19mm x 10mm). The drawer will be $4\frac{5}{8}$in. (118mm) deep. Therefore the runners must be positioned to hold the drawer between the runners and the middle joint battens. The front ends of the runners should be positioned $1\frac{1}{4}$in. (31mm) in from the front edges of the panels. Screw and glue the runners into position on each of the two side panel inside surfaces.

Note that all exposed cut edges must be covered with edge trim before assembly. Whichever material you have chosen to use there will be a matching edge trim available. If it is plastic, read the instructions carefully and follow them. Probably it will be only a matter of pulling off a strip of grease paper and sticking the edge trim into place. To apply veneer edging strip, position, then place a piece of ordinary brown paper over it. Apply a warm iron and move it slowly over the surface. Remove the iron every two feet and rub down with a cloth to ensure even contact. After 30 minutes, remove any overhanging edges with a flat fine-cut file, using quick down-strokes.

Assembly

Mark the position of the shelf, its top surface being 9in. (229mm) from the top edges of the two side panels.

Fix the shelf panel to the inside surface of the two side panels by screwing and glueing the side battens to the side panels, the front edge of the shelf being $\frac{1}{2}$in. (13mm) in from the front edges of the panels.

Fix the base panel to the inside surface of the two side panels by screwing and glueing the side battens to the side panels.

Note that the under-surface of the base panel is $1\frac{1}{4}$in. (31mm) from the bottom edges of the panels and that the front edge of the base panel is $\frac{1}{2}$in. (13mm) in from the front edges of the panels. Cut a plinth member 15in. x $1\frac{1}{4}$in. x $\frac{5}{8}$in. (381mm x 31mm x 16mm). Fix the plinth mem-

Left. *This handy unit occupies a minimum of floor space and can double as a bedside table, writing desk, dining table for one person, and as a book case.*

ber to the inside edges of the two side panels, the under-surface of the base panel and pinned to the 10in. (254mm) batten.

Place the back panel into position between the side panels, ends level at top and bottom. Attach by screwing and glueing to the top and bottom 10in. (254mm) battens, and to the side battens below the shelf and the base panel.

Cut the flap support bracket to shape and fix to the flap side of the unit, using a length of piano hinge. Note that the top may be fitted with the flap to either left or right, or, indeed, both sides. Fit the support so that when folded the front edge is flush with a front of the side member.

Position the upturned main structure on to the top and flap. Locate so that when folded, the flap falls flat to the bracket support. Secure by screwing through the three internal joint battens.

Drawer assembly

To make the drawer, cut the two sides $12\frac{1}{2}$in. x $4\frac{1}{2}$in. x $\frac{5}{8}$in. (318mm x 115mm x 16mm). Cut the drawer back panel $13\frac{3}{4}$in. x 4in. x $\frac{5}{8}$in. (349mm x 102mm x 16mm) and the drawer front panel $14\frac{7}{8}$in. x 6in. x $\frac{5}{8}$in. (378mm x 152mm x 16mm).

Cut two joint battens 4in. x $\frac{3}{4}$in. x $\frac{3}{4}$in. (102mm x 19mm x 19mm). Screw these to the inside surfaces of the two side panels, one

1

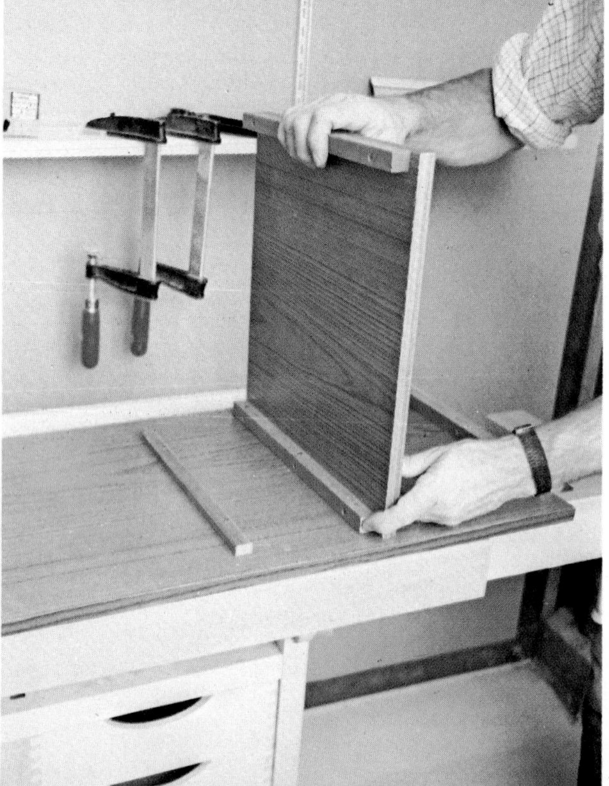
2

3

5

6

7

vertical surface flush with the front edge of the panels. Glue the rear panel to the two side panels, its ends butting the inside edges. Roughen the plastic surface so as to present a key where the joints occur. Screw the front member into position, and at this stage check the assembly with the unit for accurate fit.

To make the drawer bottom, cut a panel of hardboard $14\frac{7}{8}$in. x $12\frac{1}{2}$in. x $\frac{1}{8}$in. (378mm x 318mm x 3mm). Cover the rough side of the panel with self-adhesive plastic sheet. Pin the base into position to the bottom edges of the side and front and end members.

In choosing a handle for the drawer make sure that it will fit in with the decor of the room; as the appearance of the handle can, indeed, give specific character to the unit and tie in with the general motif of the room decor.

Follow the instructions that come with the fitting. In most cases you will need to bore a hole in the face of the drawer front panel. Fit in the threaded bolt and apply the nut and washer to the bolt at the inside surface.

4

From a piece of $\frac{3}{8}$in. (10mm) ply cut two squares 4in. x 4in. (102mm x 102mm). On each piece, rule a diagonal line from corner to corner. Cut along this line. You now have four triangular pieces. With the unit upside down, screw and glue these triangular plates to the battens beneath the base member and making a 90° junction with the side members and the plinth and rear members.

Should you decide to fit castors to the unit, and it is recommended that you do, choose a neat unobtrusive and sturdy product which moves and pivots easily. There are many such products available at hardware stores. Fit the four castors to the triangular plates.

Cutting list

Material	Imperial	Metric
Veneered chipboard		
(3) panels	28 x 15 x $\frac{5}{8}$	710 x 381 x 16
(2) panels	15 x $13\frac{1}{2}$ x $\frac{5}{8}$	381 x 343 x 16
(1) panel	$17\frac{1}{2}$ x 15 x $\frac{5}{8}$	444 x 381 x 16
(1) panel	12 x 15 x $\frac{5}{8}$	305 x 381 x 16
(1) piece	15 x $1\frac{1}{4}$ x $\frac{5}{8}$	381 x 31 x 16
(1) piece (shaped)	9 x 7 x $\frac{5}{8}$	229 x 178 x 16
(2) pieces	$12\frac{1}{2}$ x $4\frac{1}{2}$ x $\frac{5}{8}$	318 x 115 x 16
(1) piece	$13\frac{3}{4}$ x 4 x $\frac{5}{8}$	349 x 102 x 16
(1) piece	$14\frac{7}{8}$ x 6 x $\frac{5}{8}$	378 x 152 x 16
hardboard		
(1) panel		
hardwood	$14\frac{7}{8}$ x $12\frac{1}{2}$ x $\frac{1}{8}$	378 x 318 x 3
(2) battens	$12\frac{1}{2}$ x $\frac{3}{4}$ x $\frac{3}{4}$	318 x 19 x 19
(4) battens	13 x $\frac{3}{4}$ x $\frac{3}{4}$	330 x 19 x 19
(3) battens	10 x $\frac{3}{4}$ x $\frac{3}{4}$	254 x 19 x 19
(2) battens	4 x $\frac{3}{4}$ x $\frac{3}{4}$	102 x 19 x 19
(2) runners	12 x $\frac{3}{4}$ x $\frac{3}{8}$	305 x 19 x 10
(1) dowel	1 x $\frac{3}{8}$ diam.	25 x 10 diam.
plywood		
(4) triangles	4 x 4 x $\frac{3}{8}$	102 x 102 x 10
brass piano hinge		
(1) piece	15	381
(1) piece	7	178

You will also need:

4 castors, 1 brass chain, screws, pins, plastic surfacing, edging strip, adhesive, knob fitting.

8

Fig.1. *Screw the joint battens to the centre and lower shelves.*
Fig.2. *Screw the joint battens to the side members.*
Fig.3. *Screw the top and centre shelves to the side members.*
Fig.4. *Slide the back member into place and fix in position.*
Fig.5. *Turn the assembly upside down and secure the back through the joint batten.*
Fig.6. *Add the triangular plywood corner brackets and the castors.*
Fig.7. *Lay the top and flap upside down and cramp together, then screw a brass piano hinge to the angled edges.*
Fig.8. *Cut the flap support bracket to shape and fix to the flap side of the unit, using a length of brass piano hinge. Note that the top may be fitted with the flap to either right or left. This will dictate the positions of both hinges.*

HARRY BUTLER

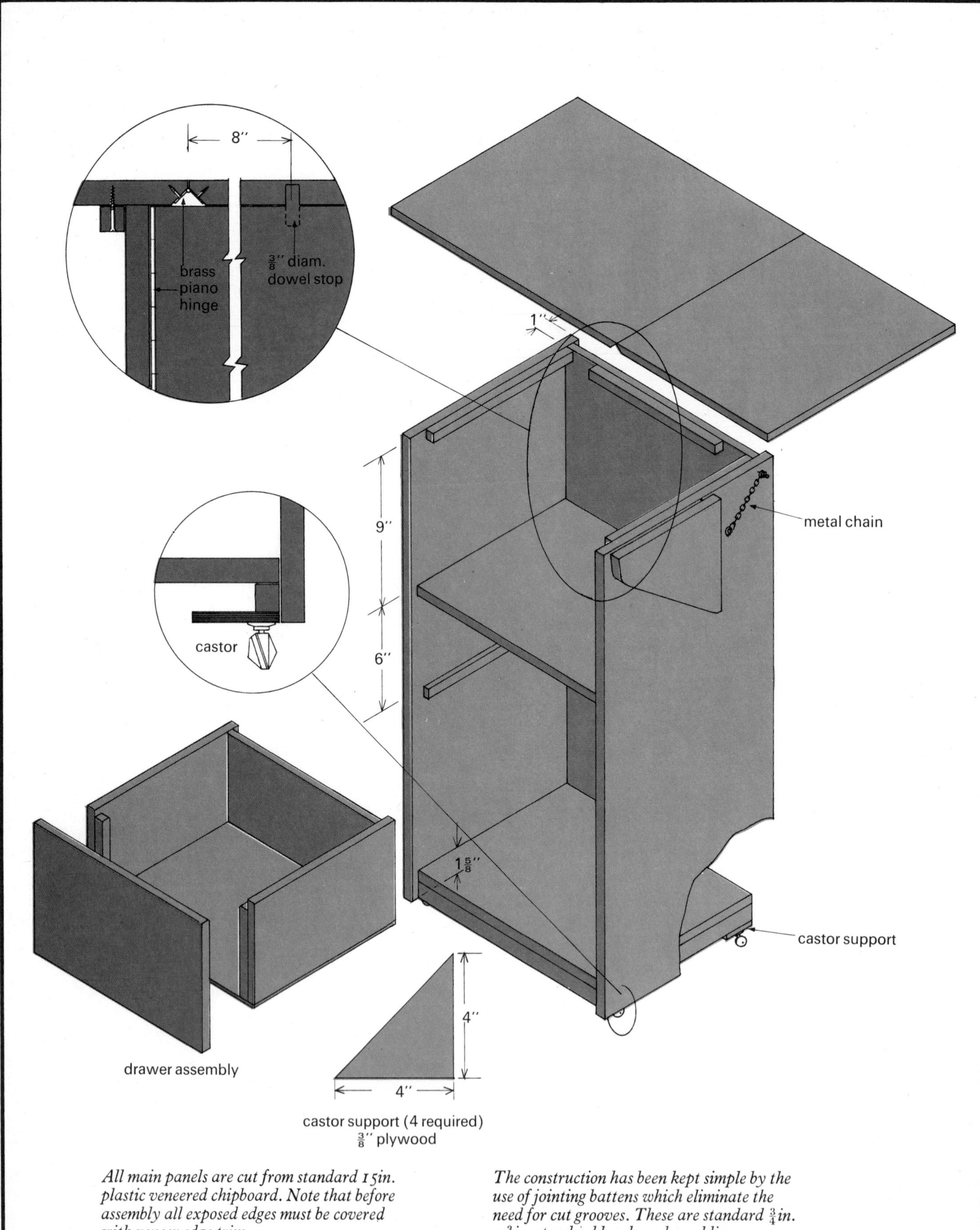

All main panels are cut from standard 15in. plastic veneered chipboard. Note that before assembly all exposed edges must be covered with veneer edge trim.

The construction has been kept simple by the use of jointing battens which eliminate the need for cut grooves. These are standard $\frac{3}{4}$in. x $\frac{3}{4}$in. standard hardwood moulding.

Fig. 9

NELSON HARGREAVES

__Above.__ The basic construction of this large elegant couch is of old wooden packing cases. A layer of foam rubber was laid over the cases, and the whole thing was covered with a brown carpet. A comfortable couch is the result.

Inexpensive furniture

Many people are of the opinion that to furnish a home comfortably and attractively will cost a lot of money. This need not be the case. With a little imagination—and a few ideas—you can make some very good looking furniture from next to nothing. Your home can be greatly improved once you have mastered the art of make-do.

Whether you are furnishing your home from scratch, or just wishing to add a few useful items, you'll find that many bits and pieces can be incorporated into basic and inexpensive designs for furniture. Don't throw away bulky items such as wooden beer crates, orange boxes, timber offcuts and the like. These may be commonly regarded as rubbish, and therefore disposable, but they could come in extremely handy in furnishing your home cheaply. Furniture for living rooms, dining areas, bedrooms and nurseries can be made quite solidly with inexpensive materials and some useful bits and pieces. First, sit down and think about what you need in any particular room in your house. Once you have a reasonably good idea of what's required you'll be surprised at the possibilities that readily spring to mind. The first thing to do is to decide on the kind of furniture you want, and to plan where it is to go.

Planning your furnishings

The size and shape of your home, and the rooms within it, is an all-important consideration when it comes to trying to furnish it at minimum cost. Many designs, while being attractive in themselves, may look totally out of place in your house.

Make a mental note of the rooms in your house which most need furnishing, and draw plans showing the size and shape of the room as well as the rough dimensions and position of any existing furniture and fittings. A scale of 1:10 or 1:15—depending on the size of a particular room—should be about right. Many unusual ideas can be created at the drawing board stage of planning.

Once you have drawn up the plans you can move on to deciding what furniture is needed, and where is the best place to put it. For the sake of simplicity it is best to concentrate on built-in units for larger items of furniture. These have the added advantage of taking up far less space than free-standing furniture. Mark the intended position of these larger pieces of furniture on your plans. Also indicate the approximate length, height and depth of each item. Now you can begin to furnish your house—room by room.

The living room

In living areas the main type of furniture you should think about initially is seating accommodation. This should be made spacious enough to be comfortable, but not so large as to dominate the room.

The best way of providing a generous amount of seating accommodation in a relatively small space is to make a built-in couch. A built-in couch can be made to seat as few as two, or as many as six people. What size you decide on will largely depend on the size of your room, as well as the amount of use you can reasonably expect the couch to be put to.

The first step is to make the base of the couch. For this you will need some wooden orange boxes. The number of orange boxes you will need will depend on the intended length of the couch. For a short two-seater couch two boxes will be enough, while a longer couch will require four boxes.

Building the base of the couch is a very simple matter. The best thing to do is to form the base in units of two boxes. Screw the boxes together—side to side. For a long couch two sets of two boxes should be placed end to end.

The two sets of boxes should now be screwed together. If you wish you can just place the two units end to end without fixing. By making a separate seat for each unit you can increase the versatility of the couch.

Once you have built the base of the couch you can begin to make a seat for it. For this you will need a sheet of $\frac{1}{4}$in. (6.5mm) ply. This will act as a base for the foam seating. A series of holes should be drilled in the ply. These will give a little more 'spring' to the wood, and improve the comfort of the seat. The holes should be about $\frac{3}{4}$in. (19mm) in diameter. They should also be regularly spaced over the sheet of ply at approximately 8in. (200mm) centres.

The sheet of plywood should overlap the orange box base by approximately $\frac{1}{4}$in. (6.5mm) all round. If you do this you will be able to fit stretch covers over the assembled couch. The exposed box sides of the base must be covered in some way. You could use quilted plastic sheeting for this. Alternatively, use a coarse weave fabric like hessian. Such fabrics will stand up well to the inevitable kicks and scuffs.

The next step is to stick the foam rubber seating to the plywood base board. For this use a contact adhesive such as Evostik impact. Check that the adhesive suits the foam—some adhesives will corrode certain foams. The adhesive should be spread over the plywood. Next, lay the foam seating down on the plywood base. This must be done with care, as you must get the foam in the right position first time.

To make a really comfortable seat you should use foam in three grades—soft, medium and hard. The soft foam should be laid around the whole of the outer edge of the seat. Medium hard foam is laid within this, as well as along the back edge of the seat. Hard foam should now be fixed into the remaining central area of the seat. If you make the seat of your couch in this way it will have a certain amount of bounce, and will give you adequate support—whereas if you sit on a seat made entirely of soft foam you will sink down on to the hard plywood base board. This will prove most uncomfortable.

Whether you intend the base to be a single movable unit, or built in two sections as described earlier in the chapter, the fitting of nylon running strips to the bottom of the base will prove a great advantage. They will make cleaning very much easier for you. Also, it will make it possible for the base and seat of the couch to be moved out from the wall. This will give you a useful spare bed to accommodate the overnight guest.

As the couch is intended to be built-in, the back should be fixed to the wall. To make the back use a sheet of $\frac{1}{4}$in. (6.5mm) ply as a base board. A piece of medium hard foam rubber is glued to the ply in the same way as that used for the seat. However, before sticking the foam on the base board you should screw the ply on to deal battens fixed to the wall. All that remains, once the couch has been assembled, is to cover it in an attractive and resilient fabric.

Always useful in any living room is a footstool. This will enable you to relax completely. With a little bit of imagination and effort an ordinary wooden box, or beer crate, can be transformed into an attractive footstool.

A major problem in living rooms, especially for the younger family or those with teenage children, is the safe and convenient storage of records. Again, orange boxes will prove ideal. They will hold a great many records. All that needs to be done is to paint the box in an attractive colour, and perhaps partition it off with hardboard glued in place with an epoxy adhesive—other adhesives just won't take the strain of many records.

For the dining area three or four orange boxes, fixed one on top of the other, will make a very serviceable shelf unit for the storage of crockery. A colourfully painted beer crate will, without any adaptation, make a perfect wine rack. For a more decorative effect, you could use adhesive plastic sheet to cover the exterior. Plastic milk crates are also good for this purpose, and are often in attractive colours in the first place; you will have to purchase them through your milkman or dairy—they are not on sale generally.

Another problem in living rooms is that of providing storage space for books. An unused alcove will prove a perfect site for a set of bookshelves. Fruit boxes can be fixed—one on top of the other—to extend to the full height of the room. These will make sturdy and spacious bookshelves, and can be painted to suit the decor.

The bedroom

In a bedroom there are numerous possibilities for making furniture cheaply. You may have an old wardrobe made of boxwood. This may serve a useful purpose in storing clothes, but still look dull and unattractive. There is no need to throw this eyesore away. These wardrobes are usually of a pretty flimsy construction. Because of this the whole of the front can easily be prised away from the frame—using only a hammer and an old chisel. This will leave you with the top, sides and bottom of the wardrobe intact. Fill the nail holes with stopper, then it can be painted in a bright colour. Replace the front with a cheerful curtain. You will still have a perfectly serviceable wardrobe—but with a greatly improved appearance.

In a small house it is a good idea to provide some space for a domestic office in one of the bedrooms. One of the few solidly made parts of a wardrobe like this is the door. This can be put to good use as a desk top for a domestic office, provided it has no mirror. For a really firm fixing screw a length of 2in. x 1in. (50 x 25mm) batten onto the wall. The old door hinges should be fixed ot the batten and the door rehung on them. Chains should be fixed to the wall with screws and plastic plugs. The other end of the chains should be fixed at each end of the wardrobe door. This should give adequate support. When not in use the desk top can be lifted up against the wall and secured by a clip.

Alternatively, you could fix the top over two small white wood drawer units. Once this has been painted, or varnished, you will have made a practical and attractive desk with very little trouble.

If the wardrobe door has a mirror, hang it on the wall to provide an attractive mirror and surround.

Some sort of rudimentary filing system is essential in a domestic office. This problem can be overcome by using one, or more, beer crates. These can be adapted into a pigeon hole filing system. Paint them in colours to suit the surroundings.

A sturdy bed platform can be made using orange boxes as a base. All you need is four orange boxes—two for each long side of the bed. Wooden slats should be placed across the orange boxes to form the bed platform itself. The best timber to use for the slats is parana pine. The slats should be approximately 6in. (150mm) wide x 1in. (25mm) thick. Leave a gap of about $1\frac{1}{2}$in. (38mm) between each slat. The slats should be screwed down firmly. As a mattress is to be laid over the slats the screws should be countersunk. This will prevent the mattress being damaged by the screw heads.

All that remains is to disguise the orange box base of the bed. The simplest and cheapest way of doing this is to paint the exposed parts of the orange boxes. Choose a polyurethane based paint. This type of paint is very resilient, and will

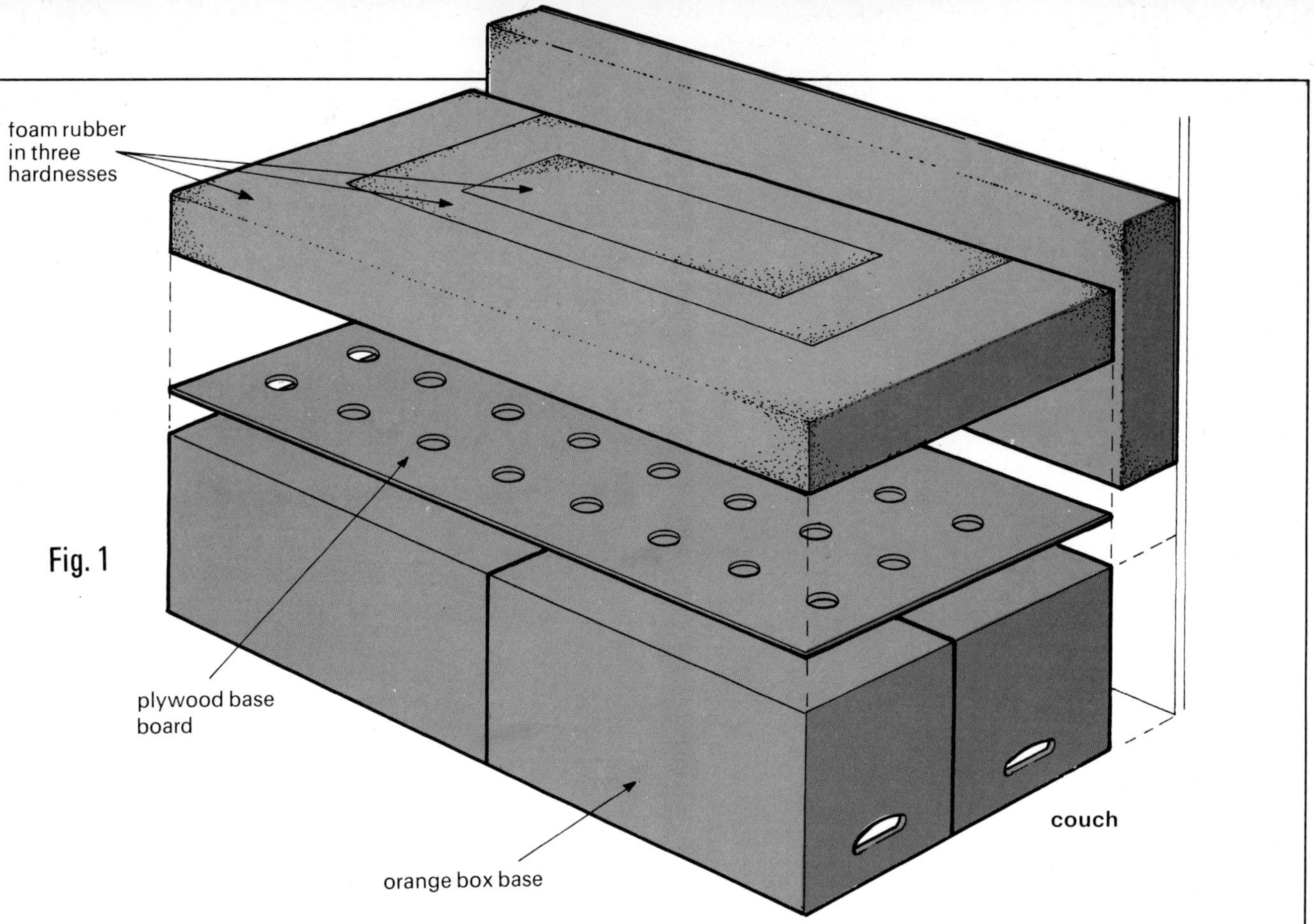

foam rubber in three hardnesses

plywood base board

orange box base

couch

Fig. 1

Figs. 1 to 3. Three excellent examples of pieces of furniture that can be made quite easily, and for very little cost. The couch and the bed base both use orange boxes as the basic material, while the desk is nothing more than the door from an old wardrobe.

withstand the scuffs and kicks that will inevitably occur.

An alternative to painting the boxes is to fit a bedspread which hangs to the floor and hides the base of the bed from view.

Fabric like hessian can be put to attractive use in covering a bed base. The hessian should be stuck to the wood with a latex based adhesive such as Copydex. The rough edge of the fabric must be tucked under the bottom of the base and tacked into place.

The playroom

In a playroom fruit boxes can be put to good use yet again. They will make excellent shelves for your childrens' toys by stacking them on top of each other—and screwing them into position—in the same way as that used for making bookshelves for the living room.

By covering old tea chests with a gaily patterned fabric, roomy and light toy boxes can be simply made. The edges of the tea chests should be padded with thin pieces of foam rubber. This will protect your children from cutting themselves on the metal stripping used to reinforce the box.

Have a look around your home. You'll be surprised at the number of pieces of attractive and useful furniture that can be made for very little cost.

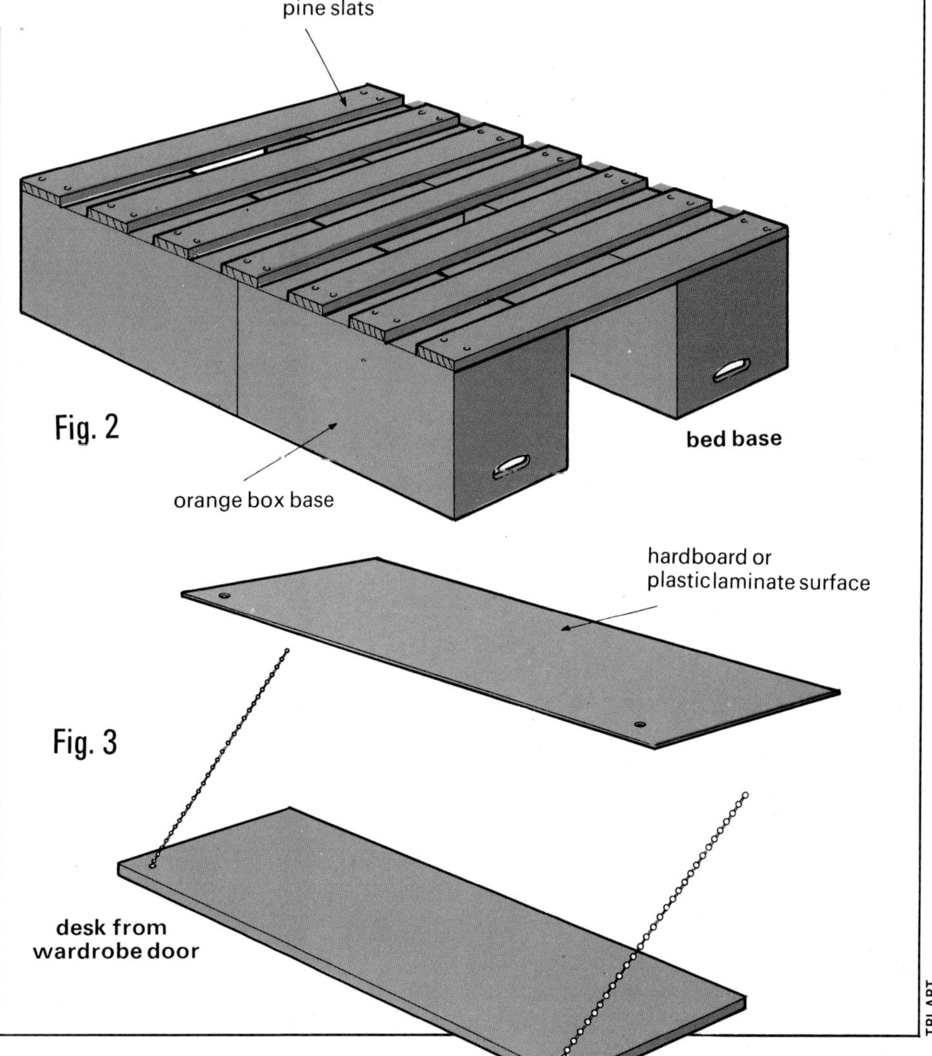

TRI-ART

More ideas for inexpensive furniture

Furnishing a house can be an expensive business—but needn't be. The previous chapter describes some attractive and money-saving ideas for furnishing your home. This chapter deals with more pieces of furniture that will help to make your home a comfortable place to live, without costing a lot of money.

Above. *Two inexpensive ideas for the home are shown here. Lengths of fabric can make striking wall designs. The shelf unit is made from wood veneered chipboard.*

The cost of moving into a new house—as well as all the extra costs and fees involved—usually leaves very little cash to spare for furnishings. If you try to buy all your furniture new it could take a number of years before your home can be made truly comfortable. You'll probably have to make do with second hand items of furniture, as well as old and bulky pieces given to you by relatives, while only gradually replacing them bit by bit.

The process of furnishing your home can be considerably speeded up. With a little patience and imagination you can make many good looking, and useful, items using very inexpensive materials. Hardboard, for example, is an excellent basic material for making some types of furniture. It can be cut to almost any shape desired, and laminated back-to-back for extra strength. Also, it has a very good painting surface. Any type of paint—emulsion, eggshell, gloss, polyurethane based and so on—can be successfully applied to the smooth surface of a sheet of hardboard.

Another inexpensive sheet material, which is becoming increasingly popular as the cost of plywood rises, is chipboard. This, as well as hardboard, can be used to good effect in a number of designs. Unless you intended to cover the chipboard with plastic laminate, or buy the type with a decorative wood veneer, the rough surface will need to be smoothed down. The best way to this is to coat the entire surface with a cellulose filler such as Polyfilla. Having done this, give the surface a sanding down with a fine grade glasspaper. The chipboard should now have an excellent surface for painting—as good as plywood at a fraction of the cost.

It should be emphasized that many of the so called temporary items that you build will end up being more or less permanent features of your home. For this reason these pieces of furniture should be well built as well as of attractive design—if you build a flimsy item it may soon fall apart. Such items must be strong enough to last a number of years at least.

And bear in mind that it's always easier to alter the appearance of a piece of furniture with a new coat of paint than to rebuild from scratch.

Colour

A good sense of colour is of prime importance in all furniture design. This is especially true of do-it-yourself items, where your own individuality can be shown off both in the design of a particular piece and in the colour scheme chosen for it. Nowadays, paints are available in a vast range of colours. Also, colour fastness has never been better. If these are used selectively, and combined together with care, they can brighten up any room considerably. In general, an area where much time is spent should have a predominantly neutral decor—with splashes of stronger colours here and there to add interest. Items of furniture could provide those essential areas of brighter colour.

It's a good idea, when buying paint, to get a little more of a particular colour than you actually need. If you do this you'll always have some spare to 'touch out' damaged areas. Also, you'll be able to use it on small items as a complement to larger pieces of furniture. Objects such as wastepaper baskets, stools and mirror frames can be painted to bring an

NELSON HARGREAVES

Top right. *The open kitchen storage unit shown here can be made from varnished lengths of deal. The top is made from hardboard over a deal frame. Storage jars and food packets will bring colour and life to a kitchen.*
Right. *A good looking and functional table is simply made—using two ordinary saw horses as legs and planks of wood for the top.*

attractive finishing touch to the decor of your room.

Another important source of colour is fabrics. Most materials are available in cheerful designs. However, probably the most effective are silk-screened patterns on cotton. If you stick to bold, simple, patterns, fabrics can make a striking addition to your decor.

Storage

Ordinary, everyday objects are usually stored behind closed cupboard doors. However, such things as tins and packages of food, crockery and pots and pans, provide an inexpensive way of bringing colour and a lively atmosphere to a kitchen or dining area.

Pots and pans can be hung over a work surface, within easy reach. You'll be surprised at the way such simple items can be used in an overall design to prevent a room from looking dull and empty. Old bottles and jars can also be used in this way to bring added colour and interest to the general decorative scheme.

As well as using open storage units to bring life and appeal to your kitchen or dining area, the same approach can be used in the living room. Your favourite ornaments can be displayed to good effect—and safely out of reach of small children.

Also, all your books can be stored here. These will look particularly good if they are in attractive bindings.

Storage can be treated in a similar way in the bathroom. Bottles of shampoo and boxes of bath salts are often attractive and can be shown off nicely if placed in a corner shelf unit. And things like towels and sweaters often come in striking shades and patterns, providing very effective splashes of colour.

If you prefer to store household objects out of sight, building cupboards with doors demands quite a degree of skill and patience. An easy and good looking alternative is to fit roller blinds across the front of your storage unit in the way shown in Fig.2. The rollers for the blinds can be obtained at most department stores or haberdasher's shops. You can get gaily patterned canvas and tough cotton fabrics to make the blinds yourself quite easily.

Another inexpensive possibility is to use hardboard to make lightweight doors. It's a simple matter to make doors out of hardboard. Its particular advantage is that you can buy it in the size you require. All you need to do is to measure at the front of the storage unit area that the doors are to cover. You can then get sheets of hardboard in the appropriate size. Add a border of deal stripping round the edge of the door. This will make the doors more solid as well as adding a touch of professionalism to the finished job. The central panel can be covered

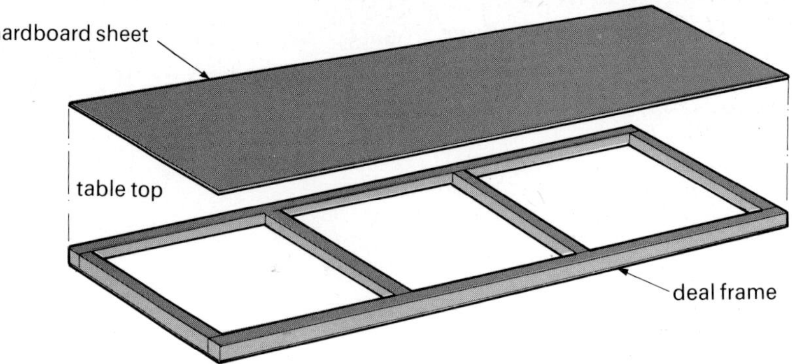

Fig. 1

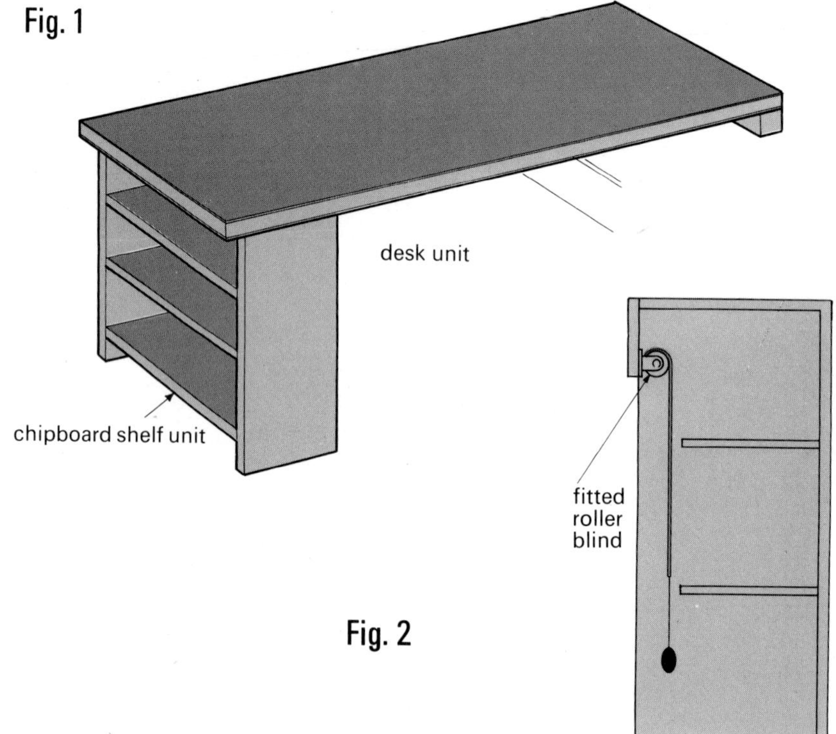

Fig. 2

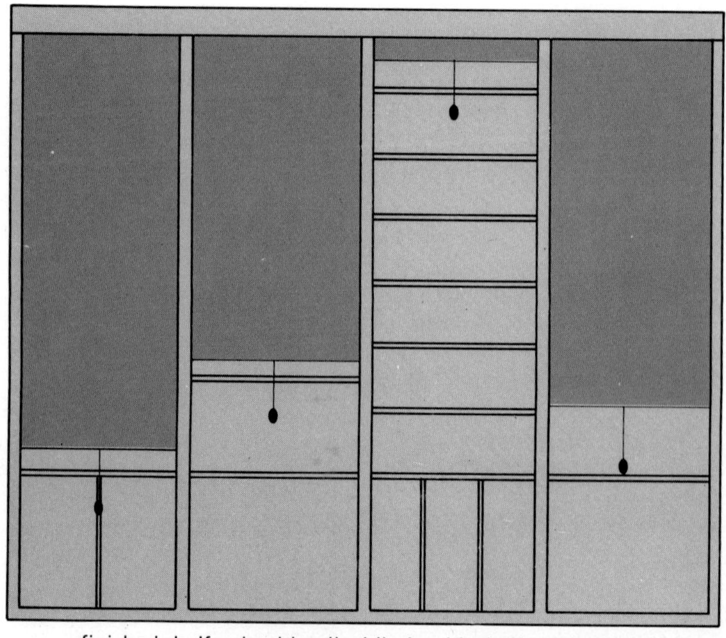

finished shelf unit with roller blinds with shelf unit at front

Fig.1. *A very attractive table top can be made with a simple deal frame, sandwiched between two sheets of hardboard. Once the table top has been made it can be put to good use in a number of projects around the home. One good idea is the sturdy and space saving desk unit shown.*
Fig.2. *Roller blinds can be used as an inexpensive alternative to doors, for cupboards and shelf units. It is easy to make lengths of material into blinds to fit onto the rollers.*

Fig.3. The basic design of an inexpensive kitchen storage unit. It is made in a varnished deal frame, and the back panel is of perforated hardboard. The working surface is a deal frame sandwiched between two sheets of hardboard. This design can be made to suit any kitchen.

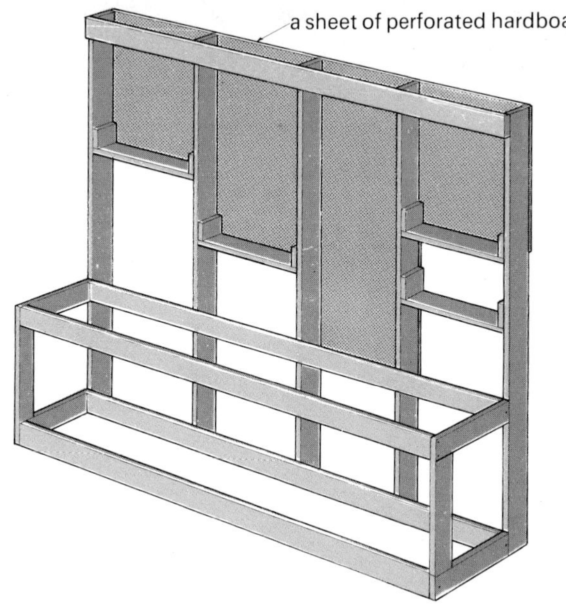

with cork sheet on which posters can be pinned. Alternatively, it could be painted in striking colours, or covered in fabric remnants. Such remnants are usually very cheap and can be combined together to produce some interesting patterns.

Table top from hardboard

Hardboard is an extremely versatile material, which can be made use of in a multitude of projects around your home. Not the least of these is in the making of light and good looking table tops. A finished hardboard table should be of 'tablet' design. The first step is to make a frame from 2in. x 1in. (50mm x 25mm) deal batten strip (see Fig.1). The frame needn't be of a really rigid construction—and only needs nailing at the corners. For a 6ft (1.83m) long table top a total of five deal cross struts should be used in the construction of the frame. Once the frame has been assembled it should be sandwiched between two sheets of hardboard—as shown in Fig.1. The hardboard sheets should overlap the deal frame by approximately $\frac{1}{8}$in. (6.5mm) all round. This is done so that the edging strip will fit flush to the frame with no rough, exposed edges.

The two layers of hardboard should be stuck to the deal frame with a contact adhesive such as Evo-stik. Once the adhesive has properly set, the hardboard sheet is nailed to the frame at 18in. (450mm) centres for reinforcement.

The next step is to fix hardboard strip round the edges of the table top. These should be 1in. (25mm) wide and cut to the length of each side of the table top. Fix this stripping with a contact adhesive and reinforce by nailing at 12in. (300mm) centres.

You now have the basic table top. All that needs to be done is to fill all the nail heads, and any places where the joins show, with a cellulose filler, then sand down. This being done you can proceed to paint the finished table top. Probably the best paint to use for this job is an eggshell finish polyurethane-based paint. The beauty of polyurethane paints is that they have a very tough finish that will stand up well to the knocks and scratches that are bound to be inflicted on any furniture.

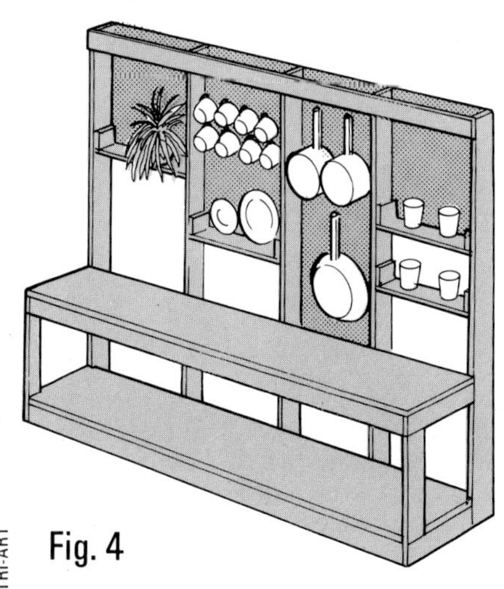

Fig.4. When the kitchen unit has been made—and stocked with utensils and crockery—it will prove good looking and useful in any home. Also, there is no reason why this idea should not be adapted to make, say, a home office.

Once you have made the table top, you'll be able to think about the inexpensive designs it can be used in.

Saw horse table

A simple and attractive idea for the table top is to use it to make a saw horse table, or desk. The top only needs to be supported by two saw horses as shown. It isn't necessary to fix the table top to the horses. As long as the saw horses are placed equidistant at each end of the top, the whole construction will be firm enough to hold up and can be taken apart for easy storage. You can either make the saw horses yourself, or buy them from your local builders' merchant or DIY dealer.

Desk and shelf unit

The hardboard top can be used to make a very good looking and functional desk or work surface. This design aims to provide as much usable work space in as small an area as possible.

Your first job is to fix a length of 2in. x 2in. (50mm x 50mm) timber batten to the wall. This is intended to support one end of the table top, and should be the same length as the width of the top—about 3ft. The screws holding the timber batten to the wall will need to be plugged into the masonry. To support the other end of the table top a shelf unit, made of chipboard, is used. The design of the finished desk and shelf unit is shown in Fig.1. To build the chipboard shelf unit, the shelves will have to be screwed to the vertical support pieces. Fibre plugs such as Rawlplugs, glued in position, should be used for this job. If they are not, the chipboard could flake and disintegrate as the screws are inserted. Once this has been done all that remains is to apply the paint. Again, use an eggshell finish polyurethane based paint. Your choice of colour is of considerable importance here. Choose bright primary shades—like red or yellow—as these will give the finished unit a cheerful appearance, as well as disguise any imperfections there may be in the chipboard.

Once the unit has been built, it will serve equally well as an extra work surface in the kitchen, as it will a desk. If you intend to use it in the kitchen you'll need to fit doors and a back shelf section. Hardboard will prove the ideal material for this job.

Wall decoration

A major problem when moving into a new home is how to decorate the walls without spending an awful lot of money. Good pictures tend to be very expensive, so you'll probably need to think of a cheaper alternative. An attractive and very inexpensive idea is fabric wall panels. The basic materials are a sheet of hardboard, a collection of fabric remnants, some fabric adhesive such as Copydex, and some deal strip. Firstly, paint the smooth side of the hardboard with two coats of emulsion, of any colour desired. Once the paint has dried, cut and lay pieces of fabric on the hardboard until you have worked out a pleasingly attractive pattern. Now proceed to stick the pieces of fabric onto the hardboard, using the fabric adhesive. Having finished sticking down the design, all that needs to be done is to make a simple frame for the panel out of the deal strip. You should now have a beautifully effective wall decoration, a good looking picture at very little cost.

Another attractive and interesting solution to the problem of inexpensive wall decoration is collage which can add a personal touch. You can make collages from a wide variety of materials at very little cost. Also, collages can be made to any size you wish, and to fit in with almost any decor and colour scheme.

There is no need to spend a lot of money to make your home a comfortable and well designed place to live. Take a hard look at the rooms in your house, and inexpensive ideas for furnishings and decor will almost certainly spring to mind.

A bed platform to make

A large proportion of today's houses consist of buildings 40 years or more old. By modern dimensions the ceilings in such homes can be exceedingly high, and the top half of each room is just wasted space. This bed platform enables you to use some of this otherwise wasted area—and add interest as well as utility to your sleeping space.

A bed platform not only uses space to the best advantage—it also economises on heating. The

COLIN WATMOUGH

top part of any room is always warmer than the lower part; so a bed situated at a high level will be that much warmer when you go to sleep.And the heat of this section might well be retained sufficiently to last the whole night through. After all, if most of your heat is 'up there'—enjoy it!

This type of structure could, if the ceiling is high enough, be used for other purposes such as a small play area for children. The flooring is not strong enough, however, to permit something like a small study for use by an adult, although it will sleep adults safely enough.

The bed platform

This particular structure has been designed to provide a platform, some 7ft or 2.1m high, covering a sufficient area for sleeping space for three adults. A large room is required for this, but you can alter the dimensions to suit your room. For example in a smaller room you could build the storage/desk unit with single bed above, as shown in Fig.1. In a small flat this could be the sleeping accommodation for the occupant, while in a larger home it might be used for the occasional visitor.

The boarded-in area at the base could provide even more sleeping space—in which case this particular section would be nothing more than a large pair of bunk beds—but here it is used as a table of sorts, with storage space underneath that is reached by doors at one side. Alternatively you could use this as a desk, in which case one of the doors should be left out to provide a recess for your knees.

Construction

The main supports consist of 3in. x 2in. (75mm x 50mm) timbers. The two rectangular frames shown in Fig.4 are of 2in. x 2in. timbers, with ½in. (13mm) tongued and grooved boarding fixed vertically at each end and on one side round the inside of the frame. And the remaining side with two doors of the same timbers and boarding, as shown in Fig.4.

The top, or platform, has a framing of 4in. x 1in. (100mm x 25mm) planking bolted to the vertical supports. The method of doing this is shown quite clearly in Fig.2 which is a 'top floor' plan.

The floor of the platform consists of 1in. (25mm) thick tongued and grooved boarding laid over an inside rim of 1in. x 1in. (25mm x 25mm) battening screwed round the planking as shown in Fig.6.

Tongued and grooved boarding, when used for flooring, is secured across the width, that is the narrowest length, of each frame. If laid across the length it would give too much in the middle. For this reason, where a frame is wider than 3ft (914mm), the underside of the flooring should be reinforced at 3ft intervals along the diagonal of the frame, as shown in Fig.7, with 2in. x 1in. (50mm x 25mm) battening.

A major safety point to note is that the combined unit, as shown in Fig.2, is a self-supporting structure. But if you wish to build only the main unit as shown in Fig.1, then it should be built against a solid wall and the main supports on one side bolted or otherwise secured to the wall. This is necessary because the weight of an adult positioned at one top edge—as happens when climbing on and off—could cause the structure to sway and possibly topple over if it were not firmly fixed to the wall.

The bottoms of the main supports should rest on something reasonably solid like a joist. It may be that some of the supports will be resting on floorboards in between joists. In this case it will be necessary to take up the floorboards at these points and skew nail some nogging in between the joists to provide a firm base for the supports.

The main frame

This is the section with a boarded-in base shown in Fig.1.

First mark out the floor area. Then mark and cut the floor support timbers, one 7ft x 4in. platform side, and one 3ft x 4in. platform end.

Stand two of the uprights against a wall, measure a line 5in. or 127mm downwards from the top of each, then drill holes and secure the platform side across the uprights with one top bolt at each end. The top of the platform side should be level with the marked line. Fig.3 shows how this will look.

Now fit the platform end, with one top bolt, to one of the uprights as shown by the dotted line in Fig.3. The platform end will be 'hanging' from this one bolt. Stand another support in position so that you can swing the platform end up and butt snugly against it pulling the other two supports upright. Drill and bolt the end in position.

You now have a 'dog-leg' consisting of three support timbers held upright by two horizontal or cross members. Because the cross members are only held by a single bolt at each end, it is possible to hold a plumb line by the side of each support and adjust the base until each timber is absolutely vertical. When you are sure that every support is vertical, use the same procedure you used for the platform end to complete the remaining side, end, and support. When this has been done, check the whole assembly for squareness and drill and fit the remaining eight bolts.

The next stage is the framing for the base boarding. This consists of 2in. x 2in. timbers. The ends of each timber are first pinned to a support with lost head nails skewed through the framing into the support, then screw holes are skew drilled through each end on the top, bottom and rear faces, into the support timber. This applies to members A and B shown in Fig.4, but not to member C, which is screwed directly to the inside of a support, as shown in Fig.4. However, member C must be fitted after the side boarding has been screwed in position because the end grain of member C actually butts against the boarding.

Fix members A and B at the bottom of the unit first. Then fix the upper members A and B at a height of 2ft 3in. Figs.1, 4 and 5 show how members A, B and C butt or join to the support timbers

When the upper and lower sections of A and B have been fixed in position, the vertical T&G boarding can be erected. This is done by direct marking, fitting each individual piece at a time. This will ensure a perfect fit all round. Each piece is direct marked, then cut, then two No. 8 screw holes are drilled 1in. or 25mm inwards from each end, the board is placed in position and the screws driven home.

When the insides of A and B, as shown in Fig.4, have had the vertical boarding fixed in position, cut and fit the two C members. These are secured at each end by two screws, skewed through the inside or back, and into the supports.

The space between the C members is filled in with two doors—or partly boarded at each side if this section is to be used as a desk. The doors are simple frames of 2in. x 2in. timbers, mitred, glued and screwed at the corners, with vertical T&G boarding at the rear. A good

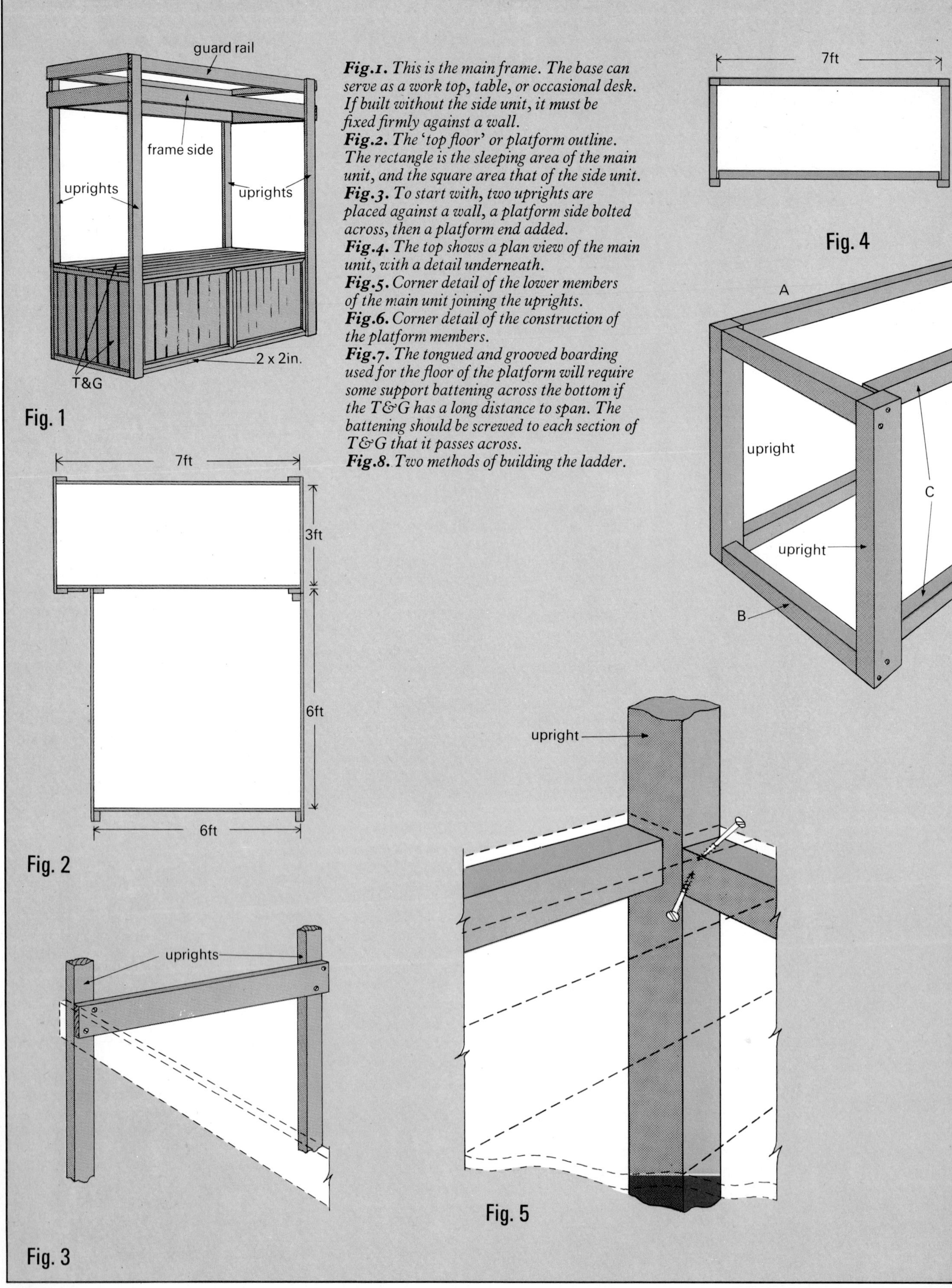

Fig.1. *This is the main frame. The base can serve as a work top, table, or occasional desk. If built without the side unit, it must be fixed firmly against a wall.*
Fig.2. *The 'top floor' or platform outline. The rectangle is the sleeping area of the main unit, and the square area that of the side unit.*
Fig.3. *To start with, two uprights are placed against a wall, a platform side bolted across, then a platform end added.*
Fig.4. *The top shows a plan view of the main unit, with a detail underneath.*
Fig.5. *Corner detail of the lower members of the main unit joining the uprights.*
Fig.6. *Corner detail of the construction of the platform members.*
Fig.7. *The tongued and grooved boarding used for the floor of the platform will require some support battening across the bottom if the T&G has a long distance to span. The battening should be screwed to each section of T&G that it passes across.*
Fig.8. *Two methods of building the ladder.*

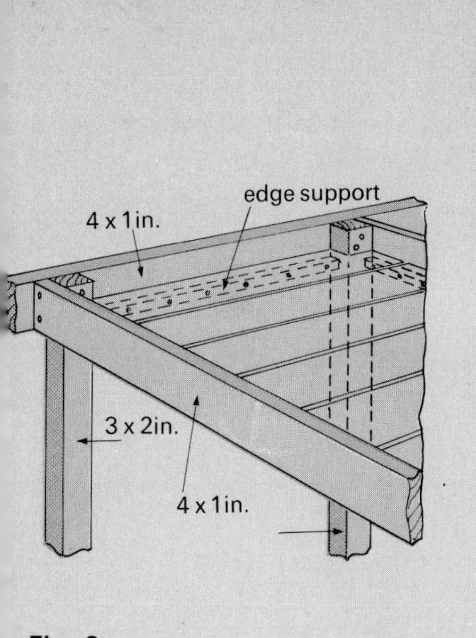

Fig. 6

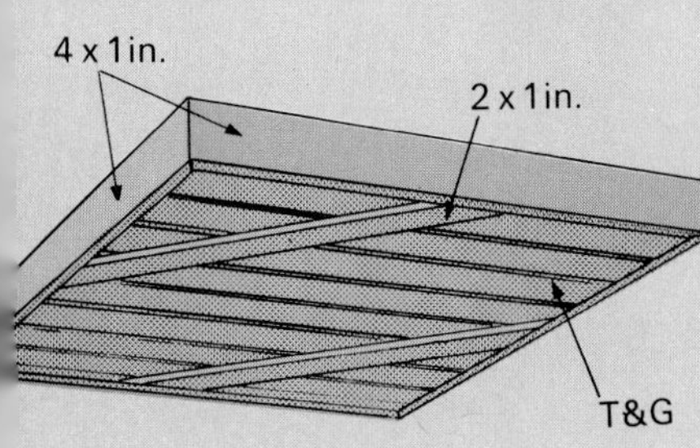

Fig. 7

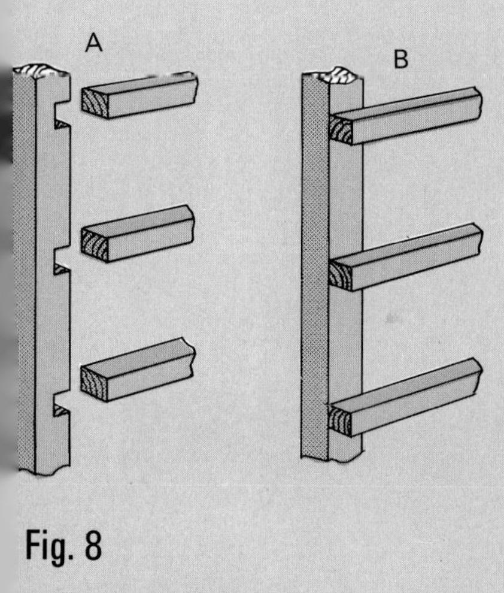

Fig. 8

woodworking adhesive is spread in the groove of each board before the tongue is inserted. When the glue has set, the run of boarding will be sufficiently strong and rigid not to require cross bracing behind. Every part of the doors should be direct fitted, because almost certainly the space it will be filling will not be a perfect rectangle.

The base is finished by laying the boarding over the top. This runs from edge to edge across the narrow width, as shown in Fig.1. The method of fixing means that the end grain of the boarding along the sides of the base will be visible. End grain is not very attractive even at its best, so ensure that the boards are cut with a fine toothed panel saw to make as clean a cut as possible. If you prefer, the boarding can be laid along the length of the base, but in this case you will need a cross member added between top timbers A and C. This is secured at each end by skew screwing through the side faces into, respectively, timbers A and C.

The platform above can now be completed. Screw a frame of 1in. x 1in. battening round

Solid wood (PAR)	imperial (ft & in.)	metric (m & mm)
Main unit		
4 uprights	8ftx3x2	2.438x75x50
4 lower frame sides	7ftx2x2	2.134x50x50
4 lower frame ends	3ftx2x2	914x50x50
Lower frame boarding		
21 tops (T&G)	3ftx4x½	914x100x13
42 sides (T&G)	2ftx3x4x½	686x100x13
18 ends (T&G)	2ftx3x4x½	686x100x13
Platform materials		
2 sides	7ftx4x1	2.134x400x25
2 sides	7ftx3x1	2.134x75x25
2 ends	3ftx4x1	914x100x25
2 ends	3ftx3x1	914x75x25
2 edge support Battens	7ftx1x1	2.134x25x25
2 edge support	3ftx1x1	914x25x25
21 flooring (T&G)	3ftx4x1	914x100x25
Side unit		
4 uprights	8ftx3x2	2.438x75x50
Platform materials		
2 sides	6ft 3x4x1	1.905x100x25
2 sides	6ft 3x3x1	1.905x75x25
1 end	6ftx4x1	1.829x100x25
1 end	6ftx3x1	1.829x75x25
2 edge support Battens	6ft 3x1x1	1.905x25x25
2 edge support	6ftx1x1	1.828x25x25
19 flooring (T&G)	6ftx4x1	1.829x100x25
2 underfloor supports	7ftx2x1	2.134x50x25
The ladder		
2 sides	7ftx2x1	2.134x50x25
10 rungs	12x2x1	305x50x25

Also needed

2 brass 3in. or 75mm angle brackets.

At least twenty-four 3½in. long ¼in. bolts, with nuts.

Wood screws, No.8, 1½in. and 3in.

Lost head nails, 1½in.

Wood adhesive.

the bottom of the inside faces of the planking you fixed first of all. The battening should be secured with countersunk 1½in. or 38mm wood screws at 3in. or 75mm intervals.

When the battening frame is finished, lay the 4in. x 1in. T&G boarding that will become the 'floor' of the platform. As with the boarding lower down, this is secured with two screws at each end and a dab of glue. But here the screw holes are drilled only ½in. or 13mm inwards from the ends of the boards. As each board is fitted, spread a little woodworking adhesive in the grooves to make the eventual floor more rigid.

It only remains to fit the side and end guard rails round the top. This is the 3in. x 1in. planking, and is bolted to the supports in the same way as the side and end planking immediately below.

The side unit

This is really only an extension of the main frame. Here it has been made wide enough to accommodate two sleeping adults, but the dimensions can easily be altered.

The method of construction is identical to that of the main unit. As shown in Fig.2, two supports are bolted to one side of the main unit, and these provide fixing points at one end for the side planking of the unit, with the two remaining supports placed at the far end as shown in Fig.6.

When a side unit is added to a main unit, as shown here, the guard rail separating the two is omitted or removed to allow easier access to both sides.

If you make a side unit as large as the one shown here, then you will have to fit underfloor supports under the T&G boarding so that it will not sag too much in the middle. This is two pieces of 2in. x 1in. timber fixed diagonally as shown in Fig.7. Each end is bevelled to fit snug against the sides of the platform and is secured to the sides with a screw at each end. Where the supports run across the boarding, drill screw holes so that a screw is driven in through each board.

The ladder

This ladder has rungs that are housed into the side supports as shown in Fig.8-A. To do this, cut all rungs to an exact length and direct mark, cut and fit so that each rung houses perfectly. The joints are secured with glue and screws skewed through the outside of the side supports into the end grain of the rungs.

A simpler version is shown in Fig.8-B. Here the rungs are laid directly over the side rails and secured at each joint with glue and two screws.

Whichever method you use, when you are finished round off the tops of the rungs with a spokeshave to make them easier on your feet.

With a bed platform you have more living space, and the concept of a home-in-a-room can become a reality. And even if you are already reasonably well off for space, a bed platform could release a bedroom to be used for other purposes. But a word of warning. If you make this bed platform for children, they'll like it so much you will have a job getting them off it!

Illuminated coffee table

A do-it-yourself coffee table is one of the easiest of projects for the home handyman. It is far more difficult, however, to design and construct one which is eye-catchingly original. This chapter gives you the opportunity to build a coffee table which is rather out of the ordinary —an illuminated, glass-topped table, which can be used as a display cabinet as well as for its usual function.

Construction of the coffee table is extremely straightforward and can be accomplished in a matter of hours. The materials, including the lights and light fittings, are readily obtainable and combine good looks with economy.

The sides of the table are made from $\frac{5}{8}$in. (16mm) veneered chipboard. A wide range of veneers is available and you can choose a type to match the overall decor of your room or a particular piece of furniture, such as a stereo unit. Ideally, cut the side panels from a single piece, so that when assembled, the grain of the veneer continues right round the table. As an alternative to veneered chipboard you can use a solid wood, such as pine, and this may be either varnished or painted. A painted finish to the unit may complement a very modern decor more strikingly than a veneered finish.

Fluorescent light fittings are recommended for illuminating the table as they cast no shadow and, more important, do not get too hot, even in an enclosed space. The light shields are constructed from plywood and softwood and these and the whole interior of the table top should be painted. Even if you have no experience of electrical work, the wiring up of the lights should present no problem.

The table top proper consists of a single sheet of $\frac{1}{4}$in. (6mm) plate glass with polished edges. When buying this item, ensure that it is of good quality and will not crack or splinter under normal use. If you do not intend to use the interior of the table as a display case, you could use smoked or stained glass for the top. This scheme would go particularly well with a painted unit.

Although it is a relatively easy job to make the table legs yourself, you will save time by buying a pre-finished leg unit. These are sold in numerous styles, but the overall design of the table is best suited to square legs.

Left. *More than just a coffee table, this illuminated glass-topped unit makes a really original display cabinet, as well as serving its usual function.*
Right. *Personal treasures, like the corals shown, deserve an eye-catching setting.*

Construction

Begin by cutting out the four side panels to the sizes given in the cutting list. As mentioned above, try to cut the panels from a single sheet of veneered chipboard to give a matching grain on all four panels. These pieces are assembled by means of rebates cut in the short edges of the end panels. The method of marking out and cutting these rebates is as follows.

Take the two end panels and mark out rebates $\frac{7}{16}$in. (12mm) deep and $\frac{9}{16}$in. (15mm) wide on their short sides. As the side panels are $\frac{5}{8}$in. (16mm) thick, they will overlap the short edges of the end panels by $\frac{1}{16}$in. (1.6mm). The reason for creating this overlap is to allow a $\frac{1}{16}$in. (1.6mm) veneer strip to be added to the raw edges of the end panels. When you have marked out the rebates, cut them out with a rebate plane, then trim and sand them to the required size. Trial assemble the panels, but do not secure them yet.

Next, mark and cut out the housing joints which accommodate the $\frac{1}{2}$in. (13mm) plywood base panel. These joints are made along one surface of all the end and side panels, are $\frac{1}{2}$in. (13mm) wide, $\frac{1}{4}$in. (6mm) deep and are located so that their bottom edges are $\frac{5}{8}$in. (16mm) from the bottom edges of the panels. Having marked out these housing joints, cut them out with a

NIGEL MESSETT

plough plane, then trim to size.

Now assemble each side panel to an end panel, remembering to match the run of the grain on each panel. For fixing, use a good quality woodworking glue initially, then secure with 1½in. (38mm) panel pins driven in at 2in. (51mm) centres. Use a punch to recess the heads of the panel pins beneath the surface of the veneer.

Having checked that each L-shaped structure is square, fit the base panel into place and secure it and complete the assembly of the side panels. Before assembling the rest of the unit, fill the cavities left by the panel pins with a stopper to match the veneer, then add matching veneer strips to the raw edges of the end panels. When cutting these veneer edging strips, do not try and cut to the exact width; instead leave a $\frac{1}{16}$in. (1.6mm) overlap which can be trimmed down.

Fitting the lights

Wiring is kept simple. A mains lead runs from a power supply to a junction box anchored on the underside of the base panel. Leads from the junction box (of three core table wiring) run to the light fittings. Although an earthed connection is not essential on an all-wood structure, you are advised to incorporate this feature as an added safety measure. Your local electrical dealer will help you choose the correct equipment and advise you on how to wire up.

Before fitting the lights, you must first bore holes in the base of the table, through which the wiring can be fed. By working strictly to the order of construction detailed below, you will save both time and temper.

First cut out four 2½in. x 2½in. (65mm x 65mm) leg supporting blocks from a piece of ½in. (13mm) plywood. Glue these to each corner of the base panel, as shown in Fig.12. Now take a brace fitted with a ¼in. (6mm) wood bit and bore holes in two diagonally opposite

Fig.1. *A detailed exploded view of one end of the coffee table.*
Fig.2. *Section through one end of the coffee table, showing the arrangement of the light, its shield and the method of fixing the legs.*
Fig.3. *A suggested wiring scheme incorporating a junction box.*

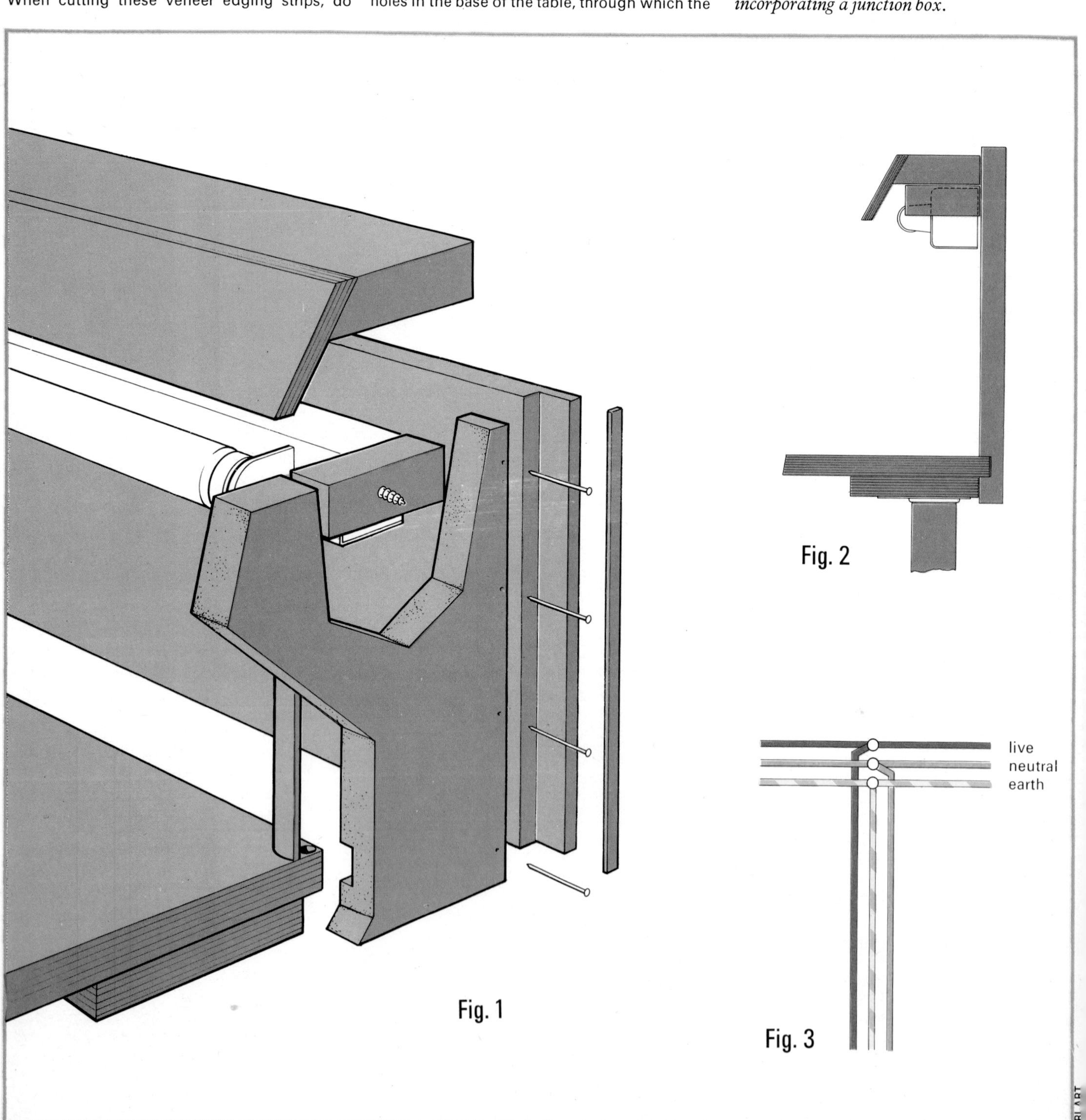

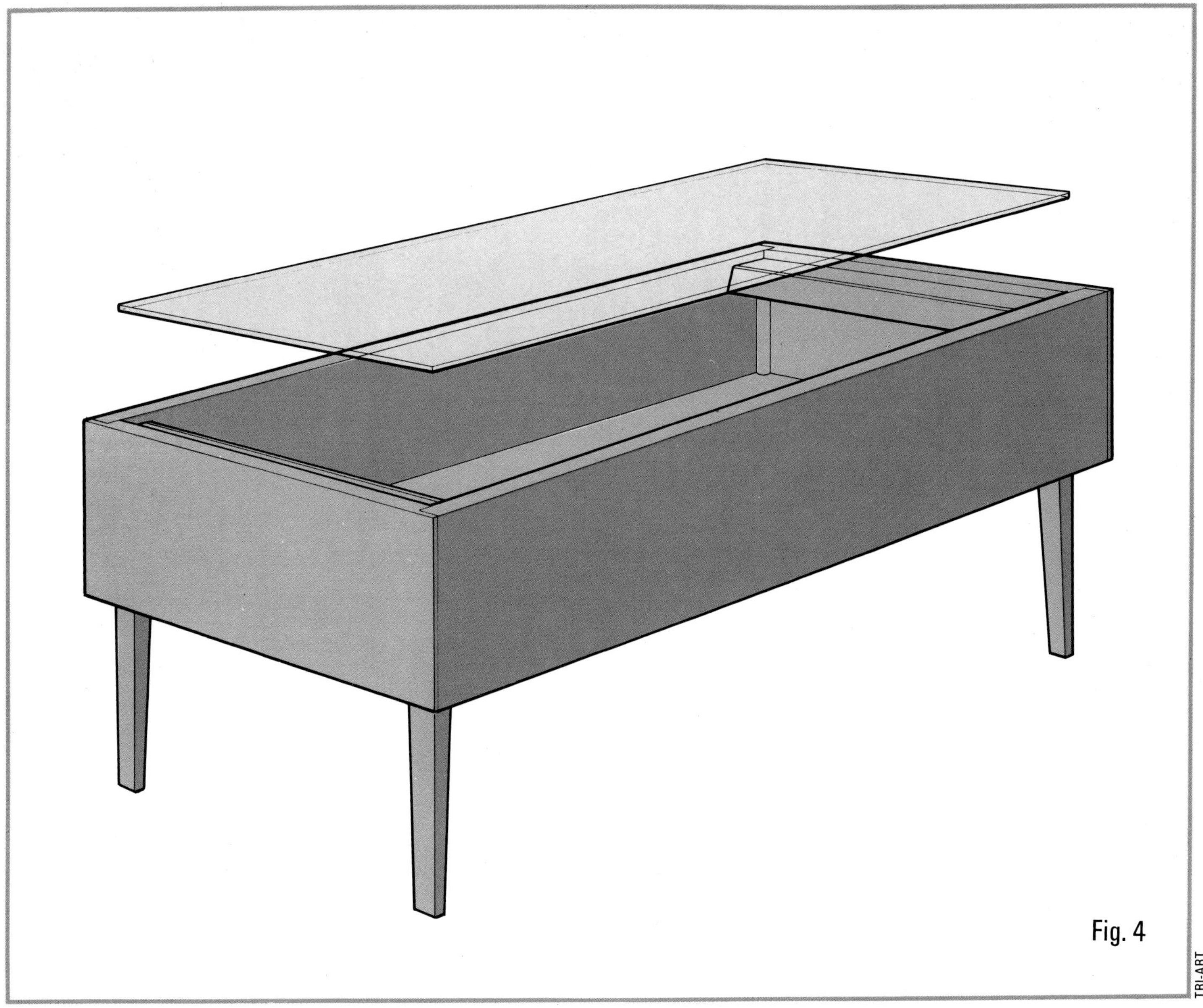

Fig.4. Construction of the coffee table is extremely straightforward. The side panels are rebated into the ends and the legs (which can be bought as a kit) are secured to blocks on the underside of the table. The glass top simply rests on the two light shields.

corners of the base panel, as close as possible to the right angle formed by the junction of the end and side panels. To prevent wiring being visible, you should also groove the underside of two leg supporting blocks to house the wires.

Feed the wiring through the bored holes and hold it in place temporarily with a dab of glue. Because exposed wiring can be dangerous as well as unsightly, you should cover it with quadrant moulding which is fitted at all four interior corners of the table. Cut $\frac{3}{4}$in. (19mm) quadrant moulding to the lengths given in the cutting list, then take two of these pieces, clamp them, right angled edge uppermost, in a vice, and plane these edges down about $\frac{1}{4}$in. (6mm). Fit the unplaned moulding to the appropriate corners first, then glue and pin the moulding over the wiring, taking care that you do not drive the pins through the wire.

Work out the exact position of the two fluorescent lights, then cut out the four light shield support blocks to the size given in the cutting list. As the light shield is not permanently fixed to the structure, but simply rests on the support blocks and is anchored by the weight of the glass top, you must secure these blocks adequately. Use glue and 1in. (25mm) screws, driven home through the blocks into the side panels, to fix these blocks in place. They are located at the interior corners of the table, with their upper edges 1in. (25mm) from the top edges of the side panels, as shown in Fig.7.

Before fitting the lights, make up the two light shields. Cut two pieces of softwood to the sizes given in the cutting list and angle one edge of each piece. To do this, set the centre point of a protractor on the end of one short edge, mark in an angle of 70°, continue the marked line down a long edge of the piece and cut out the angled edge with a panel saw. Having cut the plywood component of the light shield, fix it in place using glue and panel pins, and plane it down so that its upper long edge is flush with the top of the shield.

Try the shield by placing it on top of the support blocks and, if necessary, trim the ends for an easy fit. With the light shields in place, temporarily fit the fluorescent light and fittings in place and check that there is sufficient clearance between them and the shield. When you are satisfied that the lights fit perfectly, remove them and sandpaper the interior of the table.

Interior finishes

At this stage, before the lights are fitted to the table, you can decorate the interior of the table to suit your individual taste. For a very simple finish, paint the interior in the colour of your choice. White paint will tend to reflect the light and this increases illumination. Black paint, which absorbs light, adds a more discreet note but gives a pleasantly sophisticated effect.

For those of you who are more ambitious, the ways in which you can decorate the interior of the table are numerous. You can, for example, line the table with tiles, or a mosaic, or a piece of marquetry. If you have a favourite painting or photograph (one which will not be damaged by the small amount of heat generated by the lights), you can use the table as a striking and wholly original frame.

You can also use the interior of the table as a display cabinet to show off your treasures. One

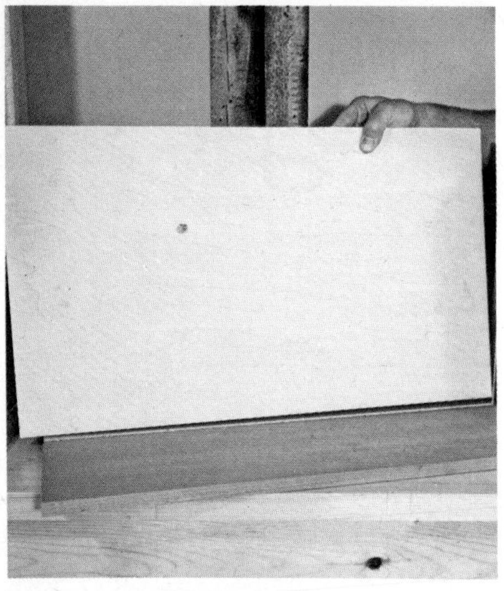
5

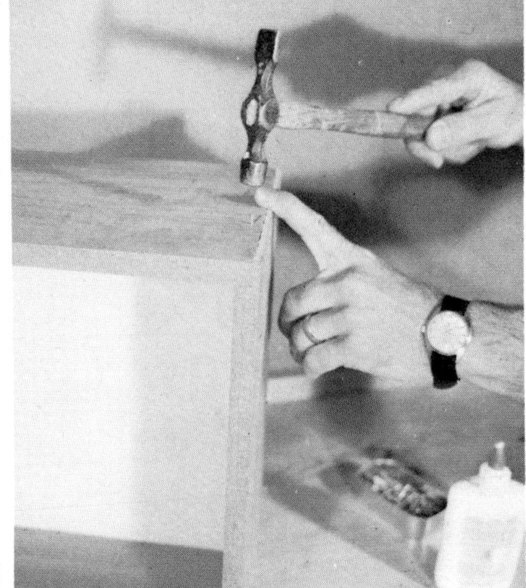
6

7

8

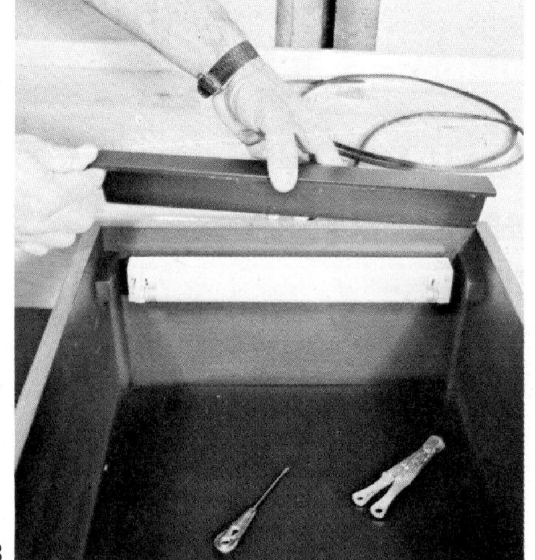
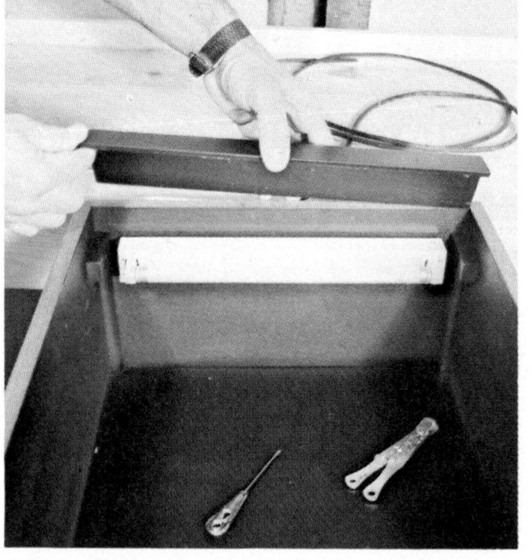
9

10

HARRY BUTLER

table built to this design housed a huge collection of ornate fishing flies which showed up beautifully under illumination. Similarly, you could display anything from small horse brasses to butterflies.

As a more practical, but no less attractive scheme, why not display a chess set in the table? By simply removing the glass top, you have a natural and flood-lit chess table! Or you could take out the chess set as it was needed and set it on the table top.

Finishing off

Turn the table top base uppermost and fit the pre-finished legs to the support blocks, according to the manufacturers' instructions. Then set the structure right way up and fit the fluorescent lights, again following the manufacturers' instructions. Connect the previously fitted wiring to the lights and to an electrical junction box, which should be secured under the base panel. Incorporate a switch if desired. Plug in the mains lead, switch on and check that the lighting functions properly.

When buying the plate glass top, take the required measurements direct from the table top. Place the top in position by dropping it onto the light shields. To remove it, make up a small hooked piece of wire which can be inserted under the top to lift it out.

Finally, to give the table a really fine finish, smooth all the side panels with fine sandpaper, then, with a soft cloth damped with turpentine substitute, wipe all the surfaces to pick up any fine dust.

Fig.5. Fix each side panel to an end, add the base panel to one half of the structure, then complete the assembly.
Fig.6. Simple rebates house the side panels and these are reinforced with panel pins.
Fig.7. The light shields are not fixed to the frame, but simply rest on support blocks which are screwed to the side panels.
Fig.8. Follow the manufacturers' instructions when fitting the lights. Fluorescent lights are preferable as they cast no shadow and give off very little heat.
Fig.9. The interior of the table can be finished in a variety of materials. Matt black paint gives a non-reflecting surface.
Fig.10. All wiring should be firmly anchored to the bottom of the base panel. When fitting the junction box, incorporate a switch. Your electrical dealer will advise you on details.

With a good quality 2in. (51mm) brush, sparingly apply a varnish of clear matt polyurethane and turpentine substitute blended 50/50. When dry, cut down with fine glasspaper, remove any dust as before and recoat with the same mixture and, when dry, finish with grade O steel wool. Clean the surface with neat turpentine substitute, leave overnight, then apply teak oil as sparingly as possible.

After a few days the unit can be polished with a soft dry cloth to give a beautiful sheen.

Cutting list

Wood	Imperial	Metric
From veneered chipboard:		
2 side panels	26 x 9 x $\frac{5}{8}$	660 x 228 x 16
2 end panels	16 x 9 x $\frac{5}{8}$	407 x 228 x 16
From plywood:		
1 base panel	$25\frac{1}{4}$ x $15\frac{1}{4}$ x $\frac{1}{2}$	641 x 387 x 13
2 light shield members	$14\frac{3}{4}$ x 2 x $\frac{1}{4}$	375 x 51 x 6
From softwood:		
2 light shield members	$14\frac{3}{4}$ x $2\frac{1}{2}$ x $\frac{3}{4}$	375 x 64 x 19
4 shield support blocks	$2\frac{1}{4}$ x $\frac{3}{4}$ x $\frac{3}{4}$	57 x 19 x 19
From quadrant moulding:		
4 lengths	6 x $\frac{3}{4}$	152 x 19

You will also need:
Veneer edge trim. 1 plate glass table top 25in. x $14\frac{3}{4}$in. x $\frac{1}{4}$in. (635mm x 375mm x 6mm). 12in (305mm) batten type fluorescent light fittings. 1 pre-finsihed leg kit. 1 electrical junction box. 60in. (1532mm) 3 core table wiring. 1 Mains lead to suit location. 50 1in. (25mm) panel pins. 1in. (25mm) wood screws. Wood glue. Brace and $\frac{1}{4}$in. (6mm) bit. Hammer. Panel saw. Tenon saw. Protractor.
All imperial measurements in inches, all metric measurements in millimetres.

Hi-fi in a chimney breast

Although chimney breasts have largely been made obsolete by modern heating methods, they can still play an important role in home decoration. Usually, they occupy a particularly prominent position on a wall, and this can be exploited by incorporating an attractive unit into the chimney breast itself. This chapter gives full instructions on how to fit a stereo unit into a chimney breast in such a way that it becomes a striking focal point of a room.

Open fires in many town houses are a thing of the past. Modern central heating systems and enclosed fires have largely replaced the cheerful glow of open coal fires. Those people who regret the change should consider the benefits of modern systems—instant, controllable heat, no mess and waste and, of course, less polluted air.

However, it is only recently (in Britain, at least) that houses have been built to incorporate modern heating systems. Consequently, most houses are still fitted with obsolete open fires and the associated chimney work.

It is the chimney breast—the area of brickwork enclosing the fire and chimney—that is most obtrusive. Usually it is located on a long wall opposite the entrance to a room (the most prominent part of most rooms) and extends about 2ft (609mm) into the room. While an unused chimney breast need not look out of place, it certainly takes up valuable space.

In what ways can a chimney breast be modified to increase living or storage space and complement a contemporary decor? The most drastic solution—and a major undertaking—is to remove the chimney breast altogether. This is not an easy job—and certainly not one to tackle without careful planning and preparation. Also, you will need building, and in Britain, planning permission, because the work involves major structural alterations. All in all you should not consider removing a chimney breast unless you are desperately in need of extra space.

A much more practical solution is to utilize an existing chimney breast for a convenient, fitted storage cupboard or to convert the area into an attractive display area. This chapter takes a fresh look at the way in which a chimney breast can easily and inexpensively be modified to house a stereo unit.

The unit

Obviously you need not fit a stereo unit into the chimney breast. You could, for example, adapt the breast to hold a drinks cabinet or some other storage unit. However, the prominent position of most chimney breasts is ideal for siting stereo units and, because the system is recessed, you avoid damage to delicate components, keep trailing leads well-hidden, and provide a solid, vibration-free location.

The dimensions given below will have to be modified to individual requirements and are given as a guide only. The chimney breast shown is big enough to include space for storing records in the safest possible way. This is a valuable feature which should be incorporated where possible.

Construction of the unit is kept as simple as possible, and anyone with even a modicum of carpentry skill should achieve professional results. Although recessed, the system is not permanently fixed and can be taken out for servicing or cleaning.

Preliminaries

Although not absolutely essential, you will probably want to remove the fireplace if it is still in position. To do this, locate the metal plates which hold the fireplace to the surround and remove the locking screws. The fireplace should come away fairly easily, although you may need help to lift it.

Next, remove the hearth, which may also be fixed by screws through plates. Frequently, the area beneath the hearth has to be made good, either by filling with concrete or by putting in local sections of floorboarding.

At this stage, *have the chimney swept thoroughly* and remove any built up soot deposits at the base of the chimney. To prevent rain entering the chimney and damaging the unit, cap the chimney stack with a piece of slate or earthenware.

One of the drawbacks of an unused chimney is that it traps moisture which can attack surrounding brick and plasterwork. One way to prevent this is to install air bricks—one high up in each room that the chimney breast intrudes into. Alternatively, you can use metal or plastic grills, screwed into place over a gap in the brickwork.

A comprehensive DIY manual should be read in conjunction with the following information.

Opening the chimney

To accommodate the unit shown, only a small part of the chimney breast has to be removed. For maximum accessibility, the base of the stereo unit should be located 4ft (1219mm) above ground level, but this position can be modified to suit individual requirements and tastes. Once you have established the proposed location of the unit, mark out the area of brickwork to be removed, remembering that ideally, the recess should be 1in. (25mm) wider than the width of the unit and $1\frac{1}{2}$in. (38mm) taller than the height of the unit.

The brickwork on the front of a chimney breast is supported, just above the fireplace opening, by either a pre-cast concrete lintel or a chimney bar. If you intend fitting the unit above the fireplace and wish to remove the lintel prior to construction work, you must replace it before the bricking up stage. Your local authority will instruct you on what type of lintel is required for your chimney.

Another consideration is whether the chimney structure in your home is load-bearing. It isn't in most cases, but some open-plan houses use the chimney stack as a central support pier, and in some very old (or badly built) houses it could be used to carry the ends of floor joists. An examination of the floor joists in all rooms will resolve this problem. If you are in the tricky position of possessing a load-bearing chimney you could, with approved planning, modify the floor support system.

If your chimney is reinforced by a concrete lintel, mark out the position of the new lintel and remove the brickwork over this area, in a strip two bricks, about 6in. (152mm), high. As you remove each brick, pack the cavity with waste timber, placed at the back of the slot, to support the brickwork above. Now push the lintel into place, dislodging the packing pieces, fill any gaps with slate or tile and secure it with mortar.

If your chimney is fitted with an angle-iron chimney bar, replace it with a similar piece. To fit it into position, knock out one brick on either side of the chimney at the proposed height of the new chimney bar. Push the bar through the holes so that its horizontal surface is supporting one row of bricks across the face of the chimney. Secure it in place by replacing the two bricks (cut down, if necessary) and mortaring in.

Removing the bricks

With the lintel or chimney bar in position, remove the brickwork over the proposed location of the unit. In some older properties, a lime mortar, which is very soft, was used and consequently the bricks are easily dislodged. To avoid displacing too many at once, slice through the mortar with an old hacksaw blade, enabling the bricks to be lifted out one at a time.

Making good

Ordinary bricks are suitable for bricking in a chimney opening. The bricks should be 'keyed' into the surrounding brickwork, either by removing a brick every three courses from the existing brickwork and bonding a brick between new and old brickwork (known as toothing), or by bonding the brickwork by means of metal wall ties. Make sure the new brickwork is flush with the original, or you will encounter problems when plastering for a smooth finish.

An alternative method of making good is to fix plasterboard over the chimney aperture. First nail a timber frame to the brickwork on either side of the opening, then cover with a sheet of plasterboard, recessed a little to allow for surface plastering. While this method is cheaper than bricking-up, it is not so strong.

To finish the exterior of the modified chimney breast, plaster the new brickwork, taking special care to leave a smooth surface.

Making the stereo unit

As mentioned above, the dimensions of the stereo unit described will probably need to be adjusted to individual requirements. The techniques, though, for making and fitting the unit are similar for all types and sizes of unit.

Mark and cut out the pieces to the sizes given in the cutting list. Take the middle and base panels and, using a plough plane, cut a housing joint in each to house the front panel. These housings run the length of the panels, are $\frac{3}{8}$in. (10mm) deep, $\frac{3}{4}$in. (19mm) wide and are set back 1in. (25mm) from the leading edges of the panels. The lower back panel is housed in rebates of the same dimensions as the housing joints, cut into the long rear edges of the base and middle panels with a rebate plane.

The top and bottom panels are housed in rebates cut into the short edges of the side panels. In cross-section these rebates have the same dimensions as those described above. The middle panel is not housed in the side panels at all. It butts between them and is fixed in such a way that it can easily be removed.

You must provide the cabinet with ventilation to allow the small amount of heat generated by the electrical equipment to disperse. 1in. (25mm) holes, bored into the base and lower back panels, will satisfy this need.

The methods of fitting different types of hi-fi equipment will vary. All types, however, come with instruction for fitting, and a template for the opening for the stereo deck. Do all the necessary cutting out before assembling the unit.

Assembly

Take the lower panel and glue and screw it into the rebates on the lower edges of the side panels, using 1$\frac{1}{4}$in. (31mm) wood screws. In the same way, add the top panel. Then glue and screw the front panel into the housing on the base panel and the lower back panel into the rebate on the back panel.

As mentioned above, the middle panel is fitted so that it can easily be removed to enable you to clean or service the equipment. To fit it, first glue and screw $\frac{1}{2}$in. x $\frac{1}{2}$in. (13mm x 13mm) battens to the side and back panels at the locations shown in Fig.2. Place the middle panel in position so that the front and back panels are loosely housed in the joints cut in the middle panel. Do not screw or glue the middle panel to any part of the assembly.

Next, glue and screw the plywood back panel to the assembly. This piece reinforces the whole structure, so ensure that is fitted properly. Remove the middle panel from the unit and screw plastic tracks to the front edge of this piece, at the location shown in Fig.2. Similarly, fix tracks to the underside of the top panel. These tracks house the sliding glass doors (of 32oz glass) which help prevent dust or dirt getting into the unit. Do not add the doors until you have fitted the hi-fi equipment.

Make up the external frame from 1$\frac{3}{4}$in. x $\frac{3}{4}$in. (45mm x 19mm) veneered chipboard. The dimensions of the external frame members given in the cuttings list are only approximate. To make a tightly fitting frame, measure directly from the sides of the cabinet. The frame is fitted together using mitre joints at all four corners. When fitted together it is slid over the cabinet and set back 1in. (25mm) from the front edges of the cabinet. Use 2in. (51mm) screws, driven through the cabinet panels, to secure it to the unit.

Apart from installing the hi-fi equipment, all that remains to do is to veneer the raw edges of the chipboard. Use a matching veneer of the stick-on or iron-on type and trim to size. Add the stereo equipment according to the manufacturer's instructions.

Installing the unit

If, as is likely, the new brickwork in the chimney breast is only one skin deep, you will have to fit additional support for the unit. This is best provided by screwing a timber frame to the interior of the chimney breast, at a height which enables you to use the frame as a runner for the unit. Because the cavity is hidden by the unit (the external frame round the cabinet completely hides the opening) there is no need to plaster or finish the cavity itself.

With the frame in position, slide the unit into the recess so that the back of the external frame butts against the chimney breast. Check that the cabinet is level and, if necessary, adjust the fit. Finally, connect the equipment to the electrical supply, by leading the wiring through holes cut in the chimney breast.

Once you have installed the cabinet, you will fully appreciate the advantages of this project. Safely recessed in the chimney breast, there is no risk of damage to sensitive equipment. The unit becomes a striking feature of any room without encroaching on valuable living space. Finally, the cost of the project is offset by the bold contemporary touch that this system adds to your home and the increased pleasure you receive from your hi-fi.

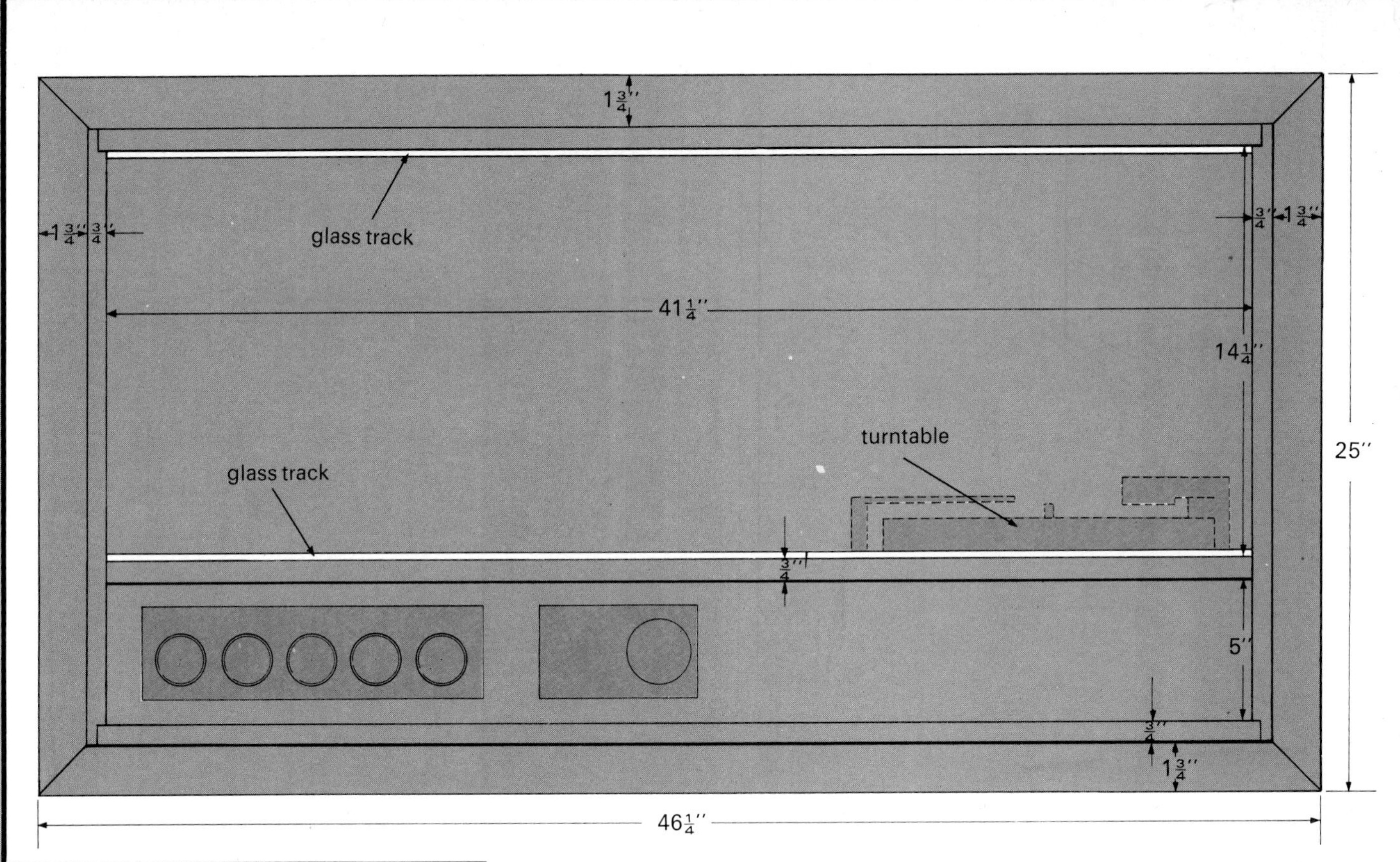

Fig. 1

Above left. By recessing your hi-fi unit in a chimney breast, you provide a vibration free location and transform an empty wall into an interesting focal point.
Fig.1. *Front elevation of the unit. You will probably have to modify the dimensions shown, and cut the centre panel to the manufacturers' template, but the basic design will accommodate most standard equipment and leave plenty of space for storing records.*
Fig.2. *Section through one side of the unit.*

Fig. 2

Cutting list : stereo cabinet		
¾in. (19mm) veneered chipboard	Imperial	Metric
1 bottom panel	42 x 15 x ¾	1067 x 381 x 19
1 top panel	42 x 15 x ¾	1067 x 381 x 19
1 middle panel	41¼ x 15 x ¾	1047 x 381 x 19
1 lower back panel	41¼ x 5¾ x ¾	1047 x 381 x 19
1 front panel	41¼ x 5¾ x ¾	1047 x 381 x 19
2 frame rails	46¾ x 1¾ x ¾	1187 x 45 x 19
2 frame rails	25 x 1¾ x ¾	635 x 45 x 19
From ½in. x ½in. (13mm x 13mm) hardwood :		
2 battens	12 x ½ x ½	350 x 13 x 13
1 batten	39 x ½ x ½	990 x 13 x 13
From ¼in. (6mm) faced plywood :		
1 back panel	42¾ x 21½ x ¼	1085 x 546 x 6

You will also need :
Veneer edging strip. 320z glass doors and plastic tracks. 12 ½in. (6mm) wood screws. 36 1¼in. (31mm) wood screws. 24 2in. (51mm) wood screws.
Tenon saw. Rip saw. Rebate plane. Plough plane. Jig saw. Brace and bit.
All imperial measurements in inches, all metric measurements in millimetres.

TRI-ART

NIGEL MESSETT

A telephone table to make

A properly designed table provides a permanent, safe place for your telephone, and a home for all those directories. In this way it will help create a neater, more attractive, home. And making a 'phone call becomes much easier when the telephone rests firmly on a surface which has room for a note too. If you have ever spent half an hour looking for a particular telephone directory, tripped over a telephone that was on the floor or dropped the telephone during the middle of a call, you will realize the advantages of a telephone table.

This table has been built to a traditional design, and the baroque scroll round the rear and sides of the top lends a rather exotic touch that would enliven a modern hallway. If you prefer a more simple style, just omit the scroll or alter the outline to a more modern pattern.

Under the table top, one half comprises a directory storage cabinet, and the other half provides a drawer and a recess to enable a small stool to be housed—out of the way and ready for those long conversations!

Construction

The joints for the legs, uprights and cross members are all glued mortise and tenon. The mortise and tenon is a relatively simple joint and details on exactly how to construct it can be found in a comprehensive DIY manual. If you prefer, you could use a different joint such as a dowelling joint.

Tongued and grooved (T&G) boarding runs vertically up each side of the table. This is laid across the inside of the cross members and is glued and pinned.

The top is formed from 5 pieces of 4in. T&G boarding, glued and cramped together, then cut and trimmed to size.

A jig-saw will be required to cut the curved baroque pattern on the scroll. This is quite easy to mark if you use the template outline shown here, but considerable care is needed in the cutting if you don't want to end up trying to remove irregularities in the curves with a spokeshave.

The joints for the corners of the drawers are of the tongue and grooved type which can be seen in a do-it-yourself manual.

Whenever possible, purchase dressed timber, or plane and sand down all pieces before you commence construction. This is necessary because it would be extremely difficult to obtain a good finish to this unit when it is complete.

Materials

If the table is to be left in a natural finish, varnished, then a suitably attractive wood, or combination of wood, will be needed. Knotty pine has been used for this table, because it is attractive and easy to obtain. (The smaller picture shows this natural finish while the main illustration gives an alternative of painting the table to match your decorative scheme.) But if you use something more exotic, such as teak, then you may have difficulty in obtaining T&G boarding in this particular wood. But bear in mind that T&G is not essential for the table top if you use the techniques mentioned below.

Tapering the legs

Cut all four legs to the finished length. On one end of the grain of each piece make a mark. The marked ends indicate the tops of the legs.

Place one of the legs on a table and mark off a line 18in. (457mm) downwards from the top of the leg. Continue the line round all four sides.

On the end grain of the bottom of the leg, mark off a square, $\frac{1}{4}$in. (6mm) inwards all round, as shown in Fig.3.

Place the leg horizontal in a wood vice, with sufficient standing clear of the vice to enable you to plane the leg.

With a bench plane set to fine, carefully plane from the 18in. marked line down to the bottom of the leg. Start with slight pressure on the plane, increasing slightly towards the end of the stroke. This will ensure that you take off more wood progressively as the blade travels towards the bottom, creating a tapering surface. The limit of the taper can be seen by one side of the square marked on the end grain—when the plane has cut down to this line, the correct degree of taper has been reached. Repeat on the remaining three sides, and on the remaining three legs.

The table top

The procedure for joining the five pieces to form the table top is the same whether using T&G or boarding with flush edges.

The butting edges are glued and placed together, then held by at least two sash cramps while the adhesive sets. This technique is quick and effective.

When the adhesive binding the five pieces has set, don't start trimming the panel to size immediately. Leave this until you have built the frame, then you can direct trim the top to the correct size.

The side frames

First build the two side frames. The outline for these is shown in Fig.1. Cut four cross members (D) to size, then cut tenons on both ends of each. The dimensions for these are shown in Fig.4.

Lay two legs down on a flat surface, about 14in. (356mm) apart, then place two cross members (D) in position in between. One member must run between the leg tops, flush with the end, and the other one below this, with 12in. (305mm) in between as shown in Fig.1. Mark off the positions of the mortises, using the tenons on the cross members as templates, then cut out the mortises in the legs. Repeat this with the remaining two legs and cross members.

When everything fits properly, glue and fit all joints, place the frames one on top of the other, and hold the joints in place with two sash cramps while the adhesive sets.

Finish off by fitting the T&G boarding between the D members of each frame. The ends of the T&G are cut to fit flush with the top of the upper D member, and flush with the bottom of the lower one. They are fixed with glue and panel pins.

The centre frame

Using the same procedure described above, construct the centre frame which comprises the uprights (A), the remaining two D members, and the T&G boarding.

To ensure that the eventual fit will match, lay the right hand frame (on the left in Fig.2) down on a flat surface, and mark and fit the centre frame using the frame underneath as a guide.

Left. *Don't make the mistake of thinking of a telephone table as a luxury. It will fill many other functions, and after a while you will be wondering how you ever managed without one.*

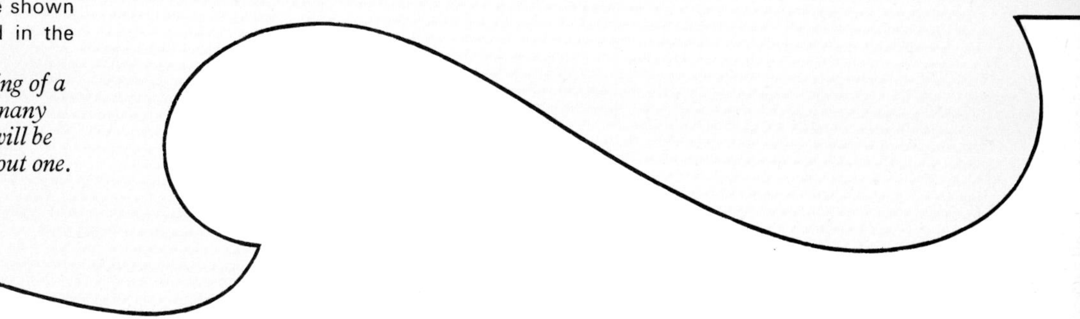

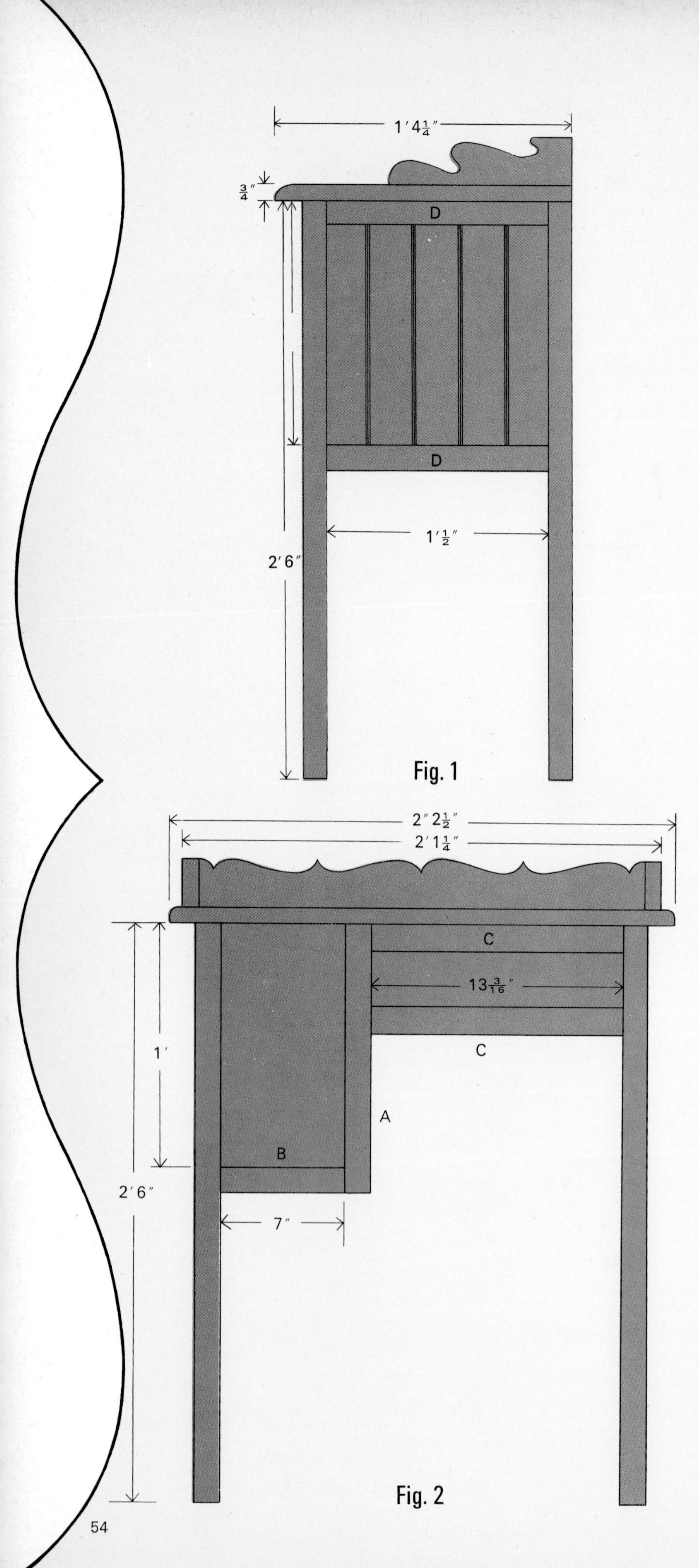

The directory cabinet

The next stage is to build the directory cabinet on to the right hand frame.

Stand the right hand and centre frames on their back edges on a flat surface, about 7in. (178mm) apart. They should be in the same positions as shown in Fig.2, but resting on what will eventually be the back of the table.

Mark and cut the 4 cross pieces B, then cut tenon joints in both ends of each piece.

Using the same procedure as that described above, use the tenon joints as templates to mark out mortise joints in the legs and uprights. When this has been done, glue and cramp all joints until the glue has set.

Finish off this section by cutting and fitting the plywood base of the cabinet. This must overlap the cross members and is glued and pinned in position.

Finishing the frame

When the adhesive has set properly, use the same technique to fit the 4 cross members (C) in between the cabinet and the left hand frame.

While the glue is setting, mark the lengths of the drawer runners, then cut them to size. The drawer runners lie in between the inside ends of the lower C runners, and are simply butted, glued and pinned in place. Do this when the glue has set on the C members.

Fitting the top

Stand the frame upright, on its legs. Place the uncut table top in position, and cut and trim where necessary.

Take the top off and, with a bench plane set to fine, round off the four top edges so that each edge has a bevelled surface.

Drill screw holes at 3in. (76mm) intervals round the top frame members, place the table top back in position and drive the screws home from underneath.

Fitting the back

There will be two openings left in the rear of the frame—the cabinet and drawer spaces. Mark a line ½in. (13mm) away from the edges of these openings. Then rebate a ¼in. deep step or recess round each opening. This is best done with a router, clearing the corners out with a sharp chisel.

Cut the plywood backs to fit into these recesses, and pin and glue in place.

The drawer

The drawer shown here has tongued and grooved joints, but you could use mortise and tenon joints, if you prefer. The technique for

The outline on the sides of these pages, and along the bottom of the previous pages, can be transferred to plain paper and used as templates for the baroque surround.
Fig.1. *Side construction view of the table.*
Fig.2. *Front construction view showing the overall dimensions and storage space.*
Fig.3. *The legs are tapered by marking round the leg ends and planing down to the mark.*
Fig.4. *The finished dimensions for the mortise and tenon joints.*
Opposite, top left. *The table with a natural finish of clear varnish.*

building drawers may be adapted from the instructions given on pages 30 to 32.

The front panel of this drawer has had a 1in. (25mm) border planed away round the edges for a decorative effect. This is done by marking a line, 1in. inwards, all round, then planing down with a bench plane set to fine.

When the drawer is ready and fitted, the drawer runners can be pinned in place.

Cutting the scrolls

These are an optional part of the structure. The baroque pattern is marked out using the outline shown here. Run over the outline with tracing paper, then transfer the outline to the $2\frac{1}{2} \times \frac{3}{4}$in. battening.

Use a jigsaw for cutting along the outline, smoothing down any rough edges with a spokeshave.

The scroll is held in position with screws through the underside of the table top. But there is no reason why it should not be glued with a good woodworking adhesive. Using the latter method, there will be no holes to fill if you should tire of the scroll and wish to get rid of it.

It remains but to varnish or paint the unit, and add an attractive handle to the drawer. You will soon be wondering how on earth you ever managed without a telephone table.

Cutting list

Solid wood	**imperial**	**metric**
4 legs	$30 \times 1\frac{1}{2} \times 1\frac{1}{2}$	762 x 38 x 38
2 uprights (A)	$14\frac{1}{2} \times 1\frac{1}{2} \times 1\frac{1}{2}$	368 x 38 x 38
4 cross pieces (B)	$8 \times 1\frac{1}{2} \times 1$	203 x 38 x 25
4 cross pieces (C)	$14 \times 1\frac{1}{2} \times 1$	356 x 38 x 25
6 cross pieces (D)	$13\frac{1}{2} \times 1\frac{1}{2} \times 1$	343 x 38 x 25
5 table top T&G	$26\frac{1}{2} \times 4 \times \frac{1}{2}$	673 x 102 x 13
2 drawer runners	$74 \times 1 \times \frac{3}{4}$	356 x 25 x 19
2 drawer runner beading	$14 \times \frac{1}{4} \times \frac{1}{4}$	356 x 6 x 6
2 drawer front and back	$13 \times 3 \times \frac{3}{4}$	330 x 76 x 19
2 drawer sides	$13\frac{3}{4} \times 3 \times \frac{3}{4}$	349 x 76 x 19
1 rear scroll	$26\frac{1}{2} \times 2\frac{1}{2} \times \frac{3}{4}$	673 x 69 x 19
2 side scrolls	$10 \times 2\frac{1}{2} \times \frac{3}{4}$	254 x 69 x 19
Plywood		
1 storage box base	$13\frac{3}{4} \times 8 \times \frac{1}{4}$	349 x 203 x 6
1 storage box rear	$12\frac{1}{2} \times 7\frac{1}{2} \times \frac{1}{4}$	317 x 191 x 6
1 drawer space rear	$13\frac{1}{2} \times 3\frac{1}{2} \times \frac{1}{4}$	343 x 89 x 36
1 drawer bottom	$12\frac{1}{2} \times 11\frac{3}{4} \times \frac{1}{4}$	317 x 279 x 6

Imperial measurements are in inches, and all metric measurements in millimetres. All measurements are approximate, add 10% for wastage when ordering.

Also required : Screws, panel pins, adhesive.

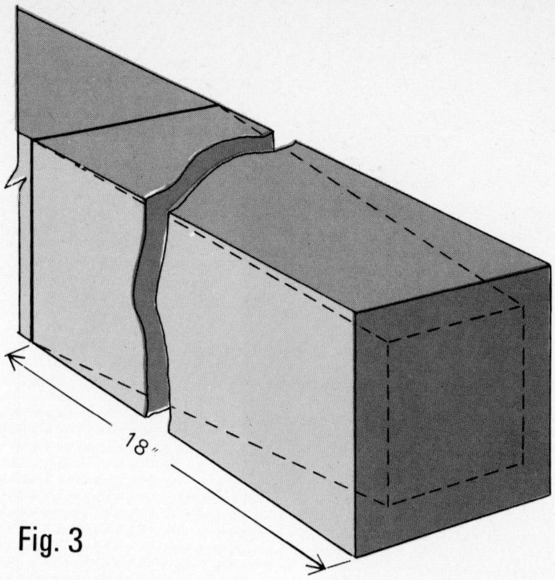

Fig. 3

Fig. 4

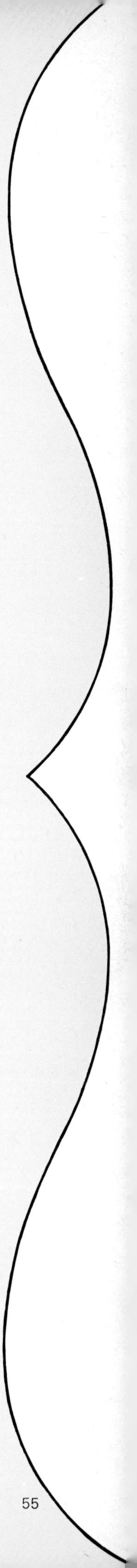

A modern Wardian case

With the introduction of home central heating, the cultivation of indoor plants has become quite difficult. The atmosphere is usually too dry. One answer is a permanent miniature garden which does not need constant attention and which provides an ideal environment — hence the popularity of bottle gardens and Wardian cases. The construction of this modern version of a Wardian case will introduce a fascinating and rewarding hobby into your home.

Invented over a hundred years ago by Dr. Nathaniel Ward, the Wardian case is a miniature conservatory, based on the principle of enclosing plants within glass walls to ensure a close damp atmosphere. This combats not only air dryness but also gas fumes and smog, draughts, and to some extent fluctuations in temperature.

The Wardian case, whether on its stand or installed on a table, will provide a bright and attractive focal centre as well as an interest-provoking conversation piece.

The unit illustrated has been designed as an elegant and pleasing addition to the living-room, drawing-room or hall. It would be ideal in a flat or bedsitter. It can be provided with legs, and stand as an individual unit or placed directly on the floor, in which case it can double as an attractive and original occasional or coffee table.

Before involving yourself in the purchase of materials, you should choose the ultimate location of your Wardian case, for this will have an important bearing on size, height and appearance.

In many homes, the fireplace, once the main design feature of the living room, has been made redundant by the introduction of compact heating units and unobtrusive air conditioning systems; and, of course, the television set has won pride of place as centre of attention. Thus, the fireplace and hearth may well be the ideal location for your Wardian case, in which case the unit illustrated would probably need to be modified, or used without the leg-platform.

Your Wardian case should not be thought of merely as an ornament. Try to put it to some other use, such as serving as a base for a table lamp. If you should decide to use it in this way, be careful to choose a low-wattage bulb. Then you have an unusual feature for your room, combining soft light with attractive foliage. In any case, you should not let the bulb heat the plants. Considerations such as these may influence you to alter or modify the design of your Wardian case.

Left. This Wardian case makes an elegant and pleasing addition to the home; it is based on the principle of enclosing plants within glass walls to ensure a close damp atmosphere.

The unit illustrated comprises—

(a) the soil tray;
(b) the glass case;
(c) the timber base;
(d) the stand, or leg-platform.

NIGEL MESSETT

***Above.** In many homes the fireplace is the ideal location for a Wardian case. The unit illustrated would need to be used without the leg-platform if sited in this way.*

The soil tray

The dimensions of your unit will be governed by the external dimensions of an available soil tray. Ideally, this should be made of plastic or a similar waterproof material. You will probably find a suitable tray at your local hardware or garden supply store.

If a plastic one is not available, you may decide to make or purchase a metal one. Ideally, it should be at least 5in. (127mm) deep. It should have a lip round the top edge wide enough to provide a solid base for the glass case to rest on. It would be necessary to protect a metal tray from rust by painting it with a high-gloss water-resistant paint.

You may, of course, create an attractive soil tray from some other material, such as terrazzo floor tiles bonded together with cement or plastic adhesive. But you must be sure that your tray is completely waterproof.

As stated, the shape and size of the tray will dictate the design of the other units, and may be the inspiration for an unusual design. A circular tray, for instance, may necessitate the use of a cylindrical or hexagonal case made of perspex in preference to glass.

Having obtained a suitable tray, place it upside down on a sheet of paper and accurately trace its overall exterior shape. By applying a ruler to this tracing, you will be able to obtain the dimensions of the glass case, the timber base and the stand.

In the unit illustrated, the soil tray measures 16in. by $16\frac{5}{8}$in. (407mm by 423mm), and these dimensions dictate the size of the other pieces.

The glass case

The glass specified for the housing is 24oz., or 3mm ($\frac{1}{8}$in.). Float glass is recommended, as it is strong and free from distortion. However, before finalizing your choice of glass, make sure you can obtain the specified plastic corner and edge channel which is sold by most DIY shops. Otherwise you will have to fashion your own from wood battens heavily varnished.

You will need a large flat surface to lay the glass on, such as a kitchen or dining table. Place a blanket on the table to protect it and the surface of the glass from being scratched.

A steel-wheel glass-cutter is adequate for the job. Try to choose one on which the wheel is clearly visible while the tool is in use, as this will promote greater accuracy. If you have never cut glass before, it would be better to order the glass ready cut.

Before cutting, clean the surface of the glass by wiping it with a proprietary glass cleaner, or with methylated spirits. Mark the cutting lines on the surface and re-check the dimensions before cutting.

The sides of the glass case are 15in. (381mm) deep. Cut as follows:

Two pieces for front and rear to a width of $16\frac{3}{8}$in. (416mm).

Two side pieces $15\frac{3}{4}$in. (390mm).

One piece for the case top: $15\frac{1}{2}$in. x $14\frac{7}{8}$in. (394mm x 378mm).

Before cutting, lubricate the glass cutter by wiping it over with a piece of felt which has been soaked in light machine oil. With a straight-edge held $\frac{1}{8}$in. (3mm) from the marking line (to allow for the thickness of the wheel) score the surface of the glass along the line with the cutter. Cut with a firm, smooth stroke, drawing your arm back while keeping the rest of your body still. Do not backtrack as the glass may break at a point other than where you want your cutting line. For more detailed instructions on glazing, including how to remove rough edges to get a true finish, see a DIY manual.

Using a fine-toothed hacksaw, cut four lengths of plastic corner channel, allowing $\frac{1}{4}$in. (6mm) for the top hardwood moulding. The length, therefore, is $14\frac{3}{4}$in. (375mm). Trim to accuracy with a handyman's knife.

Select a $16\frac{3}{8}$in. (416mm) glass panel as the front of the case. Apply an epoxy resin to one of its 15in. (380mm) edges and along a $\frac{1}{4}$in. (6mm) strip on each face. Slide the panel into one channel of the plastic corner moulding, leaving $\frac{1}{4}$in. (6mm) at the top to allow for the hardwood moulding to be fitted later. Secure temporarily

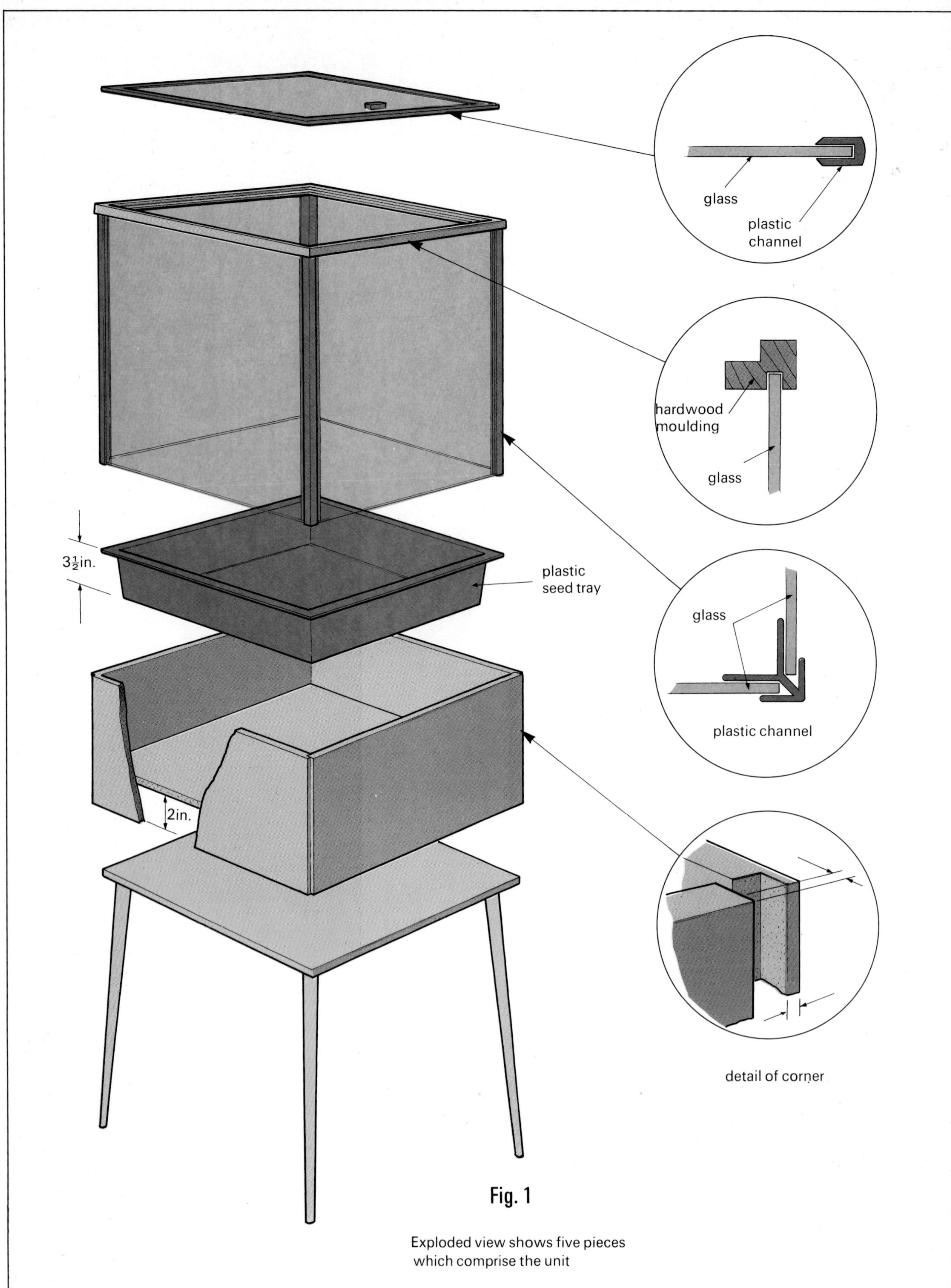

Fig. 1

Exploded view shows five pieces which comprise the unit

with adhesive tape on both surfaces and leave to harden.

Select a side panel. Apply epoxy resin to a 15in. (380mm) edge. Slide into the second channel of the plastic corner moulding. Secure with adhesive tape and leave to harden.

Using the same method, fix the glass panels at all four corners.

In the illustrated example, $\frac{1}{2}$in. (12mm) dull finished black adhesive tape has been applied vertically on the outside panel adjoining both sides of each corner join. This is purely decorative and may be left off if desired.

The back tape has also been applied to the bottom perimeter to achieve a snug fitting at the junction of the glass case and the soil tray.

With a fine-toothed panel saw, cut the four lengths of hardwood moulding at 45° angles. Fix to the top edges of the four glass panels, using epoxy resin. Secure temporarily with adhesive tape and leave to harden.

Check the lid aperture. Cut the plastic edge moulding at a 45° angle with a fine-toothed hacksaw. Using epoxy resin, apply the moulding to the edges of the glass top. Secure temporarily with adhesive tape. Leave to harden. Apply epoxy resin to handle bottom and surface of the lid. Place handle in position under weight. Leave to dry. Remove all temporary adhesive tape.

The timber base

The base unit is a chipboard surround with a false floor. It provides the housing in which the soil tray is concealed, holds the glass case in place on the lip of the tray, and fits snugly over the stand or leg-platform. If no legs are required, it provides an attractively finished base for the unit.

The base is constructed of $\frac{11}{16}$in. (17mm) chipboard, (see cutting list).

Mark the groove lines along the 8in. (200mm) sides of the two side members. Cut with a tenon saw and finish with a bevel-edged chisel.

Fit the front and rear members by pinning and glueing into the rebated side members. Cut veneer edge strips and apply to exposed edges.

Fig.2. *Cut four lengths of hardwood moulding at 45° angles. Fix to the top edges of the four glass panels, using epoxy resin. Secure temporarily with adhesive tape and leave to harden. Check lid aperture. Cut the plastic edge moulding and apply to glass top.*
Fig.3. *Check internal dimensions of the base unit and cut false bottom as per cutting list. Mark its position from the top edge of the base. Apply woodworking adhesive below this line to the thickness of the chipboard. Place the false bottom in position. Pin and glue.*
Fig.4. *The leg-platform does not have to be trimmed with veneer edge since it is concealed beneath the base unit. This is a chipboard surround with a false floor. The first step in assembling the case is to fit the base unit over the leg-platform.*
Fig.5. *The dimensions of your unit will be governed by the external dimensions of the soil tray. Ideally, this should be made of plastic or a similar waterproof material. To assemble, place the soil tray into the top of the timber base unit.*

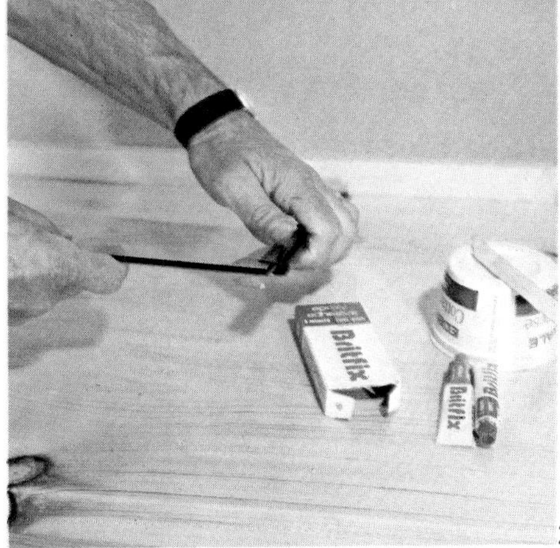

2

3

4

5

HARRY BUTLER

Check the internal dimensions and cut the false bottom as per cutting list.

Mark the position of the false bottom 5in. (127mm) from the top edge of the base. (This may vary with the depth of your soil tray). Apply woodworking adhesive below this line to the thickness of the chipboard. Place the false bottom in position. Pin and glue.

Cut and fix veneer edge trim to exposed edges. Glasspaper and finish as desired.

Your Wardian case is now complete except for the stand or leg-platform.

The stand

Cut the stand top. This does not have to be trimmed with veneered edge, since it is concealed beneath the wooden base unit. But if you do provide an attractive top, it will be possible to ring the changes occasionally by placing the Wardian case on a table, or the floor, and use the stand as a separate small table.

A variety of timber, metal and plastic furniture legs with purpose-made steel fittings is available from hardware and department stores, packaged as 'kits'. Each kit comprises four legs, four fixing-plates and the requisite screws.

These precision-made legs and plates give rigidity without the use of ugly cross-rails, and the result is a slim clean line. They are time-saving and very simple to fit.

To assemble your Wardian case:

(a) stand the timber base on the stand;

(b) place the soil tray into the top of the timber base;

(c) fit the glass case into the base so that the lower edge of the case rests on the top edge lip of the seed-tray;

(d) locate the lid in the top hardwood edge moulding.

You are now ready to plant out your indoor garden. Make certain you obtain information on care of plants and ferns before you begin. You will find that with a little imagination and a certain amount of initial effort you will be able to create a miniature conservatory which will bring you years of pleasure.

Cutting list

Material	Imperial	Metric
2 panels veneered chipboard	$17\frac{3}{8}$x8x$\frac{11}{16}$	440x203x17
2 panels veneered chipboard	$16\frac{7}{8}$x8x$\frac{11}{16}$	429x203x17
1 panel veneered chipboard	$16\frac{5}{8}$x16x$\frac{11}{16}$	423x406x17
1 panel veneered chipboard	16x15x$\frac{11}{16}$	407x381x17
2 strips hardwood moulding	$16\frac{1}{8}$x$\frac{3}{4}$x$\frac{1}{2}$	411x19x12
2 strips hardboard moulding	$16\frac{13}{16}$x$\frac{3}{4}$x$\frac{1}{2}$	424x19x12
1 hardwood handle	$1\frac{1}{2}$x$\frac{1}{2}$x$\frac{1}{2}$	38x12x12
2 panels Float glass	$15\frac{3}{4}$x15x$\frac{1}{8}$	400x381x3
2 panels Float glass	$16\frac{3}{8}$x15x$\frac{1}{8}$	416x381x3
1 panel Float glass	$15\frac{1}{2}$x$14\frac{7}{8}$x$\frac{1}{8}$	393x378x3
4 lengths plastic corner channel	$14\frac{3}{4}$x$\frac{1}{8}$x$\frac{1}{8}$	375x3x3
2 lengths plastic edge channel	$15\frac{3}{4}$x$\frac{1}{8}$	400x3
2 lengths plastic edge channel	$15\frac{1}{8}$x$\frac{1}{8}$	384x3
1 plastic seed tray	$16\frac{5}{8}$x16x$3\frac{1}{2}$	423x407x89

Easy build hall stand

If you have ever rummaged for your overcoat among a pile of coats hanging on a solitary hook in the hallway, or stumbled over carelessly left shoes, then this hall stand is for you. It has plenty of space for all the family's outdoor coats, and room to store shoes and umbrellas. It also looks good, and is very easy to make.

The hall stand has ample room for hanging coats, space for storing shoes in the base, and an umbrella stand. The lower part of the stand can be used as a telephone table, or simply a stand for a flower pot.

All the major parts of the hall stand are cut from one sheet of 8ft x 4ft, or 2440mm x 1220mm, ½in., or 13mm, birch plywood. You will need a small extra sheet of plywood for piece F—see Fig.3. The only other timber you need is 1in. x 1in. or 25mm x 25mm PAR or 1in. triangular moulding. The clothes rail of the hall stand can be made from 1in. timber dowel, but a length of round tubular steel will carry the coats better.

The construction of the hall stand, with its butted joints, is straightforward. The only difficult job is accurate cutting of the pieces from the sheet of plywood. A power jigsaw is an essential tool for this project.

Marking out the panels

Accurate marking out of the plywood sheet is essential, or the finished construction will not be square. To mark out the sheet you will need a tee square, a large set square, and a hard pencil or an indelible pen. You will also need a steel tape measure and a straightedge, or a 3ft or 1m rule.

First, make sure that the plywood sheet is perfectly square, by measuring the diagonals. If it is not, you will have to plane it square with a long smoothing plane. Large boards can be propped upright while planing, using a block of wood and a wedge as support.

You can now mark out the sheet, taking all dimensions from the marking out diagram (Fig.1). Mark out the boards in a series of straight lines, marking right angles from the edges of the sheet with the tee square, and from within the edges of the sheet, from lines already marked, with the set square.

All the curves shown in Fig.1 have a radius of 4in. (102mm). The best way of marking these is to make a cardboard template of the curve. Draw a circle with a 4in. (102mm) radius on a piece of cardboard, and then square a horizontal and a vertical line through the centre point. Cut out the circle.

At the points where the curve is to be drawn (see Fig.1), measure a distance of 4in. (102mm) from the corner along the two lines that form the right angle. Lay the cardboard template on the sheet of plywood with the ends of the squared lines touching the marked points. Then draw round the template to form the curve in the corner.

Cutting out the components

You will need a power jigsaw to cut out the panels for the hall stand. You must cut accurately, and follow the order of cutting shown in Fig.2. To help make the first cuts you can pin a timber straightedge to the plywood, along the marked lines. This will guide the blade of the jigsaw. When you come to the end of the first cuts, and start to make the second cuts, curve the saw out into the waste area of the plywood (see Fig.2). These corners can be trimmed square with a tenon saw later.

When you have cut the panels for the two large sides of the hall stand, clean them up. Trim off any waste plywood. Then lay the two panels together, one on top of the other, and clamp them with a few G cramps. Plane the straight edges square with a smoothing plane and shape the curves neatly with a spokeshave.

Then unclamp the boards. The edge of long curved area on the 'inside' of the two large sides should be rounded slightly—this looks better than square edges. Don't do this on any of the outer edges of these sides, though, as the other components of the hall stand are butt jointed to these.

The other panels for the hall stand can now be cut from the plywood sheet. Refer to Fig.1 for the dimensions. Trim the panels square.

There is an alternative method of construction if you are not sure whether you can cut two identical panels for the large sides. This method uses two sheets of plywood which are clamped together and cut, after the shape of the large side has been drawn on to one of the sheets. This, of course, wastes more timber than the proceedure described above. Another alternative, which involves altering the dimensions of the unit, is to cut one plywood sheet in half across its width and cut out the outline of the sides, with scaled down dimensions, with the two parts clamped together. This will give you a hall stand about 3ft 10in. (1169mm) high—ideal for children's overcoats.

Left. *Good looking and modern, this unit provides super storage where it can be most useful. It banishes overworked clothes hooks and the often untidy jumble of coats that drape from them.*

TUBBY

Fig. 1

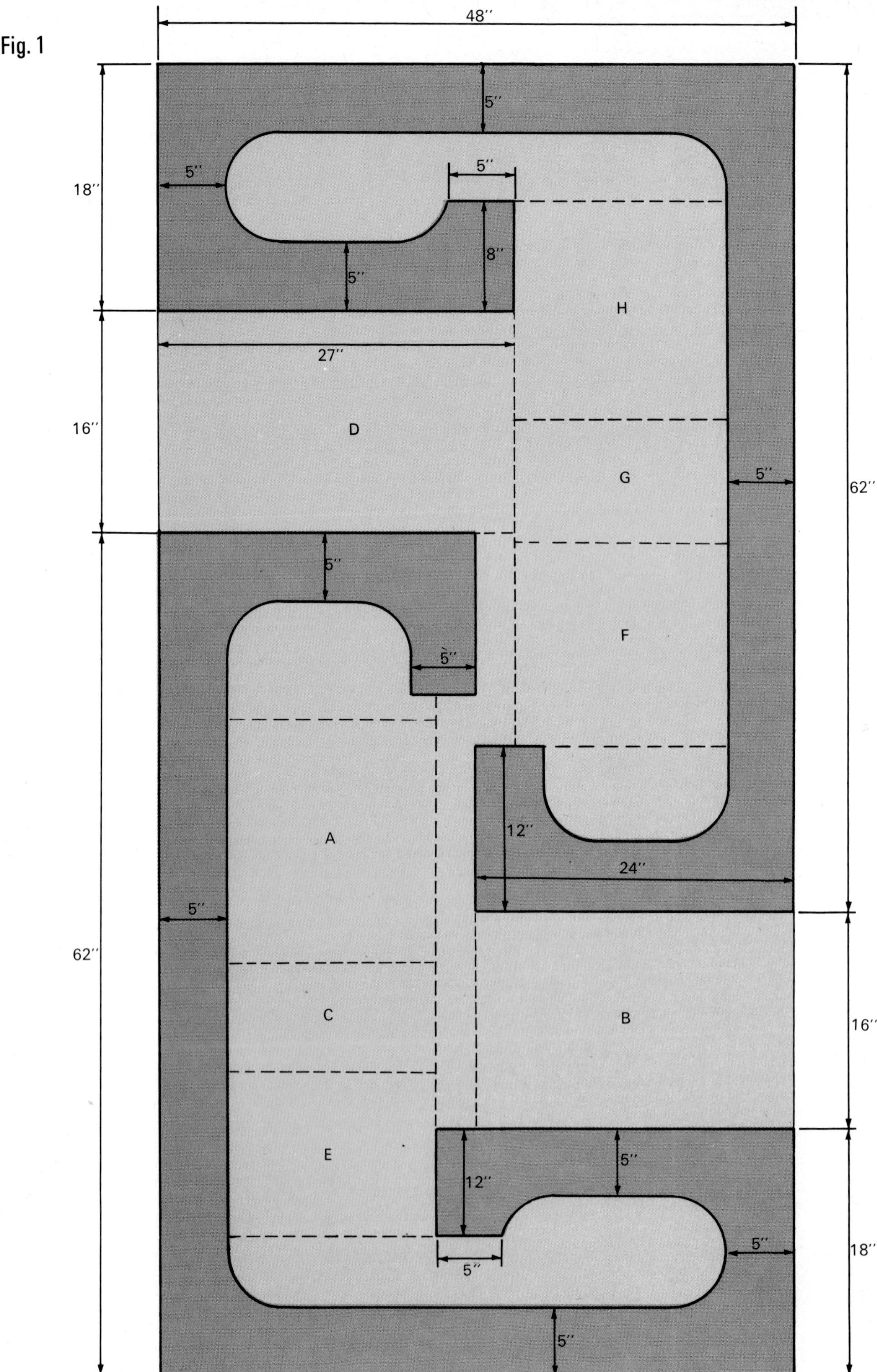

Fig.2

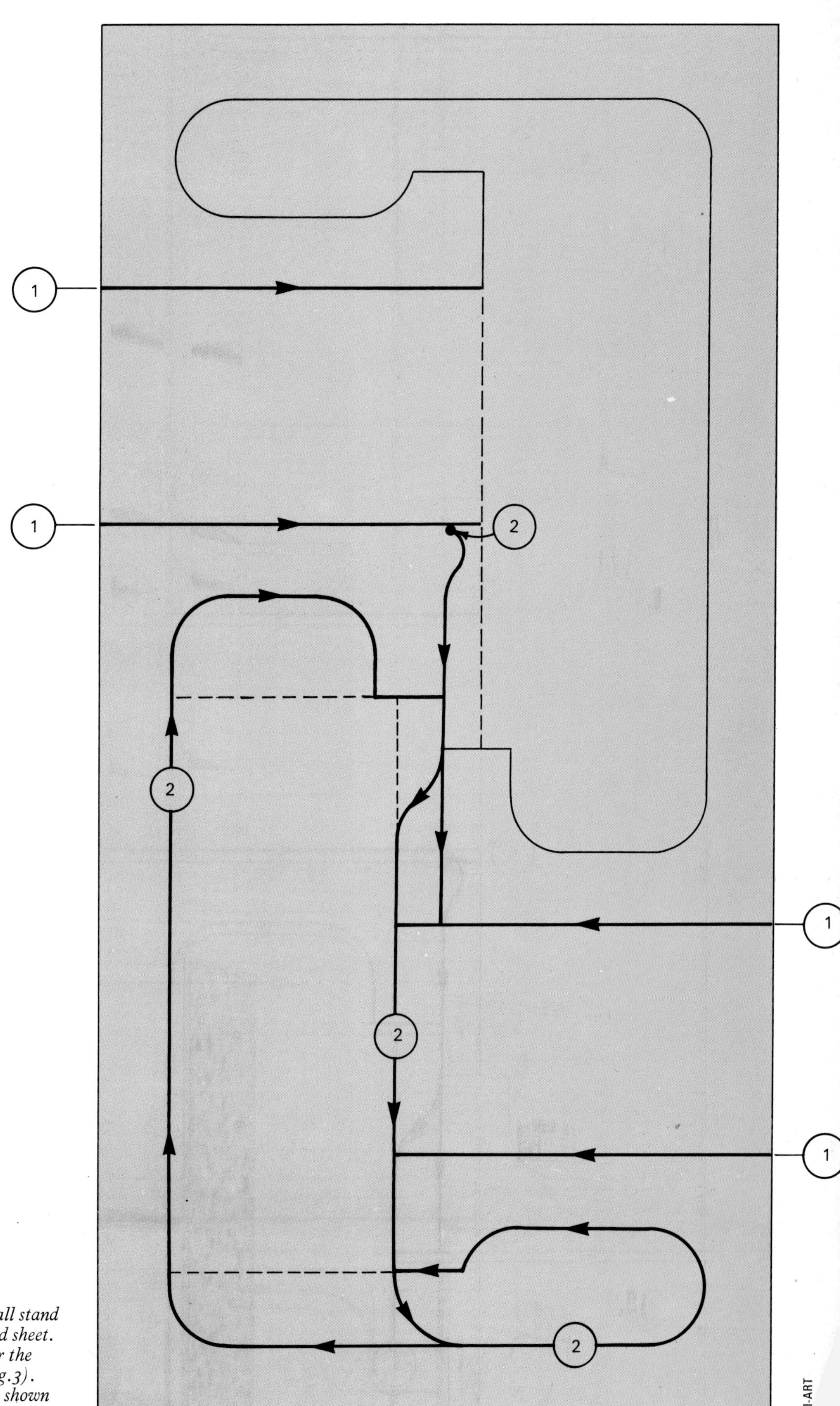

Fig.1. *Nearly all the parts of the hall stand can be cut from one 8ft x 4ft plywood sheet. You will need a small extra piece for the back of the hall stand (piece F in Fig.3).*
Fig.2. *Follow the cutting procedure shown here to make the sides of the hall stand.*

TRI-ART

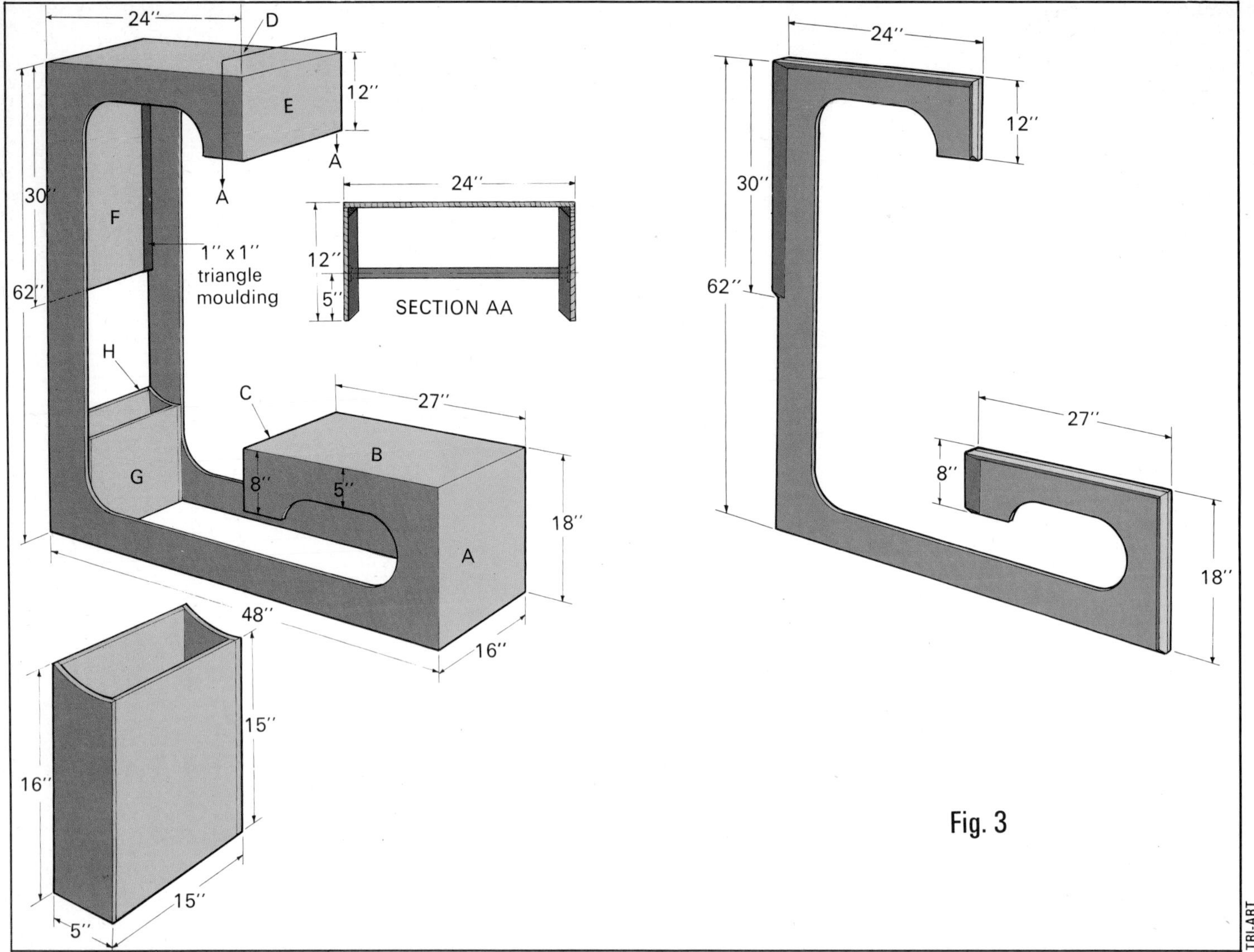

Fig. 3

Fig.3 (left). *Perspective view of the hall stand and of the umbrella stand.*
Fig.3 (right). *Pin strips of timber to the sides as shown to strengthen the butt joints.*

Assembling the unit

All the joints used in the construction are butted and pinned with extra fixing provided by 1in. x 1in. (25mm x 25mm) strips of timber. If you use square sectioned timber for these fixing strips, you should cut it to a triangular section with a bench saw. Alternatively, buy triangular shaped moulding. You will have to mitre the ends of the timber at joints, so do not cut the pieces of fixing strip yet—'direct measure' and cut them to length just before you pin them in place.

Lay one large side of the unit on a flat surface and glue and pin the fixing strip to it with 1in. (25mm) panel pins, in the position shown in Fig.3. Mitre the ends of the strip where necessary. One square edge of the strip should be flush with the edges of the large sides.

When you do this job on the other large side, make sure you pin the fixing strip to the right surface. Lay the second side down on the flat surface with its long edge butting that of the first side. Then pin the moulding in place on the second side.

The next step is to pin the other panels to the two large sides. This job can be a little awkward, because the large sides are unwieldy, so you may need some help. Pin piece A (see Fig.3) from the table, or lower, section in place, and piece E and F from the canopy, or upper, section. Piece C from the table section comes next, followed by pieces B and D, the tops of the table and canopy sections.

The umbrella stand

The next stage is to make and fix the umbrella stand. This is a simple box construction, glued to the inside face of the two large sides.

Cut the pieces for the box to the size and shape shown in Fig.3. You can mark the curve on the top of the narrow sides of the box using the cardboard template made earlier. Cut the curve with a jigsaw with the two narrow sides held together in a vice.

Now glue these sides to the inside face of the large sides of the hall stand. The bottom edge of these narrow sides should be flush with the bottom edge of the large sides of the hall stand. One long edge of the narrow sides of the umbrella stand should be set ½in. (13mm) in from the back long edge of the large sides of the hall stand. This allows the back of the umbrella stand box construction to fit flush with the back edges of the large sides. Pin the wide sides of the umbrella stand in place.

The coat rail

The coat rail for the canopy section of the hall stand is 16in. (407mm) long. It can be made from 1in. (25mm) timber dowel or 1in. tubular steel rod. This can be fixed at the ends with small blocks of plywood with a 1in. wide U shape cut into them. These blocks can be made from off-cuts from the plywood sheet, and glued and pinned in place. Alternatively you can choose one of the proprietary wardrobe rail fixings available. One of the simplest consists of a small chrome or brass disc with a screw hole drilled off-centre and a raised rim around half the circumference. These are screwed in place through the hole and the rail lifted in place to rest on the rim. Whatever fixing you choose, it should be fixed in place about halfway along the canopy sides, and about 2in. (50mm) up from the curved bottom edge of these pieces.

Finishing

Rub down the edges of the hall stand with glasspaper and trim up any irregularities with a finely set smoothing plane. Fill any gaps at the joints with wood filler. Then paint the unit in the colour of your choice, taking care that you make a good choice of brush and paint.

You now possess an original and attractive hall stand.

HEDRICH BLESSING/ARCHITECT ALDEN & DOW ASSOCIATES

Above. *Room dividers vary from attractive and useful units made from whitewood cupboards to this luxurious purpose-built piece of furniture. Here, the divider is built from the same wood as the ceiling and designed so that it becomes an integral part of the room.*

Room dividers to make space—and save it

Whitewood cupboards are more than storage units. You can paint them, group them on your walls and link them with vertical boards to make an attractive wall unit. Better still, hang them between vertical boards and decorate them imaginatively to provide a contemporary-style room divider with built-in storage space. You can design your room divider to look exactly as you like and the right size to take all those things you want to store in it.

It is easy to build cupboards into wall units and room dividers; a drill, screwdriver, set-square and saw are about all the tools you need. And this system of hanging cupboards from vertical boards makes the units easy to construct. If the vertical boards project slightly beyond the front edge of the cupboards, it will not be so noticeable if the cupboards are fractionally out of line.

Choosing a type

Room dividers come in all shapes and size

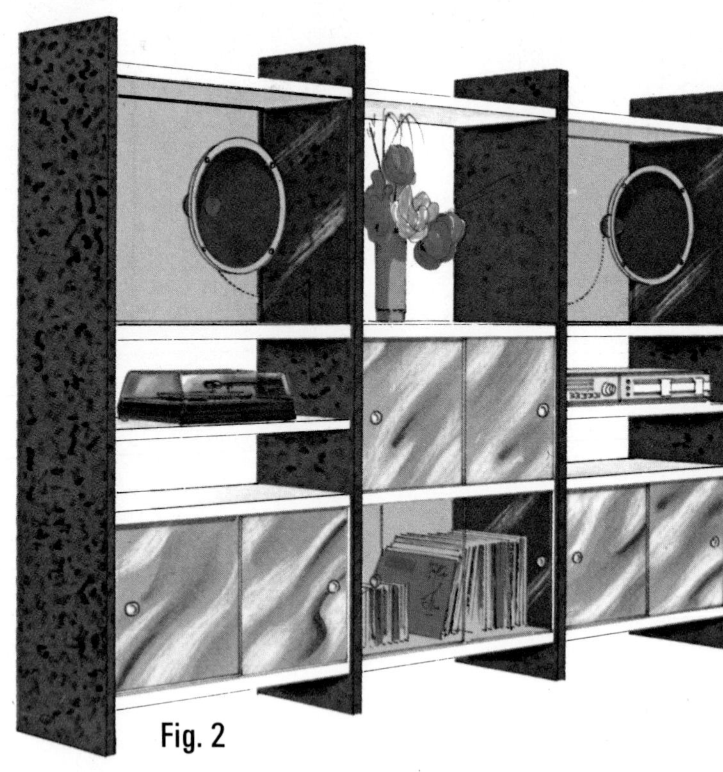

Fig.1. *A gay and practical room divider especially suitable for a nursery. Built from six whitewood cupboards—three on each side—with a space behind each cupboard, this unit looks the same from both sides. It also gives plenty of storage space and is very strong.*
Fig.2. *A slimline, single width but less robust divider constructed around three whitewood cupboards faced with foil. Sliding doors fitted to a shelf make a record cabinet. Speakers fitted here in sheets of plastic could also be fitted in wooden units.*

Fig.3. *Ten cupboards (five either side) make an attractive and strong divider. The prights are tongue and grooved boards nailed attens.Keep the space behind the ision open to prevent overheating.*

Fig.4. *A slimline divider with a double row of cupboards placed back to back and hung from very narrow uprights. Stability is sacrificed for looks and so the unit must be securely anchored to the floor and ceiling.*

opposite side in the same way as the cupboards. Hidden or adjustable shelf supports may also be installed.

Fixing cupboards to walls

When constructing a wall unit as in Fig.6, you should design it so that the weight of the cupboards is taken by the wall and not by the uprights. The uprights need not then reach right down to the floor; they serve merely to break up the units visually. The system of fixing the cupboards described below and shown in Fig.5 enables the cupboards to be fixed exactly level with each other, and makes it possible to remove the units easily if you want to redecorate behind them. Cut a length of wood say 150mm x 25mm or 6in. x 1in. lengthways at an angle of 45°. Fasten one length to the wall with the narrowest side against the wall and the slanting edge upwards, so that it forms a long hook. It should be screwed to the wall with plugs and screws every 4in. (110mm). Then cut the other batten into pieces the same length as the cupboards. Screw the pieces to the top of each unit at exactly the same level, and with the groove at the bottom and the narrowest side against the unit. Nail a length of narrow batten the same thickness as the top batten to the bottom rear edge of the unit. Then simply lift the cupboard into place and hook the batten at the top over the batten on the wall. The cupboards can be slid along the batten, which allows you to space them as you wish. If you want to have uprights between the cupboards, screw them to one of the cupboards. A notch will have to be cut in the rear edge of each upright to fit over the wall-mounted batten; this will not show when everything is in place.

Height of the units

The easiest way to assemble a room divider is to lay the pieces horizontally on the floor, screw them together and then raise the complete unit to its feet. But the diagonal length from corner to corner of a board is longer than the straight length. So the height of the room from floor to ceiling must be at least the diagonal length of the dividers. If you want a floor-to-ceiling divider, you will have to build it in position, piece by piece, which is harder, or else make it under size and finish it with an extra piece at the top to bring it to the full height, as shown in Fig.4.

A room divider with a solid row of cupboards at the bottom could be raised on a plinth instead which would give an attractive and unusual look. This should contain wide cross-pieces to support the bottom of the vertical boards. But it would be quite difficult to lift a complete divider on to a plinth. You might even have to use car jacks. And the designs shown here, which have gaps at the bottom, would look wrong mounted on a plinth.

Very tall, narrow units such as the one shown in Fig.3 may have stability problems if they are just resting on the floor and not fastened down in any way. The best way to cure the trouble is simply nail them lightly to the ceiling. Three or four nails to every vertical board should be enough, but they must pass through the plaster into a joist.

You can find the joists in a ceiling quite easily by tapping the plaster lightly with a stick—the area over a joist makes a duller sound than the rest—and then drilling a few test holes with your narrowest drill to find the exact spot. When you have found a joist above most of the vertical boards—you may not manage to find one above all of them, but this doesn't matter—skew nail the top of the board in place as unnoticeably as possible from both sides of the board. Use lost head nails and punch their heads below the surface of the wood. Fill the dents with wood filler if they show. Make good the holes in the ceiling with cellulose filler.

Assembling the unit

Take the pieces of board you are going to use for the uprights and check that one end of each is square. Then cut the other ends to the right length in the following way. If the unit is to reach the ceiling, or the floor is noticeably irregular, the uprights will not be the same length as each other, because of the slight irregularities in floor and ceiling levels found in all houses. The best way to get these the right length is to mark their positions on the floor, cut them just over length, and (if they are ceiling height) jam them between floor and ceiling as near vertical, and as near their right place, as you can. Then scribe the top to the ceiling as if fitting a shelf into an alcove (see a DIY manual for more detailed instructions. Cut ceiling height uprights to length at this stage, but leave shorter ones above.

Now prop the uprights temporarily in the place they will occupy and use a long spirit level, or a level and a straight edge, held horizontally between them to make a mark on the edge of each upright at exactly the same level a few inches from the floor.

Number the uprights and mark their left and right sides to make sure you don't get them mixed up. Now lay them down on top of one another in their right relative positions and slide them about until the marked horizontal line is level on the edge of each of them. Then square a line across all the edges at the level of the bottom of the shortest upright, and take this as a base line to measure all distances from, including the total height in the case of uprights that do not reach the ceiling.

Working from the base line upwards, mark across the edge of all the uprights the height of the top and bottom of all the cupboards and shelves at their different levels. Then separate the uprights and square the lines across their faces. You only need to draw lines where cupboards will actually fit, of course, so it is not necessary to square all the lines across all the uprights. Non-ceiling height uprights should be cut to their final length at this stage.

Where cupboards are staggered, as in Fig.1, don't forget to allow for the overlap when marking the uprights.

The next stage is to insert dowels in the chipboard uprights to take the mounting screws of the cupboards and shelves. But you can omit this step is you are using materials into which you can screw directly.

To avoid marking the surface of the uprights, all the cupboards should be screwed to them from the inside of the cupboards themselves, and not from the opposite side of the uprights. Lay each cupboard down on its side on an upright in the position it will occupy, making sure that the overlap at front and back is correct. Drill four or more pilot holes through the strong side battens of the cupboards (not the flimsy ply sides) into the chipboard a short way so as just to mark its surface. At this stage you should number the cupboards so as to be sure of putting them back in the same place during final assembly.

When you have marked all the uprights through the sides of the cupboards in this way, insert dowels under the marks to provide a strong fixing point for the screws. If the board you are using is to be edged later, insert the dowels from the edge wherever possible, as this will aid edging later. If the board is already edged, or the dowel is to be inserted a long way from the edge, put the dowel straight into the face. Make sure you don't drill the dowel hole right through the board. Glue the dowels in with a very strong adhesive, preferably an epoxy resin.

At the same time, insert dowels for the shelf mountings. The easiest way of mounting non-adjustable shelves is on aluminium angle strip (this can be done invisibly by using various methods described in DIY manuals.) Adjustable shelves should be mounted on proprietary shelf mounting tracks.

If the unit is to be built as one piece and raised into place, lay all the cupboards on their backs on the floor—or, if the divider is to be two cupboards deep, lay the cupboards for one side face down and those for the other side on top of them face up. If the fronts of the cupboards are to be recessed behind the front edges of the uprights, pack the cupboards up on scrap wood blocks to a height equivalent to the overlap you plan to have.

Now insert the uprights between the cupboards and carefully line everything up in its right place. If the uprights are to be recessed behind the cupboards, as in Fig.1, then the uprights will have to be propped up on blocks instead.

Screw everything together and put in the angle brackets and shelf tracks. When everything is assembled, call in at least two helpers, lift up the unit and set it on its feet. Put the shelves on their mountings and it is complete, except for any final decorative work you may wish to do. If the unit seems unstable, you might fasten it to the floor with angle strip and screws.

If the divider is a floor-to-ceiling type, it will have to be assembled upright and in place. Follow the above instructions up to the point of actual assembly, and then get helpers to hold the cupboards up while you screw them between a pair of verticals. It should be possible, if not particularly easy, to get the whole unit together in this way. It will help if you pre-drill all the screw holes in the dowels before starting work; this should be done through the sides of the cupboards to ensure accuracy. You might also install the shelf mountings at this stage.

Don't attempt to nail the unit to the ceiling joists until it is completely assembled, or you will probably rip the nails out by accidentally pressing too hard on an upright.

NIGEL MESSETT

A cabinet for corners

Here is an attractive and elegant corner cupboard which is ideal for holding and displaying some of your best pieces—Venetian glassware, decanters, pewter mugs etc. Of simple, trim design, this unit solves the problem of utilizing that often-wasted corner space, and at the same time adding a colourful and functional feature to your living room or dining room.

As this unit will become a design feature of almost any room in which it is introduced, care should be taken in the selection of the location. Firstly, does the room need a corner cabinet. Could the room carry the unit from a design point of view. Would the cabinet harmonise with the rest of the furnishings?

As for the corner you have chosen: is the angle of the walls accurate, at right angles. Are the wall surfaces smooth, free from bumps, clear of conduits, light-switches. Will they accept wall-plugs or screws. On which side will the door of the cabinet open? It may be necessary for you to make some minor adjustment to the walls before you commence work on the cabinet.

Taking the project through still further, you may decide that the cabinet as illustrated would not be sufficient for your needs. Your requirement may call for a full-size corner cabinet. If so, you can plan to build two versions of the unit, and stand one on top of the other.

Having cleared up all these points, the next thing you have to decide before purchasing your materials relates to the appearance of the cabinet. You have to be sure that it will not clash with the room aesthetically. A room with antique furniture or dark wall panelling would call for a unit made of dark-stained timber.

This unit is made in high density veneered chipboard, which is available in a variety of timbers, and, of course, can be stained or painted.

Chipboard is the ideal material for your purpose. It is easy to work with and will give a professional finish. Having no grain direction, it can be cut without danger of splitting, and, being a mass-produced precision-made product, can be relied upon for the accuracy of its thickness and the flatness of its surfaces. All exposed edges should be covered by matching veneer edge trim, which is readily available and easy to apply.

Chipboard lends itself to the use of all hand tools, saws, planes and chisels. While drills and hand-held power-tools may be used with confidence.

The chipboard used in this unit is veneered with oak. A range of other tonings is available, including teak, mahogany and white. And, of course, the unit may be painted if you wish.

Construction

Apart from mouldings, all members for the construction of the unit can be cut from a sheet of $\frac{5}{8}$in. (15mm) veneered chipboard 6ft by 18in. (1830mm x 457mm). After scoring the cutting line on both faces and edges with a sharp knife, cut with a fine toothed saw.

Be sure to cut to your own measurements and markings. On no account rely on the supplier's cutting or squaring of edges.

First cut the vertical side members (A and B). Stand the two sides together at right angles, B butting A. This makes the general shape of the unit, and you may care to place it in position in

Left. *Neatly designed to fit snugly into a corner, this triangular cabinet is ideal for displaying selected china pieces. The coloured cloth covering the interior panels makes a flattering background for the designs.*

the corner where it will be ultimately located. This is the time for any minor corrections to size.

A first step in joining members A and B is to accurately mark the hole points for the screws. The screws to be used are 1½in. No. 6. Mark a line $\frac{13}{32}$in. (10.31mm) from a long edge of member A. Now mark with cross lines the screw points along it, the first at 2¼in. (57mm), the others at intervals of 6in. (152mm). Using an awl, mark the screw holes.

Using a $\frac{5}{32}$in. (4mm) drill or bit, drill all holes. Place members A and B together, B butting A along a long edge. Using an awl, mark the first and last holes in the edge of member B. Now, with the point of the drill inserted through the first hole in A, drill a ½in. deep (12mm) hole into the first screw position along the edge of B. Butt B to A; insert screw and tighten a few turns. Insert drill through the last hole in A into the edge of B, drill a ½in. deep (12mm) hole; insert screw and tighten a few turns.

At this point, check the accuracy of your work so far. Check the 90 degree angle of the two members with a set-square. Stand the unit on a smooth surface and check that the ends of both members stand flushly onto it.

Now, inserting the drill through the holes in A, drill the remaining ½in. deep (12mm) holes in the edge of B, insert screws, tighten a few turns.

Check once again for accuracy, then remove all screws. Using a counter-sink bit, modify all holes for countersinking the screw heads.

Apply woodworking adhesive at the junction-line of both members. At the specified time, butt together, then insert screws, tighten the first screw, then the last, then the remaining screws. Screw in tightly to countersink screw-heads. Fill in the holes with matching wood-stopping (such as Brummer). Allow to set, then shave flush with a chisel.

Cut the end triangular members (C and D). Place the base piece in position; glue and pin directly to the ends of the assembled side members. Place the top member in position; glue and pin. Countersink nails and fill holes with matching wood stopping.

At this point you will have built the basic cabinet, and all that is needed now is to add the mouldings, edge trim and door.

To prepare the aperture to receive the door, pin and glue the triangular moulding to the inside front edge of the two side members.

Add veneer edge trim to all front exposed edges. Self-adhesive edging strip is available in cut lengths in white or teak. To apply, position the edging strip, place ordinary brown paper on top. Now apply a warm iron and move slowly over the surface. Remove the iron every two feet and rub down with a cloth to ensure even contact. After 30 minutes, remove any over-hanging edges with a flat fine-cut file, using quick down-strokes.

The shelves

Measure the interior depth of the sides of the cabinet, and mark for positioning of the shelves.

Right. *Apart from mouldings, all members used in the construction of the cabinet can be cut from a single sheet of ⅝in. (15mm) chipboard. It is easy to work with, does not split and gives a professional finish to the job.*

Fig. 1

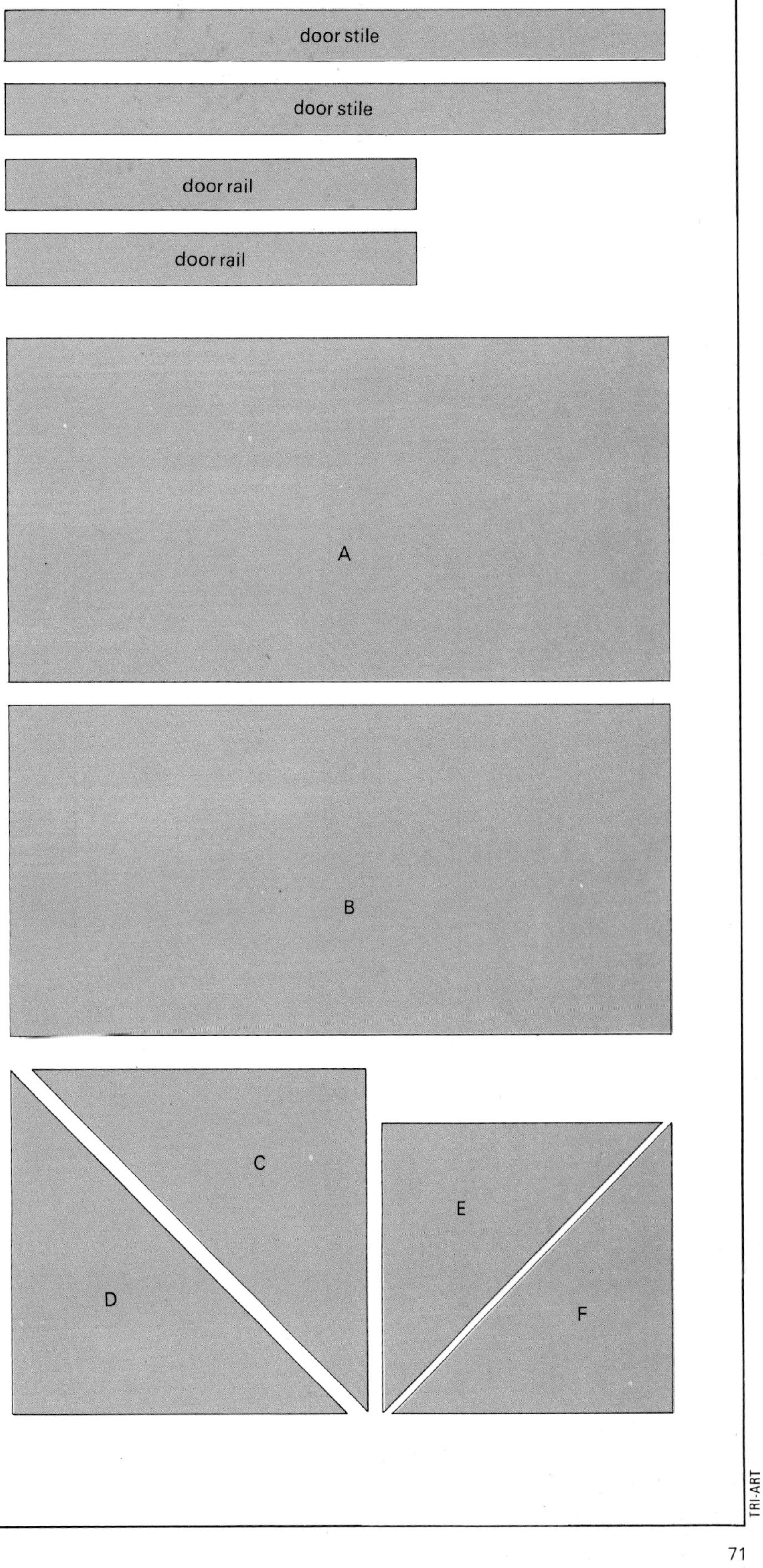

door stile

door stile

door rail

door rail

A

B

C

D

E

F

TRI-ART

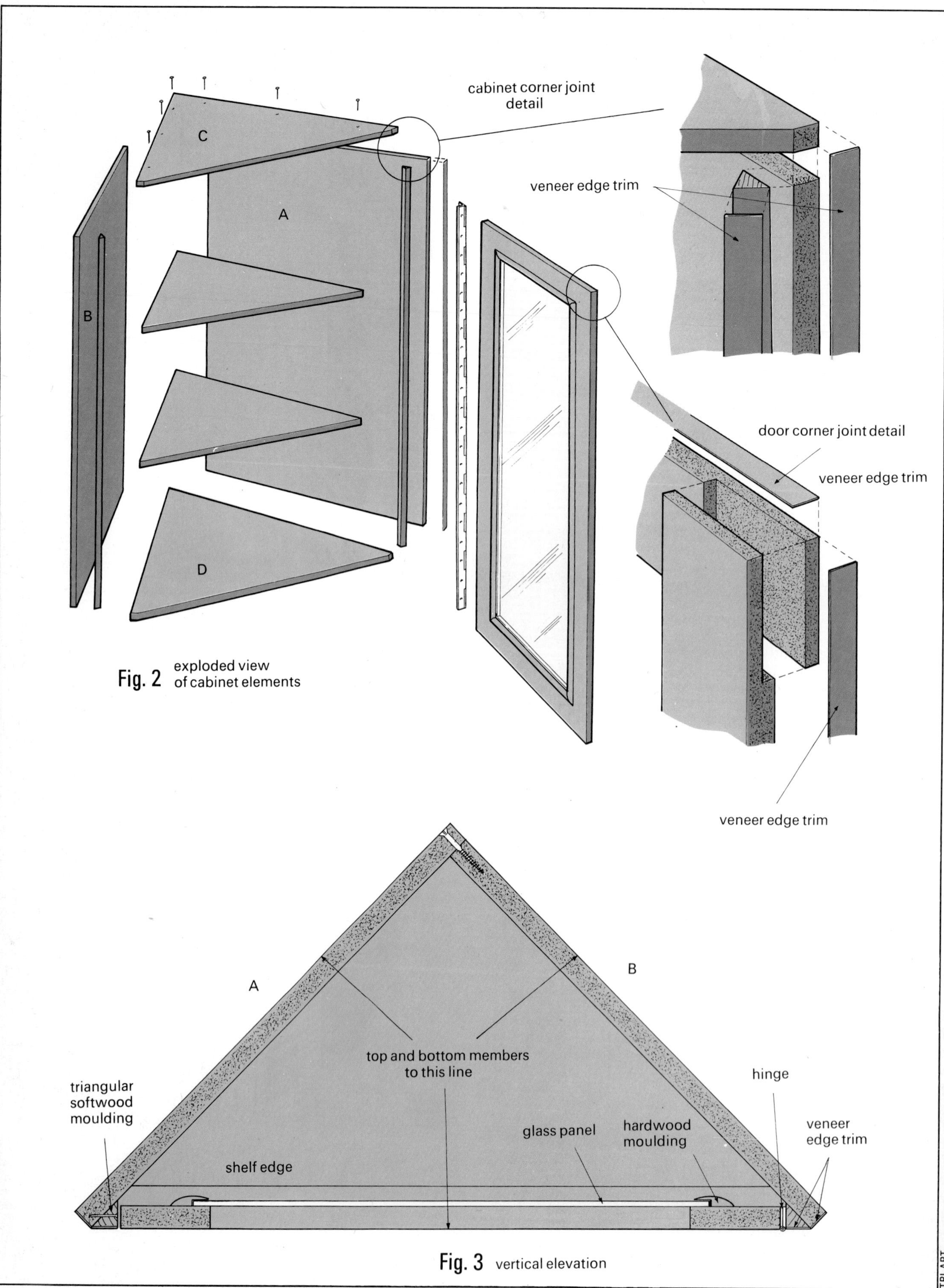

Fig. 2 exploded view of cabinet elements

Fig. 3 vertical elevation

Mark a line 9⅜in. (240mm) from the top, and again from the bottom.

Cut and temporarily fit the shelves into position by screwing through the side members and into the shelf edge.

The door

Check the door aperture and cut the door members to fit.

Cut the door joints (see Fig.2) and assemble by glueing and screwing from inside. Use ½in. No. 4 screws and countersink slightly below the wood surface.

Clean up the door joints and fit the full length brass piano hinge to one edge of the door, taking into consideration the positioning in the room of adjacent furniture, windows, etc.

Note that this design has carried the top and bottom rails of the door fully across instead of using the conventional construction of running the stiles full length. This has been done deliberately, in order to make the door appear wider. However, should you wish to be professionally 'correct', simply turn the door back-to-front so that the stiles run full length, and the rails are shortened at the front.

Temporarily place the hinged door into position in the aperture. Trim as necessary to provide a good fit, making due allowance for the veneer trim to be applied to three edges of the door. Withdraw the door and add veneer edge trim to the three exposed door edges.

Countersink nails and fill all holes with matching plastic wood, or any proprietary wood filler.

Glazing

Now you are ready to prepare the door ready to receive the glass panel. The special moulding used is ¾in. (19mm) rebated half-round ramin moulding. Measure, mark and cut at 45 degree

4

5

6

7

8

9

10

11

12

HARRY BUTLER

13

Fig.4. *Place members A and B together, B butting A along a long edge. When screwed together, these make the general shape.*
Fig.5. *Place base member D in position; glue and pin directly to the ends of the assembled sides. Glue and pin member C.*
Fig.6. *To prepare the aperture to receive the door, cut two 30in. (762mm) lengths of ¾in. triangular moulding; add basic unit.*
Fig.7. *Pin and glue the triangular moulding to the inside front edge of the two vertical members to serve as a door frame.*
Fig.8. *Add veneer edge trim to all front edges which are exposed. Self-adhesive edging strip is available in white or teak.*
Fig.9. *Cut and temporarily fit the shelves in position. Attach by screwing through the side members and into the shelf edges.*
Fig.10. *Cut the door joints and assemble by glueing and screwing from inside. Use ½in. No. 4 screws and countersink.*
Fig.11. *Clean up the door joints, fit the full length brass piano hinge to one edge of the door, then place the door into position.*
Fig.12. *Prepare the door ready to receive the glass panel by fitting special rebated half-round ramin moulding.*
Fig.13. *Fit the door to the main unit, placing cardboard at top and bottom. Fit screws in, remove cardboard, check clearance.*

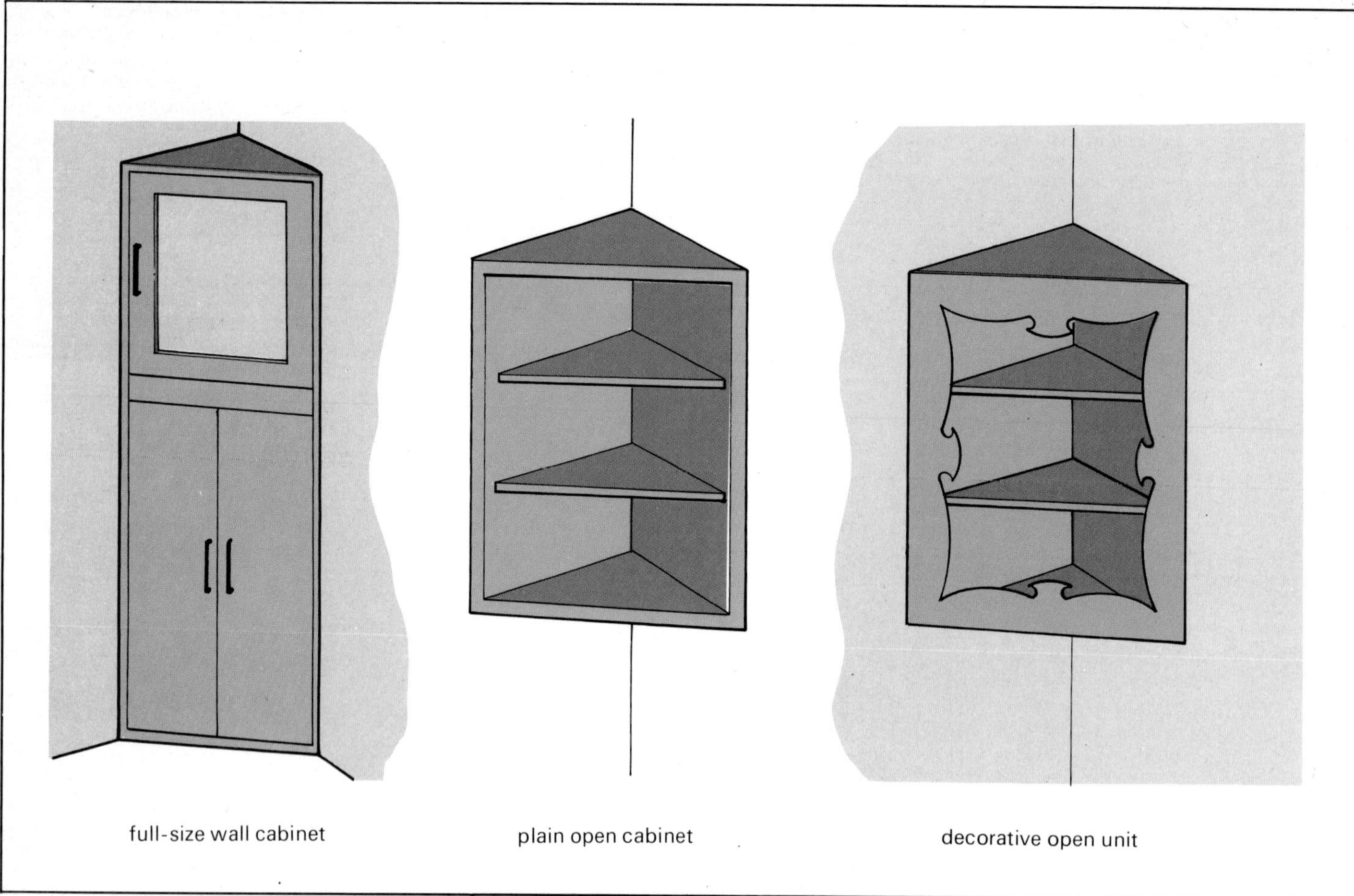

full-size wall cabinet — plain open cabinet — decorative open unit

angles. Place glass panel in position, place mouldings around both sides and bottom, mark position on door, remove glass, then pin and glue the mouldings into position.

Sandpaper the structure and apply semi-matt clear finish to front, top and bottom. Allow to dry thoroughly before further handling.

The interior

Remove shelves and cover all internal faces with self-adhesive baize material. This unit has a deep wine-red, but you may choose a colour to suit the decor of the room. Since the unit provides an additional colour mass, the colour chosen should pick up one of the colours from the drapes, furniture or floor-coverings.

Re-fit the shelves and secure with screws and adhesive.

Fitting the door

Fit the door to the main unit, placing a thickness of cardboard at top and bottom to ensure clearance. Fit screws in, not fully tightened; remove cardboard pieces. Swing door and check for clearance. Screw the magnetized unit to the under-surface of member C. Fit the metal plate to the inside of the door. Swing door and check the magnetic catch. Make any minor adjustment necessary.

Undo the hinge screws and take off the door. Add the handle, using a single Phillips self-tapping screw, plus woodworking adhesive, for secure fitting. Slide the glass panel into the door moulding (see Fig.3). Add top moulding. Fit the door to the main unit and tighten hinge screws. Make final check of door clearance.

Left. *Full-size wall cabinet; made by building another version as a base and standing the glass-front version on top of it.* ***Centre.*** *Plain open unit; leave the door off to achieve a clean open and modern look.* ***Right.*** *Decorative open unit; make a frame of ¼in. (6mm) ply, scrolled or scalloped.*

Fixing

This corner cabinet may be placed on a corner table, or it may be fixed to two corner walls. Should you decide on the latter, it is vital that a secure attachment be made, since the finished unit is quite heavy and will presumably contain some of your valuable pieces.

The choice of fixing will depend largely on the type of walls the unit will be attached to. There are three basic methods of fixing: for solid walls, masonry nails and plugs and screws (or bolts in the case of very heavy objects) are used, and for hollow surfaces such as panelled walls cavity devices can be used. For methods of fixing, types of wall plugs, and tools to use, see a comprehensive DIY manual.

Alternative designs

Full-size wall unit. Construct another version of the cabinet measuring 36in. (0.91m) in height, with two solid doors instead of the single glass door. Use this version as the base, and stand the glass-doored version on top of it.

Plain open unit. If your room has modern Swedish or Italian type furniture, you may wish to give the unit a lighter and simpler look. You can achieve this by leaving the door off altogether and painting the front, top and bottom exteriors in a white gloss, leaving the interior coloured as described.

Decorative open unit. If your room has colonial-type or frilled upholstered furniture, or if you decide to build the unit for a chintzy kitchen, you may dispense with the door and make a scalloped, scrolled or curly-queued decorative frame. Use ⅜in. (9mm) plywood. Make the frame to fit onto the front aperture of the unit.

Cutting list

Veneered chipboard	Imperial	Metric
1 panel	72x18x⅝	1830x457x15
Cut to give:		
1 cupboard side (A)	30x15x⅝	762x380x15
1 cupboard side (B)	30x14¾x⅝	762x374x15
2 triangular ends (C&D)	15x15x⅝	380x380x15
2 triangular shelves (E&F)	12¾x12¾x⅝	324x324x15
2 door stiles	29⅞x2¼x⅝	758x57x15
2 door rails	18⅝x2¼x⅝	470x57x15
Other pieces		
2 triangular moulding	30x¾	762x19
2 ramin moulding	26¾x⅛	670x4
2 ramin moulding	15¾x⅛	390x4
1 veneer edge trim	30x¾	762x19
1 float glass	25⅞x14½	657x368

You will also require a piano hinge at least 30in. (It is easily cut down with a hacksaw). All imperial measurements in inches, all metric measurements in millimetres.

A luxurious lounge chair: 1

Comfort and good looks are the qualities to look for in a chair—this luxurious lounger has them both. It has been ergonomically designed for maximum comfort and has the sort of looks which make it ideal for those lazy days in the house or garden. This first chapter explains how to construct the chair frame; in the next part you are told how to make a rather different fitted cushion for it.

Generally, chairs are manufactured for use either in the home, or in the garden—only rarely can you obtain a dual purpose chair. The reason for this is that most of the materials used in the construction of household chairs are badly damaged by rain and other adverse weather conditions. This chair does not suffer from this defect. It is constructed entirely of wood, has no glued joints and the system of using slatted rails for the seat allows the structure to expand and contract without distortion. The cushioning, which is described in the second part of this chapter, is made up from foam rubber

Below. *The chair's novel design features combine ease of manufacture with bold, modern styling. Its mode of construction makes it well suited to both indoor and outdoor use.*

NIGEL MESSETT

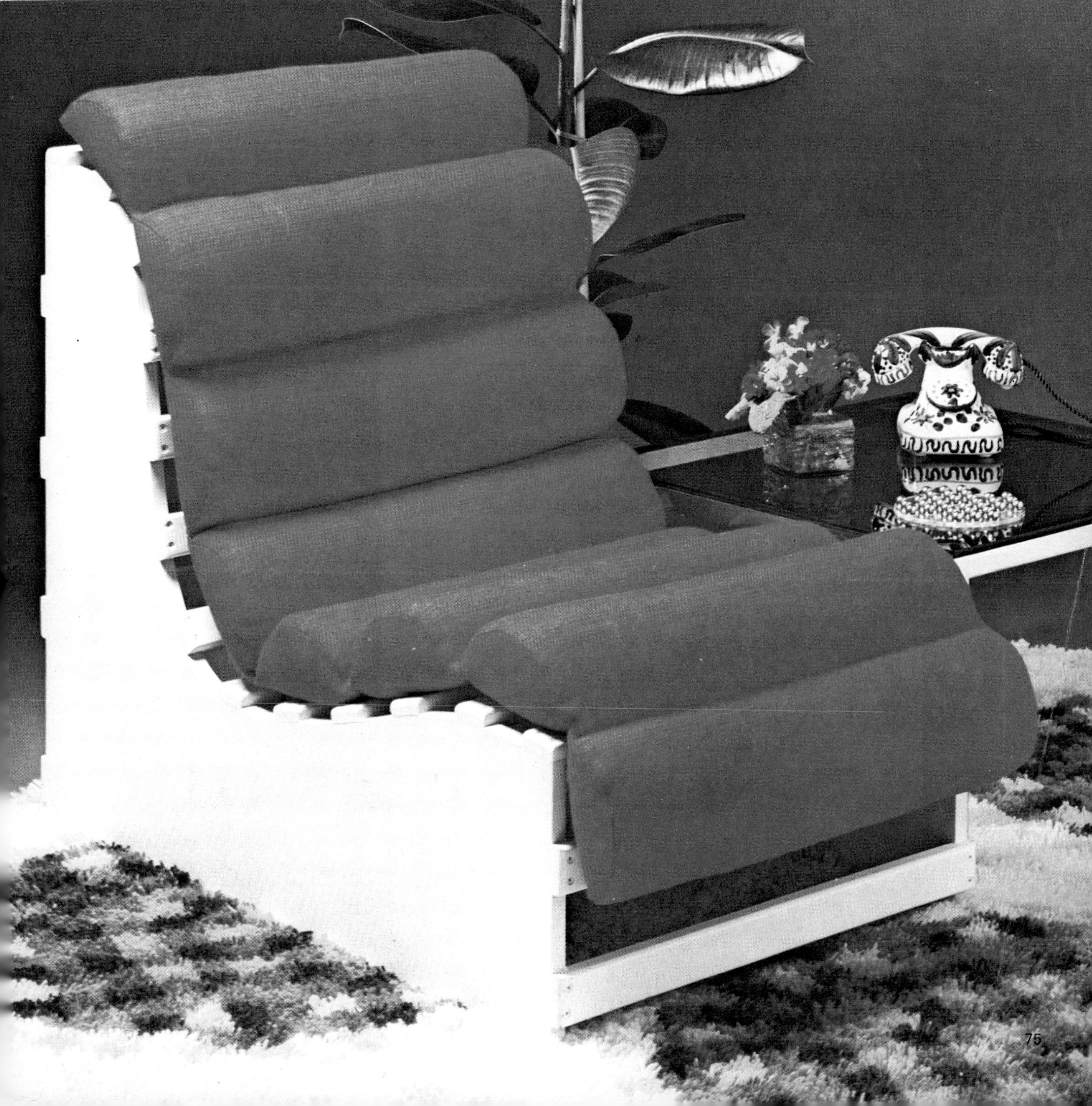

foundations and is covered with a washable material.

The chair is equally at home in the living room, where its bold contemporary lines will enhance a modern decor. Wherever you use it though, the chair is perfect for lounging away those leisure hours.

Design and modifications

The chair has been designed to fit naturally the curves of a person sitting in a semi-upright, but relaxed position. It is an easy job to modify the design so that the back slopes more, allowing you to lie back more. By using slats instead of a solid seat, you not only produce an attractive result more economically, but also avoid the need for elaborate glued joints.

One useful addition to the main structure is a foot rest. This can be constructed on the same principle as the chair and will add that extra touch of luxury.

Materials and general construction

Your choices of materials for the shaped side panels is wide. If expense is not important, a solid wood, such as pine, can be used, but

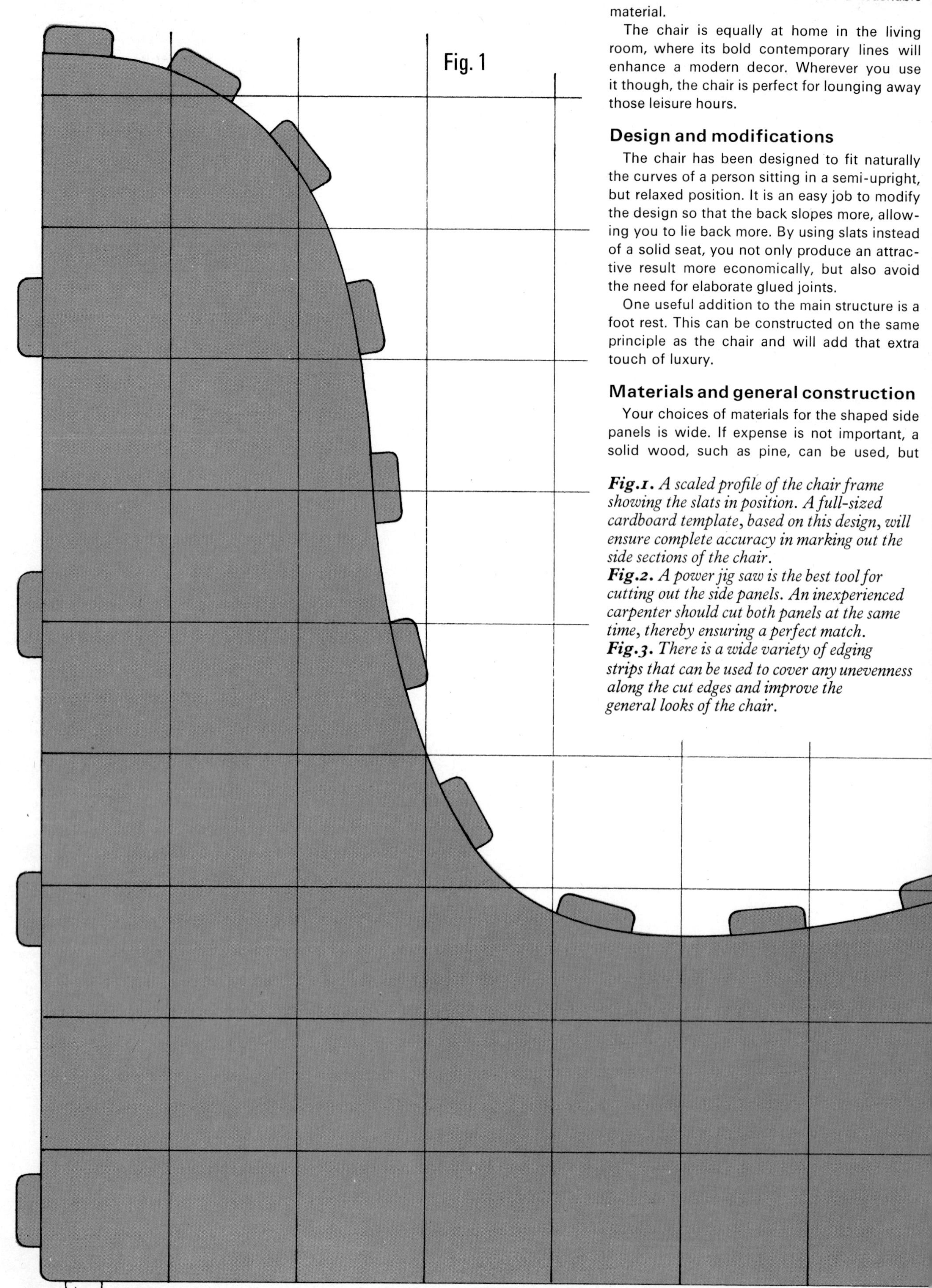

Fig.1. *A scaled profile of the chair frame showing the slats in position. A full-sized cardboard template, based on this design, will ensure complete accuracy in marking out the side sections of the chair.*
Fig.2. *A power jig saw is the best tool for cutting out the side panels. An inexperienced carpenter should cut both panels at the same time, thereby ensuring a perfect match.*
Fig.3. *There is a wide variety of edging strips that can be used to cover any unevenness along the cut edges and improve the general looks of the chair.*

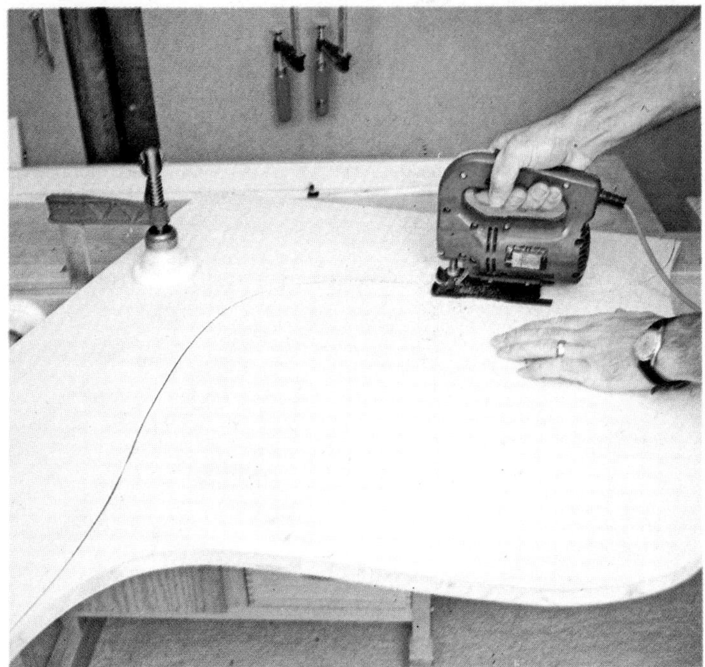

2

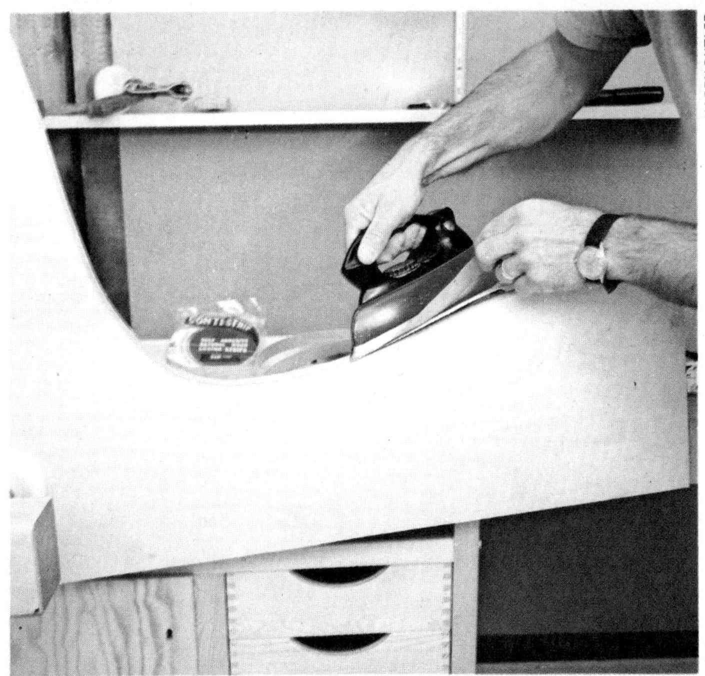

3

HARRY BUTLER

man-made boards will look just as good when painted and are comparatively inexpensive.

Plywood can be used, but its exposed edges tend to split and chip and do not take a good screwed joint. Perhaps blockboard is the most suitable material for the sides. It is a strong board made up of $\frac{3}{4}$in.—1in. (19mm-25mm) wood strips glued together between thick veneers of solid wood which give the board a smooth surface. The grain of alternative wood strips in blockboard is reversed to even out the pull of their expansion and contraction. As a result, the board is exceptionally stable and unlikely to warp. One disadvantage of blockboard is that its cut edges are unsightly. Not only do the ends of the internal wood strips show, but also there are occasional gaps between strips. This defect is easily remedied, however, by applying an edging strip to the cut edge.

The only other pieces to be cut are the slats. These form the seat; the back and additional slats give added reinforcement. They are best made from 2in. x 1in. (51mm x 25mm) softwood.

Cutting out

Fig.1 is a scaled template of a side panel. Each square measures 3in. x 3in. (76mm x 76mm) and thus the height and length of the chair are 28in. (711mm) and 34in. (863mm) respectively. You may wish to alter these dimensions, but the construction process remains the same. Draw out a full-size template of one of the sides on a stiff piece of cardboard, then trace out the two sides on $\frac{3}{4}$in. (19mm) blockboard. Before cutting out, make sure your tools are sharp, as blockboard, in common with most man-made materials, blunts cutting tools quickly. A power jig saw is the correct tool for cutting out the sides—it is a long and laborious job to achieve the correct shape of the sides using a hand saw. However, if you do not possess a power saw, you can cut the sides out with a pad saw or, alternatively, some timber merchants will cut the panels to shape for you. To cut out the sides, first clamp the panels together and cut them out as one piece, thus ensuring they are exactly the same size and shape. Hold the saw at right angles to the wood surface so that the edges of the side panels are completely flat.

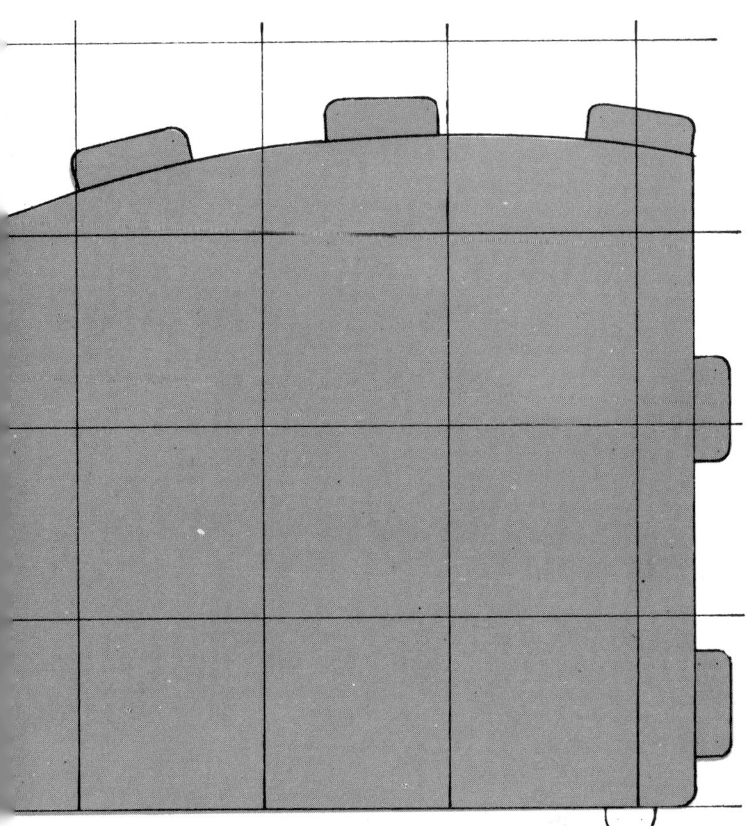

Having cut out the sides, do not unclamp them, but plane and sand the edges flat then take each piece in turn and smooth all the surfaces, using coarse, then fine sandpaper. You will find it easier to finish the sides at this stage rather than when the rails are assembled to them. A wide range of finishes is available, including natural, laminated and painted finishes. Whichever one you choose, first add an edging strip to all the cut edges of the blockboard.

Once the side pieces have been finished, cu
out the slatted rails from 2in. x 1in. (51mm
25mm) softwood. There are nineteen of the
and all are 22in. (559mm) long. A halving is c
in each end of these pieces so that a neat jo
can be made between the rails and the s
panels. Each half-lap is $\frac{3}{4}$in. (19mm) long,
wide and $\frac{1}{8}$in. (3.2mm) deep. To make them
cut along the base of the joint with a fine to
tenon saw, cut down the length of the
then clean up the cut edges with a $\frac{3}{4}$in. (1
chisel.

4

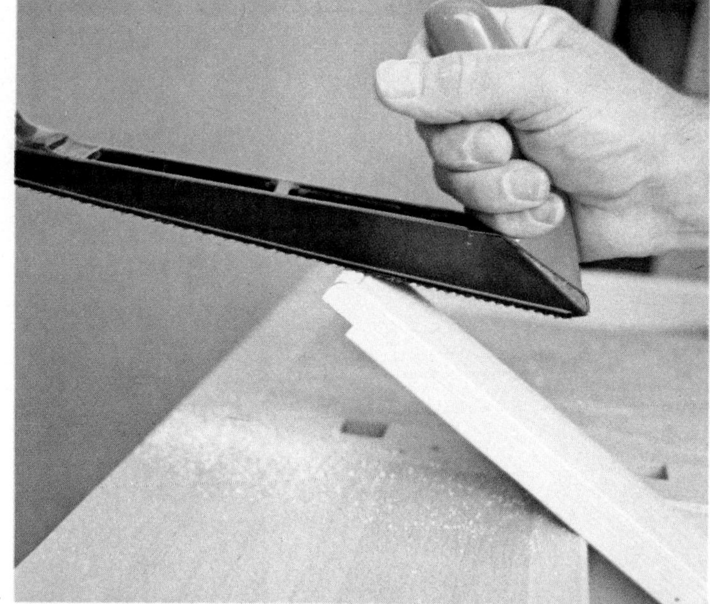
5

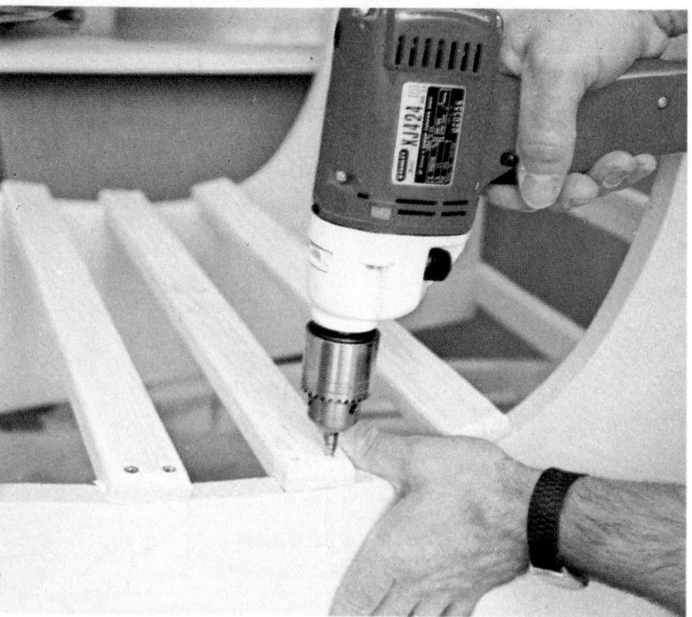
6

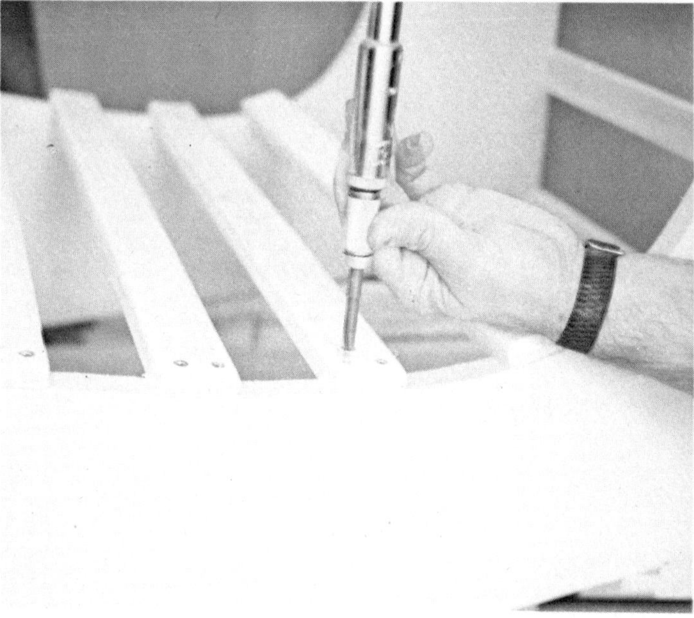
7

HARRY BUTLER

Assembling the chair

Each rail forming the seat and back is set an equal distance from its neighbours. Because the top edges of the side panels are curved, ou cannot measure and mark the centres of ese rails using a straight rule. Instead, take air of compasses, set them at a radius of (102mm), then, starting at the top rear of the side panel, mark in points on the edge at 4in. (102mm) intervals. These epresent the positions of the rear the rails; it is important to ensure that ions are identical on both side panels. ces of the half-laps cut in the rails d the edges of the side panels are t joint cannot be made unless half-laps to the curve. Curvature length of the top edge of the ail must be matched to its You can easily achieve this face of each half-lap till it sed site on the side panels. oints at once, but modify it in position.

Fig.4. *Halvings should be cut into the ends of the slats. This will ensure that the slats and the side sections meet in a secure and neat joint.*
Fig.5. *To improve the looks of the chair and prevent torn clothing, round off all the exposed edges of the slats with a rasp or bench plane, and glasspaper.*
Fig.6. *The slats are secured to the side panels with two screws on each side. For a tight fit, each slat end should be planed to match the curve of the side panel.*
Fig.7. *The screw heads are recessed into the slats to give a neat finish, and then covered with edge-trim plugs or wood filler.*

As well as forming the seat, rails are secured across the front and back of the chair, as shown in Fig.1. Those across the back are fixed 5in. (126mm) apart, those across the front are fixed at 3in. (76mm) intervals. As they are fitted to straight edges, the joints cut in their ends need not be shaped.

To fix all the rails, bore their ends to receive two $1\frac{1}{4}$in. (31mm) No.8 steel screws, place them in position and drive home the screws, recessing the heads for a neat finish. You can hold the unit stable while you work, by adding the rails at each corner of the side panels first. Once the rails are all in position, cover the recessed screw heads with edge-trim discs or wood filler. If any of the joints between the rails and sides are not true, fill the gaps with a wood filler.

Now round off the long edges of each rail. Use a bench plane to take off the right angle, then finish off with sandpaper. Finally, paint the rails in the colour of your choice.

Cutting list

Wood	Imperial	Metric
2 blockboard sides	34 x 28 x $\frac{3}{4}$	864 x 711 x 19
19 softwood rails	22 x 2 x 1	559 x 51 x 25

You will also need:
38 $1\frac{1}{4}$in. (31mm) No.8 steel screws. Jig saw. $\frac{3}{4}$in. (19mm) chisel and mallet. Tenon saw. Wood filler. Bench plane. Glasspaper.

A luxurious lounge chair: 2

This project describes the design and method of construction of a novel easy-chair, for use indoors and in the garden. This chapter explains how to upholster the chair—for indoor use only—in order to make the most of its design advantages for both comfort and good looks.

The main features of the upholstery's design are that it follows perfectly the contours of the chair and allows easy removal of the cushions.

Materials

The upholstery for the chair is made up from eight semi-cylindrical blocks, 22in. (559mm) long and 6in. (152mm) in diameter at the base, of latex (natural rubber) or polyether foam. The shape and positioning of the blocks is shown in Fig. 1. on the following page. The major differences between these two cushion materials is basically that latex, depending on its density, is soft and compresses immediately, while polyether foam gives firmer support—and is cheaper to buy. Polyether foam can be moulded and cut at home but in this case it is wise to buy it ready-cut, for the sake of accuracy.

Below. *The chair frame and upholstery. The cushion cover contains eight separate cushion pads so that the upholstery as a whole moulds well to the contours of the chair and gives firm support to the body.*

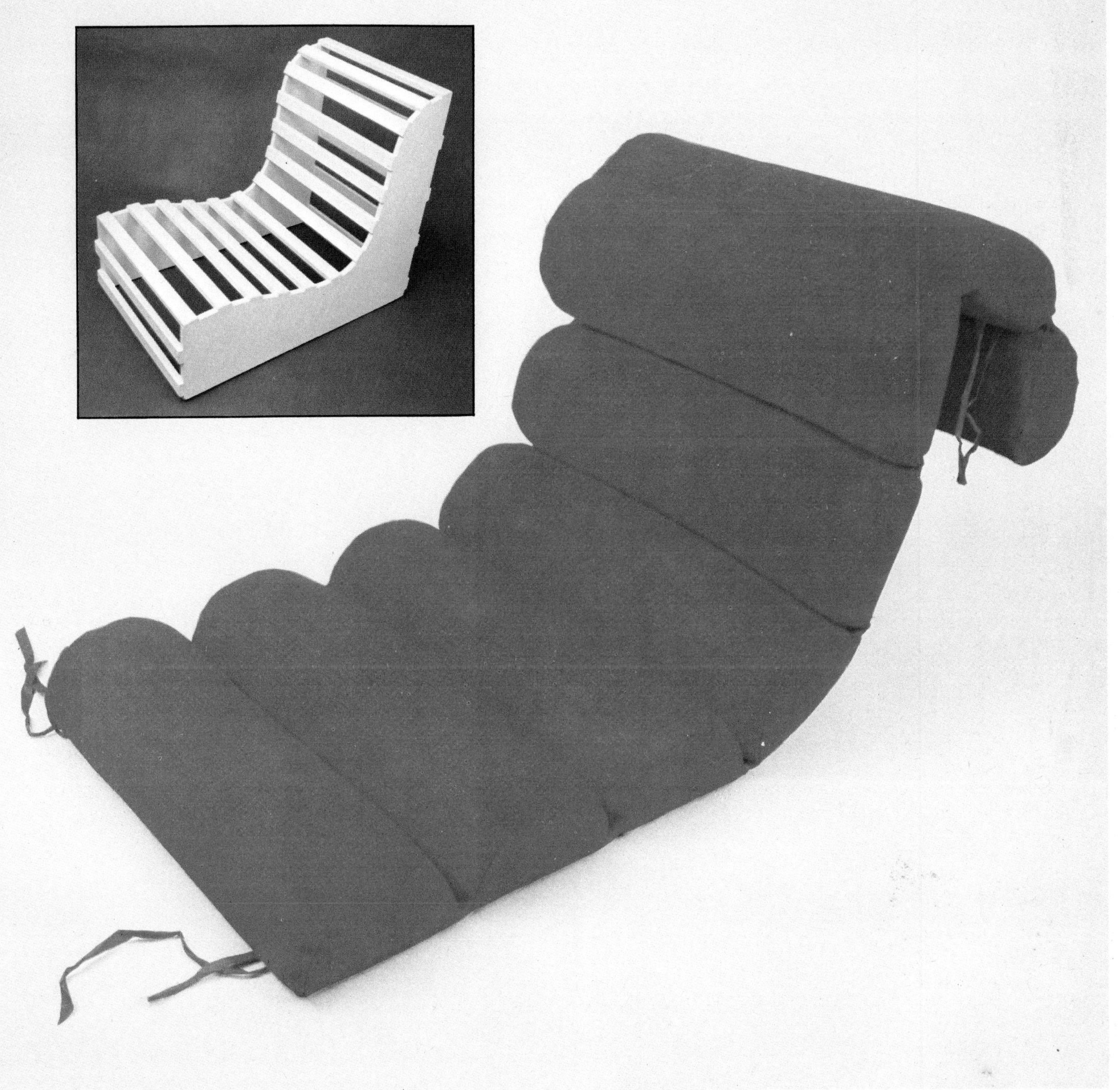

Fig. 2

line of stitching ½'' above base of side section

Fig. 3

bottom strip, attached to top along one edge only

cover top

side section

Fig. 1

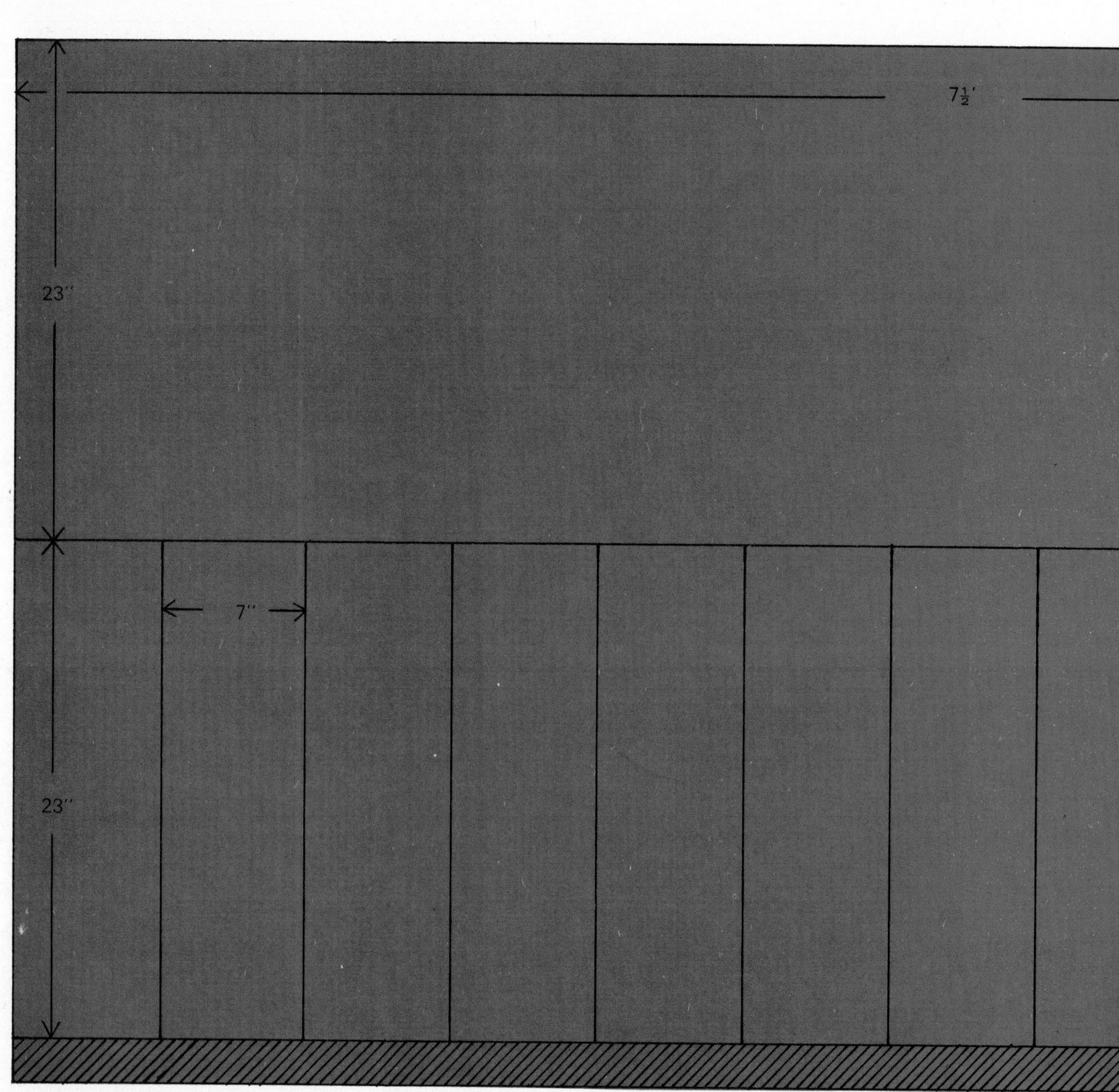

For the cushion cover you will need 2½yds (2286mm) by 48in. (1219mm) of any furnishing fabric suitable for loose covers, so long as it is not too thick or heavy, since this will make the cover lumpy at the joins. If you use a patterned fabric, remember to cut it so that the motif is centrally displayed. The following cover-design is not suitable for stiff water-proof fabrics, but the cushion as a whole is easily detachable from the chair so that it can be removed if the chair is left out of doors.

Cutting out the cushion cover

Fig.2 shows how to cut out the material. Cut out two equal pieces from the fabric, each 23in. (584mm) by 2½yds (2286mm). Set one piece aside: this will form the top side of the cover, running for the length of the chair over the circular tops of the cushion blocks.

From the other piece cut out eight strips of 7in. (178mm) by 23in. (584mm), as shown in Fig.2, for the bottom part of the cover—one for each cushion block. The fabric remaining over from this piece will provide material for the sides of the cushion cover. To make these, first make a paper pattern by drawing a half-circle with a radius of 3½in. (89mm) and extend the straight bottom edge by ½in. (13mm). With the aid of this pattern, cut sixteen pieces.

Take the main piece of fabric, which is going to form the top of the cover, and make a line of stay stitching along each long side by machining ½in. (13mm) from the edge. Next clip into the edge up to this line at ½in. intervals.

Stitching the cover together

The cover is made with eight individual pockets, one for each cushion, so that these are held firmly in place and mould well to the curve of the seat. To make the pockets for the cushions, while leaving openings for their insertion and removal, each of the strips which form the bottom of the cover is stitched to the top along one edge only. When the cushion has been inserted, the remaining edge is turned under and slip-stitched in position. This slip-stitching can easily be unpicked when the cushions are removed for cleaning the covers.

Start by pinning the round edges of the side sections to the long sides of the cover top, eight along each side. Then stitch them together to within ½in. (13mm) of the straight bottom edges of the side sections as shown in Fig.3. Always start and finish the stitching by reversing for 1in. to give the join added strength, and attach the pieces so that there are no gaps between them. Check across the width of the fabric to ensure that the joins along each side correspond to those opposite and are on the same grain and pattern. Trim the turnings to within ¼in. (6mm) of the stitching and press the turnings on to the top side of the corner.

When all the side sections have been attached to the cover-top in this way, join the strips along their short sides to the straight edges of the side sections as illustrated in Fig.4. Stitch to within ½in. (13mm) of the straight edge of the circular sections, as before, so that the two rows of stitching meet exactly.

Now join the strips at the bottom, to the cover-top. Attach the first strip along its length to one of the cover-top's short sides. Take ½in. (13mm) turnings and stitch the cover-top to within ½in. of each strip end, so that this stitching meets the stay stitching on the cover-top. Leave the opposite edge of the strip open.

Pin the top edge of the second strip flat on to the top cover and machine stitch ½in. (13mm) from the raw edge. This stitching should correspond with the junction of the two circular side-pieces at each end of the strip. Again, leave the opposite side open.

After the eight strips have all been attached in this way, with one side being left open, insert the cushion pads. Then fold the turnings under on the open sides of the strips and slip stitch into position. For this you should use a strong thread and a curved needle.

Alternately, you can attach ½in. seam binding ribbon along these edges and stitch this ribbon to the cover-top. This will add strength to the join and prevent fraying on the edge through repeated insertion and removal of the cushions.

Try the cushion in position on the chair and attach ties where necessary. Three pairs of these will probably be required—a pair at the top of the chair, in the middle and at the bottom. Straps of leather or plastic, whether stud-secured or simply buckled around the chair struts, may add to its overall attraction. Alternately, coloured ribbon, perhaps picking out the colouring of the fabric used for the cover itself, may be preferred.

Fig.1. *One piece of fabric, 2½yds x 48in., provides material for the eight bottom strips, sixteen side sections and cover top.*
Fig.2. *View of side sections and top. Sew to within ½in. of the side sections' straight edges so as to leave no gaps between them.*
Fig.3. *The underside of the cover. Each strip is stitched to two side sections, ½in. from their straight edges, and to the cover top along one side only.*

A modern sofa/bed

Compact and comfortable, this inexpensive couch doubles as a bed and is the perfect solution to the problem of putting up a guest in a single bedroom flat.

People who live in small flats frequently encounter the problem of how to put up a guest, or unexpected visitor, for the night. The most obvious solution—to buy a spare bed—is not only expensive, but also is not practical where space is at a premium. There are alternatives. You can buy a fold-away bed or one of the expensive sofa/beds now marketed, and if your friends are sufficiently spartan they will make do with a camp bed.

However, if you possess even the bare modicum of carpentry skill, you can easily devise a more satisfactory solution yourself by building this attractive couch/bed. By day it is a luxurious seat for lounging on, yet it is compact and stylish enough to fit unobtrusively into any but the smallest room. At night it can quickly be made up into a comfortable, full-size single bed.

Design and materials

The design of the couch has been kept as simple as possible and this is reflected in the wide choice of materials available for the construction. Depending on how much you are prepared to spend and the particular finish you desire, you can use hardboard, plywood, softwood or hardwood for the basic frame—or any combination of these materials. For example, you could use laminated hardboard for the sides, back, base and fascia, and softwood for the base supporting frame. In this way you reproduce the design economically, and the finished couch lends itself well to a fine paint finish. Alternatively, you can use solid wood throughout to produce a more solid and sophisticated result. This latter method lends itself to further modification. The sides can be built of single wood panels or can be made up of separate strips of wood laminated together, as shown in Fig.5. It is this laminated construction which is described below, but the basic construction method is the same whatever materials you use.

There are several different ways of making the cushion-supporting base. Perhaps the simplest is simply to fit a single hardboard panel across the frame. Provided you supply adequate cushioning, the result will be perfectly comfortable. Another, but more expensive method, is to fit rubber webbing across the frame.

Shop bought cushions are expensive and it is unlikely that you will be able to obtain them in a size to fit the couch. By following the instructions given in this project, and referring to an upholstery magazine for further information, you can easily make up the necessary cushioning yourself.

NELSON HARGREAVES

***Left.** Built to a simple design which allows you to use a variety of materials, this couch makes an ideal spare bed for the smaller home.*

Making the sides

Having decided on what materials to use, begin by cutting out the side panels or, if you intend making up the side panels from strips of timber, cut each piece to the size given in the cutting list. Each side consists of four parallel members with a cross-section of 6in. x 1½in. (152mm x 38mm), which are flanked by two vertical members of the same section. Fig.5. shows how the side and top members are mitred together for greater strength, and also shows the tongued and grooved joints by which the separate pieces are assembled together.

To make these joints, first take each of the vertical side members and, having marked in a line from one corner, at an angle of 45° to the long edge, cut with a tenon saw to produce the mitred end. In the same way, mitre the ends of the top horizontal member, but remember that this piece has a tongue cut on it and must, therefore, be cut 1in. (25mm) overlength at each end.

Now take the vertical members and, using a plough plane, make a groove 1in. (25mm) deep and ½in. wide down each mitred and inside long edge. Clean up these grooves with a chisel and sandpaper. Then take the top horizontal member and, with a rebate plane, cut a tongue on each mitred end 1in. (25mm) deep and ½in. (13mm) wide. Similarly, make tongues on each short edge of the other horizontal members as shown in Fig.5.

With the pieces of both side panels cut to shape, trial assemble and, when you are satisfied that each joint fits perfectly, begin construction by glueing the three lower horizontal members into the grooves on the vertical members. Complete the construction by adding the top in the same way. Allow the glue to set, then trim off that part of the tongue which protrudes beyond each outer edge of the vertical members.

Sides and back assembly

Assembling the side panels to the back is straightforward. However, you must take steps to ensure that the butt joints between side and back panels are completely secure, and this cannot be achieved by simply screwing through the side panels into the end-grain of the back panel. Instead, you must first bore the short edges of the back panel (at 4in. (102mm) centres) to receive fibre Rawlplugs. Glue these Rawlplugs into position, then fit the sides into position and screw through them, at previously marked locations, into the plugs. 3in. (76mm) wood-screws countersunk below the surface are most suitable, and the cavities they make should be filled with a suitable stopper.

Making the base frame

The frame which supports the seat is constructed separately, then fitted, pre-assembled, to the back and sides. To make it, begin by cutting out the rails to the sizes given in the cutting list, then mitre all the ends to an angle of 45°. Ensure that each mitred end is smooth and plain, then glue and pin the rails together, checking that the structure is square. A fascia panel is fitted across the front rail, but this piece is not added until the base of the seat has been fixed to the frame.

Next, fit the frame inside the side and back panels, with its lower edges located 7in. (178mm) above the base of the sides and back. Fix the frame with 2½in. (64mm) woodscrews driven through the frame members at 6in. (152mm) intervals.

Because the couch is long and must bear the weight of a person, reinforcement members must be fixed across the frame to maintain strength and rigidity. Conduit tubing cut and bent to the shape shown in Fig.4 is ideal. To make these pieces, cut ¾in. (19mm) tubing to the lengths given in the cutting list, flatten the ends with a hammer, drill the ends to receive screws, then screw the tubing across the underside of the frame at the locations shown in Fig.1.

Making the base

As mentioned above, you can make the base from a single sheet of laminated hardboard or plywood. ½in. (13mm) plywood is the stronger and, therefore, the most suitable material. Simply cut the base panel to the correct size and screw it onto the top edges of the frame.

The only disadvantage of plywood as a material for the base of the couch is its rigidity. It will not yield under pressure and consequently you must make the cushions extra thick. An alternative, more luxurious base is provided by rubber webbing stretched between the frame. Webbing can be obtained in a continuous roll and there are several methods of fixing it in place. The easiest way is simply to tack or staple it to the top edges of the frame, having first removed any sharp edges with which the rubber comes in contact. Another method is to fit clips, of the type shown in Fig.1, to the ends of the webbing, then anchor the clips in a groove cut in the top of the frame. Whatever method you choose to fix the webbing, make sure that it is fitted under the correct tension and will give complete support.

Making the cushions

Both the seat and the back cushions use rubber foam as a foundation. This is both inexpensive and easy to cut and the only problem occurs in choosing a foam filling of the correct density. It is this density which determines the resilience and 'give' of the finished cushion. As the unit will be used for sleeping on, you must take extra care in choosing and making up the foundation.

For best results you require at least three layers of foam for the seat. The top and bottom layers should have a density of about 1.8lb per cubic foot, and sandwiched between these should be a layer with a density of no less than 2.5lb per cubic foot. This arrangement gives ample support while being extremely comfortable. The back cushion or cushions can be cut from a single piece of foam and, because it does not support so much weight, need not have a density exceeding 2lb per cubic foot. Comfort also depends on the thickness of the cushions. The base cushion must be at leat 4½in. (115mm) thick, the back cushion 3in. (76mm).

Cut out the foam to size, using a fine-toothed hacksaw or an electric carving knife. All the foundations should be cut slightly oversize, the reason for this being that when they are covered by fabric of the correct size, they will be slightly compressed and thus prevent wrinkles forming.

Your choice of fabrics for the cushion covers is very wide—bold designs will complement the contemporary lines of the chair. Making the covers is far easier than you would imagine, but the beginner should refer to a comprehensive sewing manual for instructions on how to achieve really professional results.

Fig.1. *An exploded view of the couch, which shows the method of springing the base using rubber webbing clipped into grooves in the long rails. To save time, the back panel can simply be cut from a single piece of wood.*

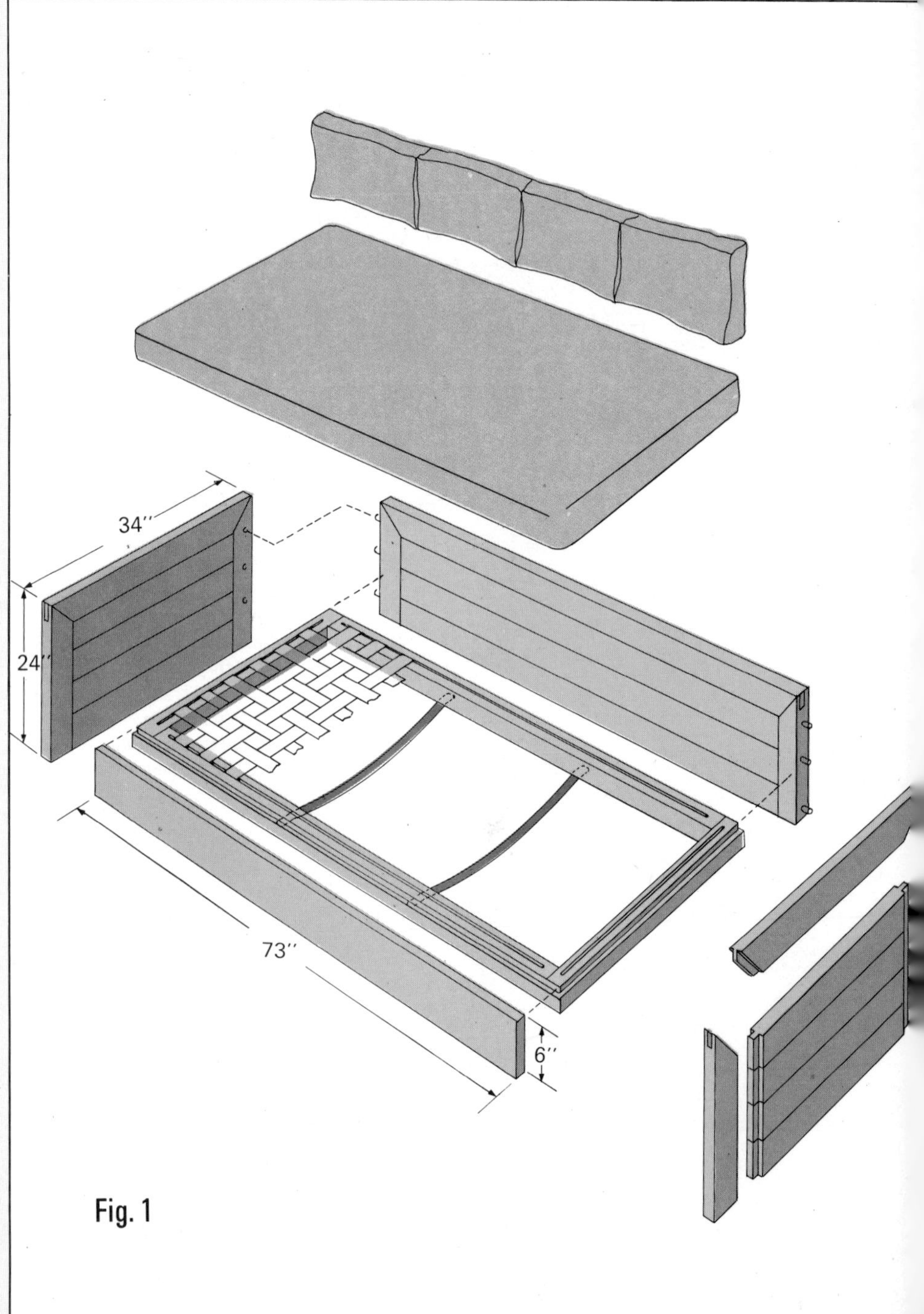

Fig.2. *The base frame is made up separately and fitted, pre-assembled, to the sides and back.*
Fig.3. *There are several ways of making up the side panels and there is a wide choice of suitable materials. Here, four horizontal members are fitted to two vertical members.*
Fig.4. *Adequate reinforcement must be given to the base frame. The simplest method is to fit two lengths of strong metal tubing across the long rails—conduit tubing is ideal.*
Fig.5. *To assemble the side members, cut tongues on all the horizontal members and corresponding grooves on the vertical pieces, then glue the structure together.*
Fig.6. *When screwing the side panels to end grain, use fibre wall plugs for a secure joint.*
Fig.7. *An alternative method of assembling the sides is to use the 'loose tongue' technique.*

Cutting list

Solid wood	Imperial	Metric
2 top side members	34 x 6 x 1½	836 x 152 x 38
6 horizontal side members	22 x 6 x 1½	559 x 152 x 38
4 vertical side members	24 x 6 x 1½	609 x 152 x 38
1 back panel	73 x 24 x 1½	1854 x 609 x 38
2 frame cross rails	29½ x 3 x 1½	750 x 76 x 38
2 frame long rails	73 x 3 x 1½	1854 x 76 x 38
1 fascia panel	73 x 6 x 1	1854 x 152 x 25

The size of the couch can be modified to suit individual requirements. For economy, man-made wood, such as plywood, can be substituted for solid wood.

You will also need:
Rubber webbing or a plywood base panel. 3 lengths ¾in. (19mm) conduit tubing. Foam cushion foundations and fabric covers. Wood glue. 12 fibre Rawlplugs. 3in. (76mm) wood screws. Plough plane. Rebate plane. 1in. (25mm) chisel and mallet. Wood filler. Sandpaper. Wood stain and varnish, or paint.

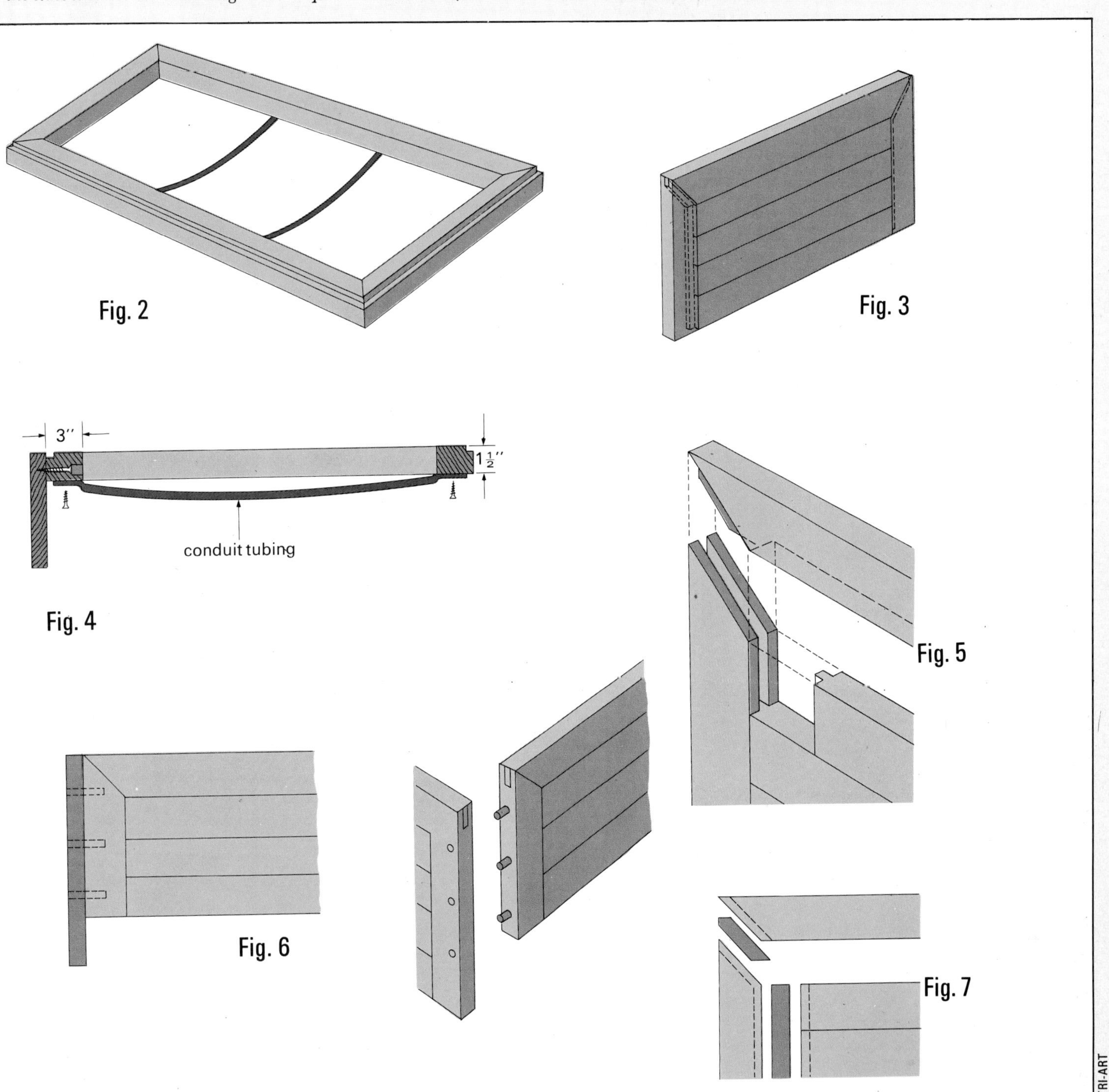

***Above.** The basic unit is the wall cabinet (Model A); for the complete sewing centre, add the specially designed gateleg cutting table, and C, the cupboard with mirror.*

Space-saving sewing centre

In these days when 'getting by' financially depends to an appreciable extent on savings made possible by the housewife and her golden hands, there is a need to create for her a 'homemaker's centre' where she can work comfortably, with adequate working space, good lighting and the right facilities. This chapter describes a wall unit you can build which has been especially designed as a needlework, sewing and ironing centre.

Before you go to the trouble and expense of buying the materials for this unit, discuss the project fully with your wife and get the benefit of her ideas. Since she is the one who will actually be using the centre, she will know what she wants. Her existing ironing facilities may be perfectly satisfactory, or she may be quite happy using the kitchen table or dining table for cutting. There is, of course, the question of the location, as you will need 6ft (2m) of clear wall space for the basic sewing centre and a further 2ft (600mm) if you want to add the ironing cupboard.

Being a wall unit, the centre takes a minimum of floor space and can be used for a multitude of purposes. Being well lit, and having a clear work surface, plus bookshelves and drawers, it could double as an office for yourself, or a desk where the children can do their homework.

The basic unit (Model A) accommodates the working area, a separate compartment for storing the sewing machine, drawers for holding cottons, bobbins, needles, tapemeasures, dockets, patterns, etc., a book shelf for holding your favourite sewing journals and magazines, and spacious lower drawers for storing all sorts of items from linen, materials, unfinished projects to a handy area for a rag-bin.

To this basic unit can be added:

Model B, a specially designed gateleg table which adjoins the unit to become a cutting table.

Model C, a cupboard containing a full-length mirror, an ironing board, cleaning cloths, brushes and fluids, and even a tailor's dummy.

Before commencing the construction, study the design to see whether the sewing machine you already have will fit into the storage space allocated. Should you need more depth, you may either make the whole unit a little taller or take a little space from the book shelf above it. But before you do this, check with your wife on which books she wishes it to hold.

Materials

Once again, the material chosen for the desk is high-density chipboard, which is available in a variety of veneers, and, of course, can be stained or painted. Chipboard is the ideal material for your purpose, being easy to work with and, with the addition of veneer edge strips, it will give you a professional finish. However, the choice of material depends on what is available, and at what price; and planed timber, hardboard or plywood can be used just as effectively.

In this instance, teak has been chosen as the finish; but a range of other finishes is available, including oak, mahogany and white. And of course the unit may be painted to suit the decor of your room.

The basic unit

The basic assembly (Model A) comprises a wall unit measuring 77¼in. x 56in. x 15in. (1960mm x 1422mm x 380mm). To make the main assembly, cut the following panels: Two end panels: 56in. x 15in. x ¾in. (1422mm x 380mm x 19mm). Top and bench panels: 75¾in. x 15in. x ¾in. (1925mm x 380mm x 19mm).

To cut chipboard, score the cutting line on both faces and edges with a sharp knife and cut with a fine-tooth saw. Be sure to cut to your own measurements and markings. On no account rely on the supplier's cutting or squaring of edges. Examine the corners closely to make sure that they have not been damaged in handling.

At the base of the left-hand end panel, cut a rebate for a lapped joint to take the front and rear plinth battens: 1½in. x ½in. (38mm x 13mm). Cut the mid-support panel 27in. x 15in. x ¾in. (687mm x 380mm x 19mm). In the base of this member cut the rebates for the lapped joint to take the front and rear plinth battens, as above.

Use this mid-support panel to make a line 27in. (687mm) from the base on the inside surface of each end member as the position for the work-bench.

On the outside of each panel, rule a similar line, then rule a line ⅜in. (10mm) above it. Along each of these top lines mark the points for five screws. Rule another line ⅜in. (10mm) from the outside top edge of each end member and mark the points for five screws along each line.

Use an awl to mark the screw hole positions. Using a 5/32in (4mm) drill or bit, drill all 20 holes. With an awl poked through the holes, mark the positions of the first and fifth screw hole in the end edges of the top and bench members. Insert screws and tighten a few turns. With the awl, mark the positions of the other 12 screw holes. The screws used are 1½in. (38mm) No. 6 screws.

Now, one by one, remove each screw, and, using a snail-head bit, make the conical depressions for countersinking; re-insert screws, tighten. Having tightened all screws, fill in the holes with woodstopping, such as Brummer. Allow to set, then carve off with a chisel.

Along the bottom of the bench panel rule a line across the width at 42in. (1070mm) from the left-hand end panel inside edge. This is the position of the inside edge of the mid-support panel.

On the top surface of the bench panel rule a line across the width at 42⅜in. (1080mm). Mark five screw holes, drill holes for the screws. Butt the mid-support edge to the panel at this position and glue and screw to make a permanent join, countersinking all screw-heads and filling with wood-stopping.

From ½in. (13mm) planed timber or plywood, cut two plinth battens 43½in. x 1½in. x ½in. (1108mm x 38mm x 13mm). Pin and glue them to the rebates at front and rear of the left-hand end and the mid-support members to make completed lapped joints.

Divisions

To make the main division member in the upper section of the unit, cut a panel 28¼in. x 15in. x ¾in. (720mm x 380mm x 19mm). Mark its position on the under surface of the top member and the top surface of the bench panel at 21½in. (546mm) from the inside edge of the end member. Mark the screw positions ⅜in. (10mm) to the right of these lines on the top surface of the top panel and the bottom surface of the bench panel. Mark with an awl, then drill the 10 holes. Glue and screw the panel into position.

To make the book-case, cut the horizontal panel 20½in. x 15in. ¾in. (521mm x 380mm x 19mm) and the vertical panel 12½in. x 15in. x ¾in. (318mm x 380mm x 19mm). Butting the edge of the shorter panel to the longer panel, screw and glue into position. Mark the position of the unit on the under-surface of the top member at 20½in. (521mm) from the inside edge of the left end member, and on the inside edge of the left end member at 12½in. (318mm) from the undersurface of the top member.

Mark the screw positions ⅜in. (10mm) from these lines on the outer surfaces. Mark with an awl, then drill the holes. Glue and screw into position.

You have now made the general shape of the assembly, and it is a good idea to place the unit in the position it will occupy. This is the time to find out whether any modification is needed. Such things as skirting boards and light switches may have escaped your notice, and it may be necessary to make some compensating alteration.

Cut a panel of 3/16in. (5mm) ply 77¼in. x 29¾in. x 3/16in. (1960mm x 754mm x 5mm). Pin and glue to the edges of all members so far assembled. This will hold the assembly square and stop it from yawing. For this reason, the carpentry has been kept simple, with no grooves or difficult joints, all members so far being butted and joined by screwing. The only other elements to be added are in the form of movable drawers.

Drawers

All drawers have been designed to allow the edges of the vertical panels to be seen and to fit flush with them.

Cut the faces of the three top drawers 21½in. x 7in. x ¾in. (546mm x 178mm x 19mm).

Make three drawer trays with exterior dimensions 19¾in. x 13½in. x 5½in. (502mm x 343mm x 140mm) as follows: Using planed softwood cut two end members 18¾in. x 5 5/16in. x ½in. (477mm x 135mm x 13mm), and two side members 13½in. x 5 5/16in. x ½in. (343mm x 135mm x 13mm). Pin and glue together. Cut a panel of 3/16in. (5mm) ply 19¾in. x 13½in. (502mm x 343mm) and pin and glue to the bottom edges of the side and end members.

If you wish, you can join the corners of the drawers using grooved and tongued joints or lapped joints.

To join the drawer trays to the faces, place the tray end panel and the rear surface of the face member together, the bottom surface of the tray being ½in. (13mm) above the bottom edge of the face and with an overlap of the face of ⅝in. (16mm) at each end. Screw and glue, using four screws at top and bottom.

Make the runners from ¾in. x ½in. (19mm x 13mm) hardwood planed and glasspapered. Cut them 13in. (330mm) long, two pairs for each of the nine drawers.

Mark the positioning line of the tray 1in. (25mm) from the top edge of each side panel. Screw and glue one of the runners to each side, top edge level with the positioning line and screwed through the panel into a ¾in. (19mm) edge at three points.

The top drawer face should clear the edge of the top member of the unit by ⅛in. (3mm). Thus the top edge of the runners on which the drawer will slide must be 2⅞in. (73mm) down from the edge of the top member.

These runners are positioned at ¾in. (19mm) from the front edge to butt the rear surface of the drawer face. They are fixed at their ½in. (13mm) edges by screwing and glueing.

Position the second drawer to clear the top drawer face by ⅛in. (3mm), then each other drawer as it is installed. The three lower drawers in the top section have faces only 2⅜in. (61mm) deep, and the drawer trays are 1¾in. (44mm)

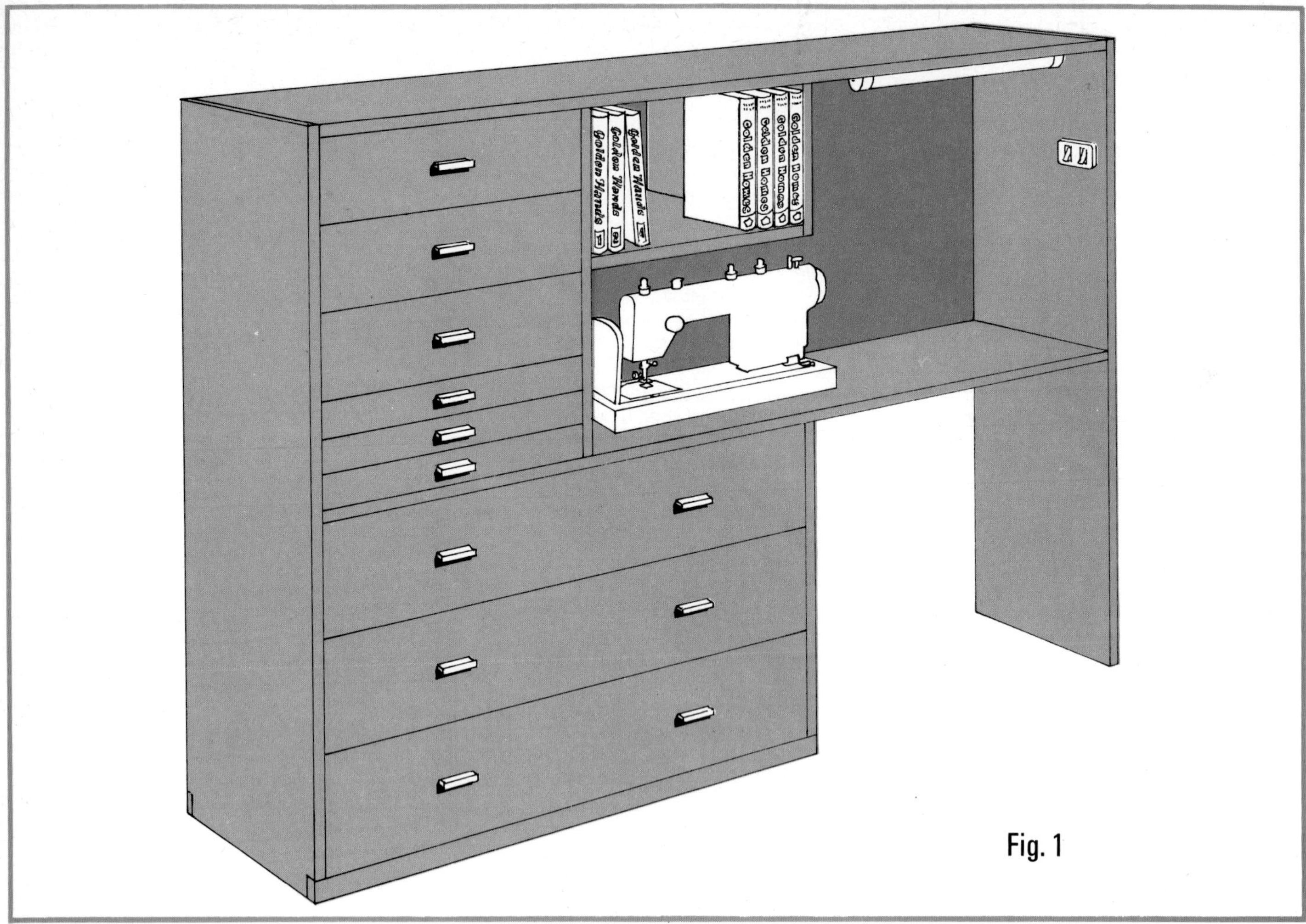

Fig. 1

deep. The other dimensions are the same as that of the three top drawers.

The faces of the three large lower drawers measure 42in. x $8\frac{1}{2}$in. x $\frac{3}{4}$in. (1070mm x 216mm x 19mm) and the drawer trays measure 40in. x $13\frac{1}{2}$in. x 7in. (1020mm x 343mm x 178mm).

Follow the procedure to make all drawers, fit runners and slide the drawers into place. If any adjustment is necessary, alter the depth of the plinth battens accordingly.

Finishing

Add veneer edge trim to all front exposed edges. Self-adhesive edging strip is available in cut lengths. To apply, position the edging strip, place ordinary brown paper on top. Now apply a warm iron every 18in. (460mm) and rub with a cloth to ensure even contact. After 30 minutes, remove any overhanging edges with a flat fine-cut file, using quick downstrokes. Pin and glue ramin handles to the faces of all drawers.

Fit electric light fittings under the top member for lighting, and also in the area where the sewing machine is stored, for when this is slid out onto the working area, the surface it occupied extends the working surface and needs to be lit. You will also need a power-plug for the machine.

Model AB

This is Model A, as described above, plus a gateleg table (B) which is used as a cutting table. Made from the same teak chipboard, it is

Fig.1. The basic unit needs 6ft (2m) of clear wall space, plus a further 2ft (600mm) if you wish to add the ironing cupboard. Model A accommodates the working area, with a space for storing the sewing machine. This space should vary in height to suit your machine. The unit features a book-shelf for holding magazines, patterns and books, special shallow drawers for housing cotton-reels, etc., and large lower drawers.

42in. (1070mm) wide and $27\frac{3}{4}$in. (706mm) deep. The top panel, between each of the fold-out panels, is only 4in. (102mm) wide. For full details of the construction procedure, see Page 1409. An important addition is the 36in. (or 1m) steel rule fixed at the edge of the working surface. The advantage of this unit is that it can be moved away from the wall unit and used as an extra dining table, or moved, perhaps, to where the lighting is better, or where it is more convenient for working on.

Model AC

This is the wall unit extended to include an ironing cabinet (C), including a full length mirror, fold-out ironing board, shelves for cleaning fluids, cloths and brushes, and perhaps a tailor's dummy.

In this case, it would have been advantageous to have made the top panel 8ft (2440mm) long. The right hand end panel of Model A would thus become an intermediate partition and would be shorted by $\frac{3}{4}$in. (19mm).

Model ABC

This is the wall unit, plus both the ironing cabinet and the gateleg cutting table.

Cutting list

Material	Imperial	Metric
Veneered chipboard		
(2) panels	$56 \times 15 \times \frac{3}{4}$	1422 x 380 x 19
(2) panels	$75\frac{3}{4} \times 15 \times \frac{3}{4}$	1925 x 380 x 19
(1) panel	$27 \times 15 \times \frac{3}{4}$	687 x 380 x 19
(1) panel	$28\frac{1}{4} \times 15 \times \frac{3}{4}$	720 x 380 x 19
(1) panel	$20\frac{1}{2} \times 15 \times \frac{3}{4}$	521 x 380 x 19
(1) panel	$12\frac{1}{2} \times 15 \times \frac{3}{4}$	318 x 380 x 19
(3) pieces	$21\frac{1}{4} \times 7 \times \frac{3}{4}$	546 x 178 x 19
(3) pieces	$21\frac{1}{4} \times 2\frac{3}{8} \times \frac{3}{4}$	546 x 61 x 19
(3) pieces	$42 \times 8\frac{1}{2} \times \frac{3}{4}$	1070 x 216 x 19
Ply		
(1) panel	$77\frac{1}{4} \times 29\frac{3}{4} \times \frac{3}{16}$	1960 x 754 x 5
(6) panels	$19\frac{3}{4} \times 13\frac{1}{2} \times \frac{3}{16}$	502 x 343 x 5
(3) panels	$40 \times 13\frac{1}{2} \times \frac{3}{16}$	1020 x 343 x 5
Softwood		
6 pieces	$18\frac{3}{4} \times 5\frac{5}{16} \times \frac{1}{2}$	477 x 135 x 13
6 pieces	$13\frac{1}{2} \times 5\frac{5}{16} \times \frac{1}{2}$	343 x 135 x 13
6 pieces	$18\frac{3}{4} \times 1\frac{3}{4} \times \frac{1}{2}$	477 x 44 x 13
6 pieces	$13\frac{1}{2} \times 1\frac{3}{4} \times \frac{1}{2}$	343 x 44 x 13
6 pieces	$13\frac{1}{2} \times 7 \times \frac{1}{2}$	343 x 178 x 13
6 pieces	$41 \times 7 \times \frac{1}{2}$	1045 x 178 x 13
38 pieces		
Ramin	$13 \times \frac{3}{4} \times \frac{1}{2}$	305 x 19 x 12

You will also need:
Ramin drawer handles, light fittings and bulbs, $1\frac{1}{2}$in. (38mm) No. 6 screws, panel pins, veneer strip, woodworking adhesive, wood-stopping.

A wall desk to make

In these days of budgeting and form-filling, every home needs a conveniently placed and immediately accessible desk. Accounts are generally stored out of sight in various parts of the house—household dockets in a kitchen drawer; insurance policies, taxation records, car repair bills and receipts in a shoe-box in the china cabinet; medical accounts in a drawer of the dressing table, and so on. Here is an attractive and compactly designed wall desk which will fit into a minimum of space, and allow you to organise all accounts and records in one spot in the house to help solve your budgeting problems.

Below: *This easy-to-make wall desk utilizes room space to the best possible advantage, taking up no floor-space and thus allowing for a chair to be placed beneath it.*

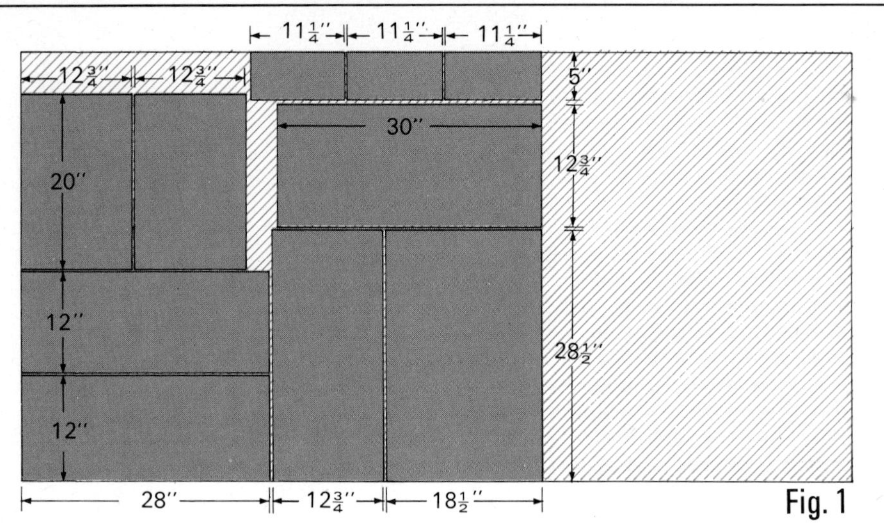

Fig.1. By careful cutting you will be able to cut all the main panels from a single 8 x 4ft. (2440 x 1220mm) sheet of ¾in. (19m) chipboard. All partitions are made of ¼in. (6mm) plywood.

Fig.2. The desk should be compartmented to cater to the needs of your family, with compartments carefully allocated for receipts, accounting books, title deeds, correspondence, household accounts, diaries, and so on.

Cutting list

Materials	Imperial	Metric
chipboard		
2 panels	20 x 12¾ x ¾	508 x 324 x 19
1 panel	28½ x 12¾ x ¾	724 x 324 x 19
2 panels	28½ x 12 x ¾	724 x 305 x 19
1 panel	28½ x 18½ x ¾	724 x 470 x 19
3 panels	11¼ x 5 x ¾	285 x 127 x 19
1 panel	30 x 13½ x ¾	762 x 343 x 19
plywood		
4 panels	7 x 4⅞ x ¼	178 x 124 x 6
2 panels	12¾ x 10½ x ¼	324 x 267 x 6
3 panels	10½ x 10 x ¼	267 x 254 x 6
hardwood moulding		
8 pieces	10½ x ¼ x ¼	267 x 6 x 6
6 pieces	10 x ¼ x ¼	254 x 6 x 6
veneer edge trim	210 x ¾ x 1/32	5940 x ¾ x 1/32
2 top and bottom		
nylon running strips	28½ x 2(¼)	724 x 2(6)
brass piano hinge	28½	724

You will also need:
Ramin moulding for handles; 1½in. (38mm) No. 6 screws; 1½in. (38mm) and ½in. (13mm) panel pins; woodworking adhesive, glasspaper, wall plugs and screws, wood-stopping; sharp knife, panel saw, awl, drill, snail-head bit, chisel, pin punch, moulding plane or spindle cutter, cramp, lock fitting, 2 angle-stays.

Before deciding on the design of your desk, give consideration to your family's accounting problems. If you or your wife are self-employed or have a money-making hobby, you may have tax problems, or you may have to maintain efficient systems for keeping a check on customers and prospects, and for filing correspondence. If either of you uses a typewriter, the fold-out desk and the wall supports will have to be strong enough to hold a machine. These and other considerations will have a bearing on dimensions, materials, design, etc.

The site for your desk should be selected with care. Make sure that the wall surface is smooth, free from bumps, clear of conduits and light-switches, that you know its composition and that it will accept wall-plugs or screws.

The next thing you have to decide before purchasing your materials relates to the appearance of the unit. You have to be sure that it will not clash with the room aesthetically. A room with antique furniture or wall panelling would probably call for a unit made of darkstained timber.

Materials

The material chosen for the desk is high-density chipboard, which is available in a variety of veneers, and, of course, can be stained or painted. Chipboard is the ideal material for your purpose, being easy to work with and, with the addition of veneer edge strips, it will give you a professional finish.

The main advantage with chipboard is that,

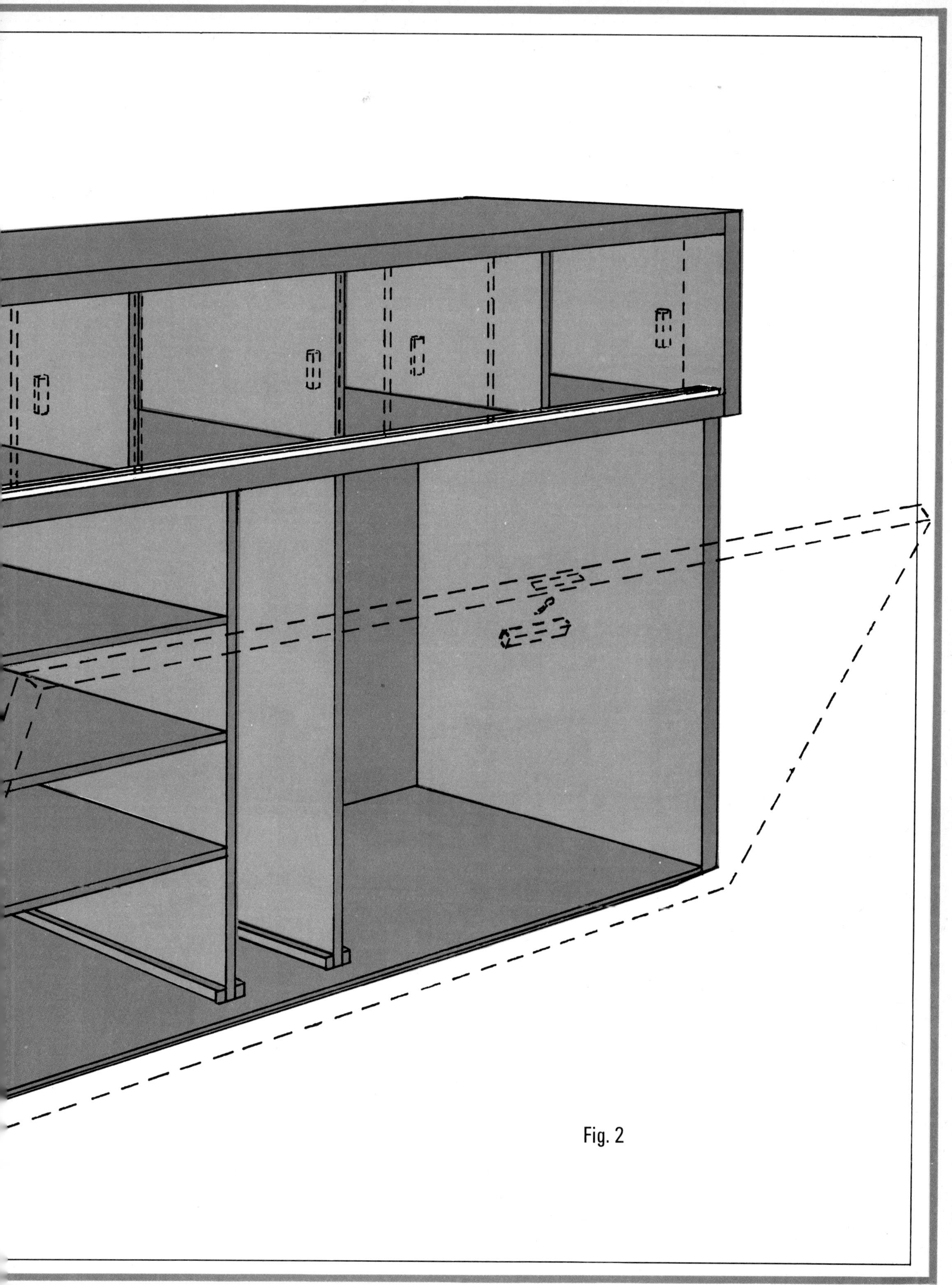

Fig. 2

being a mass-produced precision-made product, it can be relied upon for the accuracy of its thickness and the flatness of its surfaces. Chipboard lends itself to the use of all hand tools, such as saws, planes and drills, and hand-held power-tools may be used with confidence. The matching veneer edge trim for covering exposed edges is readily available and easy to apply.

Teak has been chosen as the finish for this unit. A range of other finishes is available, including oak, mahogany and white. And, of course, the desk may be painted if you wish.

The maximum exterior dimensions of the unit are 30 x 20 x 12¾in. (762 x 508 x 324mm), and all members, apart from interior partitions, can be cut from one sheet of ¾in. (19mm) chipboard 8ft x 4ft (2440 x 1220mm), with plenty left over for another project.

To cut chipboard, score the cutting line on both faces and edges with a sharp knife and cut with a fine-tooth saw. Be sure to cut to your own measurements and markings. On no account rely on the supplier's cutting or squaring of edges. Examine the corners closely to make sure that they have not been damaged in handling.

Construction

Cut the two vertical end members to shape (see Fig. 1) 20 x 12¾ x ¾in. (508 x 324 x 19mm). Cut the top member: 28½ x 12¾ x ¾in. (724 x 324 x 19mm). Cut the base member: 28½ x 12 x ¾in. (724 x 305 x 19mm).

Butt the two horizontal members to the sides of the end members. A first step in joining the members is to mark accurately the hole points for the screws. The screws to be used are 1½in. (38mm) No. 6.

Mark a line ⅜in (9.5mm) in from the edge. Mark the screw point locations with cross lines: the first at 1in. (25mm), the second at 4¼in. (108mm), the third at 7¾in. (197mm) and the fourth at 11in. (279mm). Using an awl, mark the screw positions.

Using a $\frac{5}{32}$in. (4mm) drill or bit, drill all 16 holes. Using an awl, mark the first and last holes in the short edges of the top and bottom members. Now with the point of the drill inserted through the first hole in one of the side members, drill a ¼in. (6mm) deep hole at the first screw position, insert screw and tighten a few turns. Insert drill through the last hole in this side, drill a ¼in. (6mm) deep hole, insert screw and tighten a few turns.

Now, inserting the drill through the intermediate holes, drill ¼in. (6mm) deep holes, insert screws and tighten a few turns.

Repeat this operation at the four sides of the frame. This makes the general rectangular shape of the unit, and you may care to hold it in position on the wall where it will be ultimately located. This is the time to make any last minute modifications in respect to size.

Now cut the back panel: 28½ x 18½ x ¾in. (724 x 470 x 19mm). Place it into position, being completely framed within the four sides of the unit. At this point check the accuracy of your work so far. Check the 90° angles of all members. Stand the unit on a smooth level surface and check that the back panel fits snugly inside the frame.

Remove the panel and apply woodworking adhesive to the edges to be joined. Tighten the screws securing the frame, thus securing the back panel in a snug fit. Rule a line along the outside of the top, bottom and end members ⅜in. (9.5mm) from the back edge of the unit. Using 1½in. (38mm) panel pins, pin the panel into position.

Now, one by one, remove each screw, and, using a snail-head bit, make the conical depressions for countersinking; re-insert screws, tighten. Having countersunk and tightened all screws, fill in the holes with matching woods-topping, such as Brummer. Allow to set, then carve off with a chisel.

Using a pin-punch and hammer, countersink all nail-heads, fill with stopping, and carve off flush.

This is a good time to make the holes in the

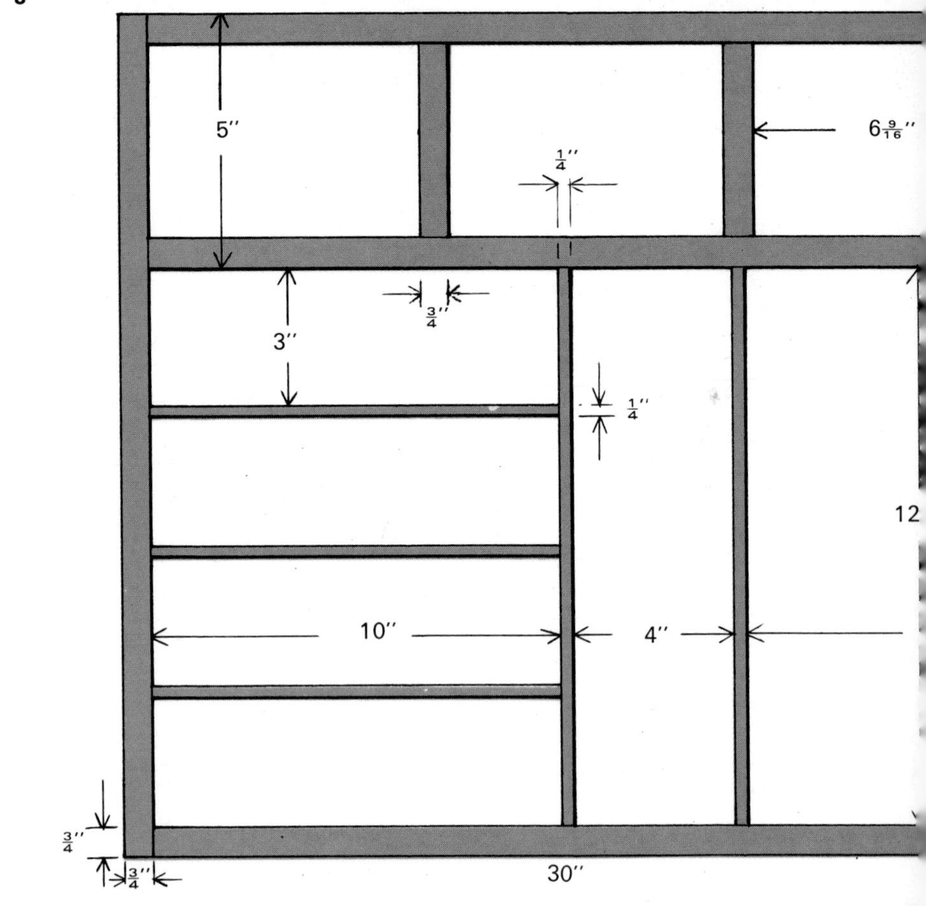

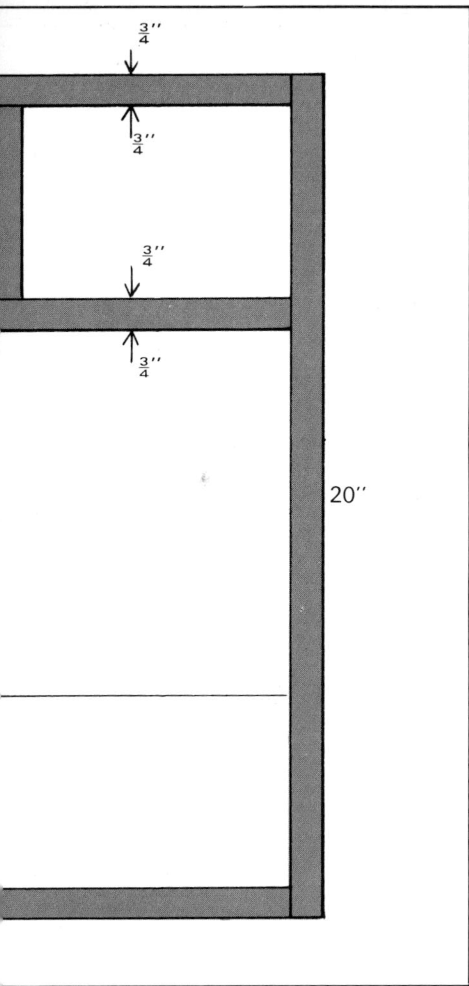

back of the unit for fixing to the wall. Using an awl, mark two hole positions in the back panel at a position 7in. (178mm) in from each end and from the top edge. Bore a ¼in. (6mm) deep hole at each position.

Cut the shelf piece 28½ x 12 x ¾in. (724 x 305 x 19mm). Rule a line inside the assembly 5in. (127mm) down from the top.

Apply woodworking adhesive to the rear edge and the two 12in. (305mm) edges of the shelf and slide it into the position marked, the top edge flush with the line. On the outside of the assembly, rule a line 6⅛in. (155mm) down from the top. Along this line, hammer in the panel pins. Countersink heads with a pin-punch, fill with stopping and carve off flush.

Wall fixing

At this point, you will have built the basic cabinet without the shelves or flap-down work surface. It is a good idea to position the unit temporarily against the wall and drill the holes and actually put in the wall-plugs or other fixings.

The choice of fixing will depend largely on the type of wall the unit will be attached to. There are three basic methods of fixing:

a) for solid walls, masonry nails and plugs, and screws;

b) in the case of very heavy units, for instance if the desk should hold a typewriter, bolts are used;

c) for hollow surfaces such as panelled walls, cavity devices can be used.

Fig.3. *The lower partitions providing shelves and divisions are made of ¼in. ply.*
Fig.4. *Position the angle-stay so as to hold the two working sufaces exactly level and secure for functional use.*

See a do-it-yourself manual for methods of fixing, types of wall plugs, tools, etc.

Top compartments

To make the partitions for the top shelf, cut three pieces 11¼ x 5 x ¾in. (285 x 127 x 19mm).

Mark their positions carefully. The space between any two partitions or end panel is 6 9/16in. (166mm). Apply woodworking adhesive to top, bottom and rear edges and slide into position. Pin through top, rear and shelf panels. Countersink nail heads on top surface, apply stopping and slice flush.

Add veneer edge trim to all front exposed edges, with the exception of the base of the unit. Self-adhesive edging strip is available in cut lengths in teak. To apply, position the edging strip, place ordinary brown paper on top. Now apply a warm iron and move it slowly over the surface. Remove the iron every 18in. (460mm) and rub with a cloth to ensure even contact. After 30 minutes, remove any overhanging edges with a flat fine-cut file, using quick downstrokes.

The partitions have been pushed back to butt the rear panel and thus allow ¾in. (19mm) for the top and bottom nylon running strips.

Cut these 28½in. (724mm) long and screw and glue into position.

From a piece of ¼in. (6mm) teak-veneered ply, cut four sliding door panels 7 x 4⅞in. (178 x 124mm). Sandpaper top and bottom edges to give easy running but not loose fit. Check their action thoroughly. Remove the doors. Glue on ramin handles. Place doors back into position for permanent installation.

Partitions

On the top surface of the base member of the unit, rule lines at right angles to the front at positions 14in. (356mm) and 14¼in. (362mm) from the inside of the right hand member.

Rule lines in identical positions on the under surface of the shelf member. These two pairs of lines indicate the position of the central partition which will bisect the interior of the cabinet.

Cut 8 pieces of ¼ x ¼in. (6 x 6mm) hardwood moulding 10½in. (267mm) long. Pin and glue two of these mouldings into position on the outside of the two pairs of lines and thus make a recess for the central partition to slide into. Cut the central partition: 12¾ x 10½in. (324 x 267mm). Apply woodworking adhesive to the shorter edges and rear edge of the panel and slide it into position between the two pairs of mouldings.

On the top surface of the base member of the unit, rule lines at right angles to the front at positions 10 and 10¼in. (254 and 260mm) from the inside of the left hand member. Rule lines in identical positions on the under surface of the shelf member. Pin and glue two of the 10½in. (267mm) mouldings into position on the outside of the two pairs of lines. Cut a second partition: 12¾in. x 10½in. (324 x 267mm).

Shelves

Mark the positions for three ¼in. (6mm) thick shelves. 3in. (76mm) apart, on the left-hand end member. Mark complementary positions on the partition. Cut six mouldings 10 x ¼ x ¼in. (254 x 6 x 6mm). Pin and glue three of the mouldings to the left end member, the top edges of the mouldings being level with the shelf lines and butting the back panel. Pin and glue the other three to the facing surface of the partition.

Apply woodworking adhesive to the top and bottom edges of the partition and slide it between the two pairs of mouldings.

Cut three shelf panels 10½ x 10in. (267 x 254mm). Apply woodworking adhesive to the side edges and the rear edge of each shelf panel, and to a ¼in. (6mm) strip along each side of the under surface. Slide the three shelves into position to rest on the mouldings.

The interior of your desk is now complete, providing four upper compartments covered by sliding doors, a large area for storing a correspondence file, a typewriter perhaps; a 4in. (102mm) wide recess which could hold account books, desk diary, etc; four shelf spaces for storing stationery and miscellaneous items. All that is needed now is to cut and fit the door-flap which provides the working surface.

Flap-down lid

To prepare the base and end members to receive the flap-down lid, with an old-fashioned moulding plane, combination plane, or spindle cutter, make a convex shape to the bottom edge of the unit, angled at 45°

Cut the lid panel 30 x 13½ x ¾in. (762 x 343 x 19mm). Fit veneer edge trim to the top and side edges. Using a moulding plane or spindle cutter (or even an electric router) which will give a complementary shape, cut the edge of the panel to a concave shape, also angled at 45°.

Cut a piano hinge 28½in. (724mm) long. Open the leaves and screw it to the inside edge at the bottom of the lid panel. Apply it to the aperture and pin it temporarily to the top surface at the edge of the base member.

Close and open the lid several times to check its position and the fit of the convex-concave edges when fully open. Mark the positions of the screw holes for an accurate fit.

Remove the panel and fit the lock. This should be of the type which is mortised into the edge so that only the keyhole is visible from the outside: either a small mortise deadlock or escutcheon.

Cut a 2½in. (63mm) length of ramin handle moulding. Apply woodworking adhesive and cramp it in position just below the keyhole.

Refit the panel: place in all screws to secure the piano hinge. Test the lock by inserting the key and turning it. Mark the position of the bolt against the under edge of the shelf member and cut a mortise groove and a rebated groove to accommodate the metal plate. Screw the plate into position. Check lock in closed position.

Fit a 6 x 6in. (152 x 152mm) angle-stay to the inside of each end member and to the surface of the open lid, 1in. (25mm) in from each side. Before screwing into position, check that when the angle-stay is fully extended the two surfaces are exactly flat.

JIM KERSHAW

Above. *Distinctively original, all the furniture described in this two-part chapter is finished to simulate the craftsmanship of an earlier age.*

Rusticated wood furniture: 1

Individually crafted furniture is almost impossible to buy and the techniques for making it are largely lost or ignored. This two part chapter revives some strikingly original aspects of the carpenter's craft, and shows how they can be applied to the construction of modern, everyday furniture. The first part explains how to make a settle (a high-backed bench seat) and a stool; the second part describes a magazine rack, a coffee table and a plant holder–all stamped with an eye-catching hand-finished look at a fraction of the shop price.

The designer of these pieces wanted to produce furniture for his semi-detached home which was both attractive and original. He disliked the modern design concept of straight lines and a smooth finish and, in his search for something strikingly different, he turned to the furniture of an older age. After a study of the furniture of the Tudor period and before, he realised that many of the techniques employed by craftsmen of the middle ages were still applicable to the construction of furniture for the modern home.

What were the characteristics of this antique furniture? Firstly, it was comparatively rough finished. Sophisticated tools, such as the smoothing plane, were unknown and carpenters finished their work with an adze. This tool—which consists of a long handle to which is fitted a large chisel blade—was used to chip away the surface of the work to give a comparatively level finish. In the hands of a skilled craftsman the adze could produce an almost plane surface, but most household furniture was left in the rough, with the distinctive cuts by the adze showing.

The second characteristic of this furniture was the simplicity of the joints. Again, the relatively primitive tools available could not cope with complicated joints, and usually mortise and tenons were used which were reinforced by pegs, as shown in Fig.2.

These two features—an adzed finish and the use of pegged joints—can be incorporated with striking effect in the construction of modern furniture. Once you have mastered the basic knowledge of techniques and materials, you can commence work on the attractive projects.

Tools

To make the pieces of furniture shown, you require not only conventional tools, but also a tool which can produce an adzed effect. A proper adze is almost impossible to obtain and, in inexperienced hands, is a difficult tool to use. One alternative is a carving gouge as used in carving wood. This tool has a 1in. (25mm) blade section shaped to a shallow U, the method of using it is explained at a later stage.

Choosing a timber

All the designs shown have a period character which is emphasised by the correct choice of wood. Most early English furniture was built from native hardwoods, such as oak, beech and elm, and any one of these is suitable for the projects below. However, oak is nowadays both expensive and difficult to obtain and these considerations, plus the fact that it is not easy to work, mean that most carpenters will seek an alternative.

Of course, you can use one of the imported tropical hardwoods. These can often be obtained more easily than the native varieties and have the same properties. Choose a wood which is open-grained, durable and which carves well—one of the mahogany family is suitable.

Making a settle

Based on the design of a mediaeval church pew, this settle could be the focal point of your living room. Alternatively, if you make a matching table, it could be used as a dining settle. Construction is straightforward and involves no complicated jointing techniques, and the number of parts to be cut out and assembled is relatively small.

Begin by making a full size template of the end panels, using the scaled drawing in Fig.2 as a guide. Then trace out the pattern on two panels measuring 39in. x 24in. x $\frac{3}{4}$in. (990mm x 610mm x 19mm).

Cut out the correct shapes with a jig saw or, if you do not possess this tool, with a coping saw. Now cut out the three long rails to the size given in the cutting list. At each end of these rails a tenon or tongue is cut which is $1\frac{1}{2}$in. (38mm) long and 2in. x 1in. (51mm x 25mm) in cross-section. These tenons joint or slot into through-mortises cut into the end panels at the locations shown in Fig.2. By themselves these joints are not secure enough to hold the unit stable, and they are reinforced by pegs, which not only add strength to the structure, but also add to its period character.

To fit these pegs, first lay the long rails on a flat surface with the wider surfaces of the tenons uppermost. Mark a point midway between the long edges of each tenon and $\frac{3}{8}$in. from the shoulder of each tenon. These points represent the centres of the holes in which the pegs fit. Now, using the marked points as a guide, bore out the holes with a brace and $\frac{3}{4}$in. (19mm) auger bit. Alternatively, you can cut the holes with a hole saw fitted to a power drill. With all the holes bored out, square them off with a chisel, but do not make the pegs or cut the mortises in the end panels at this stage.

Cut out the two cross rails to the size given in the cutting list. With a tenon saw and chisel, cut a tenon $1\frac{1}{2}$in. (38mm) long and 2in. x 1in. (51mm x 25mm) in cross-section on each end of the two cross rails. Take two of the long rails and make mortises, corresponding to the tenons on the cross rails, on their inside edges. The outer short edges of the mortises are located $\frac{1}{2}$in. (13mm) from the shoulders of the tenons on the long rails. Cut out the mortises. Do not assemble the cross rails to the long rails just yet.

Now cut out the three back slats. A tongue $\frac{3}{8}$in. (10mm) long and 4in. x $\frac{3}{4}$in. (102mm x 19mm) in cross-section is cut at each end of these. The slats slot into mortises cut on the inside surfaces of the side panels, and are glued and screwed to battens, which themselves are screwed to the side panels, as shown in Fig.2.

Having cut out the back slats, make the mortises for these pieces and for the long rails. Begin by cutting the through mortises for the lower long rail. Refer to Fig.2 for their exact location and cut them out with a brace and bit and chisel, as described above. In the same way, cut mortises for the long seat rails. The exact location of these is determined by first trial-assembling the cross rails to the long rails, measuring the distance between the centres of the tenons, and marking this distance out on the side panels at the position indicated in Fig.2. This diagram also shows the location of the mortises which house the back slats, and these should be cut to a depth of $\frac{3}{8}$in. (10mm).

Creating an adzed finish

An adzed effect is created on all the exposed surfaces of the settle, greatly adding to its appearance. Although the techniques involved are simple to master, you are advised to practice on a waste piece of timber first.

Hold the curved gouge at a shallow angle to the work surface and strike it with a short, round-headed mallet to gouge out small scoops of wood. Work *with* the grain and try to leave

Below. *Despite the period flavour of this settle, its eye-catching good looks will make it the focal point of any living room.*

JIM KERSHAW

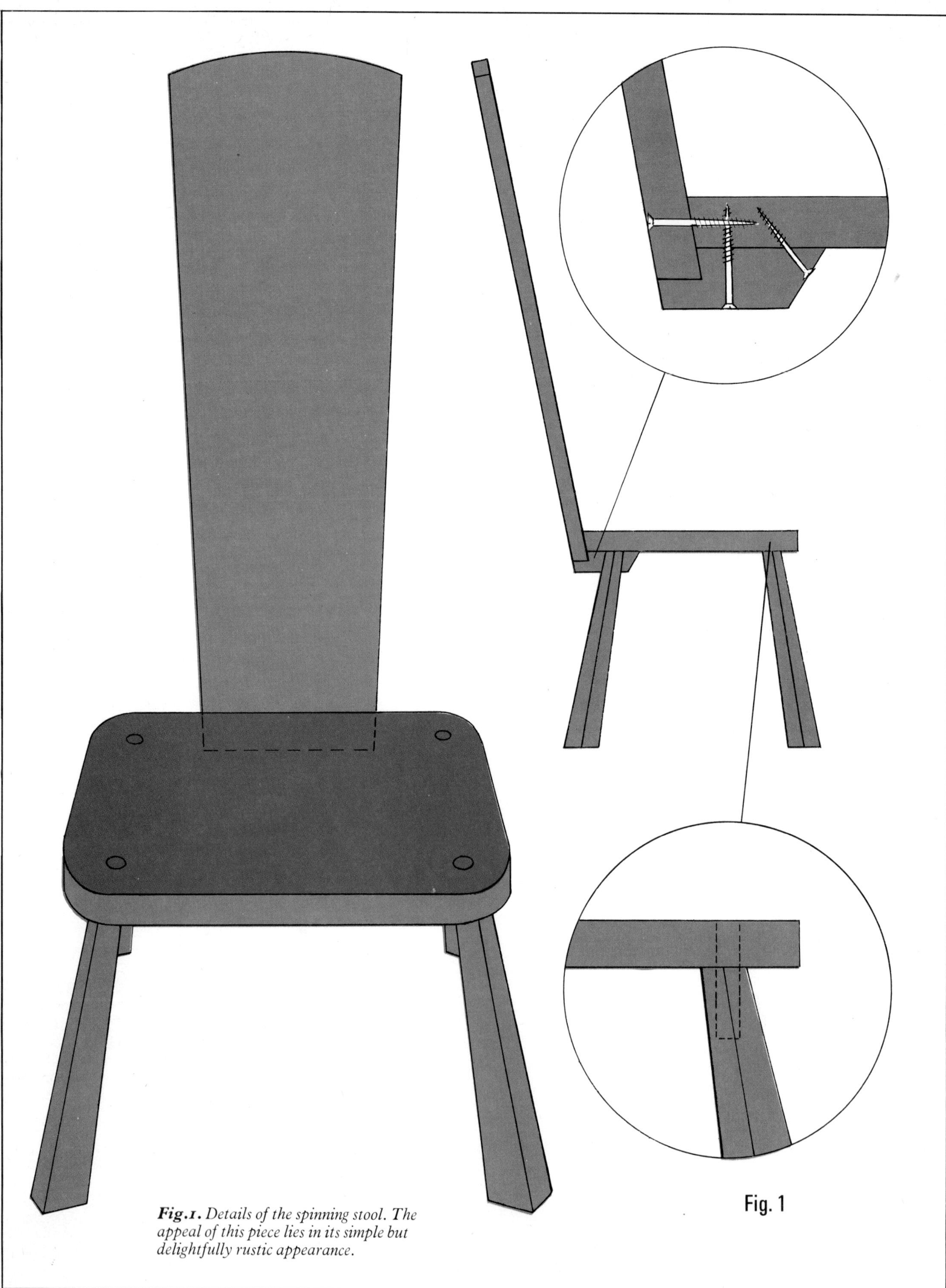

Fig.1. *Details of the spinning stool. The appeal of this piece lies in its simple but delightfully rustic appearance.*

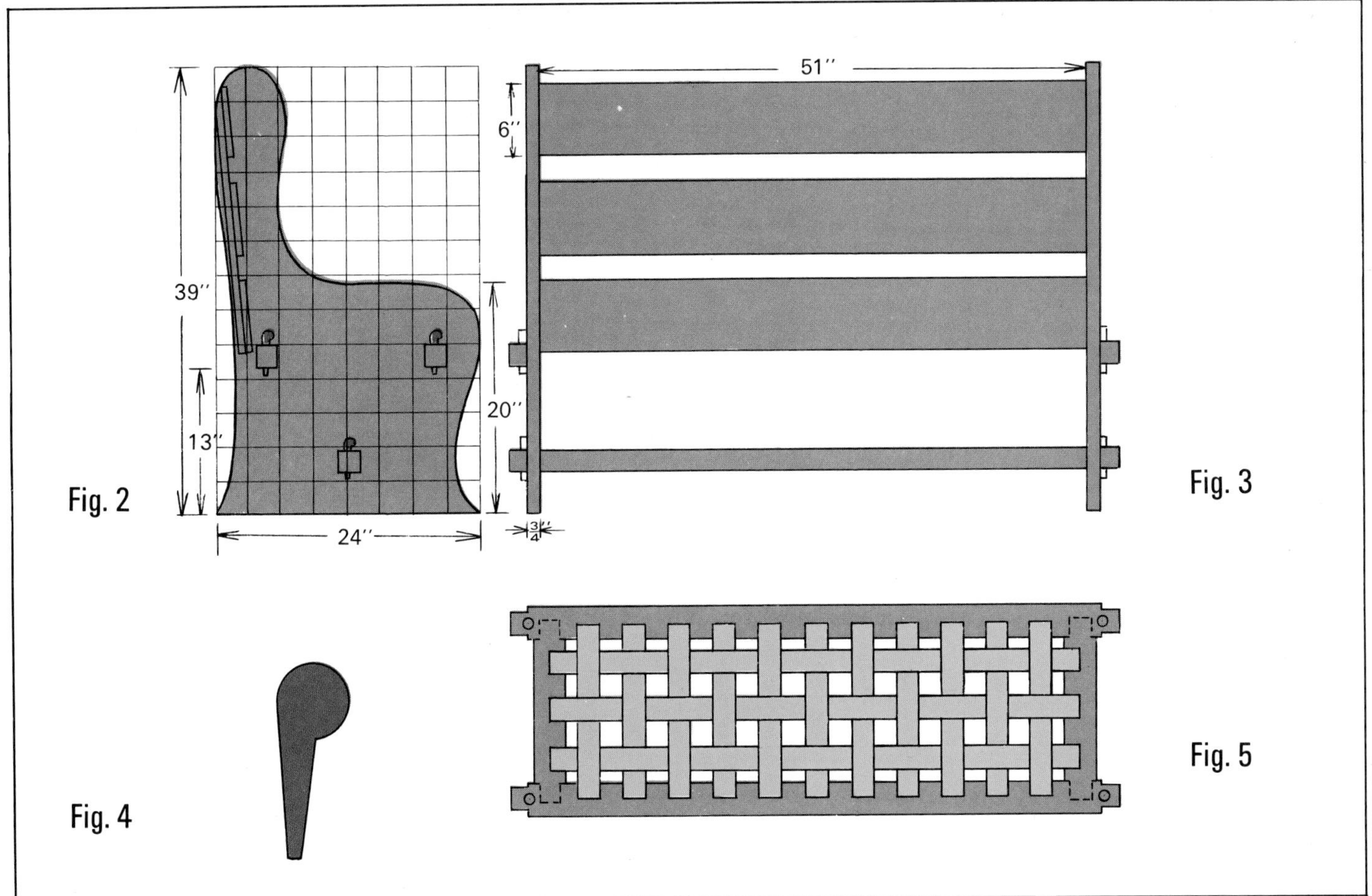

a small margin between the individual cuts. Do not cut too deep; if you find that you cannot control the depth of cut, you are either using the wrong gouge or holding it at the wrong angle. After you have adzed an area of, say, 6in. (152mm) square on the waste timber, create the same effect on both surfaces of the side panels, the front surfaces of the back slats and the exposed edges of the long rails. Obviously this is a long job which requires a lot of patience and, unfortunately, there is no short cut to creating a fine finish. Your gouge will require frequent sharpening; to ignore this will spoil the finish and, in the long run, increase the work. However, the work involved is amply rewarded by the eye-catching effect that is achieved.

Assembling the settle

Begin by glueing the cross rails into the mortises cut in the long rails. Provided you have measured and cut out correctly, the long outside edge of each cross rail should be flush with the shoulders of the tenons on the long rails. If they overlap slightly, plane them to size so that when assembled to the side panels, the cross rails and the shoulders of the tenons butt flush against the inside surfaces of the side panels. Check that the assembled seat structure fits into the mortises in the side panels.

As explained above, the long rails are held in position by pegs hammered into holes cut in the tenons on the long rails. Cut these pegs out to shape and size shown in Fig.4, using a coping saw and a sharp handyman's knife. The widest part of each wedge should be a little over 1in. (25mm) wide and $\frac{3}{4}$in. (19mm) thick. Fit the

Fig.2. *Scaled outline of one side of the settle. Each square is 3in. x 3in. (76mm x 76mm).*
Fig.3. *A view of the back of the settle.*
Fig.4. *Cut the pegs to this basic outline.*
Fig.5. *Canvas webbing gives seat support.*

long rails into the mortises on the side panels and drive the pegs home. Check that the unit is stable, with no play at the joints, then knock the pegs out and dismantle the structure. The reason for this is to allow you to screw the battens which support the back slats to the side panels, and also fit the seat with canvas webbing.

Screw the battens into position on the side panels and tack canvas webbing to the seat as shown in Fig.5. Alternatively, with a little extra work you can add rubber webbing to the seat to give extra comfort. This latter idea involves fitting a clip at the end of each length of webbing and then housing it in a slot cut in the top edges of the rails. Although it involves more work, it is a neater and longer lasting method of springing the settle.

Now re-assemble the settle, fitting the back slats into the mortises on the side panels and screwing them to the battens. For maximum strength, fix the cross rails to the side panels with black, round-headed coach bolts. The assembly is now complete and all that remains to do is to stain and varnish the timber and make the cushions.

Staining and varnishing

The settle shows up particularly well in most contemporary decors if a dark stain is applied to it. One easy and inexpensive method of making up a suitable stain is to dissolve bichromate of potash crystals in water to give a concentrated solution. Test the stain on a waste piece of timber and dilute it as required before painting it onto the settle.

Once the surfaces are the desired colour, and dry, spray or brush on a modern polyurethane furniture varnish. Use a good quality brush and work quickly to apply an even coat. When the first coat has dried, cut it down with grade 0 steel wool, then add another coat and cut this down. Repeat this process at least four times to give a really fine gloss finish which, if desired, can be dulled a little with steel wool. Finish with wax.

The cushions

Foam rubber forms the foundations of the two cushions. Of the various types of foam available, polyether is the most suitable as it can be obtained in different densities and textures. For the seat cushion, choose foam 4in. (102mm) thick with a density of at least 1.8lb per cubic foot. A thinner foundation can be used for the back cushion—2in. (51mm) is ideal—with a density of between 1 lb and 1.5 lb per cubic foot.

Cut out the cushions for both the seat and the back rest, using a sharp hacksaw or electric carving knife. They are cut slightly over-size, so that when covered in fabric of the right size they hold it under tension and thus prevent wrinkles forming. Full instructions on how to make up covers for cushions are given in various upholstery or home sewing magazines available in today's market.

Making a spinning stool

Genuine spinning stools are popular antiques and consequently are expensive to buy. Here is a chance to make an attractive reproduction.

Below. *The spinning stool is useful both as an attractive ornament and an occasional seat. The gouged surfaces simulate the adzed finish of earlier times and provide striking contrast to most modern finishes.*

Begin by cutting out the seat panel to the size given in the cutting list and rounding off the corners. Then cut out the back panel and round off the top. The legs, which are cut over length at this stage, taper from 1$\frac{3}{4}$in. (44mm) to 1$\frac{1}{4}$in. (31mm). When fitted to the seat the legs are splayed, which means that the top edge must be angled. The angle at which the legs meet the seat panel is 75°. To mark and cut out the angled edge, lay the centre point of a protractor on one long edge, at a point about $\frac{1}{2}$in. (13mm) from one end and mark this point. Mark in a line to the opposite long edge at 75° to the previously marked point, then repeat the process on the side of the leg adjacent to the first marked point. Cut down the two marked lines with a tenon saw to give the engled end.

With all the pieces cut out, 'adze' finish all exposed surfaces except the surface of the seat panel. This can be shaped for comfort.

JIM KERSHAW

Assembly

With a brace and auger bit, bore a hole $\frac{1}{2}$in. (13mm) in diameter and 1in. (25mm) deep in the narrow end of each leg. Hold the bit at right angles to the angled end, as shown in Fig.1. Bore a corresponding hole $\frac{3}{4}$in. (19mm) deep at each corner of the seat panel as shown in Fig.1.

Now glue 1$\frac{3}{4}$in. (44mm) lengths of $\frac{1}{2}$in. (13mm) dowel into the legs and, when the glue has set, fit the protruding ends of the dowels into the seat.

Cut a $\frac{3}{4}$in. (19mm) square rebate on one long edge of the support block. This houses the back rest. Glue and screw the back rest to the support block and fix this structure to the seat.

The base ends of each leg must now be levelled off. Take a waste block of wood measuring 3in. x 2in. x 1in. (76mm x 51mm x 25mm) and drill a hole through the midpoint of the 1in. (25mm) edge, just big enough to hold a pencil tightly. Push the pencil through so that about $\frac{1}{2}$in. (13mm) protrudes, and lay the block on a flat surface so that the pencil is parallel to the floor. Draw a line round the bottom of each leg and carefully cut through the legs, around the lines, using a tenon saw.

The construction is now complete and you can stain and varnish the stool in the same way as suggested for the settle. The attractive results that you have obtained will, no doubt, encourage you to construct the furniture described in the second part of this chapter.

Cutting list: Settle

Solid wood	Imperial	Metric
2 side panels	39x24x$\frac{3}{4}$	990x610x19
3 long rails	54x3x1	1371x76x25
2 cross rails	18x3x1	457x76x25
3 back slats	51$\frac{3}{4}$x6x$\frac{3}{4}$	1314x152x19
2 battens	26x1x1	660x25x25
6 pegs	3$\frac{1}{2}$x1x$\frac{3}{4}$	89x25x19

You will also need:
Canvas or rubber webbing. Wood glue. 12 1$\frac{1}{2}$in. (38mm) wood screws. 1in. (25mm) curved gouge. Short, round-headed mallet. Coping saw. Tenon saw. Brace and $\frac{3}{4}$in. (19mm) auger bit. $\frac{3}{4}$in. (19mm) chisel. 6 black coach bolts. Wood stain and varnish.

Cutting list: Spinning Stool

Solid wood	Imperial	Metric
1 seat panel	15x10x1	381x254x25
1 back rest	24x11x$\frac{3}{4}$	609x279x19
4 legs	13$\frac{1}{2}$x1$\frac{3}{4}$x1$\frac{3}{4}$	343x44x44
1 back rest support	8x3x1$\frac{1}{2}$	203x76x38

You will also need:
4 1$\frac{3}{4}$in. (44mm) lengths of $\frac{1}{2}$in. (13mm) dowel. Wood glue. Tools and finishing materials as for the settle.

Rusticated wood furniture: 2

In this second part of the chapter on hand-crafted furniture, you are given full instructions on how to make a magazine rack, a coffee table and a plant holder. All these pieces have a period flavour which is enhanced by their 'adzed' finish —a highly original touch in an age of mass-produced furniture.

Of the furniture described in this chapter, two pieces, the coffee table and the magazine rack are assembled without the aid of screws, nails or bolts. The magazine rack is constructed using simple mortise and tenon joints and is reinforced with pegs—the same technique that is used to build the settle described in the first part of this chapter. The coffee table is built to a traditional design which owes its good looks to its distinctive finish and simple lines.

Both these pieces can be easily dismantled and stowed away—a useful feature if you want to create extra space in your home, or if you have to move house.

Making a magazine rack

If you made the settle, you will not experience any difficulty in making the magazine rack. It is constructed from the same wood and uses the same construction techniques.

Begin by drawing out a full-size template of the end panels, using the scaled drawing in Fig.1 as a guide. The dimensions of the rack are suitable for holding most magazines, and

Below. *The shaped ends, 'adzed' finish and use of reinforcing pegs lift this magazine rack out of the ordinary. With a little re-styling you can modify the rack to hold records.*

JIM KERSHAW

records too, but can easily be modified. Trace the patterm out on two panels measuring 15in. x 12in. x ⅝in. (381mm x 305mm x 16mm) and cut out the correct shapes with a jig saw, or, if you do not possess this tool, with a coping saw.

Now cut out the two cross members to the size given in the cutting list, then cut the base panel and the six side members. Finally, cut out four pegs to the size and shape shown in Fig.1.

Clamp the two end panels together so that all their edges are flush. If any part of one panel overlaps the other, plane it to size. When you are satisfied that both panels are of an identical size and shape, draw a centre line down one of them. Mark points on this centre line 1¼in. (31mm) and 9in. (229mm) from the top edge of the panels. These represent the locations of the top edges of the through mortises which house the cross-rails. Mark out these mortises—they are 1½in. (38mm) long and ¾in. (19mm) wide—and cut them out.

Unclamp the end panels and clean up the edges of the mortises with a chisel. Next, mark and cut out the mortises which house the base panel. Each of these two mortises is 7in. (178mm) long, ½in. (13mm) wide and $\frac{5}{16}$in. (8mm) deep. Their lower long edges are located ½in. (13mm) from the bases of the side panels and their sides are located 1in. (25mm) from the long sides of the side panels. Now mark out the mortises which house the side members, at the locations shown in Fig.1. Cut out all these mortises to a depth of $\frac{5}{16}$in. (8mm).

Mark points on the narrow edge of each cross rail, ⅝in. (16mm) from their ends and at the midpoint between long edges. These points represent the centres of the holes which hold the pegs. Using them as a guide, bore out the holes with a brace and ¼in. (6mm) auger bit, then cut away round the holes to give mortises ¾in. long and ¼in. (6mm) wide, as shown in Fig.1.

With all the cutting completed, adze finish all the exposed surfaces of the pieces. Work right to the edges of each member and slightly blunt all the edges to enhance the period look of the finished article.

Assembly and finishing

Assembly is straightforward. Begin by glueing the base panel into its housings on the side panels. In the same way, add the side members. When the glue has set, fix the two cross rails into position, then drive home the pegs which hold the rack secure.

Like the other pieces described, the rack is

Fig.1. Views of the magazine rack end and side panels. Also shown on the end panel are the locations of the side slats and base.
Fig.2. You can cut the coffee table top to any shape you desire. The splayed legs are fitted by means of lengths of dowelling.

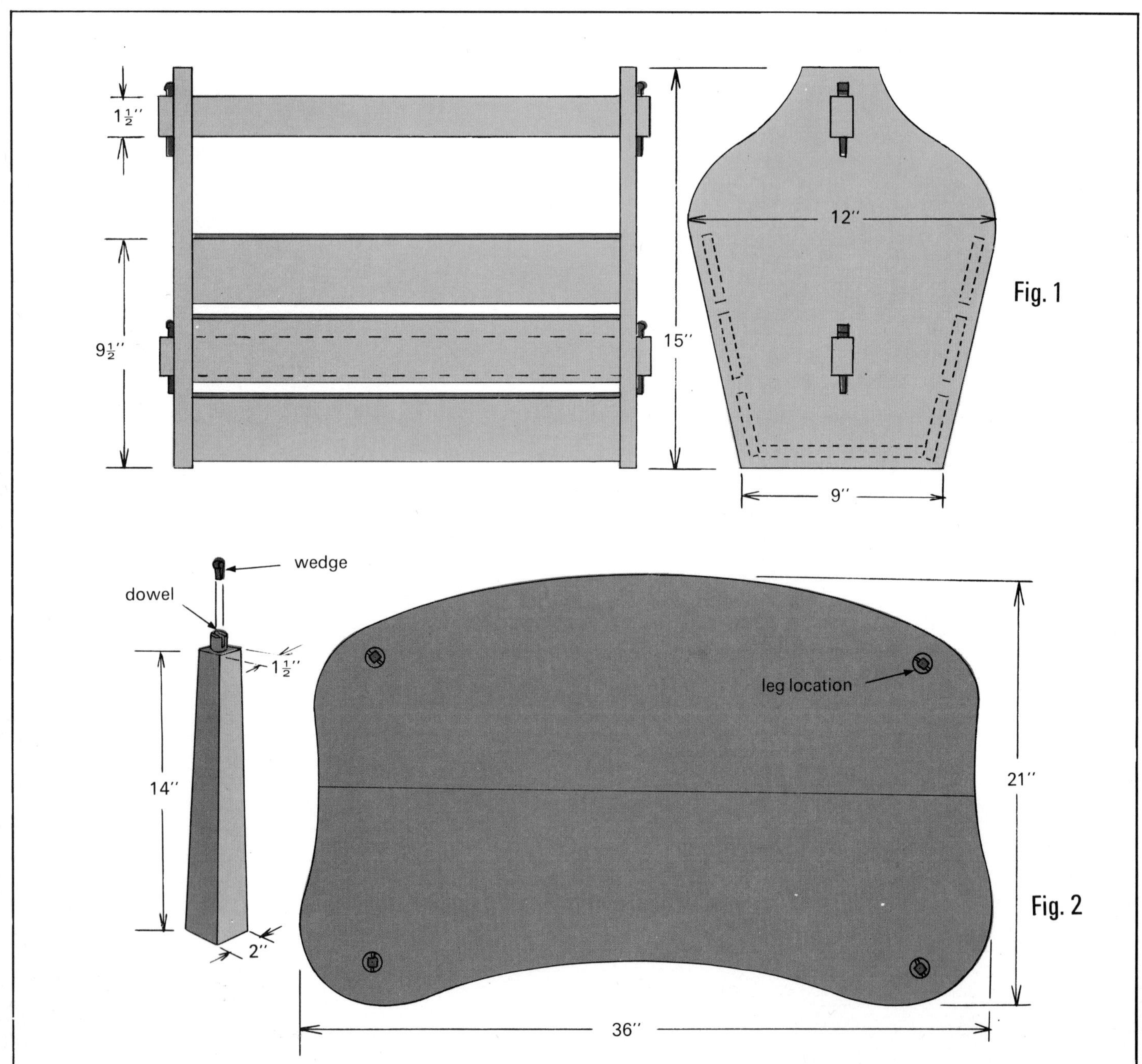

seen at its best when stained a dark colour and given a glossy polyurethane finish.

Making a coffee table

Most modern coffee tables are elegant, but rather flimsy pieces, designed to fit unobtrusively into the modern home. However, even the most contemporary decor can be enhanced by a bold touch, and this solid coffee table, finished to show off the richness of the wood, is certainly a very striking piece.

It is built entirely of a suitable hardwood, such as oak, beech or one of the mahogany family. This makes the materials rather expensive, but the finished article makes most other coffee tables look insignificant by comparison.

Construction

The dimensions of the table can be modified to suit individual requirements. Those given in the cutting list are of the table shown in Fig.2, which is large enough to hold television snacks.

There is no reason why you should cut the table top to any particular shape. If you want, you can make the top square, round or oval, or even irregular. If you decide to make an irregularly shaped top, first draw out possible shapes on a large piece of paper, then, when you have found one which appeals to you, transfer the outline to the timber and cut it out with a jig saw or bow saw.

Cut out the members which give the legs. At this stage these pieces are 1in. (25mm) overlength to allow you to cut out the angled ends. Each leg tapers from 2in. (51mm) square at the base, to 1½in. (38mm) square at the top. To cut the taper, mark in a 1½in. (38mm) square on one end of each leg, making sure that each side of the square is ¼in. (6mm) from one short edge of the member. Continue each line to the short edge and down to a corner at the base of the leg. Cut down these lines with a rip saw.

Now cut the angled ends which meet the underside of the table top. Mark a point on one long edge of a leg, about ½in. (13mm) from the narrow end. With the aid of a protractor, draw a line at 75° to this point which extends to the opposite long edge. Repeat this process on the side of the leg adjacent to the first marked point, then cut down the two lines with a tenon saw to give the angled end. Repeat with the other legs.

With all the pieces cut out, 'adze' finish all exposed surfaces.

Bore a hole 1in. (25mm) in diameter and 2in. (51mm) deep in the narrow end of each leg. Into each hole, glue a 4½in. (114mm) length of 1in. (25mm) diameter dowel. Corresponding holes, which run at 75° to the table surface, are

Below. *Although designed primarily as a coffee table, it is large enough and solid enough to hold casual meals and for this reason is ideal as a television table.*

JIM KERSHAW

cut in the table top, at the locations shown in Fig.2. Obviously, you will find it difficult to judge the correct angle by eye and there are no tools available which can hold a drill at a pre-set angle to the work-surface. However, there is a device, easily constructed by the handyman, which answers this need. To make it, cut one end of a small block of waste wood at an angle of 75°. Then cut a groove down the centre of this end, capable of housing a drill bit. On the upper surface of the block and on a centre line drawn from the groove to the rear edge of the block, drive in a screw about ½in. (13mm) longer than the thickness of the block.

To use this device, position it on the underside of the table top so that the bottom of the groove corresponds to the proposed location of the top end of a leg. Line up the line marked on the top of the block with the nearest corner of the table, then screw the block to the table. Place the drill bit into the groove and bore out the angled hole. Repeat this process at all four corners of the table top.

Clamp each leg in turn, in a vice and, using a tenon saw, cut a groove 1in. (25mm) deep in each protruding length of dowel. Insert each leg into the housings in the table, then cut off any dowel which protrudes through the top flush with the surface of the table. To reinforce these joints, drive wedges into the grooves cut into the dowels.

Cut the bottoms of the legs square then finish by staining and varnishing, as described above.

Making a plant holder

Large enough to hold four pot-plants, the 'adzed' finish on this plant holder adds a delightfully rustic touch to your home.

Begin by making a template of one end panel. Transfer this to the timber and cut out the two end panels. Cut out the other panels to the sizes given in the cutting list.

Take the two end panels and cut rebates across them, ½in. (13mm) wide and ¼in. (6mm) deep. The upper edge of each rebate is 8in. (203mm) from the top edge of the end panel. Now make rebates of the same depth and width on the long edges of the end panels. 'Adze' finish all exposed surfaces.

Assembly is straightforward. Simply glue and screw the panels (beginning with the base panel), into the appropriate rebates. Finish by staining and varnishing as described above.

Cutting list: Magazine rack

Solid wood	Imperial	Metric
2 end panels	15x12x⅝	381x305x16
2 cross rails	20x1½x¾	508x38x19
6 side slats	18⅝x2½x½	473x64x13
1 base panel	18⅝x7x½	473x178x13

You will also need:
4 hardwood pegs. Wood glue. 1in. (25mm) curved gouge. Short, round-headed mallet. Coping saw. Tenon saw. Brace and ¼in. (6mm) auger bit. Wood stain and varnish.

Cutting list: Coffee table

Solid wood	Imperial	Metric
1 table top	36x21x2	914x533x51
4 legs	15x2x2	381x51x51
4 1in. (25mm) dowel rods	2½	64

You will also need:
1in. (25mm) curved gouge. Short, round-headed mallet. Coping saw. Tenon saw. Rip saw. Brace and 1in. (25mm) auger bit. Wood stain and varnish.

Cutting list: Plant holder

Solid wood	Imperial	Metric
2 end panels	16x6x½	46x152x13
1 base panel	19½x6x½	495x152x13
2 side panels	19½x8x½	495x203x13

You will also need:
1in (25mm) curved gouge. Short, round-headed mallet. Coping saw. Tenon saw. Rebate plane. Wood glue. 16 1¼in. (31mm) wood screws. Wood stain and varnish.

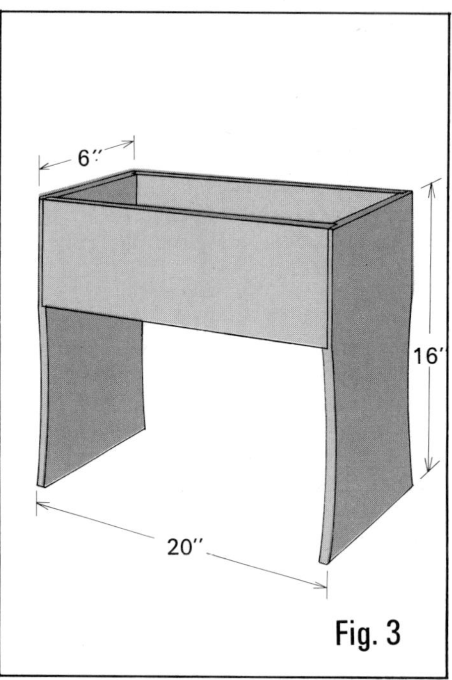

***Fig.3.** The dimensions of the plant-holder can be easily altered. The panels are simply fitted together by means of rebate joints.*
***Below.** Simple to construct and delightfully rustic in appearance, the plant-holder can be used to hold all types of household plants. The distinctive 'adzed' finish complements the other hand-crafted pieces.*

Modern furniture from angle strip: 1

One simple idea, applied to several items of furniture in the home, can lend a pleasing unity to the decor. Aluminium angle strip, used as an important part of the structure of a piece of furniture, does just this, as well as being an attractive decorative feature in itself.

The first part of this chapter gives full instructions on how to build a roomy sideboard and a good looking glass topped coffee table, incorporating 1$\frac{1}{4}$in. x 1$\frac{1}{4}$in. x $\frac{1}{8}$in. (31mm x 31mm x 3mm) aluminium angle strip as a decorative reinforcing material.

***Below.** A view of the spacious sideboard.*
***Following page.** An exploded drawing of the sideboard.*

General construction

The sideboard consists of two rectangular timber frames, the top frame of which is mitred at the corners, and the lower frame butt jointed at the corners. The top frame has a rebated groove cut in the members to take a laminated chipboard top, and aluminium angle strip is screwed to it at the corners. The lower frame and the angle strip are also fixed together, this fixing being 18in. (407mm) below the top frame. The area between the frames is filled with two cupboards, one at each end of the frame, with a central open space between them. The cupboards have sliding doors.

The coffee table is very simple. It consists of four sides with a rebated groove cut in the inside faces near the top edge to take a sheet of float glass for the table top. The table has timber legs, strengthened with aluminium angle strip.

The sideboard

The basic construction of the sideboard is described above and shown in Fig.1. The unit has plenty of room for storage and the top of the unit, and the central area between the cupboards, is covered with hardwearing plastic laminate. The timber you choose for these units is up to you, though it should be hardwood—softwood will damage too easily.

The top frame

The top rectangular frame of the sideboard has a finished size of 6ft x 2ft (1.83m x 0.61m) and is constructed from 7in. x 1in. (178mm x 25mm) timber. A rebated groove on the inner face of the frame side pieces supplies a fixing for the sideboard top. The tops of the cupboard panels fit into a rebated groove cut into the bottom edge of these pieces.

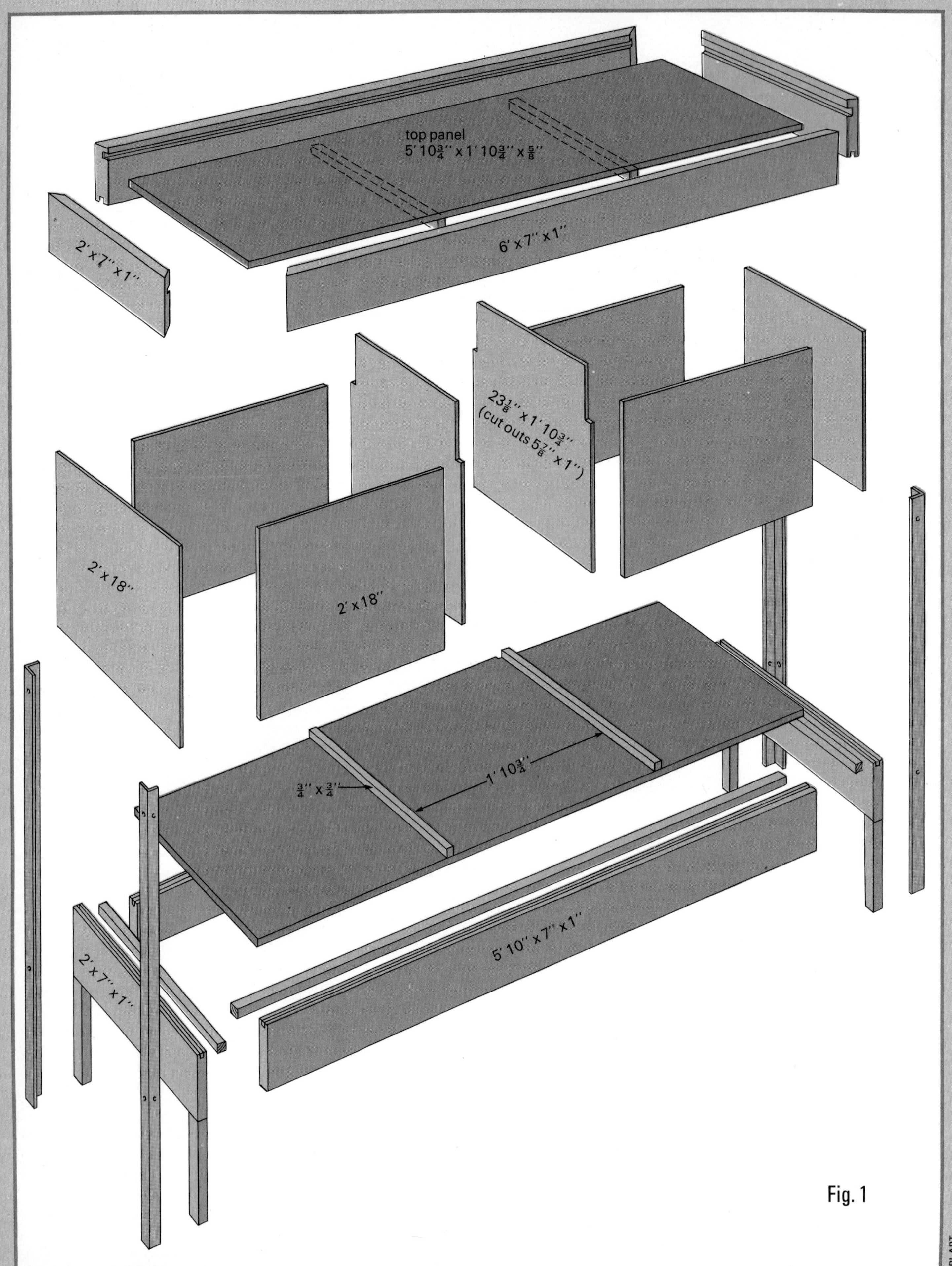
top panel
5′10¾″ x 1′10¾″ x ⅝″
2′ x 7″ x 1″
6′ x 7″ x 1″
23⅛″ x 1′10¾″
(cut outs 5⅞″ x 1″)
2′ x 18″
2′ x 18″
¾″ x ¾″
1′10¾″
5′10″ x 7″ x 1″
2′ x 7″ x 1″
Fig. 1

TRI-ART

To make the top frame, first cut the sides a little overlength and mark out the finished length of 6ft (1.83m) for the long sides and 2ft (0.61m) for the short sides. Mark the inner surfaces of these pieces also—this helps to ensure that the mitres, which can now be cut, run the right way.

You can cut the mitres with a bench saw set to 45°, or you can use a handsaw, with a mitre box to guide the cuts. The timber used here is too deep to fit inside most mitre boxes so clamp the mitre box to the timber rather than placing it inside the box. Using a mitre box in this way, and cutting a mitre with a bench saw is an effective method for this kind of job. Glasspaper the mitred ends.

The next step is to cut a rebated groove in the inside face of the side pieces, close to the top edge. Set the fence of the rebate plane to $\frac{1}{2}$in. (13mm) and use a $\frac{5}{8}$in. (16mm) blade to cut the groove. The rebate should be $\frac{3}{8}$in. (9mm) deep. The width of the rebate allows for a $\frac{5}{8}$in. thick sheet of plastic laminate covered chipboard as the top panel. You can use another material, such as plywood or wood veneered chipboard for this. Whatever you choose, the width of the rebate should match the thickness of the material used.

Cut the rebated groove on the inside face of all four pieces. You do not have to stop the grooves before the end of the pieces—you cannot see the end cut-outs when the pieces are fitted together.

The bottom edges of the side pieces also have a groove cut in them. This is to accommodate the side and back panels of the sideboard cupboards. Set the fence of the plane to $\frac{1}{8}$in. (3mm) and work from the outer surface of the pieces. Cut the groove $\frac{7}{16}$in. (11mm) wide and $\frac{3}{8}$in. (9mm) deep.

Now cut the panel for the sideboard top. Cut it oversize and carefully plane down the edges to the panel's finished size of 5ft 10$\frac{3}{4}$in. x 1ft 10$\frac{3}{4}$in. (1778mm x 579mm). The panel must be square—measure the diagonals to check this.

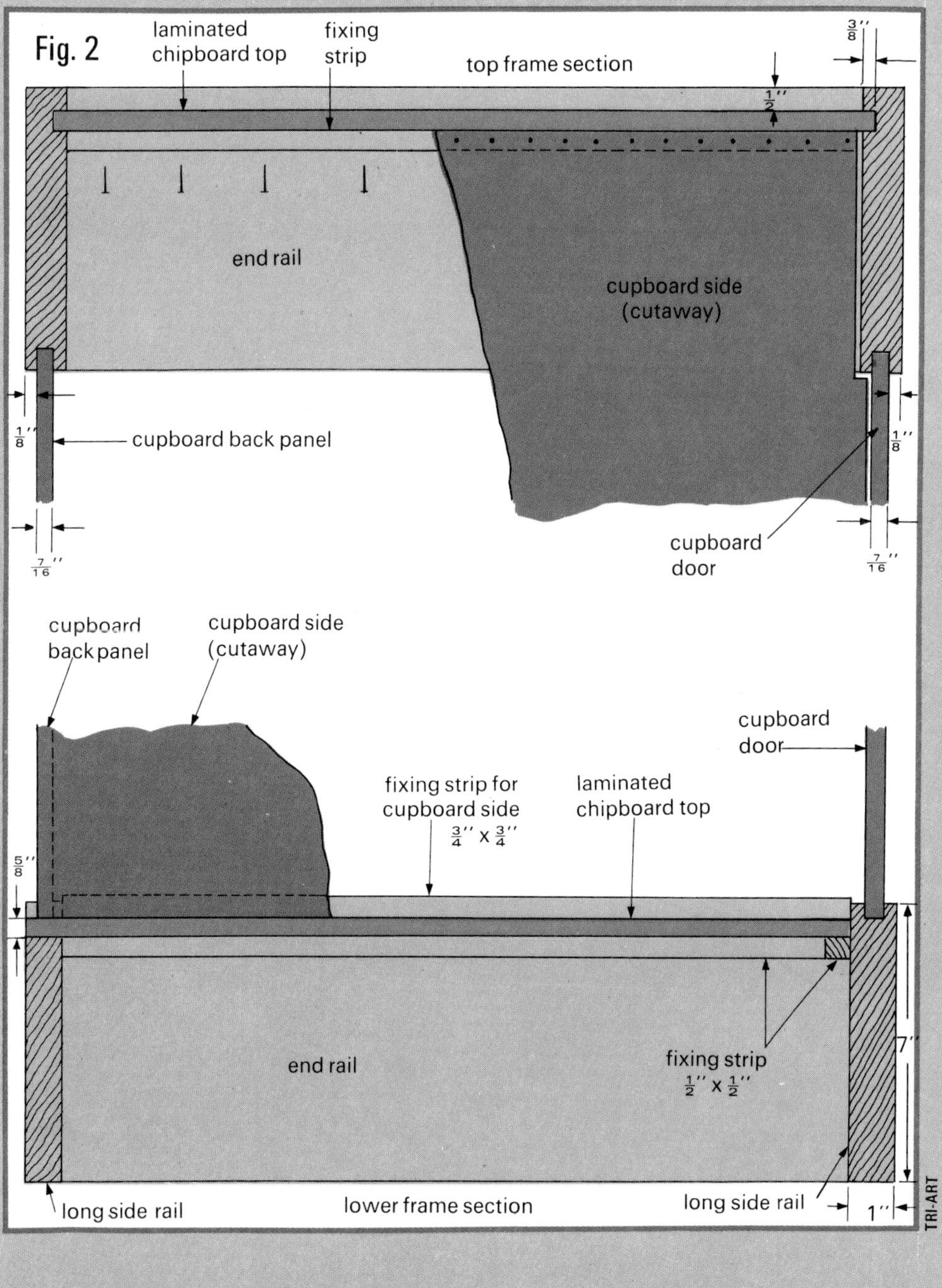

Before assembling the top frame, glasspaper the side pieces to a smooth finish and apply polyurethane varnish to the timber.

Assemble the top frame. Run some woodworking adhesive into the rebated groove and push the side pieces on to the panel. Lightly nail the side pieces together at the corners.

Fig.2. A section view of the short sides of the sideboard. The doors of the sideboard cupboard run in a single groove cut in the top edge of the front rail of the two frames.

The lower frame

The construction of the lower frame is a little more complicated than that of the top frame. The side pieces are the same width and thickness as those for the top frame, apart from the back long side which is 5$\frac{7}{8}$in. x 1in. (161mm x 25mm). In the lower frame the side pieces are butted together, not mitred—this rather unsightly joint is not visible in the finished construction.

The short rails are jointed to the wooden legs of the sideboard with halving joints. The legs are made from 1$\frac{1}{4}$in. x 1in. (31mm x 25mm) timber. Cut the halving joints on the ends of the short sides and the top of the legs in the usual way. Apply adhesive and cramp the legs and short sides.

Now cut a rebated groove right along the top edge of the two short sides and the front long side. The groove in the front long side forms the door runner. Cut the groove in the same position and to the same dimensions as described above for the top frame. A rebated groove is also cut in the top edge of the back long side, but it does not run the whole length of this piece. The groove is not cut in the part of this piece that runs along the back of the open central area. Stop the groove 2ft (610mm) from each end of the piece.

The next step is to provide a fixing for the panel that covers the lower frame. This is done by pinning strips of $\frac{1}{2}$in. x $\frac{1}{2}$in. (13mm x 13mm) timber to the inside face of the two short sides and the front long side. The back long side is narrower than the other pieces and the panel simply sits on the top edge. Position the support strips $\frac{5}{8}$in. (16mm) down from the top edge of these pieces.

The final step in the construction of the lower frame is to fix two strips of timber to the lower panel. These provide a fixing for the internal sides—those that enclose the central open area—of the sideboard cupboards. Use either $\frac{3}{4}$in. (19mm) triangular moulding or $\frac{3}{4}$in. x $\frac{3}{4}$in. (19mm x 19mm) timber. Place them so that they will butt the inside face of the cupboard sides in the finished construction. Pin strips of timber to the underside of the top frame panel also—this gives a top fixing for the cupboard sides. Position the timbers carefully so that the cupboard sides will be perfectly horizontal.

Now glasspaper the lower frame members and apply a coat of polyurethane varnish. Assemble the bottom frame. Pin the sides together but do not overnail. Check the diagonals to make sure the construction is square. Pin the lower frame panel in place, nailing through the panel into the support timbers.

The cupboards

The shape and dimensions of the cupboard sides and doors are shown in Fig.1. The panels that make up the cupboards are covered with hessian or a similar fabric in the colour of your choice. Use a fabric adhesive such as Copydex for this job as this will have the most effective visual and practical impact.

The angle strip

You can now cut the four pieces of angle strip to length. Mark the finished length on the strip and square lines through these points with a metalworking square and a scriber.

Cut through these lines with a hacksaw, with the metal held in a vice. Make sure that you use soft jaws on the vice—without these the uncovered vice jaws will mark the aluminium badly. Remove any burrs and square up the ends if necessary with a fine toothed file.

Mark on the strips the positions where they are screwed to the side pieces of the top and bottom frames. Each side of each piece of angle strip is drilled twice for No.8 1in. flat headed mirror screws or coverhead screws. Mark the positions of the holes on the strip and on the holes of the frames. Drill down these points. A good DIY magazine will give you the best techniques for drilling and sawing metal.

Assembly of the sideboard

To assemble the sideboard, stand the lower frame on its wooden legs and screw the angle strip in place. Then pin the internal sides of the cupboards to the timber strips fixed to the lower frame panel. Stand the other sides and the doors in the rebated grooves. With the aid of an assistant, lift the top frame in place so that the tops of the cupboard sides and doors fit into the groove cut in the bottom edge of the top frame pieces. Screw the angle strip to the top frame. Pin the tops of the internal sides of the cupboards to the timbers fixed earlier to the underside of the top frame panel.

All that remains now is to fix handles of your choice to the sliding doors.

The coffee table

The coffee table is a very simple construction. All you need is four lengths of timber, cut to the sizes shown in Fig.4 and mitred at the ends, a sheet of glass for the table top, and four pieces of aluminium angle strip.

Cut a rebated groove on the inside face of the four side pieces, ½in. (13mm) down from the top edge. The width of the groove depends on the size of glass you use for the top—between ¼in. (6mm) and ⅜in. (9mm) float glass should be used.

When you have cut the side pieces, finish them as described above. Cut four pieces of angle strip to the length shown in Fig.4 and drill them for No.8 1in. coverhead screws. Assemble three of the sides with adhesive and panel pins and push the glass sheet—which your supplier will cut to size—into the groove. Glue and pin the fourth side in place.

Screw the angle strip in place. Then cut four pieces of timber for the legs and glue them to the insides of the angle strip, where it protrudes below the table top. Use an epoxy adhesive such as Araldite for this.

The second part of this chapter tells how to build a long, low seat and telephone table, and an attractive hi-fi unit.

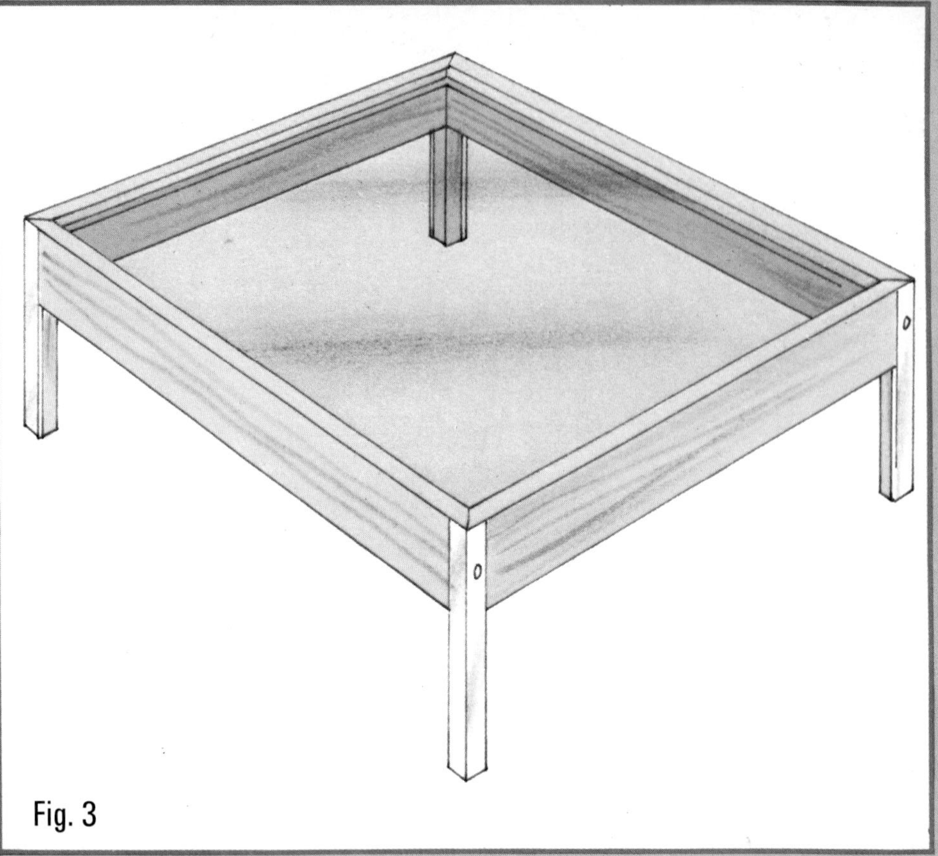

Fig.3. This good looking glass topped coffee table matches the design of the sideboard.

Fig.4. An exploded view of the coffee table showing all the dimensions.

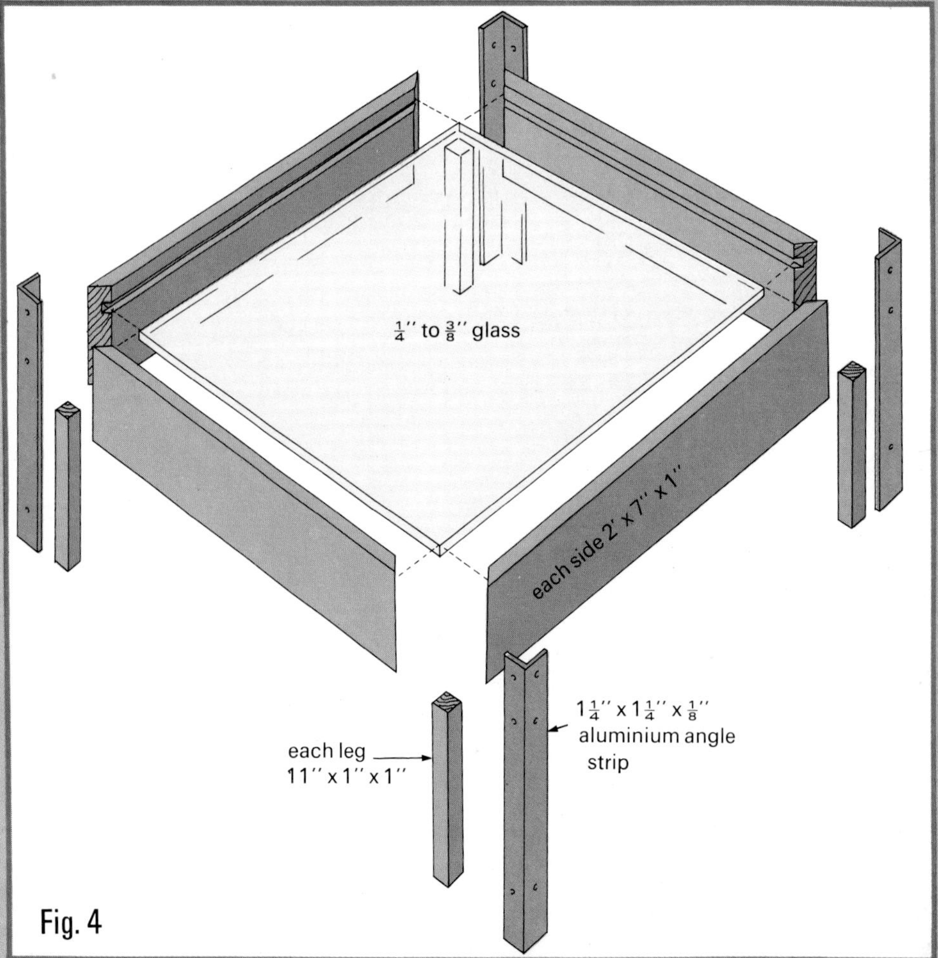

Above. *The clean good looks of this hi-fi unit and long, low telephone table will brighten any interior, and the angle strip feature will help unify the designs.*

Modern furniture from angle strip: 2

Lengths of aluminium angle strip incorporated into furniture in the home, lend unity and are an attractive decorative feature. The second part of this chapter tells you how to build a long, low seat, with a place for a telephone table and your favourite potted plant; and a good looking unit to house all your hi-fi equipment.

Both the seat and the hi-fi unit shown in the illustrations are made in oak, though any hardwood will do—the only difference will be in the finishing of the timber. The wooden legs of the furniture are reinforced with aluminium angle strip.

The seat/telephone table

The seat consists of a top rectangular timber frame mounted on wooden legs which, at the floor, are jointed to another rectangular frame. The top frame has a plywood base panel. At one end of the seat there is an upholstered foam cushion, a table section in the centre and, on the opposite side, a recess to accommodate plant pots or some other type of ornament.

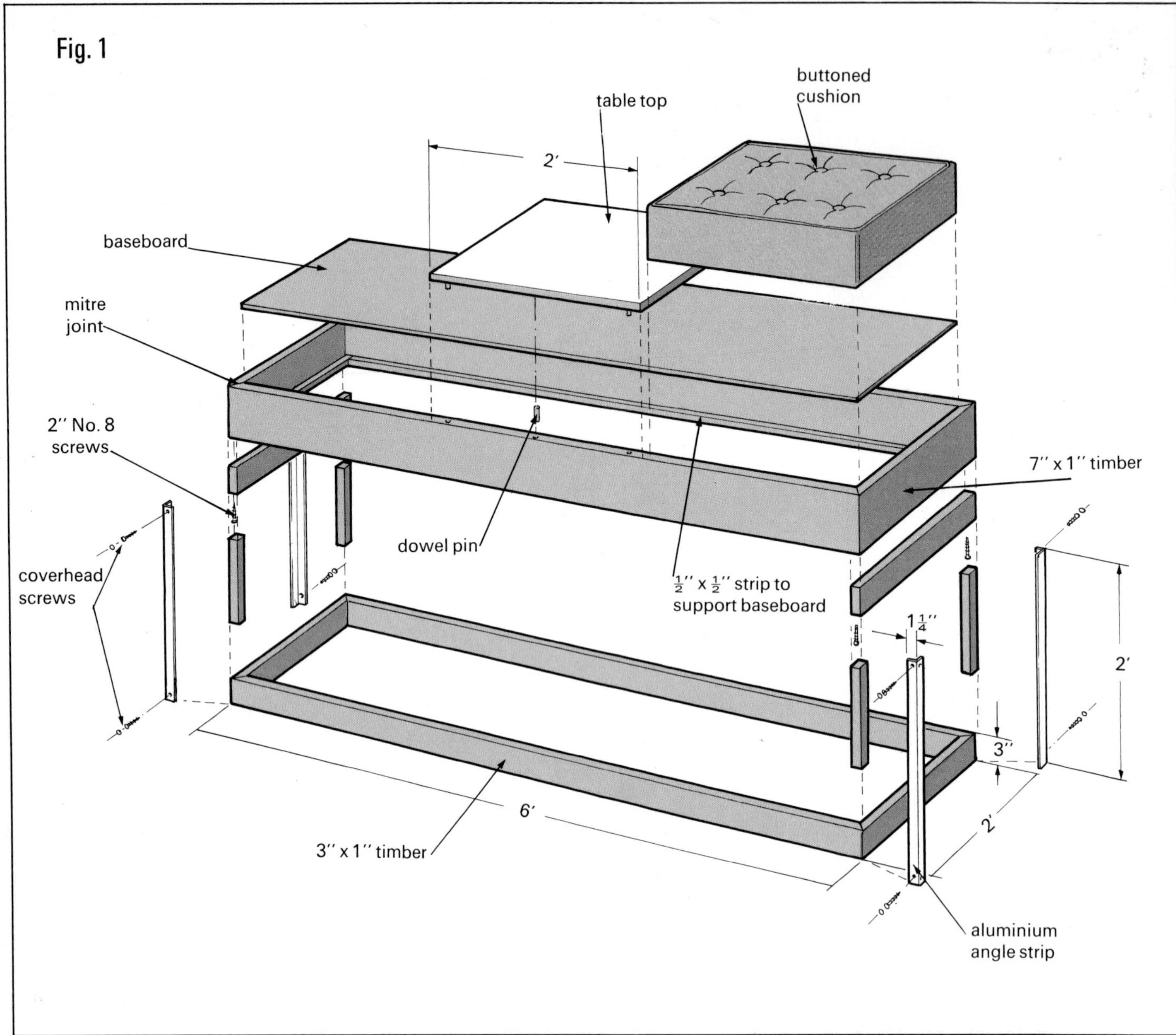

Fig.1. An exploded view of the seat and telephone table. You can, of course, alter the dimensions to suit your requirements.

The top frame

The top frame is made from 7in. x 1in. (177mm x 25mm) timber. The overall dimensions of the frame are 6ft x 2ft (1.83m x 0.61m). Cut the side pieces for the top frame a little overlength, and from points marking their finished length, mark a mitre with a bevel gauge set to 45°. Cut the mitres using a bench saw, or a hand saw and a mitre box clamped to the timber, as described more fully in the first part of this chapter. Apply a woodworking adhesive to the mitred ends and cramp the pieces together. Check the frame for squareness by measuring the diagonals. Then lightly nail the pieces together.

The lower frame

The lower frame consists of two rectangular end frames fixed to the bottom of the short sides of the top frame. These are connected by strips of timber running the length of the seat, along the floor.

First make the two rectangular end frames from 3in. x 1in. (76mm x 25mm) timber. Fig.1 shows the dimensions to use. Joint the pieces for these frames together with halving joints. Now cut the strips of timber that connect these frames, to length.

Top frame base panel

Cut the base panel for the top frame. This can be made of laminated chipboard or plywood. The size of the panel is 5ft 10in. x 1ft 10in. (1779mm x 559mm). The base panel is fixed to strips of ½in. x ½in. (13mm x 13mm) timber, pinned round the inner surface of the top frame pieces, with their bottom edge flush with the bottom edge of the frame pieces. Pin these strips in place with ¾in. (19mm) panel pins, and cut the top panel to size.

The table top

The central area of the seat is a 2ft x 2ft (610mm x 610mm) laminated chipboard panel, laid on top of the two long pieces of the top frame. It is held in place by secret dowel joints. These are simply to stop the panel moving off the top of the frame so the joint does not have to be particularly strong.

Drill holes for three ¼in. (6mm) dowels ½in. (13mm) from two opposite edges of the panel. Be careful not to drill right through the panel—use a drill stop or wrap a piece of coloured adhesive tape around the drill bit. Secret dowelling—the marking out and the cutting—is described in most good DIY manuals.

Assembly

The end frames are screwed to the bottom edge of the short pieces of the top frame. Use three No.8 2in. screws at each end of the frame. You will have to counterbore the holes, since you will be screwing through a 3in. (76mm) depth of timber in the end frame. First drill holes for the screws through the top end frame member and into the short side of the top frame. Then down the holes in the end frame pieces, counterbore with a ¼in. drill bit to a depth of 2in.

(51mm). Use one of the methods outlined above to make sure you drill to the right depth. Screw the end frames in place.

Before continuing with the assembly, finish all the timber components. Rub them down with glasspaper, apply a coat of clear polyurethane varnish and let it dry. Smooth the timber down again with fine glasspaper and apply a second coat of varnish.

You can now cut and fix the aluminium angle strip. The first part of this chapter described how to cut the angle strip to length. Cut four 18in. (457mm) lengths of angle strip and screw them to the horizontal corners of the seat with cover-head, or flat headed mirror screws, as shown in Fig.1. Both faces of each piece of angle strip is drilled twice to allow fixing to the top frame and to the bottom of the end frames.

The buttoned cushion

The seat end consists of a 1ft 10in. x 1ft 10in. x 6in. (559mm x 559mm x 152mm) medium hard foam biscuit, covered in the material of your choice. Leather looks good, but any reasonably hardwearing material will do. The cushion shown in the illustration is buttoned, and has piping running round the top corner.

The buttons are quite easy to make yourself if you use the metal button moulds with a shank that are sold for that purpose. Do not cut the material to size before you do the job—the buttoning will, of course, alter the shape of the material.

When you have made the cushion, all you have to do is drop it into the recess at the end of the seat.

The hi-fi unit

This unit is an attractive and modern adaptation of a standard radiogram design. The top of the unit has space for a record turntable, a spool-to-spool tape recorder, an amplifier and a cassette recording deck. The twin speakers for the record and tape decks are housed at each end of the cabinet.

The unit consists of an upper and lower timber frame, connected at the corners with aluminium angle strip. The space between the frames houses a cupboard for record storage and two speakers. The record storage cupboard has sliding doors.

The panels surrounding the speakers are the most critical part of the construction. The box construction round the speakers must be as airtight as possible, or the sound from the speakers will literally 'whistle' through any gaps. The speakers are fitted to the front panels of the box constructions—these panels should be covered with a material like Vynair or Tigan which are accoustically transparent. The other panels of these box constructions can be covered in the same material or with hessian in the same or a matching colour. Before you begin work on the actual construction of the speakers, make certain you have given careful

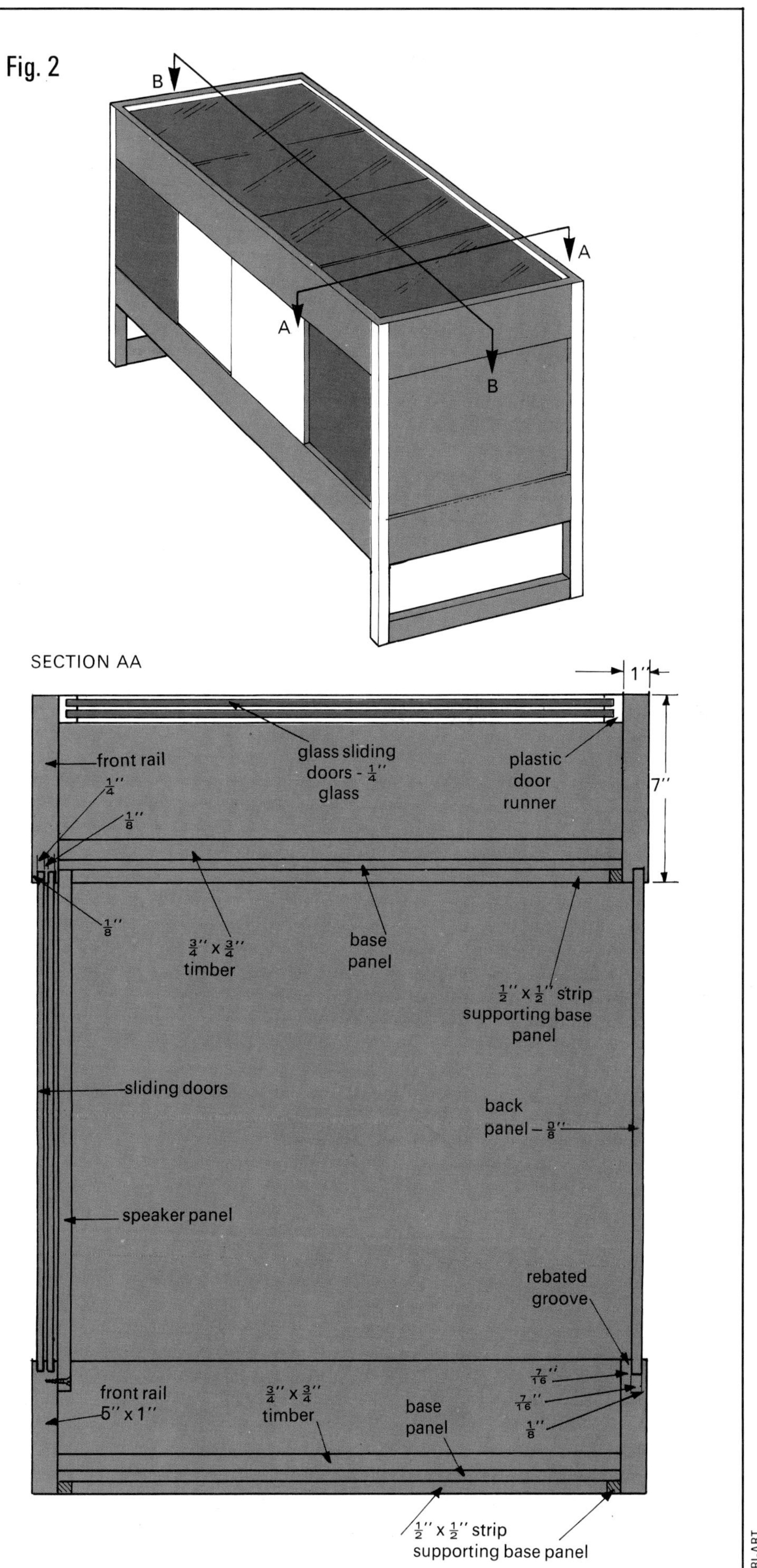

Fig.2. The top diagram shows the hi-fi unit with two cross sections marked. Section AA, shown in the lower diagram, is a view through the end of the unit. Section BB is a view through the long sides of the unit—this is shown on the following pages.

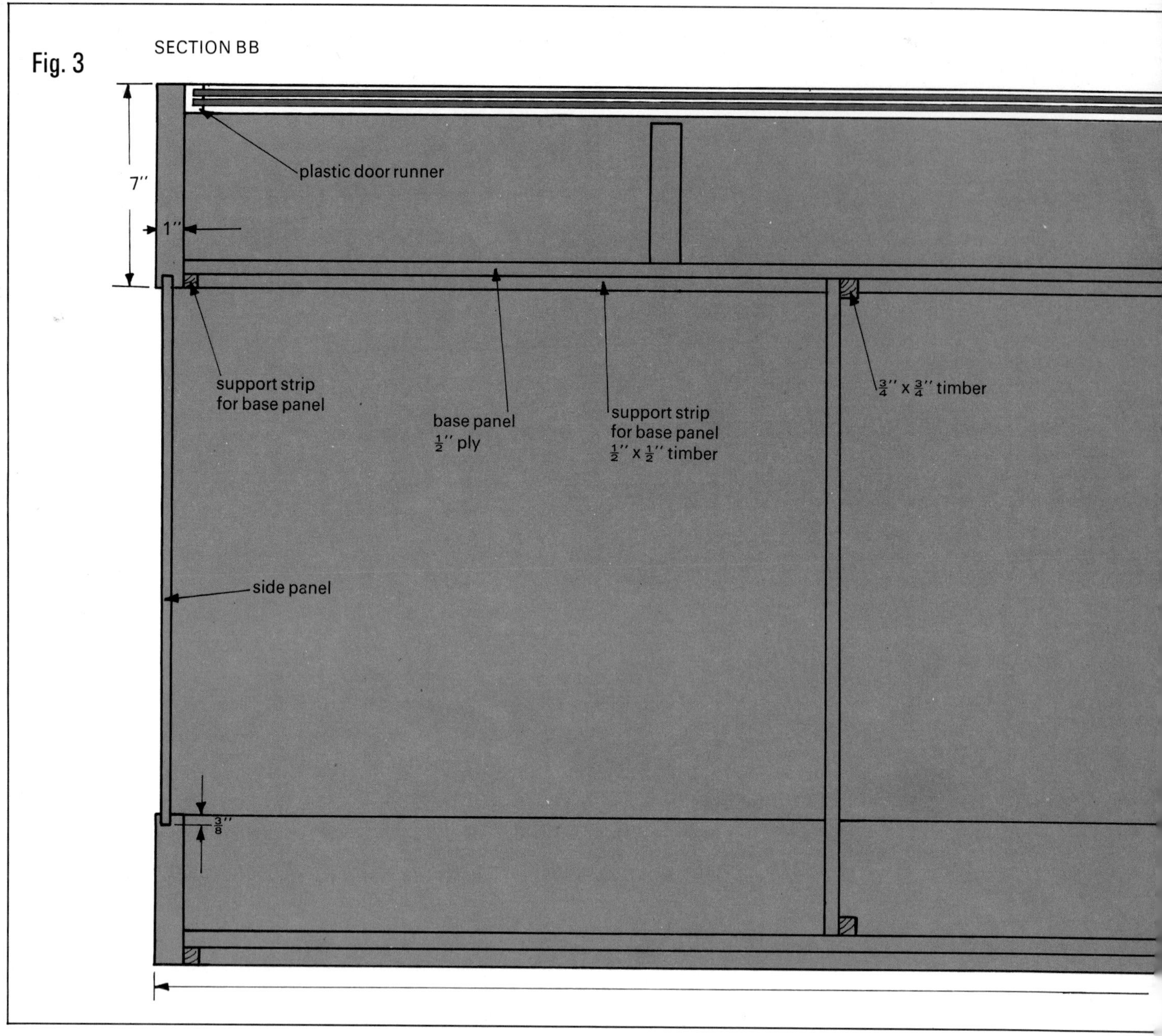

consideration to the various aspects involved in such a project.

The lower frame

The lower frame is made from 5in. x 1in. (125mm x 25mm) timber and has a finished size of 6ft x 2ft (1.83m x 0.61m). The ends of the side pieces are mitred in the same way as the frame of the seat described above.

The side and back panels of the unit are held in a rebated groove cut in the top edge of the side and back pieces. The front speaker panels are screwed to the inside surface of the front long side. The base panel of the frame—the panel that forms the bottom of the cupboard—sits on $\frac{1}{2}$in. x $\frac{1}{2}$in. (13mm x 13mm) timber supports, so that it is flush with the top edge of the frame pieces.

First cut the side pieces of the frame, and mitre the ends. Then cut a rebated groove in the top edge of the short sides and the back long side. Cut this $\frac{7}{16}$in. (11mm) wide and $\frac{3}{8}$in. (9.5mm) deep, working from the outer surface of the components, with the fence of the rebate plane set to $\frac{1}{8}$in. (3mm). The width of the groove allows for panels of $\frac{3}{8}$in. (9.5mm) plywood or high density chipboard, plus an allowance for the thickness of the fabric covering. Don't use ordinary chipboard for the panels—it is not dense enough and will effect the sound reproduction.

Cut two rebated grooves in the front long side to act as door runners. The doors are $\frac{1}{4}$in. (6mm) plywood, so cut the grooves to this width, working from each face of the component with the fence on the rebate plane set to $\frac{1}{8}$in. (3mm). Cut the door runners to a depth of $\frac{3}{8}$in. (9.5mm).

Now assemble the side pieces. Apply a woodworking adhesive to the mitred ends and push them together. Lightly nail the corners for extra fixing. Check the frame for squareness. Now cut the base panel to size. This is 5ft 10in. x 1ft 10in. (1779mm x 559mm).

The internal sides of the central cupboard area and the speaker areas—the sides parallel to the short sides of the unit—are fixed to timber strips screwed to the base panels of the upper and lower frames. Use $\frac{3}{4}$in. x $\frac{3}{4}$in. (19mm x 19mm) timber for these fixings and screw them in place in the positions shown in Fig.3. Now cut all the side panels, referring to Fig.2. Cut the sliding doors also.

The upper frame

The upper frame measures 6ft x 2ft (1.83m x 0.61m) and is constructed from 7in. x 1in. (178mm x 25mm) timber. The components are mitred at the ends. Rebated grooves are cut in the bottom edge of these components in the same positions as for the lower frame. The tops of the speaker panels are screwed to the inside surface of the front long side.

Cut the pieces and mitre the ends. Cut the rebated grooves and the three support strips for the base panel. Pin these in place but leave a 1in. (25mm) gap between the ends of the short side strip and the inner surface of the front long side.

Cut the base panel to size and screw the

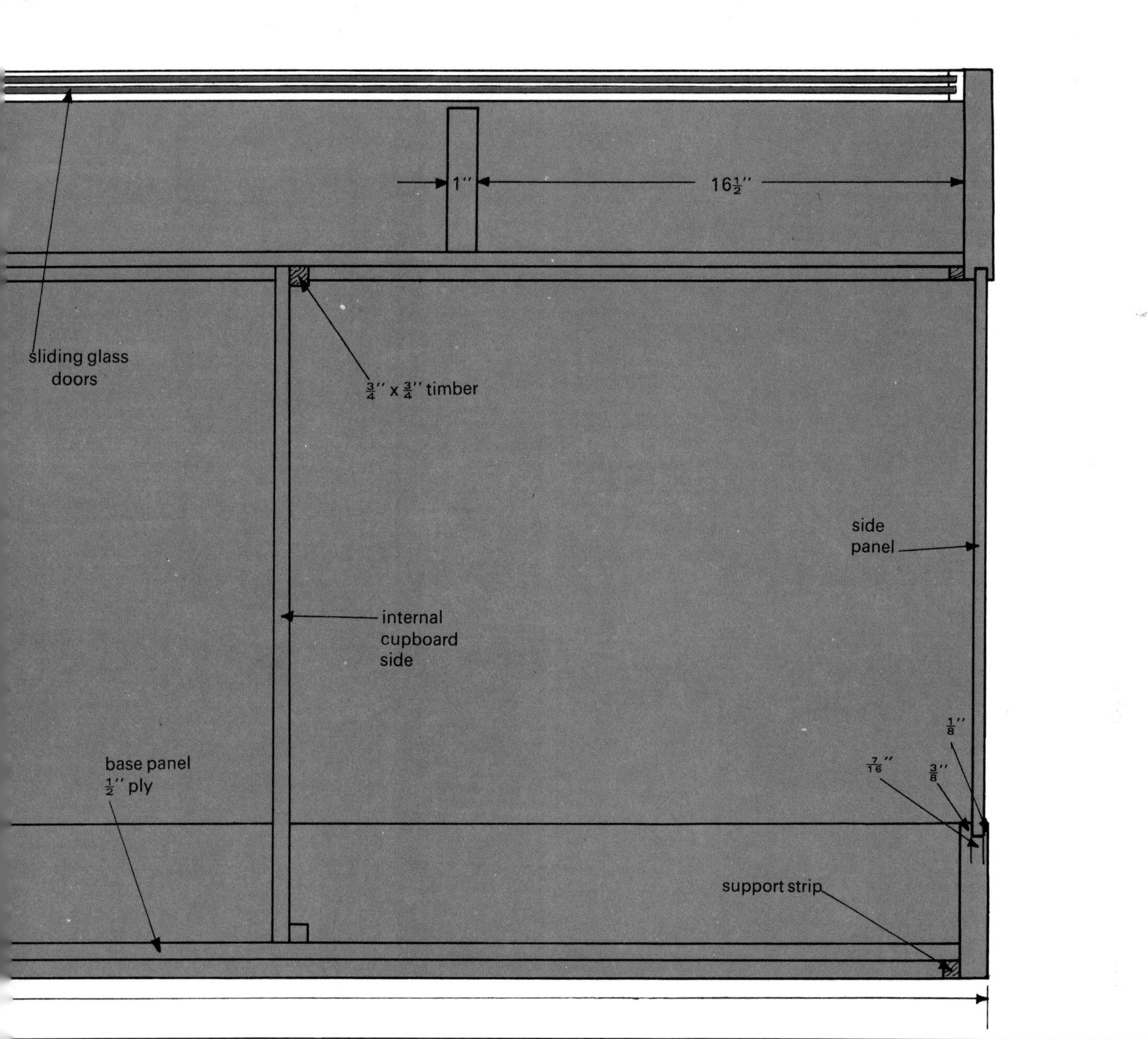

Fig.3. *Section BB, marked on Fig.2, through the long side of the unit.*

fixings for the cupboard sides in place. Refer to Fig. 3 when doing these jobs. Finish the frame as described above.

The wooden legs

The short wooden legs of the unit are dowel pinned to the bottom edge of the side pieces of the lower frame. The wooden legs are made from 9in. x 1in. x 1in. (229mm x 25mm x 25mm) timber. At the bottom the legs are housed to the cross pieces with halving joints. The cross pieces, which are shown in Fig.2, are 2ft x 1in. x 1in. (610mm x 25mm x 25mm).

Drill the bottom edge of the frame for two 1½in. x ¼in. (38mm x 6mm) dowels at each corner. Cut the timber legs and cross pieces to length. Drill the top end of each leg for two dowels. Cut the halving joints at the bottom of the legs and ends of the cross pieces. Apply adhesive to the joint and push the pieces together. Check for squareness and cramp the pieces with G cramps. When the adhesive has dried, spread glue on the dowels and push them into the holes in the lower frame. Then push the leg and cross piece constructions onto the dowels. Finish the lower frame and legs as described above.

Assembly

You can now assemble the unit. Cut the aluminium angle strip to length. The method of marking and cutting this and the general procedure for assembly is exactly the same as that described in the first part of this chapter, for the sideboard.

Fix the base panels of the top and bottom frames in place on top of the three timber supports. Then screw the angle strip to the corners of the unit as described in the first part of this chapter. Glue strips of proprietary plastic door runner around the inner surface of the top frame components. This carries the sliding glass doors of the unit.

Fit the back panel of the unit. The height of all the outer panels of the unit allow them to be pushed into the upper groove and then gently forced into the lower groove. Fit the outer short side panels and then the internal short panels. At the internal corners between the panels, glue strips of ¾in. x ¾in. (19mm x 19mm) triangular moulding. This fills any gaps. Fit the sliding doors.

Now cut the internal dividers for the equipment area of the top frame. The dimensions are shown in Fig.3. These can simply be glued in place to the base panel and the frame sides—no pressure is exerted on these so you don't need a stronger fixing.

Assemble the speaker panels, taking particular care not to dislodge any of the equipment when mounting them. Drill holes in the top frame base panel to take the wires leading from the electrical equipment. With the speaker panels face down on the lower frame, connect up the wires. Screw the panels to the inner surface of the front long sides of each frame.

Dinette table and storage cabinet to make

When you are really short of living space, for example if you have a very cramped kitchen, or a living room that has to be a dining room too, multi-purpose furniture can go a long way towards giving you enough room. This versatile unit doubles as a wall-hanging storage unit and a table that folds away when not in use. It has one particularly valuable feature—when there are objects on the table and you want to fold it up without removing them, all you have to do is push them to the back and the cutaway top can be swung up clear of them.

This unit has been designed as a kitchen storage cabinet that also provides a table top for breakfast, odd snacks, and an occasional work surface, but it can easily be adapted for other rooms. For example, in a small flat it could save the space taken by a dining table or, with doors fitted to the cabinet, it could make a useful occasional writing desk in a lounge or study.

The design

The table and cabinet consist mainly of 7 panels of 18mm (roughly $\frac{3}{4}$in.) birch plywood, all cut from one standard-sized 5ft x 5ft (1.53m x 1.53m) sheet as shown in Fig.1. Parts A and B are shaped to fit together and joined with strap hinges, then screwed to the wall to form the table when A is dropped down, as shown in Fig.5. Panel A drops down to rest on battening fixed to the front or sides of the cabinet; an exploded view of this arrangement is shown in Fig.2. The cabinet, in turn, is screwed firmly to panel B.

A small ball catch is fitted in the top edge of panel B, and the cup for this at the point where panel A butts against it. This holds panel A, in position when it is folded against the wall out of the way.

All the cabinet joints are simply butted, glued and screwed. If the unit is to be painted, the screw heads are countersunk flush with the surface and filled over with a proprietary cellulose filler, which is then sanded down to give a perfectly smooth finish. But if you want to stain or varnish the unit, the screw heads must be sunk deeper and the holes filled with matching plugs of timber cut from dowelling of a suitable size and sanded flat when in place.

Materials and tools

The unit will require one 5ft x 5ft (1.53 x 1.53m) sheet of 18mm birch plywood; one length of 3ft x 1½in. (914mm x 38mm x 13mm) hardwood; two large 12in. (305mm) strap hinges with mounting screws; one ball catch no wider than 15mm; two dozen 1½in. (38mm) No.8 countersunk head screws; and some woodworking adhesive. You will also need paint or varnish; in the case of the latter you will need some dowelling to make plugs.

For tools, you will need a power jigsaw for separating panels A and B—so you might as well use this for cutting all the pieces; a power drill; bench plane; screwdriver; spokeshave; rule; try square; and an ordinary school compass.

***Below, left.** With the table flap in the down position, there is ample room for two place settings, or a medium sized occasional working surface.*
***Bottom, right.** When the flap is in the up position, the top of the storage unit provides a small working surface, with plenty of shelf space underneath.*

NIGEL MESSETT

Cutting out

Mark out the large sheet of ply, using the dimensions in Fig.1 as a guide. To ensure that the table top will fit properly over the top of the cabinet when dropped down, it is essential that you commence marking in a particular order.

First mark out panel C. This panel has two square corners, and two with 3in. or 75mm radiuses. The method of marking these is shown in Fig.3. Mark two points, 3in. or 75mm along each edge, from the corner. Link these two points with lines drawn at right angles to the edges to make a 3in. square. The inner corner of this square will be the centre for the curve, which should be drawn with the compass.

Using the same radius method where rounded corners are required, mark out the rest of the ply sheet, but not the dividing line that will separate panels A and B.

With the jigsaw, carefully cut round the outline of panel C. When this has been done, finish the cut edges of the panel with the bench plane (fine set) along the straight edges, and the spokeshave at the radiused corners.

Mark out the dividing line between panels A and B, using panel C as a template for the central piece. This is done to ensure that when the table top is dropped down, it will fit exactly over the top of the cabinet, which will be panel C.

All the remaining panels can now be cut out of the large sheet of ply. Finish off all the cut edges of panels A and B, but leave the remainder of the panels, which will form the cabinet, until you assemble them.

Making the cabinet

This is constructed from panels C, D, E, F and G, fastened together with glued and screwed butt joints.

Trial assemble the cabinet panels as shown in Fig.2 to check that all the edges butt neatly. Where they don't, plane the high spots down. Then finish off all the edges that will be visible at the front of the unit. Trial assemble again to ensure that the cabinet is square, and that all parts fit correctly.

NIGEL MESSETT

Drill screw holes at 2in. or 50mm intervals down through the ends of panels C and F. Spread adhesive along the top and bottom of the side panels (D and E), then erect the carcase in the shape shown in Fig.2, and drive the screws home into the side panels.

Before the glue has set, lightly mark a horizontal line with a try square halfway down the outside of each side panel and drill screw holes along the lines at 2in. intervals. Trim panel G to fit in between the side panels, spread adhesive along each of its end edges, place it in position and drive the screws home.

Check that the cabinet is square, then leave it while the glue sets.

Assembling the unit

This is relatively simple except that care is required to make the table flap drop accurately over the cabinet top.

Lay panels A and B down on a flat surface and fit the strap hinges to link them as shown in Fig.5.

Lay the cabinet on its back, on top of panel B, in the approximate position where it will eventually be fixed. Lift the table flap up to a vertical position and adjust the position of the cabinet until the top fits neatly into the recess at the base of the flap. When the cabinet is in the right position, lightly mark a line round its top, base and sides onto the surface of panel B.

Take the cabinet off, then drill screw holes at 2in. intervals round the inside of the marked line. Each hole should be drilled inside the line at a distance equal to half the thickness of the plywood used for the cabinet carcase. Lay sections A and B on a table, place the cabinet in position again, ease part of panel B over the edge of the table to expose some of the screw holes underneath, then drive several screws in. Repeat this until the cabinet has been screwed all round and is securely fixed to panel B.

Finally, fit the flap-stop. This is the 3ft length of hardwood. Place it in position underneath panel C so that one third of its width protrudes beyond the front of the panel. Mark a line along the front edge of C on to the flap-stop. Remove the stop and drill holes at 2in. or 50mm intervals at a point halfway between this marked line and the back of the stop. Replace the stop and screw it in position.

There is an alternative to this method. The battening can be cut in two and fixed along the sides of the cabinet with its top surface level with the bottom surface of panel C. Either method will support the table top equally well, so choose the one that looks best in your room.

Fixing and finishing

Fill any cracks or holes with filler, allow it to dry, then rub the surface down.

To avoid getting any paint on the walls, it is best to paint the unit before fixing it to the wall. Make careful preparation in order to obtain a professional finish on your paintwork.

When the paint is dry, all that remains is to fix the unit to the wall with screws and wall plugs and you will have an original, versatile piece of space-saving furniture which will be a handsome addition to your home.

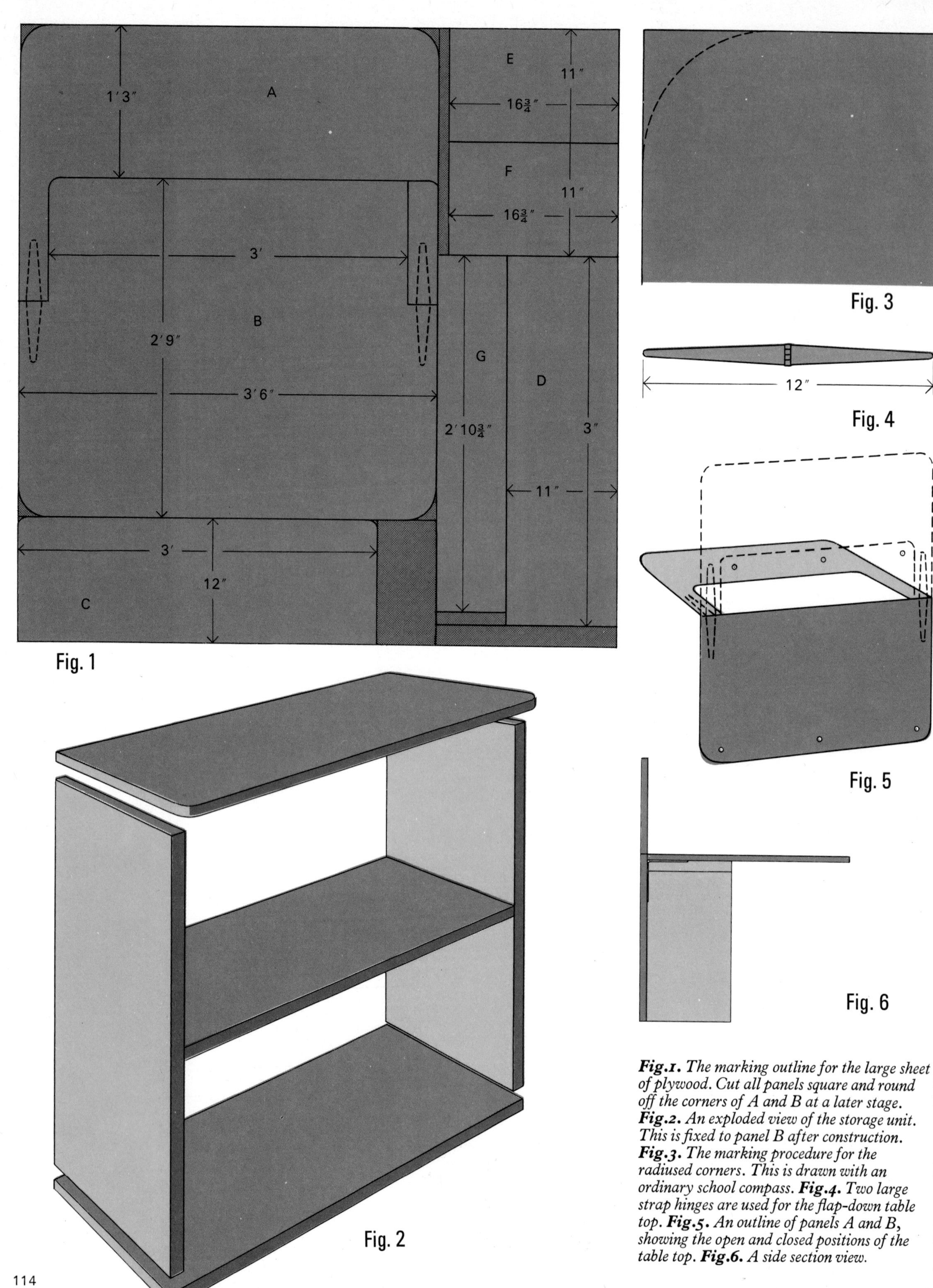

Fig.1. *The marking outline for the large sheet of plywood. Cut all panels square and round off the corners of A and B at a later stage.* ***Fig.2.*** *An exploded view of the storage unit. This is fixed to panel B after construction.* ***Fig.3.*** *The marking procedure for the radiused corners. This is drawn with an ordinary school compass.* ***Fig.4.*** *Two large strap hinges are used for the flap-down table top.* ***Fig.5.*** *An outline of panels A and B, showing the open and closed positions of the table top.* ***Fig.6.*** *A side section view.*

***Above.** One beautifully matched kitchen unit combines an eye-level oven, hob and recessed sink with a large work surface and ample space for storage. Such a system increases efficiency and aids hygiene in the kitchen.*

Kitchen unit with oven and hob

Boost your kitchen into the space-age with this ultra-efficient split-level unit. An eye-level oven, hob and sink, all recessed into an easy to clean and attractive unit help make the kitchen a pleasure to work in.

Kitchens are the busiest part of any home, and consequently their layout and fittings need to be planned and chosen with great care. Too often the arrangement of existing kitchens bears little relation to the work done in them—work surfaces are on the opposite side of the room to the cooker and sink, storage is inadequate and there are too many dirt-collecting areas. Ideally, the scheme of your kitchen should combine labour saving efficiency with hygiene and safety, and these requirements cannot be achieved without some effort and proper planning.

One way to make your kitchen a better place to work in, is to equip it with a complete work and storage system. Such a system combines the major fittings, such as the sink, cooker and hob, with a large work surface and storage areas. The advantages of this type of scheme are clear. Instead of continually having to walk across the kitchen to fetch and carry food and utensils, everything you require is close to hand in one compact unit.

It is with these considerations in mind that the split-level kitchen unit has been designed. Basically, it comprises a recessed sink and hob unit which butts onto an eye-level oven unit. An eye-level oven has decided advantages over a ground fitted oven. You don't have to bend down to take out or inspect food and you can clean it much easier. Also, if you fit a glass-fronted oven, a glance tells you if a meal is ready or not.

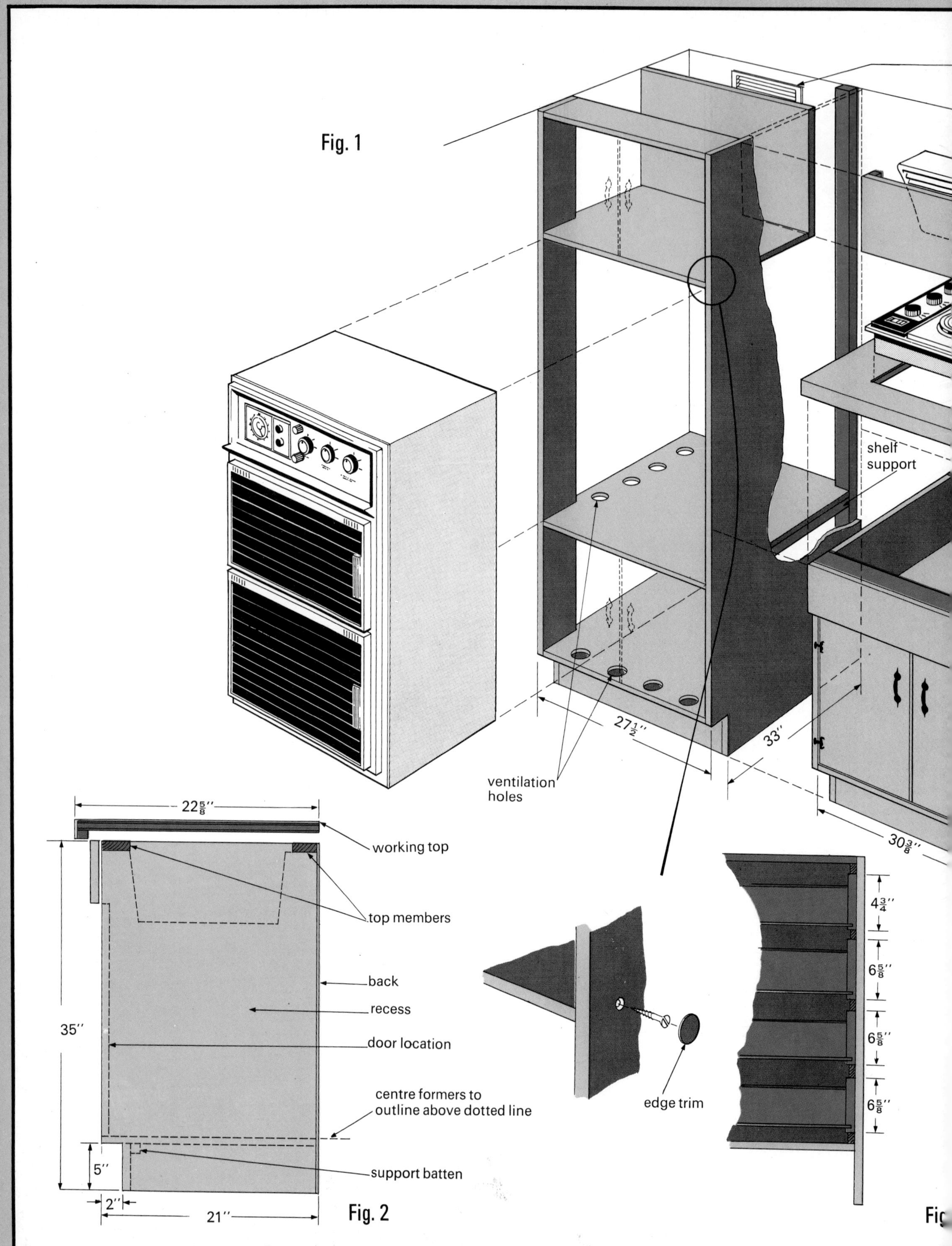

Fig. 1
shelf support
ventilation holes
27½″
33″
30⅜″
22⅝″
working top
top members
back
recess
door location
centre formers to outline above dotted line
support batten
35″
5″
2″
21″
Fig. 2
edge trim
4¾″
6⅝″
6⅝″
6⅝″

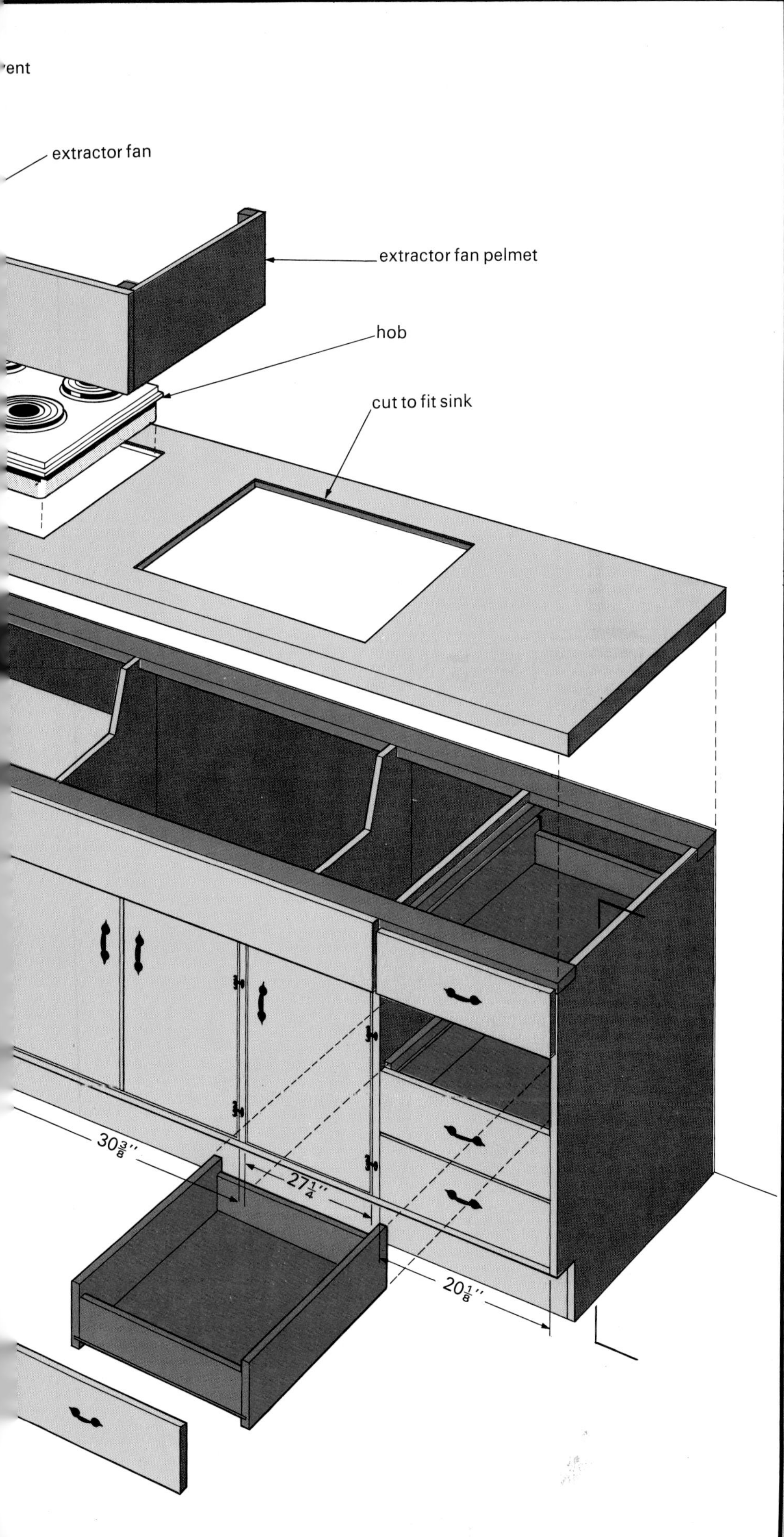

Fig.1. The whole unit is made up of two parts—a sink/hob unit and an oven unit. The number of pieces is fairly large, but the design is straightforward and allows you to modify the specifications to suit individual requirements and kitchen lay-outs.
Fig.2. Section through one intermediate former showing the cut-out for the sink.
Fig.3. Drawers are simply fitted by sliding them onto hardboard battens.

General construction

Before embarking on the construction of a large piece of furniture like this kitchen unit, remember that it will not pass through conventional doors; final assembly must be on the proposed site. A comparatively new laminated material—Conti-Plas—is used for the carcase of both sub-assemblies. This is obtainable in standard width panels and consists of a high density chipboard core, covered on both surfaces and long edges with a tough melamine coat. There are many alternative materials, but whatever type you choose, ensure that the laminate covering is heat resistant. Blockboard is used for the working top—again, when choosing a laminate covering, check that it is heat resistant.

You may wish to modify the dimensions of the unit to suit your kitchen; the simplicity of the design allows this. One cautionary word, however, before you start construction—check the oven and hob plate manufacturers instructions and specifications and amend the design shown where necessary.

The hob/sink unit

Begin by cutting out the two end formers to the outline shown in Fig.2. These have cut-outs at the top corners to accommodate the two upper long rails. Another cut-out, at the front lower corner, houses the kick-board. Now cut out the three intermediate formers to the shape represented by the dotted line in Fig.2. Again, these pieces have cut-outs similar to those made on the top edges of the end formers, but as they rest flush on the bottom shelf, they do not house the kick-board. Having decided on and checked the locations of the fitted hob and sink, make cut-outs in the intermediate formers to accommodate these fixtures.

Next, cut out the lower shelf and then the two 2in. x 1in. (51mm x 25mm) upper long rails to the sizes given in the cutting list. Lay the rails on top of the shelf so that they are parallel to its long edges and overlap both short edges by ⅝in.(16mm). Mark in the position of each former on the rails and shelf, as shown in Fig.1.

Turn the intermediate formers upside down and, referring to the previously marked locations, pin the lower shelf to their bottom short edges. Secure the formers with 1½ins.(38mm) No.6 screws. Set the structure right way up and add the upper long rails into the appropriate housings. At this point, add the end formers by pinning and screwing, and, when you have checked that the unit is square, fit the hardboard back panel.

Now you can add the kick-board. First fix a full-length 1in. x 1in.(25mm x 25mm) softwood batten to the underside of the lower shelf at the location shown in Fig.2. The kick-board butts onto this member and is fixed between the end formers. Screw it with 1½in.(38mm) No.6 screws.

The top front panel is butt-jointed to the leading edges of four formers at the location shown in Figs. 1 and 2.

Shelving

You can choose shelving to suit your individual needs, remembering that the recessed sink and hob will not leave very much space under them. The simplest method of fixing any shelves is to rest them on 1in. x 1in. (25mm x 25mm) hardwood battens glued and screwed to the formers. This method allows you to remove shelves for cleaning. Remember that under the weight of heavy kitchen utensils even chipboard can bend. To prevent this, glue and screw a 2in. x 1in.(51mm x 25mm) batten under each shelf, flush with the front edge.

Once any shelving is in place, you must effectively fireproof the area round the hob location. Different hobs require different treatment, so before starting work consult the manufacturers instructions or, if you do not possess these, the manufacturers themselves. Asbestos is the most effective fireproofing material in common use. Cut it to size with a fine-toothed saw and fix it to those areas where it is needed.

Drawer construction

Drawers are fitted at one end of the unit only. When marking out the individual drawer panels, use the dimensions given in the cutting list as a guide and take the exact measurements from the unit itself. Aim for a ⅛in.(3.2mm) clearance between the drawer sides and the formers.

When you have cut out each piece, make ¼in. (6mm) deep housings in the side panels to accommodate the hardboard drawer bottoms. The bottom edges of the housings are located ¼in.(6mm) from the bottom edges of the side panels. Once the drawer bottoms have been glued into position, add the front and back panels which simply butt between the side panels. Secure them by driving screws through the bottom panel into their lower edges.

An additional false front panel is added to each drawer, but before fixing this piece in position, check that the main drawer bodies fit satisfactorily. To do this, glue and screw a pair of hardwood drawer runners into position on the lower shelf, flush with the inside surfaces of the formers. Slide one drawer into position, slip a piece of cardboard onto its upper edges to give the correct clearance, then mark out the position of the next pair of drawer runners and fix them into position. Repeat this procedure with the other two drawers and, when you are satisfied that each drawer fits well, add the false fronts.

Door construction

Having cut out all the door panels to size, check for a good fit, remembering that each panel is hung on the inside faces of the formers on full-length, piano type hinges. Cut these hinges to length and then screw them into position on the edges of the doors. Mark the correct position of the hinges on the formers and screw the doors to the unit. Finally, fit each door with a magnetic type catch and add the handles of your choice.

Working top construction

Cut out the working top and glue and screw a 1in. x 1in.(25mm x 25mm) softwood strip to the front and right hand edge of this piece, as shown in Fig.1. Then cover the surface with a resistant plastic laminate which is easy to clean, stain resistant, and simple to apply. If desired, add a hardwood work block to the surface in a convenient position.

Now cut out spaces for the sink and the hob to the manufacturers specifications. A DIY manual describing various methods of fixing and sealing sinks and should be read in conjunction with this chapter. When you have made the cut-outs for the sink and hob, fix the working top in position by glueing and screwing it to the upper long rails—driving the screws through the rails into the top. Carry out any plumbing or electrical work at this point and then cover the area of wall immediately behind the sink with a splash-proof material, such as ceramic tiles.

Making the oven unit

Before starting to build this unit, you must check the dimensions of your oven against the dimensions of the unit shown and, if necessary, modify both the design and sizes of the various parts of the unit. Then cut out the two side members and the shelves. Take the two lower shelves and make cut-outs at one corner to accommodate the narrower side member. These shelves also house the rear 2in. x 1in.(51mm x 25mm) support batten and cut-outs must be made in their rear edges to accommodate this member. The top shelf also houses one side panel, but butts directly onto the support batten. Before fixing this shelf to the main structure, glue and screw the back panel to it.

With all the pieces cut out, begin assembly by glueing and screwing the side members to the shelves. Add the recessed kickboard and the top cross member. Next, stand the unit on its proposed site and mark out on the wall the locations of the support-battens. Fix these in place, using wall plugs, and screw the unit to them. Before fitting the oven in place on the centre shelf, add 1in. x 1in.(25mm x 25mm) reinforcing battens as shown in Fig. 1. Then bore out ventilation holes in both the bottom and centre shelves.

Doors are fitted in the same way as described for the sink/hob unit. They should be equipped with handles to match the sink unit. If you intend fitting extractor fans above the oven and hob, you can increase their efficiency by building a simple pelmet onto the oven unit. The method of construction is clearly illustrated in Fig.1.

In order to achieve a good finish, all exposed screw heads can be covered by small laminate discs cut from matching iron-on edge trim. Any exposed door edges must also be trimmed.

The construction and fitting of this unit will really transform your kitchen and make it a more pleasant place to work in. Once you have experienced the advantages of this system you may wish to make matching units to hold foodstuffs and kitchen equipment. By using the basic designs described in this chapter, this should present no problem, and the resulting scheme of your kitchen will more than match expensive, manufactured kitchen systems.

Cutting list : Sink/hob unit

Wood	Imperial	Metric
From laminated chipboard :		
2 end formers	35 x 21 x ⅝	889 x 533 x 16
3 intermediate formers	30⅜ x 21 x ⅝	772 x 533 x 16
1 lower shelf	96 x 21 x ⅝	243 x 533 x 16
5 doors	25⅛ x 15 x ⅝	638 x 381 x 16
1 top drawer front	18 x 6¼ x ⅝	457 x 159 x 16
2 centre drawer fronts	18 x 7¼ x ⅝	457 x 184 x 16
1 bottom drawer front	18 x 7¾ x ⅝	457 x 197 x 16
1 top front panel	77¼ x 7 x ⅝	1962 x 178 x 16
1 kickboard	96 x 5 x ⅝	2436 x 127 x 16
From blockboard :		
1 working top	98¼ x 22⅝ x ¾	2493 x 575 x 19
From softwood :		
2 top rails	97¼ x 2 x 1	2467 x 51 x 25
1 front edge	98¼ x 1 x 1	2493 x 25 x 25
1 front edge	21⅝ x 1 x 1	549 x 25 x 25
From hardboard :		
1 back	97¼ x 35 x ⅛	2467 x 889 x 3
4 drawer bottoms	19 x 17½ x ⅛	482 x 445 x 3
From plywood :		
6 drawer sides	19 x 6⅝ x ½	482 x 168 x 13
2 top drawer sides	19 x 4¾ x ½	482 x 121 x 13
2 top drawer ends	17 x 3½ x ½	432 x 89 x 13
6 drawer ends	17 x 5 x ½	432 x 127 x 13
From hardwood :		
10 drawer runners	20 x ¾ x ½	˙508 x 19 x 13

You will also need :
Plastic laminate. Fireproofing material. Door handles. Woodworking glue. 1 gross 1½in. (38mm) panel pins and No.6 screws. Edge trim. Tenon saw. Rip saw. Jig saw.

All imperial measurements in inches, all metric measurements in millimetres.

Cutting list : Oven unit

Wood	Imperial	Metric
From laminate covered chipboard :		
1 side panel	80 x 21 x ⅝	2030 x 533 x 16
1 side panel	80 x 6 x ⅝	2030 x 152 x 16
2 bottom shelves	31 x 21 x ⅝	787 x 533 x 16
1 top cross member	30⅜ x 6 x ⅝	771 x 152 x 16
1 top shelf	31 x 17 x ⅝	787 x 432 x 16
1 top back panel	31 x 24 x ⅝	787 x 609 x 16
2 top doors	16¼ x 15 x ⅝	413 x 381 x 16
2 bottom doors	18 x 15 x ⅝	457 x 381 x 16
1 kickboard	29¾ x 5 x ⅝	755 x 127 x 16
From softwood :		
1 rear support batten	80 x 2 x 1	2030 x 51 x 25
2 centre shelf battens	20 x 1 x 1	508 x 25 x 25

Space saving ironing board

In the small modern flat or semi-detached dwelling occupied by a growing family, coping with the week's ironing can become a backbreaking chore. This is more often than not because no adequate space has been devoted to it and the housewife has to make do with the kitchen table, or an ironing board which has to be awkwardly lifted out of a cupboard, unfolded and set up in the living room or kitchen.

Many fold-out ironing boards are badly designed, giving a rickety surface to work on, and with the trailing cord they can be a hazard among young children.

This chapter gives consideration to the whole wearisome and time-consuming task of ironing and tells you how to make a compact and functional unit which is neat, mobile, practical and attractive.

The character of the unit illustrated, perhaps, looks rather clinical, being painted white to match the appliances in the laundry and kitchen. But it need not be so; it could be constructed equally well of natural dressed timber or veneered chipboard, or painted in bright colours. Another good idea, if you're handy with a needle and thread, would be to make fitted covers which could add individuality and colourful design and also give you a nice change from time to time.

Considerations

The final design and construction must depend on your own requirements. For instance, the height of the finished unit is not adjustable; therefore it should be modified to suit the user, your wife. She will give you the height at which she will require the ironing surface.

Perhaps she has a large family to launder for, with a pile of shirts to iron every week. In this case she probably prefers to sit while she irons, and needs a lower surface to work on. If she is tall, she will probably be satisfied with the unit as designed.

The importance of making the unit the correct height cannot be stressed too greatly. The iron, being a heavy unit, has to be lifted as well as pushed and pulled. Consequently, the strain should be directed to the wrist and forearm and taken from the shoulder. Thus the ironing surface should be made low enough to give the user an easy action below the elbow.

The next point to consider is the dimensions of the ironing surface. Your wife may consider the width of 12in. (305mm) to be two narrow. She may prefer you to make it two or three inches wider. Likewise, the length. In the existing design, the ironing board folds out to a total length of 42in. (1070mm). Is this long enough? You may wish to make the flap up to 6in. (152mm) longer, in which case you will need to make an adjustment to the length of the flap and also to the length and positioning of the flap support, and the length of the members to which the wheels are fixed, for balance.

There may be other alterations or modifications you will want to build in. However, do bear in mind that the project is not a multi-purpose unit like many other designs contained in previous chapters. By reason of its function, it is an ironing table only, and is likely to be stored in the laundry where its clinical appearance is likely to match the other appliances.

The wheels and the built-in electric lead enable the user to bring the unit out of the laundry and place it in the part of the house most convenient or congenial to the user—perhaps to where she can work in sunlight, keep an eye on the children, listen to the radio, or even watch television.

Design

The unit has been designed to provide a mobile collapsible ironing table, complete with built-in cupboard space for ironing and general cleaning gear. In addition to the fold-out ironing board, it provides space for cloths, brushes, fluids, iron, sprinkler, etc.

The table is fitted with a built-in electrical fitting in that an electrical socket outlet is fitted with a 10ft. (3m) extension lead. This allows the iron to be connected to a table fitted socket, the power to the unit being provided through the extension lead.

The unit may be constructed of one material, such as plywood, chipboard or dressed timber. However, for considerations of economy and function, this unit is of plywood, chipboard and hardboard of different thicknesses for different members of the unit in order to keep the unit light and to reduce the cost. Being required in quite small panels, all material specified can probably be obtained from your nearest DIY shop.

Construction

From plywood cut the front and back members 36 x 20 x $\frac{1}{2}$in. (910 x 508 x 13mm). Rebate the top and bottom edges. Rebate the long edges to take the hardboard ends. Note that all rebates are $\frac{3}{8}$in. (10mm) deep by the thickness of the jointing material.

Mark the door shapes on the front panel. The top door is $15\frac{3}{8}$ x $11\frac{3}{4}$ x $\frac{1}{2}$in. (391 x 300 x 13mm). The bottom door is 17 x $15\frac{1}{2}$ x $\frac{1}{2}$in. (432 x 394 x 13mm).

To mark the final door shapes, having ruled the two rectangles, with a compass set at radius of $2\frac{5}{8}$in. (67mm), draw the curves on the two top corners of the top panel and the two left-hand corners of the lower panel.

Cut the doors to shape using a power jig saw or keyhole hand saw; alternatively, you could use a tenon saw for the straight lines and switch to a pad saw for the curves.

If you are using a power jig saw, begin by holding the saw at an angle of about 30° until you have cut through the material, then straighten to near 90° and cut along the line in the normal way. If you are cutting the straight lines with a tenon saw, commence cutting along a straight line, holding the saw blade almost flat, gradually raising the handle as it slices through the material. Cut to each corner.

When you reach the end of the straight line and are about to enter the curve, remove the tenon saw and insert a pad saw. Cut very carefully along the line as the cut-out pieces are to be used as doors which must fit accurately and easily into the apertures. Note that the lower door is $\frac{1}{8}$in. (3mm) narrower than the top door to allow for the hinge spine.

Cut the end members from the hardboard 36 x $11\frac{3}{4}$ x $\frac{1}{8}$in. (910 x 300 x 3mm). Slot one end of the left hand panel as per drawing to take the flap support. Note that if you decide to make the flap longer you will need to make the slot longer.

From a piece of scrap softwood cut a support batten 11 x 2 x $\frac{1}{2}$in. (279 x 51 x 13mm). Pin and glue the left hand end panel to the support, $\frac{3}{8}$in. (10mm) from the top edge of the panel. Cut the top and bottom panels $19\frac{3}{4}$ x $11\frac{3}{4}$ x $\frac{1}{2}$in. (502 x 300 x 13mm) of plywood.

Assembly

Assemble the main cupboard shell by slotting the top and bottom members into the rebated edges of the front and rear members, and to the side members, and pinning and glueing. Pin and glue the top edge of the inside batten fixed to the end panel.

Cut the centre shelf $19\frac{3}{4}$ x 11 x $\frac{1}{2}$in. (502 x 279 x 13mm) of plywood. Assemble the shelf inside the carcass, its top surface being level with the bottom of the upper aperture. Pin and glue to the front, side and rear members.

Cut the flap hinge strip support 12 x 3 x $\frac{1}{2}$in. (305 x 76 x 13mm). Screw and glue to the top of the outside surface of the left end panel. To give support, the screws should go through the hardboard and enter the inside support batten.

Counter-sink all pin heads and fill with plastic filler. Sandpaper all edges, joins and surfaces.

To arrive at the shape of the ironing extension flap, cut a rectangular piece of stiff paper $21\frac{1}{2}$ x 12in. (546 x 305mm). Fold it down the middle to make a rectangle $21\frac{1}{2}$ x 6in. (546 x 152mm). Along one edge, mark a point 12in. (305mm). Draw a curve from this point to the end of the paper at the fold. Cut along this line through both thicknesses of the paper. Unfold and smooth out.

This is the templet to use to mark the correct shape from which to cut the ironing board flap. Place the paper on a panel of $\frac{5}{8}$in. (16mm) chipboard and trace the shape and cut with a power jig saw or keyhole handsaw. Cover the exposed edge with an iron-on edge trim.

Cut the flap support batten 20½ x 2¼ x ½in. (521 x 57 x 13mm). Cut block and dowel and assemble as per inset on drawing. Fit a 1½in. (38mm) backflap hinge to the top of the support strip. Fix the ironing extension flap to the main structure with two 1½in. (38mm) backflap hinges. Fix the flap support to the underside of the ironing extension, after passing the support bracket assembly dowel through the end member slot.

The method to be used here is to hold the support strip so that the dowel passes through the slot, then twist the strip through 90° so that the dowel is trapped (see drawing and photo).

The small angled support blocks must be pinned and glued to the sides of the slot after the exact location has been determined by extending the ironing flap to the horizontal position.

Cut the wheel supports as per cutting list and drawing. These parts should be screwed and glued into position from under the main unit and arranged to extend as shown to ensure balance when the ironing flap is in use. Please note that fixed wheels are safer and more functional in this instance than swivel castors.

Fit the wheels to the wheel supports, using nuts and bolts fixed to the supports. Fit the legs to the opposite end of the structure and check that the unit stands level and solid.

Cut handle supports to shape from ½in. (13mm) plywood and countersink for the 1in.

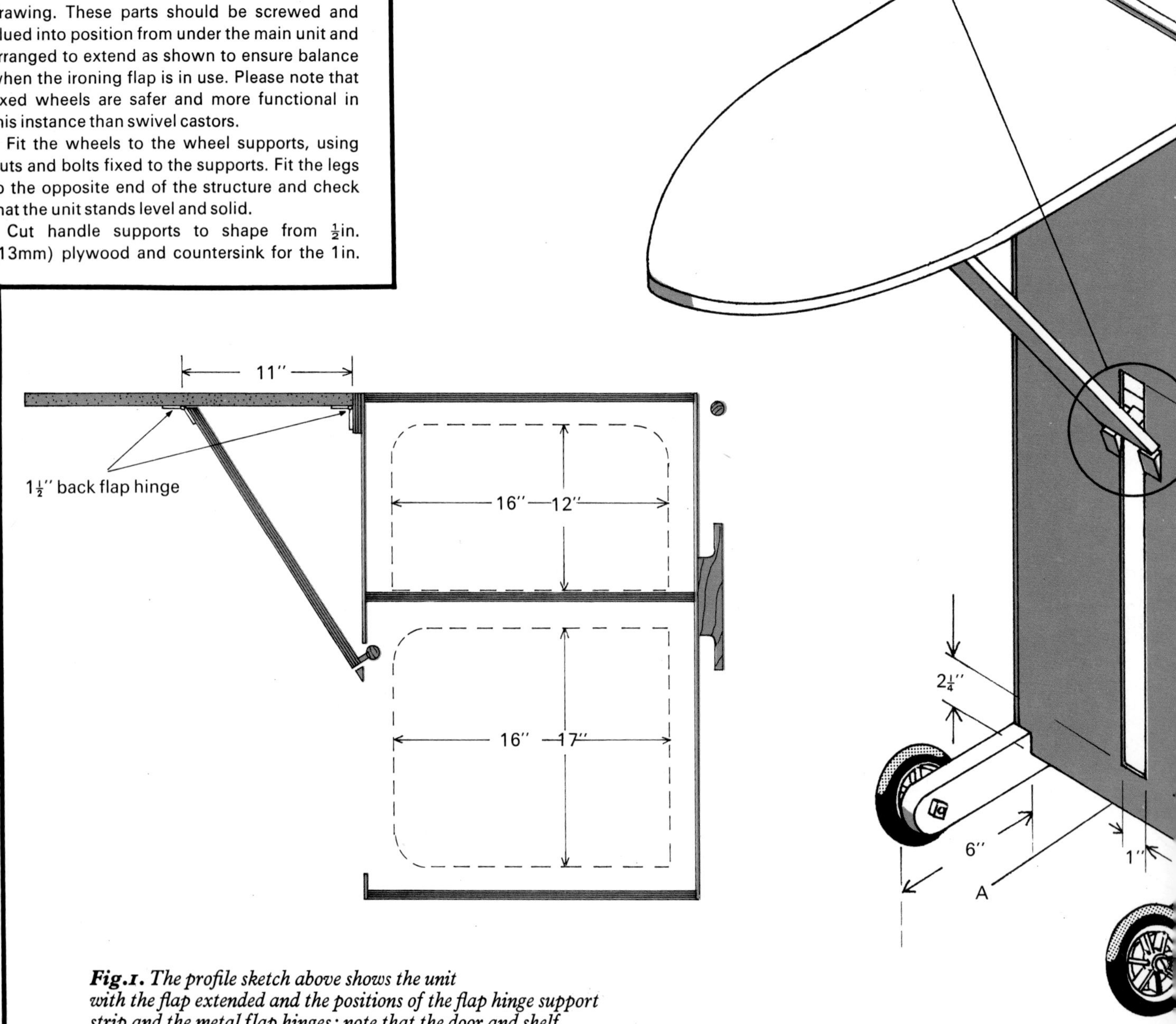

***Fig.1.** The profile sketch above shows the unit with the flap extended and the positions of the flap hinge support strip and the metal flap hinges; note that the door and shelf cut-outs are to be fitted in the apertures from which they came.*

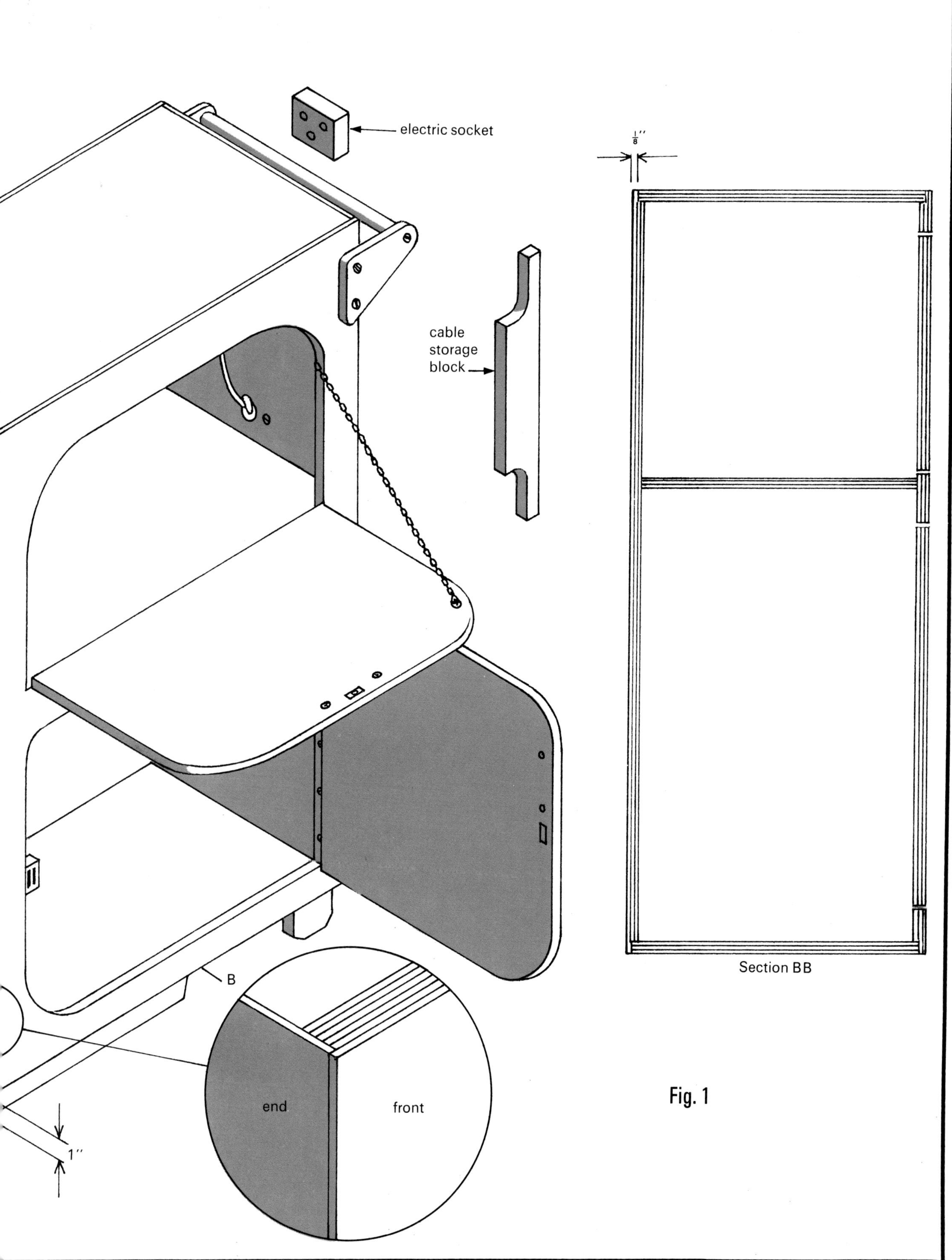
electric socket
cable
storage
block
1/8″
Section BB
B
end
front
1″
Fig. 1

2

3

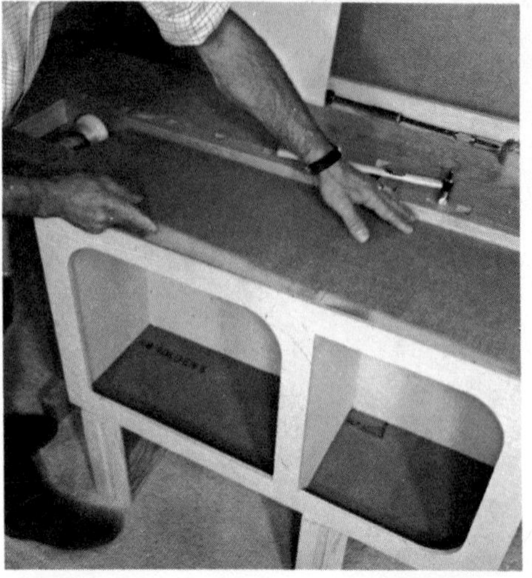

4

5

6

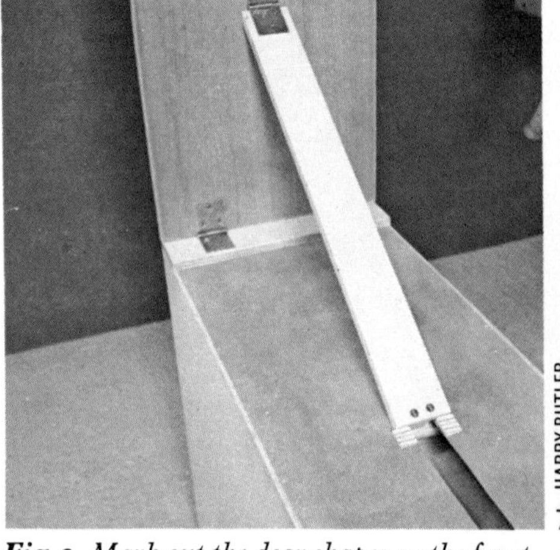

7

HARRY BUTLER

(25mm) diam. dowel handle. Screw the supports directly to the sides of the main structure. The shape and location of these parts is not critical.

Cut the cable storage block to shape and fix by screwing through the hardboard end member. Drill a hole beside the cable block and pass suitable electrical cable into the top cupboard. As this is to be handled, make sure the cable is rubber encased and that the wiring to the plugs is done properly and concealed. Allow about 12in. (305mm) of cable and knot inside.

Drill another hole near the top of the end member and pass the cable to the outside. Connect the cable to a suitable power socket and then mount the socket on the end member.

Fit the doors, using full length plastic piano hinges. The doors should present a good fit to the cut-outs, but may need trimming along the hinge edge.

Fit the catches and handles. Fit about 16in. (406mm) of chain to the inside top of the front member and to the top of the door panel, adjust to hold the door horizontal when it flaps down open. This can make a handy surface for when the ironing is being done.

Some types of catches may require the fixing of a fitting block. Remove all accessories and finish by painting.

Cover

A fitted cover for the whole of the ironing surface is the final touch which will brighten up your mobile ironing unit.

Cutting list

Material	Imperial	Metric
Plywood		
2 panels	36 x 20 x $\frac{1}{2}$	910 x 508 x 13
2 panels	19$\frac{3}{4}$ x 11$\frac{3}{4}$ x $\frac{1}{2}$	502 x 300 x 13
1 panel	19$\frac{3}{4}$ x 11 x $\frac{1}{2}$	502 x 279 x 13
1 piece	12 x 3 x $\frac{1}{2}$	305 x 76 x 13
1 piece	20$\frac{1}{2}$ x 2$\frac{1}{4}$ x $\frac{1}{2}$	521 x 57 x 13
2 pieces	3$\frac{3}{4}$ x 3$\frac{3}{4}$ x $\frac{1}{2}$	96 x 96 x 13
1 piece	1 x 1 x $\frac{1}{2}$	25 x 25 x 13
Hardboard		
1 panel	36 x 11$\frac{3}{4}$ x $\frac{1}{8}$	910 x 300 x 3
Chipboard		
1 panel	21$\frac{1}{2}$ x 12 x $\frac{5}{8}$	546 x 305 x 16
Softwood		
2 pieces	18 x 2 x 1	460 x 51 x 25
2 pieces	3 x 2 x 1	76 x 51 x 25
1 piece	11 x 2 x 1	279 x 51 x 25
Dowel		
1 piece	3 x 1 diam.	76 x 25 diam.
1 piece	12$\frac{1}{2}$ x 1 diam.	330 x 25 diam.

You will also need:
2 lengths plastic piano hinge: 15$\frac{5}{8}$in. (397mm) and 17in. (432mm); 3 1$\frac{1}{2}$in. (38mm) blackflap hinges; 2 3in. (76mm) diam. wheels; 1 electric socket; 10ft (3m) electric cable; woodworking adhesive, screws, pins, glasspaper, paint.

Fig.2. *Mark out the door shapes on the front panel and cut to shape using a power jig saw or a keyhole handsaw. If you are using a power jig saw, begin by holding the saw at an angle of about 30° until you have cut through the material, then straighten to near 90° and cut along the line in the normal way. If using a tenon saw, cut along a straight line until about to enter the curve, then remove tenon saw and insert a pad saw.*

Fig.3. *Assemble the main cupboard shell by pinning and glueing; rebate the top and bottom edges. Rebate the long edges to take the hardboard ends.*

Fig.4. *Cut ends to shape from hardboard; slot one end of the left hand panel to take the flap support. Pin and glue end panels into position.*

Fig.5. *From a piece of scrap softwood cut a support batten. Pin and glue it to the left hand end panel. Cut the ironing extension flap from $\frac{5}{8}$" thick chipboard. Fix to main structure with two 1$\frac{1}{2}$" back-flap hinges.*

Fig.6. *Pass support bracket assembly dowel through end member slot by holding support strip so that the dowel passes through slot; twist through 90° so that dowel is trapped.*

Fig.7. *The small angled support blocks must be pinned and glued to the sides of the slot after the exact location has been determined by extending the ironing flap to the exactly horizontal position, making a complementary surface with the top of the cabinet.*

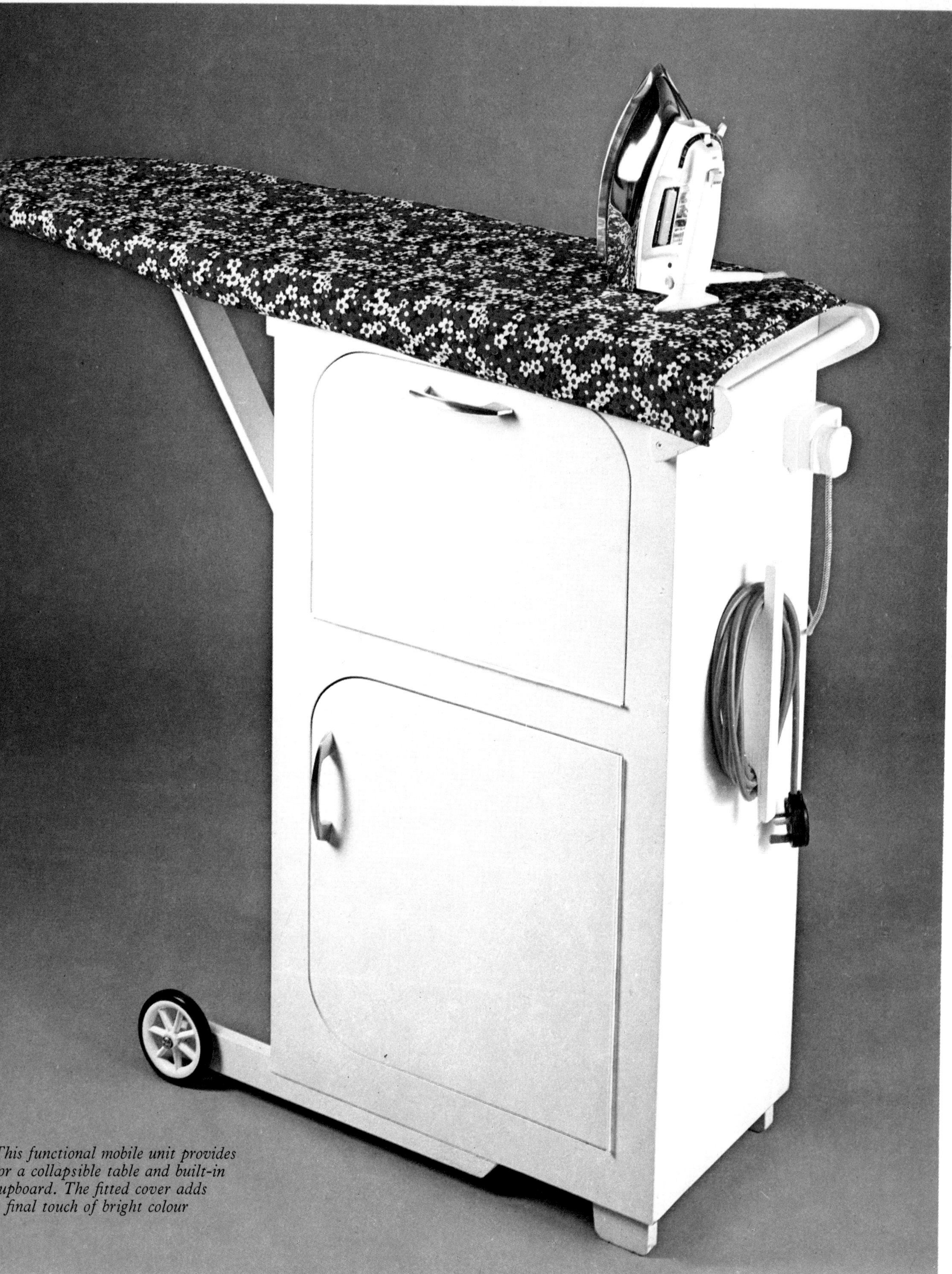

'his functional mobile unit provides or a collapsible table and built-in upboard. The fitted cover adds final touch of bright colour

Space-saving fitted wardrobe

With the building of smaller family units and the remodelling of old homes into small flats and bedsitters, space is often at a premium. As children grow up into their teens, they need their own rooms, with adequate space to hang and store their clothes and other possessions, as well as to do their home-work and carry on their leisure activities. There isn't room these days for bulky single-purpose units. The accent is on built-ins which fulfil more than one function.

This unit will provide a complete fitment which makes the maximum use of space, incorporating wardrobe hanging room, cupboard space, plus a writing table or dressing table.

Utilizing a small section of the wall and ceiling of the room, the construction saves on materials and makes maximum use of the area.

Preparation

Before starting construction, carefully survey the room and work out the best position for the unit. Points to take into consideration are the shape of the room, the contours of the walls, location of doors, windows, fireplace, and the essential furniture the room must carry. If possible, choose an area of wall which is at present being wasted; for example, a recess between the fireplace and corner, or a corner which is hidden by a diagonally placed wardrobe.

Having decided on your location, make a thorough examination of the wall and ceiling area the unit will occupy. If plastered, would surface powder come off on hanging clothes? It may be necessary to seal the wall surface with a high-gloss paint. Make sure you know the composition of the wall and ceiling, since they will have to carry battens, and consequently be drilled and plugged.

In the illustrated model, the unit has been designed to fit into a corner in which the wall returns on the left. If in the room for which your unit is intended the wall returns on the right, you will have to amend the design accordingly.

Be sure to take note of the existing picture rails and skirting boards which are within the confines of the projected construction. Note also whether warpage or shrinkage has affected the levels of the floor, walls or ceiling. You may have to take some of these factors into consideration and to make the appropriate modifications to your design.

NELSON HARGREAVES

Left. *Utilizing a small section of the wall and ceiling area of the room, this built-in unit makes the maximum use of space.*

Make a sketch or floor plan of the location, then, with a coloured pencil, sketch in the unit and see the effect the additional feature will have on the room. This may give you an idea of how to finish the completed unit—in natural wood grain, or paint. Note that if painted the same colour as the walls, the unit will tend to disappear, thus making the room look larger.

Construction

The main point to bear in mind is that the construction is basically a frontal frame fitted with two shelves and anchored to the walls and ceiling, with partitions and doors added. The unit provides wardrobe hanging space, shelves, and a working surface suitable for use as a writing table or dressing table.

Since the rigidity of the construction depends on a solid junction with the ceiling, it is necessary to measure accurately the ceiling height. Take no dimension for granted. Measure the height at intervals of 2ft. (600mm) across that section which is to be used as a junction with the frame.

In the model illustrated, the ceiling has been given a height of 7ft 6in. (2290mm). You will probably have to alter this to suit the specifications of your room.

Cut the three vertical front frame members from 2in. x 2in. (51mm x 51mm) planed timber. Two are the main floor to ceiling uprights 7ft 6in. (2290mm) in length; the other is the left frontal member on the overhanging section of the upper shelf, and measures 2ft (610mm).

Cramp the three pieces together and mark and cut 1in. (25mm) deep rebates to the rear face to accommodate the 4in. x 1in. (102mm x 25mm) horizontal members and the 3in. x 1in. (76mm x 25mm) front plinth member. The first 4in. (102mm x 25mm) horizontal members and the 3in. x 1in. (76mm x 25mm) front plinth member. The first 4in. (102mm) wide rebate is at the top of all three verticals. The second is level with the bottom of the 2ft (610mm) upright. The 3in. (76mm) wide rebate accommodates the plinth member at the bottom of the two full length uprights.

Assemble temporarily by laying the three uprights on the bench or floor in position and placing the two horizontal members and the front plinth member across them on the rebated surfaces. The first vertical member fits flush with the right hand outside end of all three horizontals, including the plinth.

The second vertical member should be exactly 4ft (1220mm) from the first (inside edge to inside edge). The third (short) vertical member will accommodate the rebated sections of the

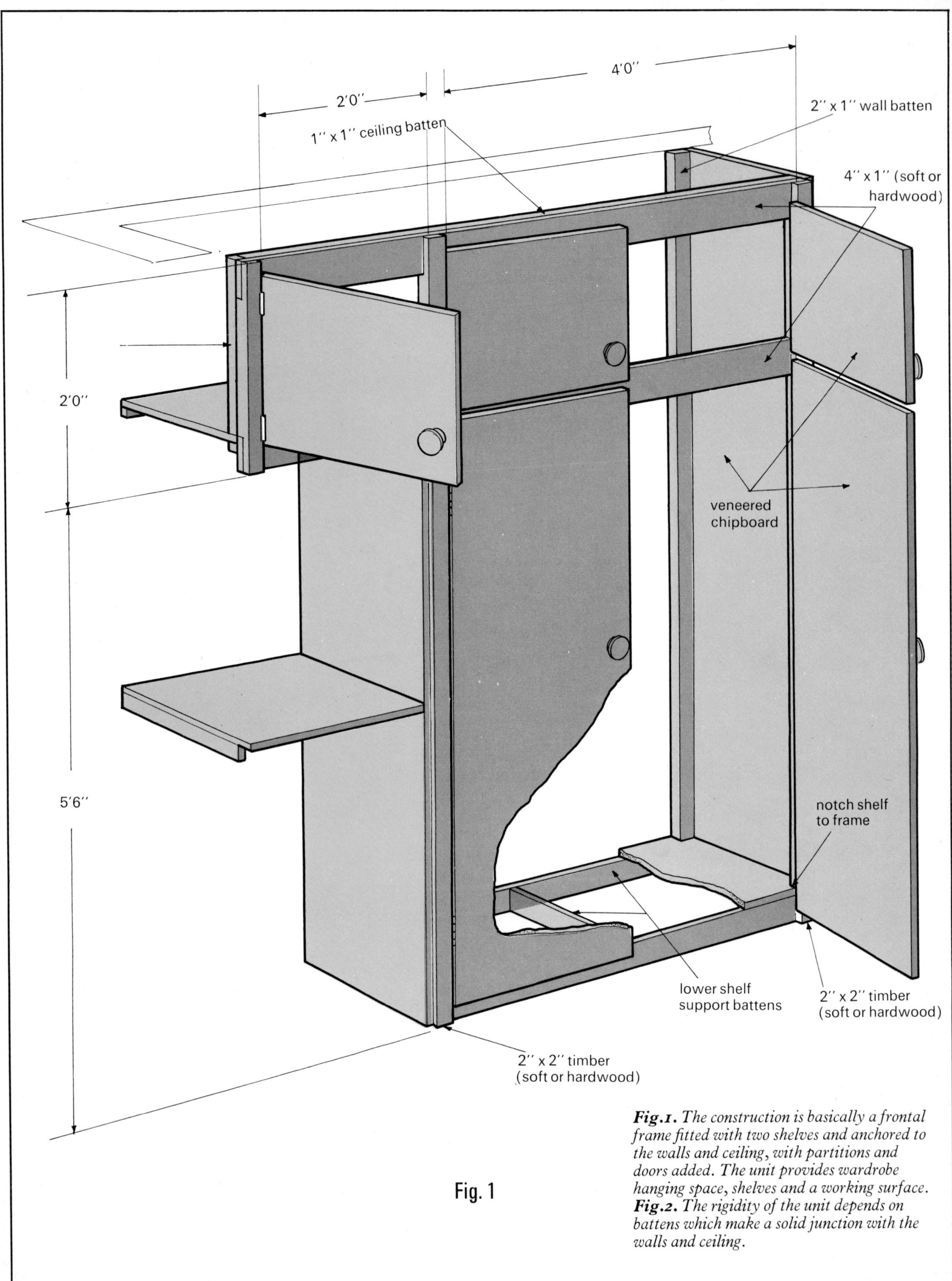

Fig.1. *The construction is basically a frontal frame fitted with two shelves and anchored to the walls and ceiling, with partitions and doors added. The unit provides wardrobe hanging space, shelves and a working surface.* ***Fig.2.*** *The rigidity of the unit depends on battens which make a solid junction with the walls and ceiling.*

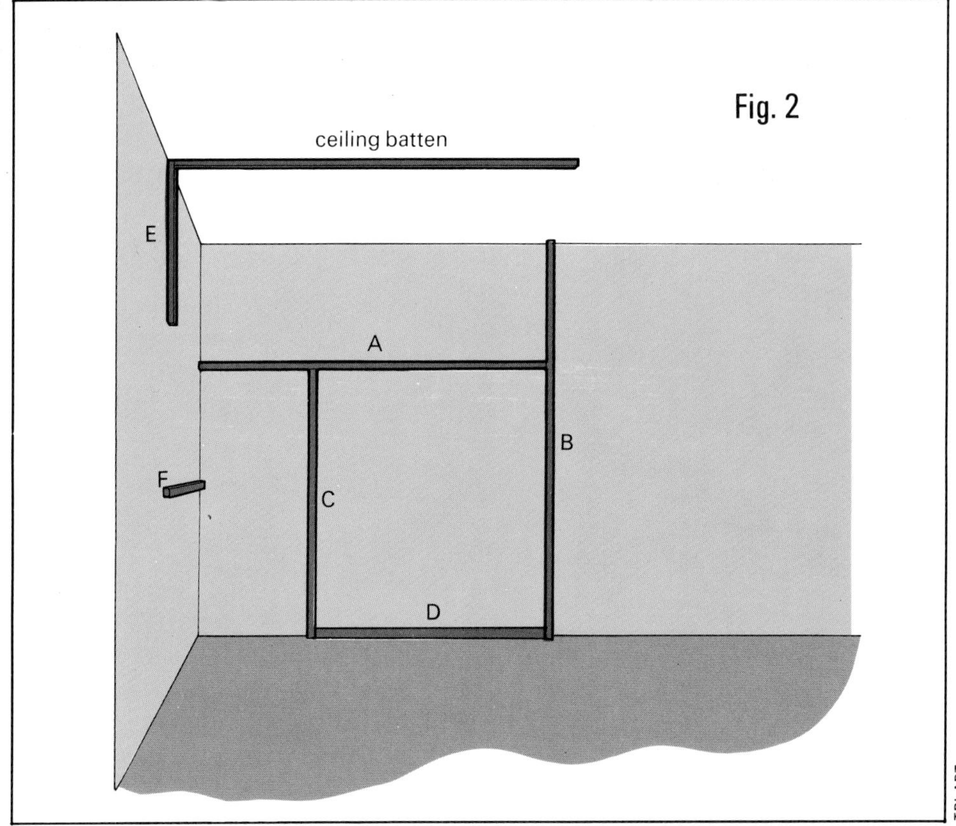

two top horizontals. Place the front plinth member across the bottom rebates of the two 7ft 6in. (2290) members. Temporarily assemble this frame by screwing the horizontal members to the vertical members.

Cut the main frame ceiling fixing 6ft 5in. x 1in. x 1in. (1955m x 25mm x 25mm). Pin this batten temporarily to the rear surface of the top horizontal member, one end flush with the right end, and the top surface being level with the top edge of the horizontal member.

This is the time to position carefully the assembled frame at the intended floor location. To ensure accuracy in the final construction it would be as well to cut the three top door panels and the two lower door panels (see cutting list). Check these against the frame. Adjust for accuracy and temporarily pin a batten diagonally across the frame to hold the angles at 90°.

Lift the frame to the vertical position and check its position on the site. Check the junction of the frame with the ceiling. With a spirit level, check horizontal and vertical levels, then transfer the locations to the wall for positioning the battens, again using the spirit level. Rest the frame down, having made any final adjustments necessary, and screw the ceiling batten permanently to the inside of the horizontal, positioned to make a flush contact with the ceiling.

Measure and cut all wall battens. These are as follows:

(a) top shelf wall batten;
(b) right end partition (vertical) wall batten;
(c) left end partition (vertical) wall batten;
(d) plinth wall batten;
(e) main frame (vertical) end batten;
(f) working top support batten.

Mark batten positions carefully on the wall, matching the dimensions of the frame. Fix all wall battens, using wall plugs and screws. A DIY manual will describe methods of fixing, types of wall plugs, and tools to use.

Cut the top shelf frame panel and screw to the horizontal member 1in. (25mm) below the top edge. Cut the top shelf panel and the lower shelf panel.

Assembly

Hold the frame in its correct position and place the top shelf panel in position, resting on the wall batten and the frame batten. It may need very minor trimming to make the shelf panel fit flush to the wall without distorting the frame. Pin temporarily in position.

Next, fit the lower shelf support members, connecting the two plinth members; one at extreme left, another at extreme right, and the third midway between them. Pin and glue these supports to the front and rear plinth members. Notch the lower shelf panel to the front and rear frame uprights, and check for fit against the wall. Trim as necessary. Note that this shelf fits on and flush with the edge of the front plinth member.

Fix the main frame to the ceiling by screwing through the 1in. x 1in. (25mm x 25mm) batten and plugging it to the ceiling. Remove the lower shelf and anchor the frame to the floor, using scrap 1in. x 1in. (25mm x 25mm) blocks pinned behind and to the front plinth member. Replace the lower shelf panel on the top edge of the two plinth members and fix, using $1\frac{1}{2}$in. (38mm) panel pins. Permanently fix the top shelf in a similar fashion.

Cut the full length end partition. Check its fit to the vertical wall batten and trim as necessary. The location of this member to the end of the front frame is not critical within about $\frac{1}{4}$in (6mm), but note that this panel conceals the end grain of the horizontal frame members. Screw the partition onto the vertical wall batten, the right front frame upright, the top end grain of the horizontal frame members. Screw the partition onto the vertical wall batten, the right front frame upright, the top shelf end support and the plinth end support.

Cut the left end partition. Screw it onto the end partition wall batten and the front vertical, the top shelf end support and the lower end plinth support.

Refit all doors, making any minor adjustments necessary to ensure that the doors close properly. With a largish structure of this type, satisfactory door alignment can often prove difficult. However, adjustment during construction should achieve a perfect fit. Screw the hinge leaves to the carcass, then to the doors, one by one, checking the position of each door in relation to the frame and the other doors.

Add the working top batten support to the outside of the left partition member. Pin the working top panel to the top edge of this batten and of the corresponding wall member.

Fit magnetic catches to the doors, on the top edge, and small rubber buffers to the frame opposite the lower door edge. Tap washers fixed with contact adhesive are suitable. Fix handles to choice.

Countersink all nails and fill with matching stopper before sanding with glasspaper. Additional internal shelving should be added at this stage, if required. Finish by painting, or with clear varnish.

A small fluorescent light fitting fixed under the top main shelf and over the working top is a useful feature which could be added.

If the fitment is to be used as a dressing table, fix a mirror to the back wall above it.

Cutting list

Material	Imperial	Metric
Planed timber		
2 pieces	90x2x2	2290x51x51
1 piece	24x2x2	610x51x51
2 pieces	78x4x1	1980x102x25
2 pieces	52x3x1	1322x76x25
3 pieces	20x3x1	508x76x25
1 piece	76x2x1	1932x51x25
1 piece	78x2x1	1980x51x25
1 piece	85x2x1	2155x51x25
1 piece	65x2x1	1655x51x25
2 pieces	21x2x1	534x51x25
1 piece	77x1x1	1955x25x25
1 piece	20x1x1	508x25x25
Veneered chipboard		
1 panel	90x22x$\frac{3}{4}$	2290x558x19
1 panel	69x22x$\frac{3}{4}$	1750x558x19
1 panel	78x21x$\frac{3}{4}$	1980x534x19
1 panel	52x22x$\frac{3}{4}$	1322x558x19
1 panel	25$\frac{3}{8}$x22x$\frac{3}{4}$	645x558x19
3 panel	23$\frac{1}{8}$x19$\frac{1}{2}$x$\frac{3}{4}$	607x496x19
2 panel	64$\frac{1}{2}$x23$\frac{1}{8}$x$\frac{3}{4}$	1640x607x19

You will also need:
$1\frac{1}{2}$in. (38mm) panel pins, 1in. (25mm) and $\frac{1}{2}$in. (12mm) wood screws, plugs and screws for wall battens, 10 hinge fitments, 5 magnetic catch sets, 5 rubber buffers, woodworking adhesive, stopper, varnish or paint, a small fluorescent light fitting.

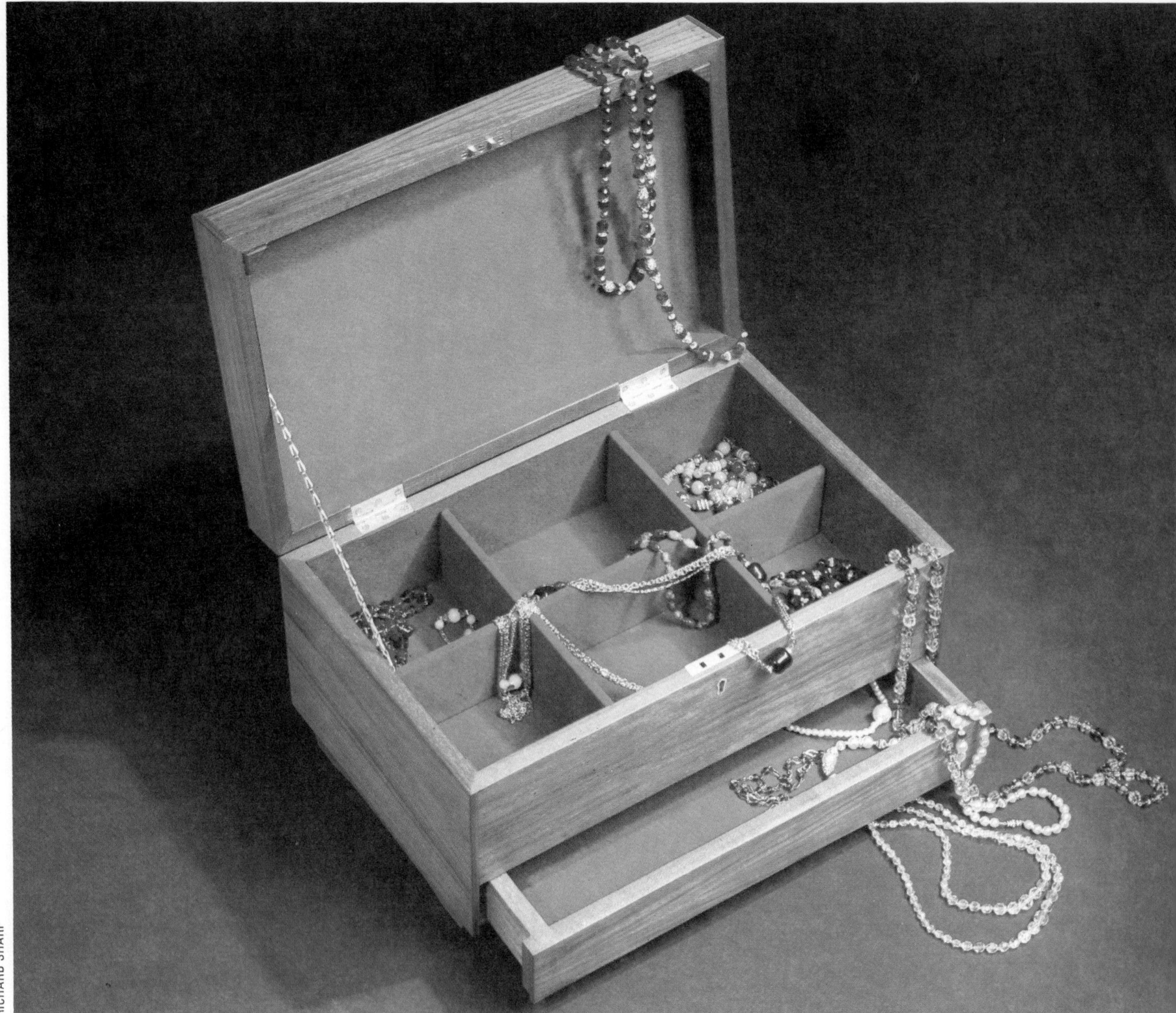
RICHARD SHARP

A Victorian fitted case

Every bit as attractive as a genuine original, this reproduction Victorian fitted box is just the thing for holding your treasures. Ideal for safeguarding jewellery, cosmetics or personal letters, it evokes the more gracious age of furniture design.

A genuine Victorian fitted box can be a magnificent addition to any decor giving a handsome touch, although it can be rather expensive to buy. Many of them were ornately decorated with inlays and silver fittings and are now much sought after by collectors.

Usually, the more elaborate boxes were used by ladies to hold their jewels; or as vanity units. The reproduction is ideal for both these functions, or it could be fitted to hold writing equipment or a matched set of glassware or cutlery. Whatever use you put it to, the fitted box will enhance your furniture and give a lifetime's elegant service.

The design

One of the reasons why antique fitted boxes are so sought after is that they do not have the rather vulgar over-elaboration characteristic of much Victorian furniture. They look just as good in the most contemporary home as in a Victorian dressing room. This reproduction faithfully copies a design, while modifying the method of construction for simplicity's sake.

An attractive feature of these boxes was the ingenious secret drawer for holding valuables. This has been incorporated in the reproduction. Depending on what use you want to put the box to, you can fix partitions as desired. Similarly, you can line the interior with the material of your choice—velvet or baize adds a luxurious touch.

Materials

Traditionally, these units were made of a hard wood such as mahogany or rosewood. Nowadays, the quality of veneered composition boards is so high that a material such as veneered chipboard allows an excellent finish.

Above left. *Your personal treasures deserve to be housed in something special, such as this reproduction Victorian fitted box. It is fitted with a secret drawer, and partitions can be added to suit individual requirements.*
Above. *Designed to allow easy construction, the elegant lines of the box are complemented by the distinctive grain of the veneer.*

The box illustrated is constructed from teak veneer chipboard, a popular and easily available finish, but you can choose from any of the wide range of veneers now marketed.

For economy's sake, the base of the secret drawer and the partitions are cut from $\frac{1}{4}$in. (6mm) and $\frac{1}{8}$in. (3mm) plywood.

Construction

Because Victorian furniture makers did not have the really strong woodworking glues available today, most of their work was constructed using strong and elaborate joints. Nowadays, there is less need for these jointing techniques and the box is fitted together by glueing and pinning the panels into simple rebates. Not only does this give an equally strong finish, it also allows the inexperienced carpenter to make the box to a professional finish.

Cutting out the box panels

Mark and cut out the side, front and back panels to length from a 9 in. (229mm) wide panel of $\frac{5}{8}$in. (16mm) thick veneered chipboard. Be sure to cut out to the exact sizes given in the cutting list. Take one of the side panels and cut out the rebates which house the front and back panels and the plywood base. The rebates on the short sides are $\frac{3}{8}$in. (10mm) deep and $\frac{9}{16}$in. (14.3mm) wide. As the front and back panels housed in these rebates are $\frac{5}{8}$in. (16mm) thick, they will overlap the edges of the side panel by $\frac{1}{16}$in. (1.6mm), as shown in Fig.10. This overlap is made to allow a $\frac{1}{16}$in (1.6mm) strip of veneer to be added to the cut edges of the side panels. The rebate which houses the $\frac{1}{4}$in. (6mm) plywood base is $\frac{3}{8}$in. (10mm) deep, $\frac{1}{4}$in (6mm) wide and extends the length of the side panel. Repeat these rebates on the other side panel, then cut a rebate of the same size along the base of the back panel.

Cutting out the lid panels

Panels for the lid member may now be cut from the rebated side and front members simply by ripping a 2" (50mm) wide strip from the top of each piece. This will ensure accurate alignment of the assembled box and lid and neat, all round continuation of the wood grain. Note that the top edge of the lid parts must be rebated to take the top member. Now cut the drawer front from the front panel by ripping a $2\frac{1}{2}$" strip (68mm) from the bottom edge.

Cutting out the drawer panels

Having cut out all the pieces for the drawer, take the front panel and make the housing joints for the side panels. These joints are located $\frac{5}{16}$in. (8mm) from the short edges of the front panel, and are $\frac{3}{8}$in. (10mm) deep and $\frac{5}{8}$in. (16mm) wide. On the lower, long edge of the front panel, make a rebate $\frac{3}{8}$in. (10mm) deep and $\frac{1}{4}$in. (6mm) wide, to house the plywood base panel

1

2

4

5

7

8

of the box when the drawer is shut.

The $\frac{1}{8}$in. (3.2mm) thick plywood base for the drawer is fitted into housing joints cut in the front and side panels. The housing joint on the front panel is $\frac{1}{4}$in. (6mm) from the bottom of the rebate which houses the base of the box. The housing joint on each of the side panels is $\frac{1}{4}$in. (6mm) from the long, lower edge. All these housing joints are $\frac{1}{8}$in. (3.2mm) wide and $\frac{1}{4}$in. (6mm) deep. When the base panel is fixed into these housings, it stands $\frac{1}{4}$in. (6mm) clear of the long edges of the side panels which thus act as runners.

Assembling the box

Begin by assembling the framework of the box, using $1\frac{1}{2}$in. (38mm) panel pins and a strong woodworking glue. The long edges of

Fig.1. *The front and back box panels are housed in simple rebates cut in the short edges of the side panels. These rebates are* $\frac{1}{16}$*in. (1.6mm) narrower than the thickness of the panels, to allow a veneer strip to be added to the short edges of the side panels.*
Fig.2. *As in most genuine antique fitted boxes, a false bottom is fitted.*
Fig.3. *After checking the plywood base for fit, make a shallow cut-out in the front edge.*
Fig.4. *Add the plywood drawer base by glueing it into the housings cut in the side and front drawer panels.*
Fig.5. *Matching veneer edging strips are glued to all the exposed edges. Where they meet at the corners, the edges of the veneer strips are angled to simulate mitre joints.*
Fig.6. *Mark out and cut the housings for the box lock and, when the lock has been fixed in position, bore out the keyhole.*
Fig.7. *To hinge the lid to the box, first clamp both parts together securely and mark out and cut the housings.*
Fig.8. *Elegant shaped feet are screwed to the base panel.*
Fig.9. *To add a luxurious touch to the interior of the box, line it with baize.*
Fig.10. *While faithfully copying the design of a genuine Victorian fitted box, the method of construction is modified for simplicity. Veneered chipboard, which combines good looks with economy, is the most suitable material to use, and matching veneer is added to exposed edges. Depending on what use you wish to put the box to, you can fit the interior with baize-covered plywood partitions.*

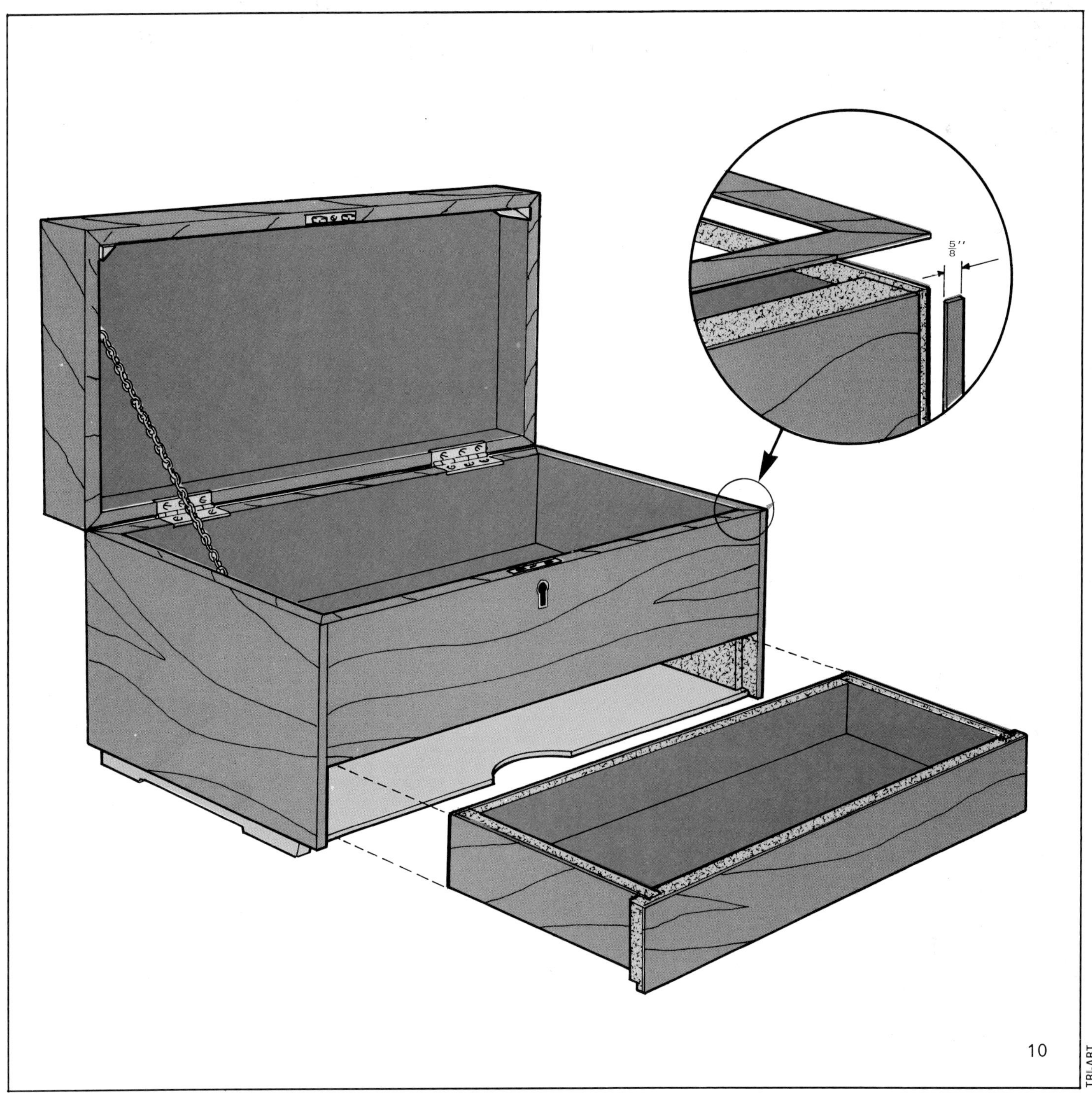

the front and back panels should be flush with the long edges of the side panels, but, as detailed previously, their short edges should overlap the side panels by $\frac{1}{16}$in. (1.6mm).

Before fitting the plywood base into position, make a shallow cut-out at the centre of the leading edge. This cut-out enables you to grasp the bottom edge of the drawer front panel when opening the drawer.

With the basic box assembly complete, assemble the lid. First glue and pin the front and back panels into the rebates cut in the side panels. When the glue has dried, add the lid top panel by fixing it into the rebates which are cut in the top edges of the front, back and side panels. The top panel should fit perfectly, if it is slightly too large at any point, trim it to size.

At this stage, add the lid locating blocks at the internal front corners of the lid, as shown in Fig.10. These are simply triangular pieces of waste hardwood about $\frac{1}{8}$in. (3.2mm) longer than the depth of the lid.

Assembling the drawer

Take the side panels and glue (but do not pin) them into the housings in the front panel, so that their long edges are flush with those of the front panel and the housings for the drawer base are correctly aligned. Now add the plywood base by glueing it into the housings cut into the front and side panels. All that remains is to add the back panel. This piece butts flush between the side panels and rests on the plywood base. Glue and pin it securely. Try the drawer to the box and, if necessary, adjust for a good fit by sanding and trimming.

Adding the veneer

The basic assembly is now complete, only the veneer strips and fittings need to be added. Before fixing these, sand the whole structure smooth and check that all exposed chipboard edges are smooth and plane enough to take the veneer edging strips. The veneer you choose should match the overall finish in colour and grain. If you cannot find an exact match, use a veneer in the same wood with a lighter colour. You can always darken it to match, by first sealing it with a proprietary grain filler, then polishing it.

Veneers are sold in large sheets measuring 36in. x 18in. x $\frac{1}{16}$in. (914mm x 457mm x 1.6mm). As you require only a small amount and veneers are expensive, you would be advised to try and buy suitable offcuts. The most likely sources of these are antique shops, many of which repair their own furniture, or home handicrafts shops. Even if they do not possess exactly what you want, they may be able to give you the name of a furniture repair shop which does.

Mark out the veneer strips for all the exposed edges of the drawer. Allow at least $\frac{1}{16}$in. (1.6mm) extra all round which can be planed down later. Cut all the strips out with a sharp handyman's knife and begin by glueing the veneer strips to the recessed edges, as shown in Fig.10. When the glue has dried, plane down the strips flush with the surrounding surfaces. Now add the veneer to the upper edges of the box and the lower edges of the lid. These strips are mitred at the corners, as shown in Fig.10. Having cut the mitres and glued the strips into position, plane down any overlapping edges.

The fittings

Cut out the two hardwood feet to the shape illustrated in Fig.11. Locate them on the base of the box, $\frac{1}{4}$in. (6mm) in from each short edge, and fix with $1\frac{1}{4}$in. No. 6 countersunk screws.

Clamp the lid to the box so that all the edges are flush, then mark the position of the brass hinges. When these have been located accurately, cut out the recesses for the hinges with a small, sharp chisel. Sand the hinge housings smooth and screw the hinges into position.

Now mark out and cut the housings for the brass box lock and, when both parts of this have been screwed into position, bore out the keyhole and glue the keyhole rim into position. Sand the finished structure and fill any holes caused by the panel pins with a stained wood filler.

Apply a lining to the interior of the box and the lid. Your choice of a suitable material is wide and can be dictated by the intended function of the box. One easy to fix material is self adhesive baize sheeting, which only requires to be cut to shape and pressed into position.

Internal partitions can be cut to size from $\frac{1}{4}$in. (6mm) plywood. The cross members are fitted to the centre member by means of slots, as shown (p.128). Before assembling them, cover them with lining to match the interior of the box and lid.

Finishing

Using very fine sandpaper, smooth all the surfaces, then, with a soft cloth damped with turpentine substitute, wipe all the surfaces so that the fine dust is picked up.

With a good quality 2in. (50mm) brush, sparingly apply a varnish of clear matt polyurethane and turpentine substitute blended 50/50. When dry, cut down with fine sandpaper, remove any dust as before and recoat with the same mixture and, when dry, finish with grade O steel wool. Clean the surface with neat turpentine substitute, leave overnight, then apply teak oil as sparingly as possible.

Fig.11. Cross sections of the front and side of the box. To give a neat look overall, the edge of the bottom panel is recessed in a rebate cut in the front drawer panel.

CUTTING LIST

Solid wood	Imperial	Metric
From teak veneered chipboard:		
2 side box panels	$11\frac{1}{2}$x 9 x$\frac{5}{8}$	292x229x16
1 front box panel	18 x $4\frac{3}{8}$x$\frac{5}{8}$	457x112x16
1 back box panel	18 x $6\frac{7}{8}$x$\frac{5}{8}$	457x175x16
1 false bottom	$17\frac{1}{2}$x$10\frac{1}{4}$x$\frac{5}{8}$	445x260x16
1 lid top	18 x11 x$\frac{5}{8}$	457x279x16
2 drawer sides	$10\frac{1}{4}$x $2\frac{1}{8}$x$\frac{5}{8}$	260x 54x16
1 drawer back	$15\frac{7}{8}$x $1\frac{3}{4}$x$\frac{5}{8}$	403x 45x16
From birch plywood:		
1 bottom box panel	18 x11 x$\frac{1}{4}$	457x279x6
From $\frac{1}{8}$in. (3.2mm) birch plywood:		
1 drawer bottom	$16\frac{1}{2}$x$10\frac{1}{8}$x$\frac{1}{8}$	429x257x3.2
From hardwood:		
2 feet	10 x $1\frac{1}{8}$x$\frac{5}{8}$	254x 28x16

You will also need:
Teak veneer edging strips. 1 pair $2\frac{1}{2}$in. (64mm) brass butt hinges. 1 2in. (51mm) brass box lock. Interior lining to fit. 1 10in. (254mm) brass chain. 48 $1\frac{1}{2}$in. (38mm) panel pins. Wood glue. Wood filler. Tenon saw. Jig saw. Hammer. Screwdriver. Chisel. Sandpaper. Clear matt polyurethane. Turpentine substitute. 1 2in. (51mm) brush. Grade O steel wool.

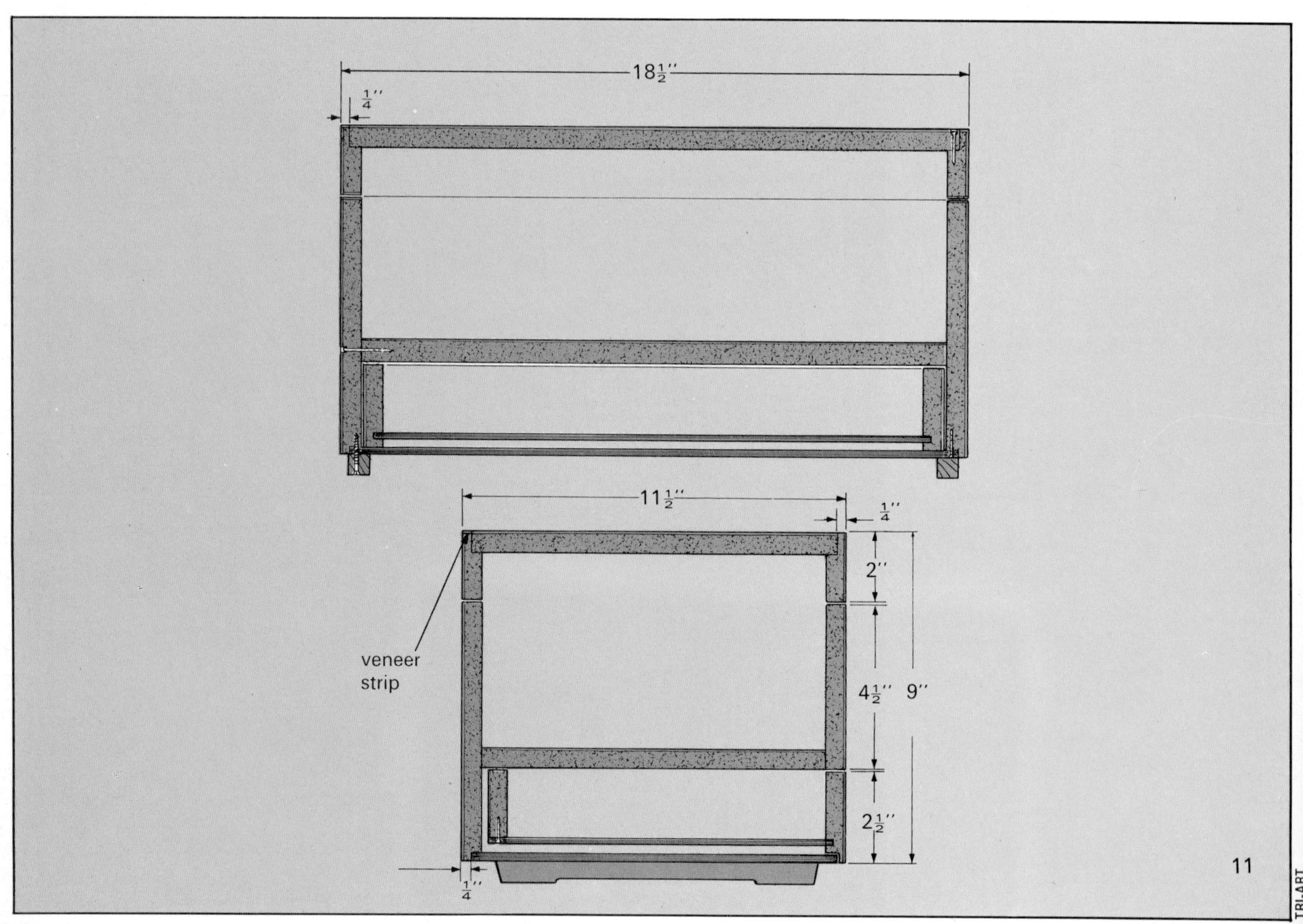

***Above.** This attractive vanity unit gives you ample storage space, a wide dressing table and mirror and a recessed wash basin. It will add a touch of luxury to any bedroom.*

Easy-to-build vanity unit

Add a flattering and up-to-date look to your bedroom with this easy to make vanity unit. Not only is it good looking and equipped with ample storage space, it has a great advantage over conventional dressing tables in that it incorporates a recessed wash basin.

Bedroom decorations and furnishings have undergone major changes in the last few years. Gone is the idea that bedrooms are only for sleeping in and need to be furnished with a bed only. Instead, bedrooms have become an integral part of the living area of a house and are now furnished and decorated accordingly.

This change has been brought about largely by the feeling that, with space at a premium nowadays, every room in the house should be used to the full. This does not necessarily mean altering the character of a room, but certainly demands more care when choosing furniture—especially bedroom furniture.

Apart from the bed itself, the most useful piece of furniture in the bedroom is a dressing table. But, even in modern homes equipped with wash basins in each bedroom, dressing tables tend to be of the heavy, old-fashioned type. Not only do these look out of place in a modern decor, they take up a lot of room and can only be used for storage.

A more satisfactory alternative is a vanity unit cum dressing table, built round a wash basin. Such a unit combines two functions in one compact and attractive structure. It provides ample storage space plus facilities for washing and applying make-up.

General construction and design

The vanity unit has been designed to match most bedroom decors and its construction is simple enough to allow some modification. The top and formers are constructed from blockboard, the rails from softwood, while the drawers are built of plywood. All exposed surfaces are laminated for easy cleaning. The two lower drawers are of the conventional sliding type, but the upper drawers swing open and shut on piano hinges.

Perhaps the only complication you may encounter is fitting the unit round a wash-basin. The wash-basin shown in the photograph on p. 133 is designed to be recessed into a vanity unit, and is supplied with a template to which the top of the unit should be cut. However, there is no reason why you should not incorporate a traditionally shaped wash-basin into the unit, provided you ensure that there is a waterproof seal between the basin and top.

Cutting list: Vanity unit

Wood	Imperial	Metric
1 blockboard top panel	61 x 20 x $\frac{1}{2}$	1549 x 508 x 13
4 blockboard formers	24 x 20 x $\frac{1}{2}$	610 x 508 x 13
2 softwood rear rails	61 x 3 x $\frac{5}{8}$	1549 x 75 x 16
1 softwood front rail	60 x 3 x $\frac{5}{8}$	154 x 75 x 16
2 plywood shelves	17 x 13 x $\frac{3}{8}$	432 x 330 x 10
1 plywood fascia	25 x 4 x $\frac{1}{2}$	635 x 102 x 13
2 softwood fascia securing blocks	$1\frac{7}{8}$ x $1\frac{7}{8}$ x $1\frac{7}{8}$	47 x 47 x 47
Fascia quadrant moulding	60 x $\frac{3}{8}$	1524 x 10
For the sliding drawers:		
2 plywood front panels	$16\frac{3}{4}$ x 9 x $\frac{1}{2}$	425 x 229 x 13
4 plywood sides	$17\frac{7}{8}$ x $7\frac{5}{8}$ x $\frac{3}{8}$	454 x 194 x 10
2 plywood backs	$16\frac{1}{4}$ x $7\frac{5}{8}$ x $\frac{3}{8}$	413 x 194 x 10
2 plywood bases	$16\frac{3}{4}$ x 18 x $\frac{1}{8}$	425 x 457 x 3
2 softwood battens	16 x $\frac{1}{2}$ x $\frac{1}{2}$	406 x 13 x 13
4 drawer runners	16 x 1 x 1	406 x 25 x 25
For the swing drawers:		
2 plywood front panels	$16\frac{3}{4}$ x $3\frac{3}{4}$ x $\frac{1}{2}$	425 x 95 x 13
2 plywood side panels	$16\frac{1}{2}$ x $3\frac{3}{4}$ x $\frac{3}{8}$	419 x 95 x 10
2 plywood side panels	28 x 4 x $\frac{1}{8}$	711 x 102 x 3
2 plywood base panels	$16\frac{3}{4}$ x $16\frac{3}{4}$ x $\frac{1}{4}$	425 x 425 x 6

You will also need:

8in. (203mm) piano type hinges. 2 drawer handles. Laminate, edge-trim and adhesive to cover all exposed surfaces. 24 $1\frac{3}{4}$in. (45mm) No 10 wood screws. 24 $1\frac{3}{4}$in. (45mm) No 6 woodscrews. Fibre Rawlplugs. Wood glue. $1\frac{1}{4}$in. (31mm) panel pins. Rip saw. Tenon saw. Jig saw. Handyman's knife. Block plane. Sandpaper. Large pair compasses.

Construction

Begin by cutting all the pieces for the carcase of the unit to the sizes given in the cutting list. Take the four formers and cut the angled cut-outs at the front lower corners of these pieces. as shown in Fig.3. Now take two of the formers and cut housings in their rear edges to take the two back rails. The exact positions of these housings are shown in Fig.3, which also gives their approximate dimensions. To find the exact dimensions, measure against the width and thickness of the rails, which, being of softwood, may vary slightly. These formers, when cut to shape, form the two outer uprights.

Like the outer formers, the intermediate formers are cut to receive the two rear rails. In addition, slots which are half the width and the same thickness as the front rail, are cut into the front edge of each of these pieces. Fig.3 shows the exact locations of these slots.

When you have cut the formers to shape, mark out their locations on the two rear rails. The end formers are fitted flush with the ends of the rails, the inside surfaces of the intermediate formers are located 18in. (457mm) from the ends of the rails, as shown in Fig.2. Having marked out these locations, fit the rear rails to the formers, using glue and $1\frac{3}{4}$in. (45mm) No. 6 wood screws.

Now take the front rail and, with a tenon saw, cut slots in it corresponding to those cut in the front edges of the intermediate formers. These slots are located 17in. (432mm) from the ends of the front rail, as shown in Fig.2. Trial assemble the rail to the formers, if necessary trim the slots to size, then secure with glue and screws. The front rail is fixed to the two end formers by No. 6 screws driven into the rail through the formers. As these screws go into end grain, a firmer fixing can be achieved by drilling holes in the ends of the rail to take fibre plugs such as Rawlplugs, glueing these into place to take the screws.

Shelving is fitted only at the base of the unit —the drawers rest on battens. Trial fit the two shelves in the positions indicated in Fig.1, and mark out the area of the front edge of each shelf which projects beyond the angled edges of the formers. Remove this section from the front edge of the shelves so that they match the angled edges of the formers. When you are satisfied that the shelves are the correct size, glue and screw them into position.

Add the battens which support the lower, sliding drawers. These are positioned so that their bottom long edges are 13in. (330mm) from the top edges of the formers. Fig.3 shows the distance by which each batten is set back from the front edges of the formers.

Place the unit right way up on a firm surface and place the top panel in position. Check that the edges of this piece are flush with the edges of the frame and, if necessary, trim it to size. If you possess a template for your wash basin, mark out the cut-out for the basin in the unit top. Cut the correct shape out with a jig-saw. If you do not have a template, you must devise your own from a piece of cardboard. Once you have sanded the edges of the cut-out, screw the top panel into place using countersunk $1\frac{3}{4}$ in. No. 6 wood screws.

Making the drawers

Make the two sliding drawers first. Take the front drawer panels and cut housings in them to receive the side panels. Each housing is $\frac{3}{8}$in. (10mm) wide, $7\frac{5}{8}$in. (194mm) long and is situated $\frac{3}{8}$in. (10mm) in from a short edge of the front panel. The rear ends of the side panels are housed in rebates cut in the short edges of the back panels. These rebates run the length of the short edges of the back panels, are $\frac{3}{16}$in. (5mm) deep and $\frac{3}{8}$in. (10mm) wide. Cut the rebates out with a rebate plane.

To assemble each drawer, first glue and screw the side panels into the housings on the front panel and the rebates on the back panel. Then add the base panel by pinning through it into the lower edges of the side and back panels. A reinforcing batten is then fixed to the base panel, flush against the rear surface of the front panel.

Try the drawers in place, having first waxed the drawer runners. The top edge of the front panel should almost touch the bottom of the front rail. Slide the drawer shut until the outer edge of the front panel is flush with the front edges of the formers, then mark the position of the edge of the back panel on the runners, and fix drawer stops at these two points.

Making the swing drawers

Rebates are cut in the short ends of the front panels to house the side panels. One of these rebates is $\frac{3}{8}$in. (10mm) wide and $\frac{1}{4}$in. (6mm) deep, the other is $\frac{1}{4}$in. (6mm) deep but only $\frac{1}{8}$in. (3.2mm) wide.

To cut the base of each swing drawer to the shape shown in Fig.7, take a panel of $\frac{1}{4}$in. (6mm) plywood measuring $16\frac{3}{4}$in. x $16\frac{3}{4}$in. (425mm x 425mm), place the point of a large pair of compasses (set at $16\frac{3}{4}$in. or 425mm), on one corner of the panel, and trace an arc out on the panel. Cut along this line.

Assemble the drawer in the following order of procedure:

Glue and pin the $\frac{3}{8}$in. side panel into the appropriate rebate, then add the base panel. Finally, fix the $\frac{1}{8}$in. (3.2mm) curved side by first glueing and pinning it into the appropriate rebate, then pinning it to the base at 1in. intervals, bending the panel as you pin. Try the two swing drawers for size, add handles of your choice, and hinge the drawers to the inner surface of the end formers, using piano type hinges.

Fixing the fascia

The gap between the intermediate formers, the top panel and the front rail is covered by a fascia panel. This panel, cut to the size given in the cutting list, is secured to $1\frac{7}{8}$in. (48mm) square softwood blocks, which are themselves

Fig.1. *A face-on view of the vanity unit.*
Fig.2. *The top, bottom and front rails.*
Fig.3. *The shape and dimensions of the inner and outer vertical panels of the unit.*

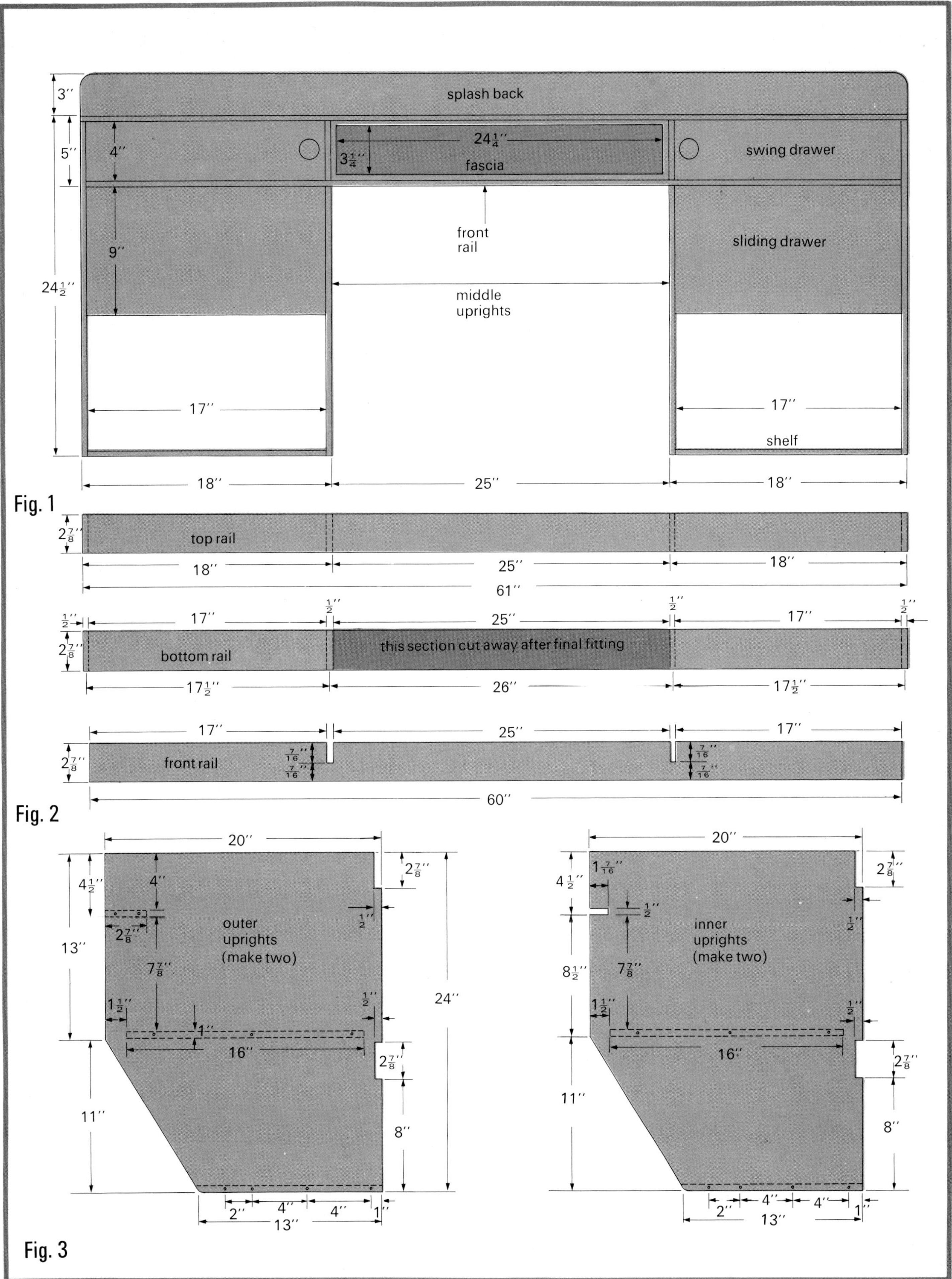

splash back
swing drawer
fascia
front rail
sliding drawer
middle uprights
shelf
Fig. 1
top rail
bottom rail
this section cut away after final fitting
front rail
Fig. 2
outer uprights (make two)
inner uprights (make two)
Fig. 3
TRI-ART

fixed to the front rail, as shown in Fig.4. $\frac{3}{8}$in. (10mm) quadrant moulding hides the joints between the top panel, front rail and fascia, but these pieces are not added until the fascia panel has been laminated.

Laminating the unit

All exposed surfaces and edges of the unit are covered with a suitable laminate, such as formica. You will need large sheets to cover the top, drawer fronts and formers, but edges can be trimmed with ready-made edging strips.

A DIY magazine will give you needed information on how to cut and apply the laminate; your task will be simplified if you bear the following points in mind.

1. Always cut the laminate slightly oversize, so that it overlaps the edges of the surface that it covers by about $\frac{1}{16}$in. (1.6mm).
2. To cut laminates, use a handyman's knife to score along the lines and finish the cut with a sharp, fine-toothed veneer saw or jig saw.
3. When cutting irregular shapes, such as the cut-out for the basin, first apply the laminate to the unit top, then cut out the desired shape from underneath, leaving a small margin which can be trimmed later.
4. Impact adhesives bond laminate and surface together almost immediately, thus obviating the need for cramps. The drawback with adhesives of this type is that once you have applied the laminate you cannot easily remove it, if, for example, it is wrongly positioned.

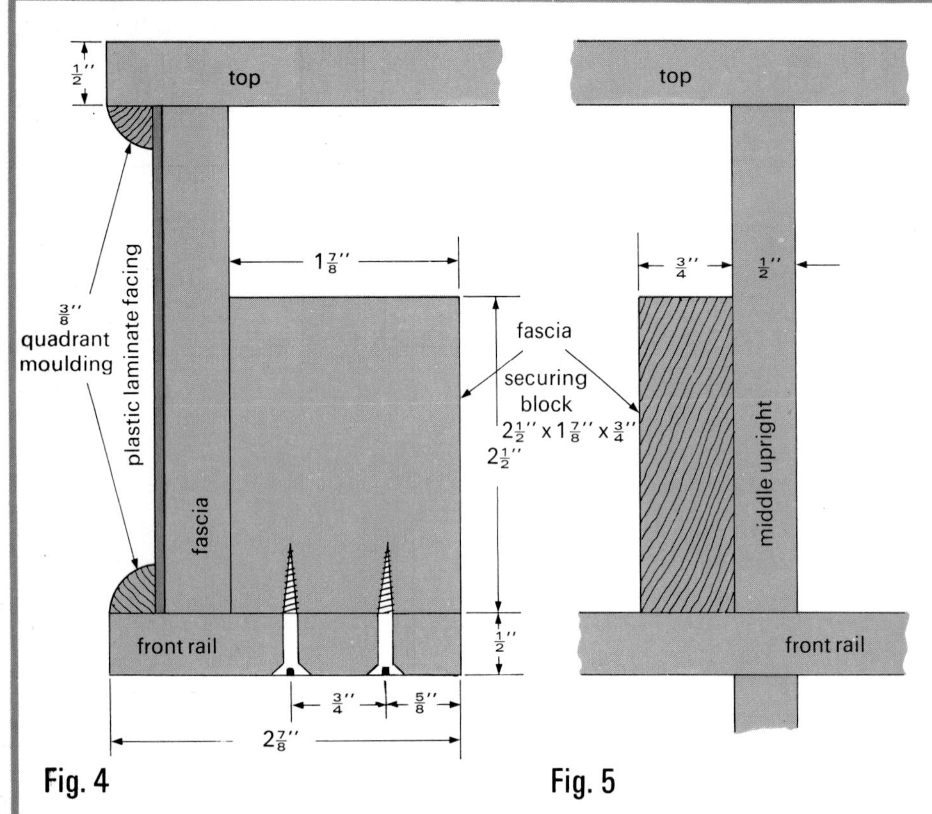

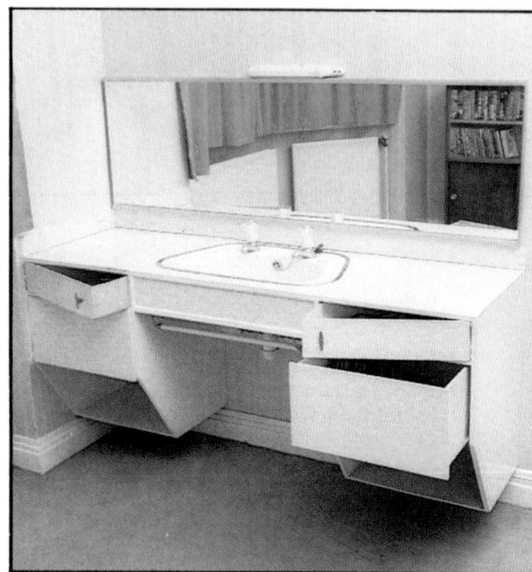

Above. *A view of the unit showing the two sets of drawers. The top drawers swing outwards on piano hinges.*

Fig. 6

61''
2'' 4 1/2'' 6'' 6'' 6'' 12'' 6'' 6'' 6'' 4 1/2'' 2''
20''
2'' 4'' 4'' 4'' 4'' 2''
17'' 25'' 17''
1/2'' 1/2'' 1/2'' 1/2''

TRI-ART

5. Work in strict order. You will find it easier to apply edging strips first and add larger sheets once these have been trimmed.
6. To apply large laminate sheets, smear the bonding surfaces with adhesive, place battens at intervals on the surface to be laminated, then press the laminate into place, starting at one end and working along the surface, removing the battens as you go.

Wall-fixing the unit

As well as fixing the unit to the wall, you must locate the wash-basin in the unit top. Unless you wish to change the location of the basin, this will only entail turning off the hot and cold water supplies, draining the pipes, unscrewing the tap and drainage pipe fittings, then fitting the basin and re-connecting the water supply.

If the basin has to be re-located, you will have to extend or shorten the existing pipework. This involves cutting and fitting pipes—an important job to take time with to get technically right. You may also have to knock through an outside wall to fit a new drainage pipe, and of course, a new drainage channel or soakaway. Because of the extra work that this involves, you are advised to fit the unit so that there is no need to re-locate the basin, provided, of course, that this is feasible.

Remove the basin and mark out the proposed location of the unit on the wall and the positions of the screws used to fix the unit to the wall. Drill for 1¾in. (45mm) No.10 wood screws, plug the holes with fibre screw plugs, then drive home the screws through the rear rails into the plugs. As additional support, you can fix 1in. x 1in. (25mm x 25mm) battens under the lower rear edge of the unit.

Once you are satisfied that the unit is properly secured to the wall, fit the basin. If this is specially designed to be recessed into a surface, follow the maker's instructions for fitting it and sealing the joint between basin and top. If, on the other hand, you are fitting a traditional porcelain basin, which has no rim or flange, simply place it in position and seal the joint between basin and top with a non-setting, waterproof sealing compound.

The area of wall immediately behind the unit should be covered with a splash-proof surface of some kind. A length of softwood covered in laminate would be adequate, or you could apply one or two courses of ceramic tiles, using the methods described in a DIY manual.

Obviously, a vanity unit should be equipped with a mirror. You could choose a long mirror like the one shown in the photograph or a smaller, square mirror and use the rest of the space above the unit for storing toiletries. Whatever style you choose, the vanity unit will greatly enhance your bedroom.

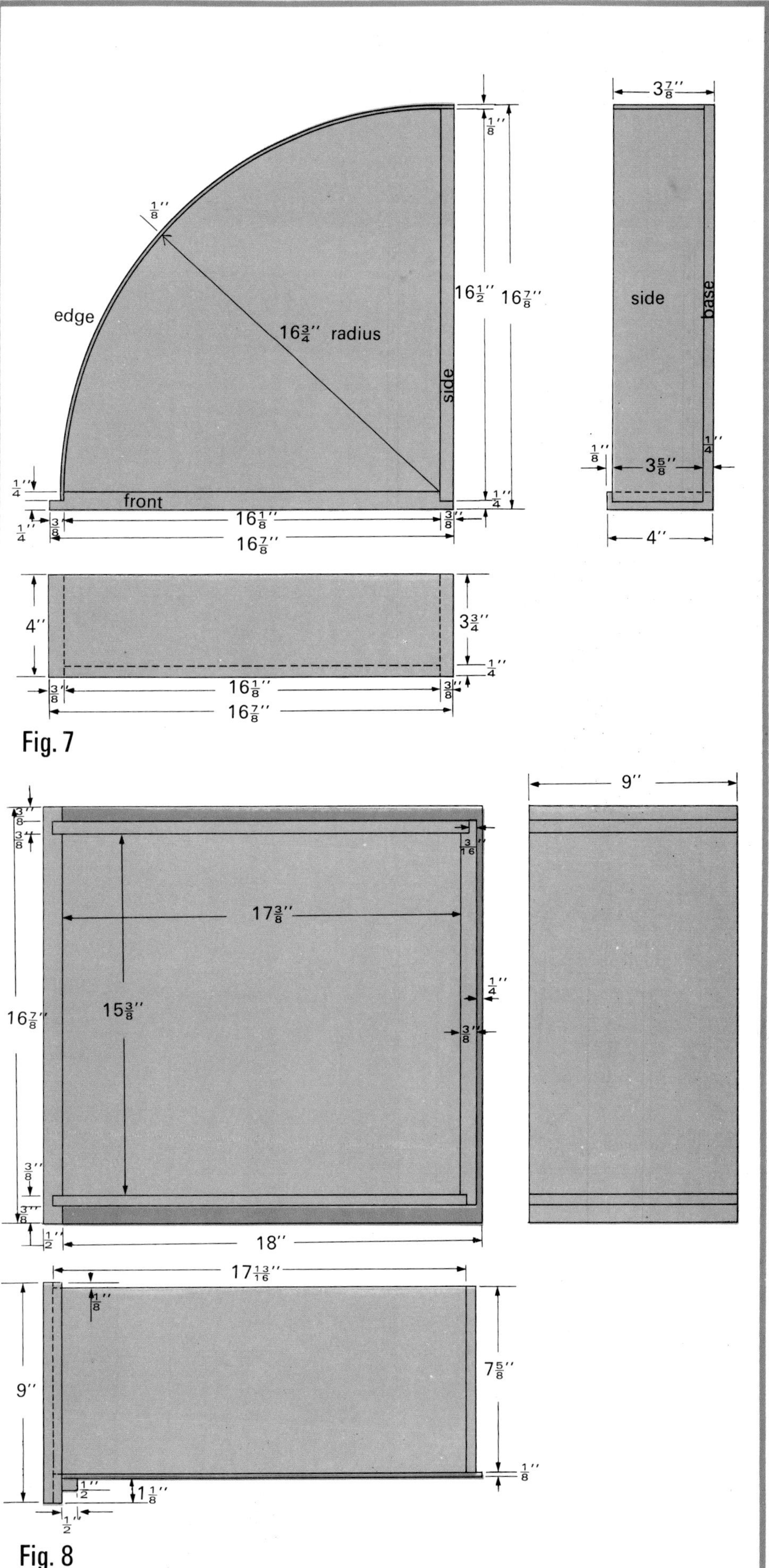

Fig.4. A cross-section through the top area of the vanity unit.
Fig.5. The view in Fig.4 turned round through 45°. The fascia has been removed.
Fig.6. A plan view of the unit top.
Fig.7. The upper drawers of the unit swing out on piano hinges. The dimensions and shape of these components are shown here.
Fig.8. One of the lower set of drawers with all the dimensions.

A modern four-poster bed: 1

The four-poster bed is the aristocrat of bedroom furniture. It has the flavour of history and an element of prestige. Unfortunately, four-poster beds are not sold by most furniture shops. Where they are, only traditional designs are available and these are expensive. This article describes how to make a four-poster of modern design that doesn't cost the earth. If you prefer, you could provide a traditional touch by adding curtains.

This is a two-part project. The first part deals with the carpentry involved in making the frame. The second part deals with the finishing, by covering the side and end panels with felt, the making of a bedspread, and the provision for curtains if you want to fit them.

Construction

This bed consists of four upright wooden posts of red deal—you could use another timber if you wish—supported and kept vertical by eight panels, four at the base and four at the top.

The panels are of plywood, and at the base, butting to the floor, there are two side panels and one foot board. The panel at the head end is raised to provide support and to act as a headboard.

The four panels or fascia running round the tops of the uprights provide rigidity for this part of the structure, but are also used for decoration. They can be painted, covered with fabric, or fitted with a curtain rail.

Plywood rarely has an attractive surface, and the end grain or cut edges look unsightly. For this bed, therefore, the plywood panels have been covered with felt, but you could use some other material, or paint. If you prefer a natural wood finish, then the plywood would have to be replaced with $\frac{3}{4}$in. or 19mm solid wood planking, but this would be much more expensive. If you do decide to do this, then each base panel will be replaced with four solid planks as wide as the panels they replace. The solid planks can be glued and cramped together—and great care should be taken—to form solid panels, or left as individual planks. The main advantage of the former method is that it prevents the planks from buckling out of line.

Support battening is fixed all round the upper inside edges of the base side panels. This provides support for the slats, which in turn makes the frame more rigid and provides the support area for the mattress. These slats are part of the structural design, and should not be replaced with something less rigid such as web springing.

Materials

The uprights are of red deal. Any other suitable timber can be used, but in any case the timber for the uprights should be ordered 'dressed'; this ensures that the timber will arrive with a good surface finish. This is essential because, in this design, the uprights are the only part of the woodwork that is visible.

The rest of the solid timber can be of a cheaper wood. This consists of the slat supports and edge battens, which are of 2in. x 2in. (75mm x 75mm) timbers, and the slats, which are 6in. x 1in. (150mm x 25mm).

All the panels are cut from $\frac{1}{2}$in. (13mm) plywood, but if you want to replace these with solid wood planking, then this should be of $\frac{3}{4}$in. (19mm) timber, because solid timber is more likely to warp than plywood. All the plywood panels can be cut from three large sheets of plywood, as shown in Figs.1-3.

Where screw heads are visible, then brass screws with screw cups are used, but where screw heads are not visible, ordinary steel screws with countersunk heads are just as good, and cheaper.

Cutting the panels

All the $\frac{1}{2}$in. (13mm) thick plywood panels can be cut from three large sheets of plywood, and the cutting plan for this is as described. This will avoid the cost of having to pay for the panels to be cut to specific sizes. But this only applies if you have done some carpentry and have access to a bench power saw. Cutting long, straight lines in wood is no job for the inexperienced carpenter. So if you have never done this sort of work, order the plywood already cut into eight individual panels according to the dimensions shown in Figs.1-3.

First prepare the two base side panels. Each panel has two recesses cut in one end, as shown in Fig.4. The recesses shown are $5\frac{1}{4}$in. (133mm) wide and $3\frac{1}{4}$in. (78mm) deep. Mark out the outline of the recesses, using a try square to ensure that all lines are straight, then cut out the recesses with a fine toothed saw. When you have finished, you will have two identical panels like the one shown in Fig.8.

Next cut the recesses in the foot board. These recesses are identical to those cut in the side panels, but in this case they are cut in each end of the foot board. When you have done this, stand one of the side panels on edge, in the position shown in Fig.8. Do the same with the foot board, as in Fig.9, and then jig-saw the two together, so that the protruding parts of one panel slide into the recesses in the opposite panel. Now add the remaining side panel to the opposite end of the foot board in the same way.

Fix the two $75\frac{1}{2}$in. battens to the side frames, $2\frac{1}{2}$in. (63mm) down from the edge of each inside face, and the 51in. batten in the same position on the foot board. Figs.8 and 9 show the battens in position.

Mark and cut the two recesses in each bottom corner of the headboard. Each recess is $3\frac{1}{4}$in. wide and $4\frac{1}{4}$in. deep (82mm x 107mm), as shown in Fig.5. Glue and screw a $55\frac{1}{2}$in. batten along the top of one side of the headboard, and a 51in. length along the opposite side, at the bottom. Figs.6 and 7 show these in place.

Fix one length of $76\frac{1}{2}$in. battening along one side of each of the top side panels. The batten should be flush with one edge, and centrally placed so that there is a space of $2\frac{3}{4}$in. (60mm) between each end of the batten and the ends of the panel, the same as with the back of the headrest. Repeat this with the top end panels and the $55\frac{1}{2}$in. battens.

Assembling the main frame

You are now ready for a dry run, to check that everything fits, and to mark and fit the slats. Do not apply glue to any of the joints at this stage and don't drive the screws in too tightly. This is because each panel will have to be removed, covered with felt, and replaced before the slats are finally screwed in place and the bed is ready.

Assemble the two base side panels and the foot rest so that the three panels are free-standing.

Where the panels interlock, the ends will protrude, forming a 'V' at each corner. Stand an upright in one of these, so that panel ends overlap two sides of the upright, then screw them together, through the panelling into the upright. Repeat this at the other end. The uprights for the foot end are now in position.

Now fit the uprights at the head end. Stand an upright at the outside end of a side panel, in exactly the same position as the upright at the opposite end. Screw this in position through the inside of the panel. Repeat this procedure with the remaining upright on the opposite panel. Stand the headboard in position on the edges of the side panels, backing on to the up-

Cutting list

Solid wood	imperial	metric
4 uprights	84 x 3 x 3	2134 x 75 x 75
11 slats	$54\frac{1}{2}$ x 6 x 1	1385 x 150 x 25
2 slat supports	$75\frac{1}{2}$ x 2 x 2	1918 x 50 x 50
2 edge battens	51 x 2 x 2	1295 x 50 x 50
3 edge battens	$55\frac{1}{2}$ x 2 x 2	1410 x 50 x 50
2 edge battens	$76\frac{1}{2}$ x 2 x 2	1943 x 50 x 50
Plywood		
2 basic side panels	82 x 21 x $\frac{1}{2}$	2083 x 533 x 13
1 foot panel	61 x 21 x $\frac{1}{2}$	1549 x 533 x 13
1 headboard panel	61 x 27 x $\frac{1}{2}$	1549 x 686 x 13
2 top side panels	82 x 12 x $\frac{1}{2}$	2083 x 305 x 13
2 top end panels	62 x 12 x $\frac{1}{2}$	1575 x 305 x 13

All imperial measurements are in inches, and all metric measurements are in millimetres.
You will also require brass screws, with cups, for the visible screw heads. Ordinary countersunk head steel screws can be used for screws that are not visible, such as the securing screws for the slats. A good woodworking adhesive will ensure firmer joints and a better finish.

***Left.** This attractive four-poster bed is a modern version of the traditional design. Here the side drapes or curtains have been omitted, but these can be added if required.*

rights, and screw it to the uprights through the front of the headboard.

The base frame is now assembled, and you can check the various panels for fit. You can also check the top frame. It isn't necessary to assemble this, it should be sufficient to hold each panel up (you'll need help) to check that it fits.

Mark, cut and fit the slats. Do this by direct marking, and as you cut and fit each one, number it on the slat and the butting batten, so that each slat will be fixed in the right place when you assemble permanently. Don't screw the slats in place—it is only necessary to drop each one into position to see that it fits.

Carefully dismantle the unit. In the next chapter the panels are covered with felt, the bed assembled permanently, a bedspread made to fit, and, if required, curtain rails fixed around the inside of the top frame.

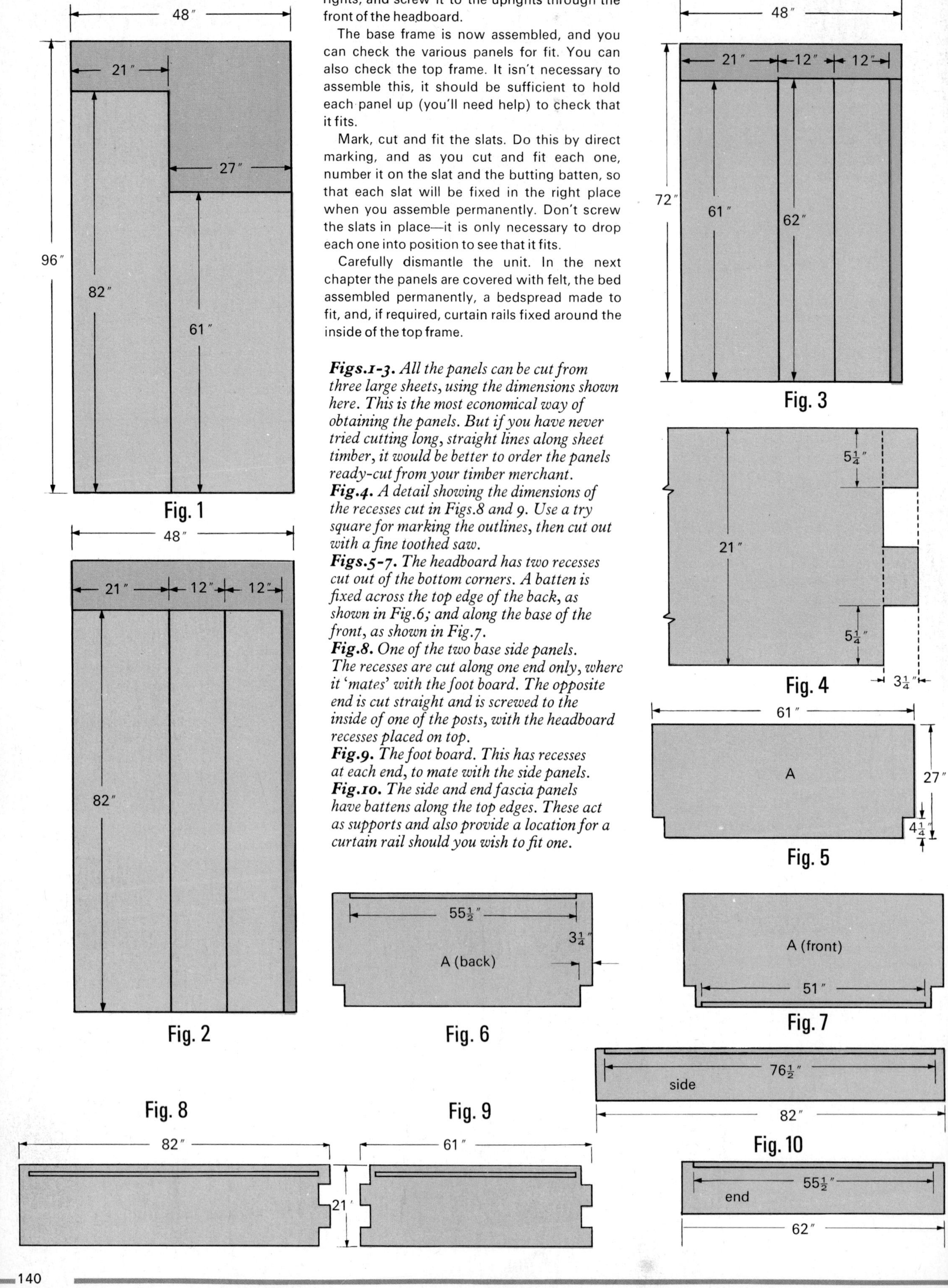

Figs.1-3. *All the panels can be cut from three large sheets, using the dimensions shown here. This is the most economical way of obtaining the panels. But if you have never tried cutting long, straight lines along sheet timber, it would be better to order the panels ready-cut from your timber merchant.*
Fig.4. *A detail showing the dimensions of the recesses cut in Figs.8 and 9. Use a try square for marking the outlines, then cut out with a fine toothed saw.*
Figs.5-7. *The headboard has two recesses cut out of the bottom corners. A batten is fixed across the top edge of the back, as shown in Fig.6; and along the base of the front, as shown in Fig.7.*
Fig.8. *One of the two base side panels. The recesses are cut along one end only, where it 'mates' with the foot board. The opposite end is cut straight and is screwed to the inside of one of the posts, with the headboard recesses placed on top.*
Fig.9. *The foot board. This has recesses at each end, to mate with the side panels.*
Fig.10. *The side and end fascia panels have battens along the top edges. These act as supports and also provide a location for a curtain rail should you wish to fit one.*

NIGEL MESSETT

A modern four-poster bed: 2

With all the components of the bed frame cut out and checked for fit, as described in the first chapter, the next stage involves glueing material—in this case felt—over the visible surface of the upper and lower panels and the headboard, before the unit is permanently assembled.

When selecting the material to cover the panels, bear in mind that the colour, and pattern if any, should be chosen to match or harmonize not only with the eventual bedspread, but also the bedroom decor.

Covering the panels

These panels are covered with felt, but any suitable material can be used. You will require 21ft or 6.40m of material, 72in. or 1.83m in width, and about a pint of fabric adhesive such as Copydex.

Although the top panels are covered all round, it is not necessary to completely cover both sides of the base and headboard panels, only the surfaces that are visible. The procedure for covering each particular panel is shown in Fig.1.

When sticking the felt in position, spread the adhesive evenly and not too thickly, in particular making sure that the edges are well covered. Stick one edge of felt down first, then work out from the centre, towards the opposite edge, stretching the felt slightly as you go to prevent creases forming.

For the fascia—that is, all four top panels—start sticking the fabric along the top edge of the batten (see Fig.1-A), then stretch the material down the outside face of the panel, round the bottom edge, up along the rear or inside face, and round the three visible surfaces of the

***Left.** The finished bed and bedspread. The design is based on a traditional pattern, but this particular unit is decidedly modern in appearance. For a slightly more 'historical' touch, drapes can be fixed to a curtain rail running round the battening attached to the inside of the fascia. This produces an effect similar to that on the opposite page.*

LEO FERRANTE

batten, finishing along the top of the batten, butting the felt at the point where you started. In this way the join will be at the extreme top of the fascia, out of sight.

For the side frames and footboard (see Fig.1-B), start at the back of the panel where the support batten butts against the panel. Stretch the felt over the top of the panel, down the outside surface, under the bottom edge, and a few inches up the inside surface. At the ends (Fig.1-D), the felt is folded over, and along the back for about 4in. or 100mm. When this has been done, cut away the recessed parts with a sharp knife or pair of scissors, and fold across.

The headboard is covered by starting at the batten-headboard join at the bottom of the front, stretching the felt up over the top edge, and round the three visible surfaces of the top batten at the rear.

Finishing the posts

Rub all post surfaces down to a smooth finish with glasspaper. Follow this with a soft cloth dampened with turpentine substitute wiping all surfaces so that the fine dust caused by sanding is picked up.

With a good quality 2in. or 50mm brush, sparingly apply a varnish of clear matt polyurethane and turpentine substitute blended 50/50.

When dry, rub down with fine glasspaper. Wipe the surface with the cloth again, re-coat with the same mixture and, when dry, polish with grade O steel wool. Clean the surface with turpentine substitute, leave overnight, then finish with a coat of neat polyurethane.

Making the bedspread

You will need 15ft or 4.57m of material, 48in. or 1.22m in width, to make the bedspread.

First calculate the amount of fabric you will require. For the width, measure from the bottom of the mattress on one side, up and across the bed, to the bottom of the mattress on the opposite side. For the length, repeat this but start at the bottom of one end of the mattress, with the pillows in place.

Because furnishing fabrics are never wider than 52in. or 1.52m, you will need to join two fabric widths, so you will have to double the length measurement to calculate how many

BAVARIA-VERLAG

***Fig. 1.** The felt should be stuck to the various panels in the proper sequence to avoid waste and ugly seams. A, shows the procedure for fascia panels. B and D, for side frames and footboard. C, for the headboard.*

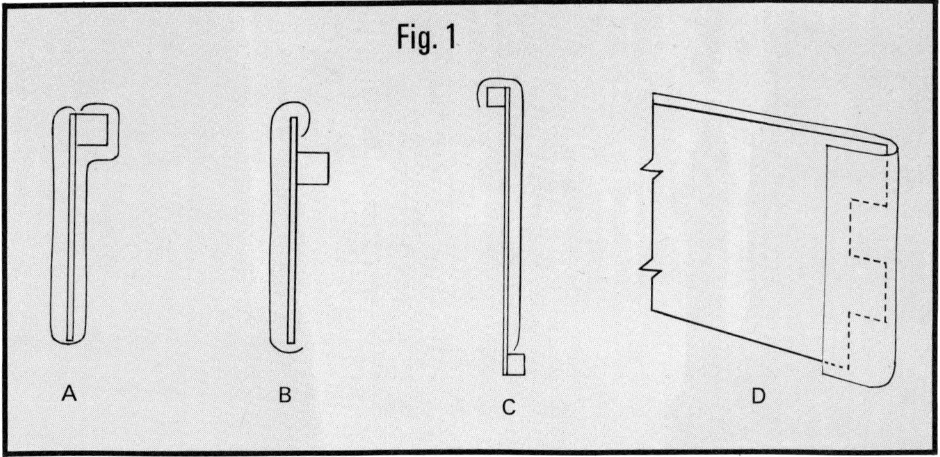

yards you will need.

If the fabric has a large design or motif, add about 3ft or 1m to the estimate to enable you to match the pattern at the seams.

To avoid having an ugly seam down the centre of the bedspread, cut the fabric across into two equal lengths and then cut one of these pieces in half lengthwise, thus making one full width of fabric for the centre panel and two half widths for the sides.

If your double bedspread is to be narrower, cut off the excess equally from each half width (take it from the raw edges rather than the selvedges if this does not affect the matching of the patterns on the seams). If the fabric is plain, the excess can be taken from one side of the centre panel, but if the pattern runs centrally down the fabric, divide the excess and take off an equal amount from each side.

Joining the panels

To join the pieces, place the 'right' sides of the fabric together, selvedge to selvedge. Make sure the pattern is matched and the fabric runs the same way on each panel. Pin and tack about ½in. or 13mm from the edge (more if the selvedges are wide). If you allowed extra on the length to match the pattern, cut off the excess fabric now (remember to allow 1in. or 25mm at top and bottom for hems).

Machine stitch the seams, using a medium length stitch, following the tacking line. Remove the tacking. Clip (cut into) the selvedges at intervals if they are tight (this helps the seam to lie flat), and press the seams open. Neaten the raw edges by oversewing by hand or overcasting by machine.

Square the corners

Make ¾in. or 19mm hems down the long sides of the bedspread. To do this fold over the raw edge ¼in. or 6mm on to the wrong side of the fabric. Make a second fold ¾in. deep, so the raw edge is now enclosed. Tack and machine stitch through three thicknesses, along the first fold. Remove the tacking and press the hems. Turn under ¾in. hems at the top and bottom, making the corners square. Tack and machine stitch them, taking the line of machining over the machined line of the side hems to finish it off. Remove the tacking and press the hems, and then press the finished bedspread all over.

When you have finished, you will have a bed that is traditional, yet modern in design, that will be the envy of all your friends.

Here are some modern examples of four-poster beds. They might have some features that you would like to incorporate in this project.
***Left.** This bed has metal posts, but one design point to note is the scalloped fascia.*
***Right.** In this version net drapes have been added, giving a light, airy effect. The gate-type head and foot boards could not be incorporated in the design outlined here without weakening the structure.*

CONWAY PICTURE LIBRARY

Cantilevered bedhead: 1

This elegant built-in bedhead unit has all the storage space a husband and wife are likely to need—and packs it into a surprisingly small area. The wife's side also contains a small dressing table with a folding mirror and generous space for cosmetics. For those with a double bed in a small room, where a separate dressing table will often not fit in beside the bed, a combined unit may be the only answer.

The unit is supported entirely by wall mountings, leaving a clear space underneath that allows the floor to be easily cleaned. It stands clear of the bed at both sides, which simplifies bed-making. The padded pvc centre section acts as a comfortable headrest for reading or eating breakfast in bed.

The two side boxes look similar when all the doors or drawers are shut, but in fact they have been designed to suit the individual needs of a husband and wife. The man's side has two drawers and a useful shallow cupboard with a drop-down lid that doubles as an extra shelf. The cupboard faces towards the bed, so that anything he may need during the night is ready to hand.

There is also a small bookshelf that holds books up to 9in. (230mm) tall, surmounted by a shallower shelf for small objects that might otherwise get lost. An alarm clock or radio is just the right size to fit on the top surface above this shelf.

The woman's side has the same drawers, shelves and surfaces. But instead of the cupboard there is a make-up drawer divided into two compartments, one for flat compacts and jars and the other for tall bottles. A folding mirror forms a lid for the drawer. When it is raised, it is at the right height and angle to act as a dressing-table mirror. A cut-out kneehole beneath the drawer allows even a tall woman to sit on the edge of the bed, with the drawer pulled out, and look into the mirror.

The design given here has the man's side on the left (seen from the foot of the bed) and the woman's on the right. But those who already have a dressing-table, and plenty of room for it, may prefer to build the unit with two cupboards.

Details of construction

The main carcase of the unit is held together by pva glue and panel pins, except where otherwise shown in Part 2. The pins should be sunk below the surface with a nail punch and the holes filled with a woodfiller such as Brummer stopping.

If you want to make the unit stronger, you can fasten it together with screws, which should be hidden in a counter bored hole and covered with a wooden plug. A plug cutter and 'screw-sink' are two items needed for this type of construction.

Other joints used are housing, stopped housing and mortice-and-tenon joints. An alternative to the last of these is to use through dowelled joints, which are less trouble to make.

Some rebates must also be made. If you do not have a rebate plane, they can be made with saw and chisel.

Materials needed

All the outer surfaces of this unit are made of veneered chipboard, an inexpensive material that looks exactly like solid hardwood when the unit is made up. The inside parts are made of Gaboon ply, birch ply and ramin or any other easily-available hardwood.

See page 148 for the list of wood parts needed for building the unit.

In addition to the wooden parts, you will also need a piece of 1in. thick foam wadding 6ft 6in. × 27in. or 2m × 700mm, and some pvc sheeting – choose 'cirrus' or some similar leather-grained material. Buy 7ft of sheeting in the narrowest width you can get, because you need a piece roughly 7ft × 1ft. The mirror should be a lightweight glass (not plastic) one 14in. (355mm) by $11\frac{15}{16}$in. (300mm). Get the glazier to cut it to size for you and finish the edges.

Other materials needed are five sunken drawer handles, three ball catches for the cupboard doors, a pair of hidden hinges, three 12in. (305mm) lengths of piano hinge and a small drop stay. The veneered cupboard should be edged with iron-on veneer edging strip, available in rolls. Accessories needed are some $1\frac{1}{2}$in. (38mm) 12 gauge panel pins, an assortment of screws and some eggshell polyurethane varnish for finishing the unit.

Tools for the job

No unusual tools are needed for this job, though if you have a *router* and *plough* and *rebate planes*, you will find the housing and rebate joints used throughout this unit a lot easier to make. It is, however, quite possible to get by with an ordinary plane and chisels. You will need:

Panel saw with 9 or 12 points to the inch
Tenon saw
Marking knife

DON KIDMAN/NELSON HARGREAVES

Try square
Marking gauge
Wheelbrace and bits
Pin hammer ($3\frac{1}{2}$oz) or a lightweight Warrington hammer
Nail punch
Rule
Chisels
Smoothing plane
Screwdriver

First stages

Select the timber for the unit with care, not only for the outer veneered parts, but also for the parts of the frame and the drawers. The smooth working of the sliding parts depends largely on getting fault-free, unwarped wood. The veneer

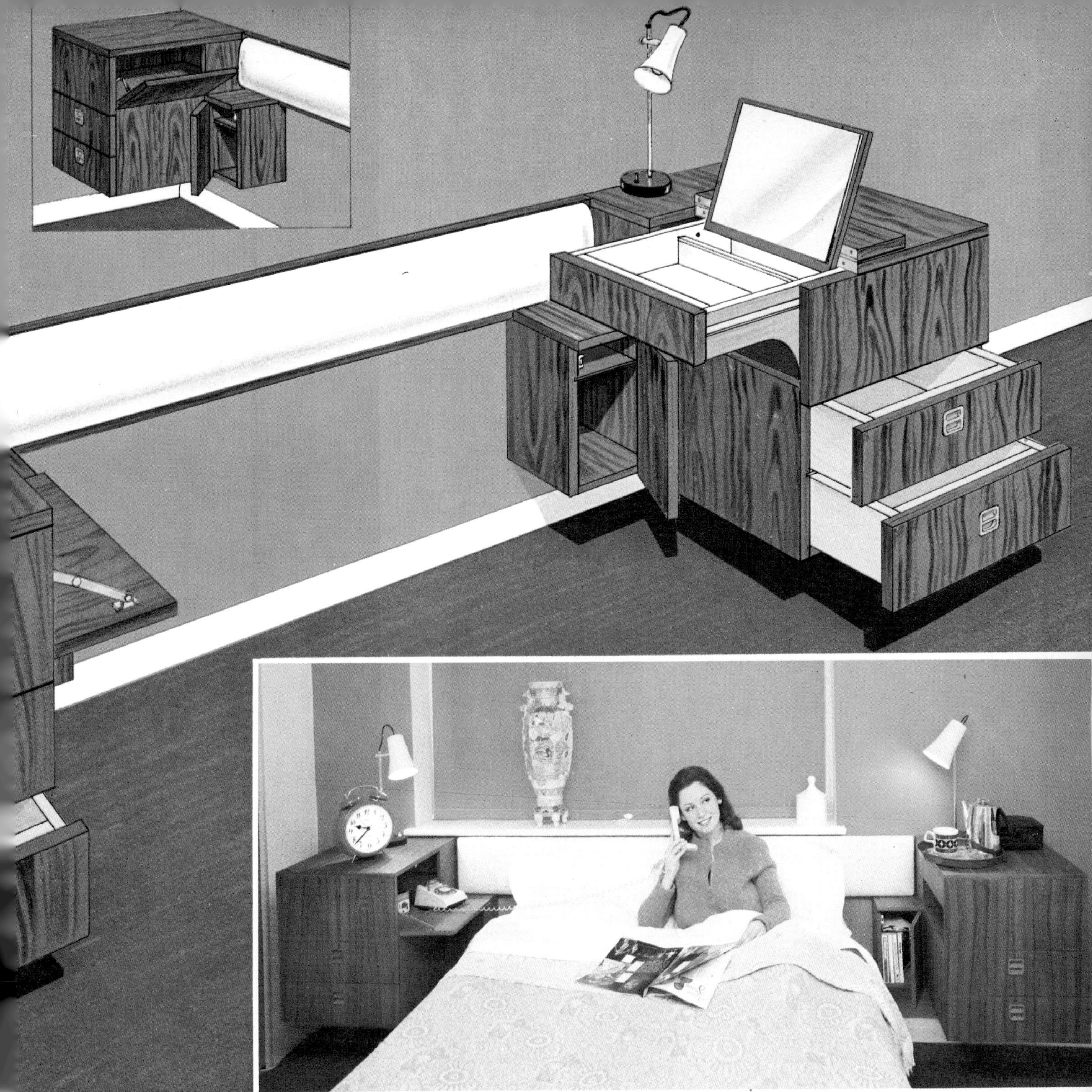

on the chipboard should be without blemishes, and the edges free from nicks or splits. Examine the pvc sheeting carefully too, to make sure there are no manufacturing marks on its 7ft length.

Mark out the timber in the usual way, paying particular attention to the accuracy of the parts of the drawers and their surrounds. When marking out the veneered chipboard, remember to allow for the thickness of the edging veneer that will later cover up the exposed edges.

Veneered chipboard is tricky stuff to cut. It is easy to tear pieces out of the edge by sawing too fast, or to start cutting off the marked line. The secret is to work slowly. It will save time in the long run. Any slight irregularities in the cutting can be smoothed out with a plane, but its edge must be set extremely fine to keep it from chewing up the board. A shooting board is useful for keeping the cut edge square when you are planing it. If you are not using a shooting board, plane from each end of the board to the middle as if planing the end grain of a piece of solid timber.

Making the joints

The housing joints used in this unit are cut by making the cross cuts with a tenon saw and chiselling out. A router, if you have one, makes it even easier.

Saw cuts for housing joints and rebates are difficult to make accurately across wide pieces of wood, because the saw blade tends to slide sideways when starting the cut. Make a groove

Above. *Neat built-in furniture like this helps you to make the most of your rooms. This bedhead not only creates a lot of much-needed space in a small room, but takes the strain off your cupboards by providing storage room for everything you need near your bed. The unique foldaway dressing-table will be a real boon to wives in a hurry, while the drop-down lid of the small cupboard on the other side becomes a shelf to hold a telephone or notepad. The lid of the cupboard shown here has a special 'touch latch' that allows you to open and shut it merely by pressing it, but a conventional handle and latch can be installed as an alternative if you prefer it.*

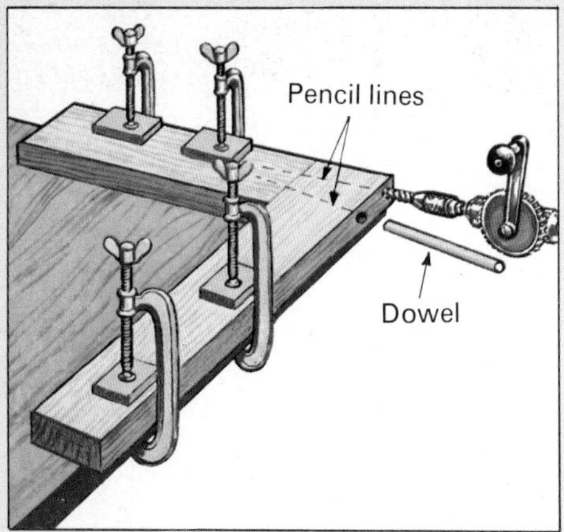

Above. *Dowelled joints are strong and simple to make. Points to watch are that the wood is firmly clamped in place during drilling, and that the drilled holes are at an angle to each other for strength.*

to guide the saw by marking the shoulder line deeply with a marking knife. Run the knife along the rule three or four times to make the cut deep enough. Then, without taking away the rule, run a chisel along the waste side of the line with its blade at an angle, so that it enlarges the cut to a V-shaped groove on the waste side only. This groove will guide the saw.

The normal way of making the stopped housing joints is to chisel out a small rectangle of wood from the stopped end of the cutout and finish the cut with very short strokes of the tenon saw, poking the end of the blade into the chiselled-out rectangle. Then the rest of the wood can be taken out with a router or chisel.

The hardwood back and base frames need to be strongly made. They can be fitted together with mortice-and-tenon joints, probably the strongest way of making them.

Through dowelled joints are nearly as strong, however, and much quicker and less demanding to make. For these, cut the timber to exact length, as if you were going to make a butt joint. Then glue the edges together and cramp the pieces together in position on a board or the corner of the workbench. Now take a $\frac{3}{8}$in. or 10mm drill (whichever matches the dowel size) and drill two holes through the edge of one piece into the end of the other. The holes should be at a slight slant, converging on each other as they get deeper, to give the joint a dovetail effect that will strengthen it (see Fig. **1**). Mark the direction and length of the holes in pencil on the top face of the wood and cut two lengths of dowel slightly longer than the holes. Run a plane lightly down the side of each dowel to make a small chamfer. This will let the air out when the dowel is forced into the hole. Fill the holes with glue and gently tap the dowels home with a mallet, or side of the hammer.

When you have wiped all the excess glue off the joints, cramp the whole frame together with sash cramps and make sure that it is dead square. Then tap panel pins into the dowels, following the pencilled lines. This will trap the dowels firmly in place, so you can take the cramps off and use them for the next frame. Leave the frames to dry thoroughly overnight before trimming the dowels.

Wood parts lists

Veneered high-density chipboard
(first dimension given is direction of grain)

Quantity	Size	Board Size	Description
4	18″×6″	6″	Drawer fronts
2	18″×9″	9″	Fascias above drawers
2	18″×21″	21″	Unit tops
1	4″×14$\frac{1}{2}$″	15″	Unit top flap R/H
4	21″×20$\frac{3}{8}$″	21″	Sides of main units
1	4″×13$\frac{5}{8}$″	15″	Vanity drawer front
1	8$\frac{3}{8}$″×13$\frac{5}{8}$″		Drop cupboard door L/H
2	16$\frac{3}{4}$″×14$\frac{1}{4}$″	30″	Main horizontal shelf
2	12$\frac{5}{8}$″×6$\frac{5}{8}$″		Backs of small cupboards
2	12″×6$\frac{3}{4}$″		Sides of small cupboards
2	5$\frac{1}{2}$″×6$\frac{5}{8}$″	21″	Bases of small cupboards
2	12″×7$\frac{1}{4}$″		Doors of small cupboards
2	16$\frac{3}{4}$″×8$\frac{3}{8}$″	9″	Interior structural member

Hardwood framing

Quantity	Size	Board Size	Description	
2	21″×2″×1″	2″×1″		
1	16$\frac{3}{4}$″×2″×1″	2″×1″	Rear frame	
1	16$\frac{3}{4}$″×3″×1″	3″×1″		
2	19$\frac{3}{8}$″×2″×1″	2″×1″		all sizes nominal
2	16$\frac{3}{4}$″×2″×1″	2″×1″	Base frame	
2	12$\frac{3}{4}$″×2″×1″	2″×1″		
2	12$\frac{3}{4}$″×1″×1″	1″×1″	Wall fixing supports	

$\frac{1}{2}$″ Gaboon plywood

Quantity	Size	Description
2	15$\frac{11}{16}$″×$\frac{1}{2}$″×5$\frac{5}{8}$″	Main drawer interior fronts
2	15$\frac{11}{16}$″×$\frac{1}{2}$″×5$\frac{3}{8}$″	
4	18″×$\frac{1}{2}$″×5$\frac{5}{8}$″	Main drawer sides
4	18″×$\frac{1}{2}$″×5$\frac{3}{8}$″	
2	15$\frac{11}{16}$″×$\frac{1}{2}$″×5$\frac{1}{8}$″	Main drawer ends
2	15$\frac{11}{16}$″×$\frac{1}{2}$″×4$\frac{7}{8}$″	
1	12$\frac{1}{16}$″×$\frac{1}{2}$″×3″	Interior front vanity drawer
1	12$\frac{1}{16}$″×$\frac{1}{2}$″×3$\frac{1}{4}$″	Interior support vanity drawer
1	12$\frac{1}{16}$″×$\frac{1}{2}$″×8$\frac{1}{4}$″	Rear vanity drawer
2	16$\frac{1}{4}$″×$\frac{1}{2}$″×8$\frac{1}{4}$″	Sides vanity drawer
1	12$\frac{1}{16}$″×$\frac{1}{2}$″×3$\frac{1}{2}$″	Base vanity drawer

$\frac{1}{4}$″ Gaboon plywood

Quantity	Size	Description
1	14″×$\frac{1}{2}$″×11$\frac{15}{16}$″	Mirror back
4	15$\frac{7}{8}$″ ×$\frac{1}{4}$″×17$\frac{3}{4}$″	Main drawer bases
2	7$\frac{1}{8}$″×$\frac{1}{4}$″×5$\frac{3}{8}$″	Small cupboard shelves.

4mm birch plywood

Quantity	Size	Description
1	9$\frac{11}{16}$″×4 mm×12$\frac{1}{16}$″	Interior front section vanity drawer
1	13$\frac{5}{8}$″×4 mm×18″	Curved vanity drawer base

If you are using dowelled joints instead of tenon joints, you will also need 6 ft of $\frac{3}{8}$″ dowel.

NELSON HARGREAVES

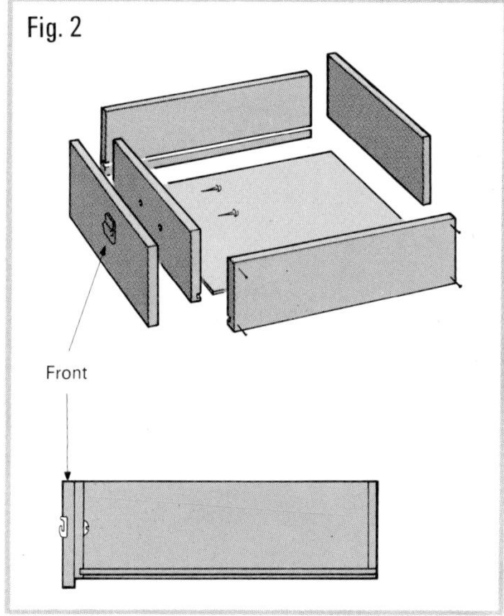

***Fig. 1** (top). Fixing the mirror to the vanity drawer, which is lined with plastic laminate.* **Fig. 2** *(above). How the main drawers are fitted together.*

Cantilevered bedhead: 2

By now you will have all the pieces cut roughly to size, and will have made the frames. The next stage is to cut the pieces to their final shape, following the exploded drawing on page 151, after which assembly can begin in earnest.

While the glue is drying on the hardwood frames, the drawers can be made. The carcases of the drawers, including the fronts, are made entirely of $\frac{1}{2}$in. gaboon plywood. The veneered fascia of each drawer is a separate piece attached later.

The four main drawers (Fig. 2) are held together with butt joints, panel pins and glue. The fascias are screwed on from inside after the glue is dry. There is quite a strain on the screws when the drawer is pulled out, so it is a good idea to spread the load on each one by putting a cup washer under the head.

The vanity drawer that goes on the woman's side of the unit does not have a flat bottom, but slides on hardwood runners that fit into grooves down the side. Rebate the grooves before putting the drawer together. They should be $\frac{3}{4}$in. wide and $\frac{3}{16}$in. deep.

Assemble the front, back, sides and central partition of the drawer first. Note that the partition is to be capped with foam plastic as protection for the mirror, and allow for the depth of both mirror and plastic when cutting the partition. When the glue is dry, steam the plywood base before curving it. It only takes a few minutes' moving the ply back and forth in the steam from a kettle to make it soft enough to bend. It is best to steam both sides of the wood to make the curve as even as possible.

When the plywood is flexible enough, glue it to the drawer frame and hold it down with cramps. If the cramps are arranged with pieces of scrap wood as shown in Fig. 4, it will help to hold the base in the correct curve. Fasten the plywood down with panel pins in between the cramps, as an extra insurance against the glue coming unstuck. When the glue is dry, take off the cramps and put in more panel pins.

The mirror top of the drawer is pivoted at the rear. The pivots should be attached before the mirror is stuck on to its plywood back.

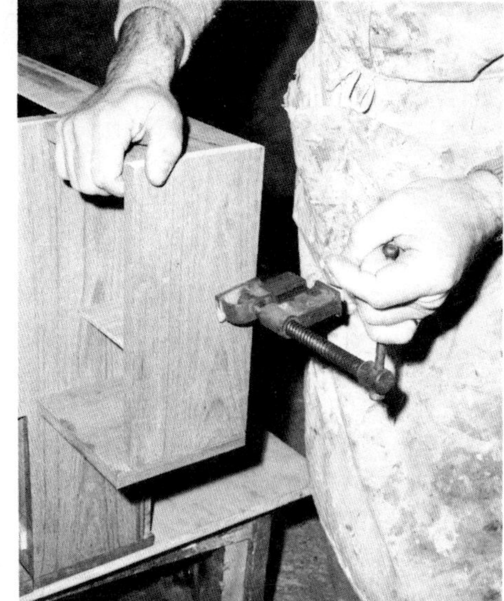

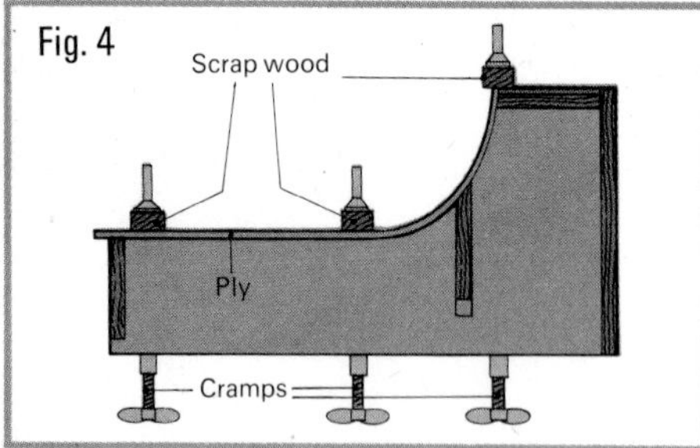

Fig. 5
Screw cup
Mirror
Backing
Washer

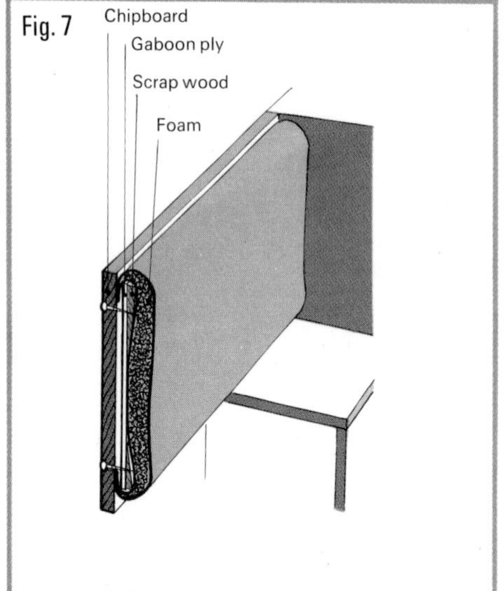

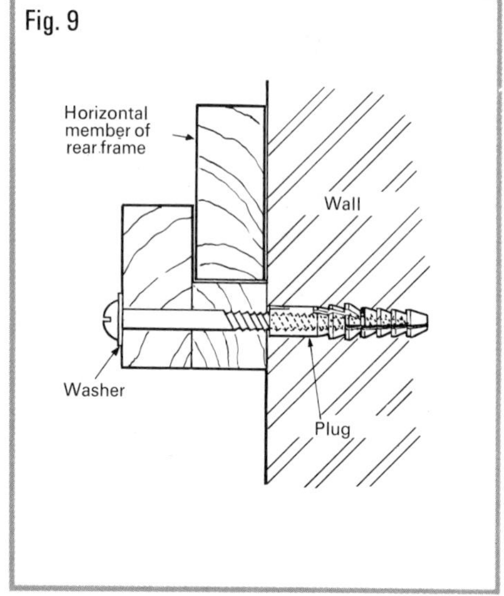

***Fig. 3** (top). Attaching the drawer slides. **Fig. 4** (next from top). Cramping the vanity drawer base into a curve. **Fig. 5** (above). An improvised pivot for the mirror.*

***Fig. 6** (top). A sash cramp holds the small cupboard in place as the glue sets. **Fig. 7** (above). A cross-section through the foam-padded headboard.*

***Fig. 8** (top). Stapling down the pvc cover of the headboard. **Fig. 9** (above). The fixing battens holding the unit to the wall, shown in cross-section.*

Proprietary pivots from a hardware shop can be used, but it is just as effective to pivot the mirror on two screws let into the plywood back through the sides of the drawer (see Fig. 5). The screw-hole should be drilled to a loose fit, and the head of the screw let into a screw cup one size too big for it, so that it turns easily. A washer between the drawer side and mirror back keeps the mirror from catching.

It is a good idea to line the inside of the drawer with plastic laminate, to protect it from spillage of cosmetics. This should be done after assembly. The mirror may be stuck to its backing with double-sided adhesive foam pads.

Assembling the cabinets

The two cabinets have quite a lot of pieces, but assembling them is straightforward provided it is done in the right order.

When cutting the cabinet components, note that the rear edge of the inner side of each cabinet is notched at the top. This notch is to take the end of the bedhead board, which passes through the cabinet side and butts up against the rear frame.

The first step in assembly is to pin and glue the hardwood drawer runners, on which the vanity drawer slides, to the inside of the front and rear panels of the woman's side of the unit.

Then screw the rear frame of each unit (marked A in the exploded drawing, Fig. 10) to the base frame B, and screw the sides C of the two large cabinets to the frames. A good carpenter would screw through the cabinet sides into the thicker frame, but this makes a mess of the veneer. You could use long screws and put them through the frame into the chipboard cabinet sides. Provided the joint is glued as well, it should have adequate strength.

Fix the interior divisions D in the two large cabinets by gluing them in place and reinforcing the joint with panel pins tapped through from the outside. The pins can be punched below the veneer and the holes filled with stopping.

Now assemble the base E, sides F, back G, top H and interior partitions I of the small side cupboards with glue and pins. When the glue is dry, glue and pin them in place, working from the inside of the main cabinets.

Fix the tops J to the main cabinets, and fasten the small lifting leaf K that folds out of the way of the mirror with one of the lengths of piano hinge. Use the other lengths to hang the doors L on the small cabinets (they open from the sides nearest the bed), and the hidden hinges to hang the fold-down flap on the man's side of the unit. The drop stay should also be fastened to this flap. Glue and pin the fronts M on each main cabinet and fit the drawers. The handles should be fitted according to the maker's instructions.

To complete the cabinets, fill all pin- and screw-holes and apply edging strip to the exposed edges of the veneered chipboard panels. Finally, lightly sand all the outside surfaces and finish with polyurethane varnish—or in any other way that appeals to you.

The headboard

While the varnish is drying, make the head-

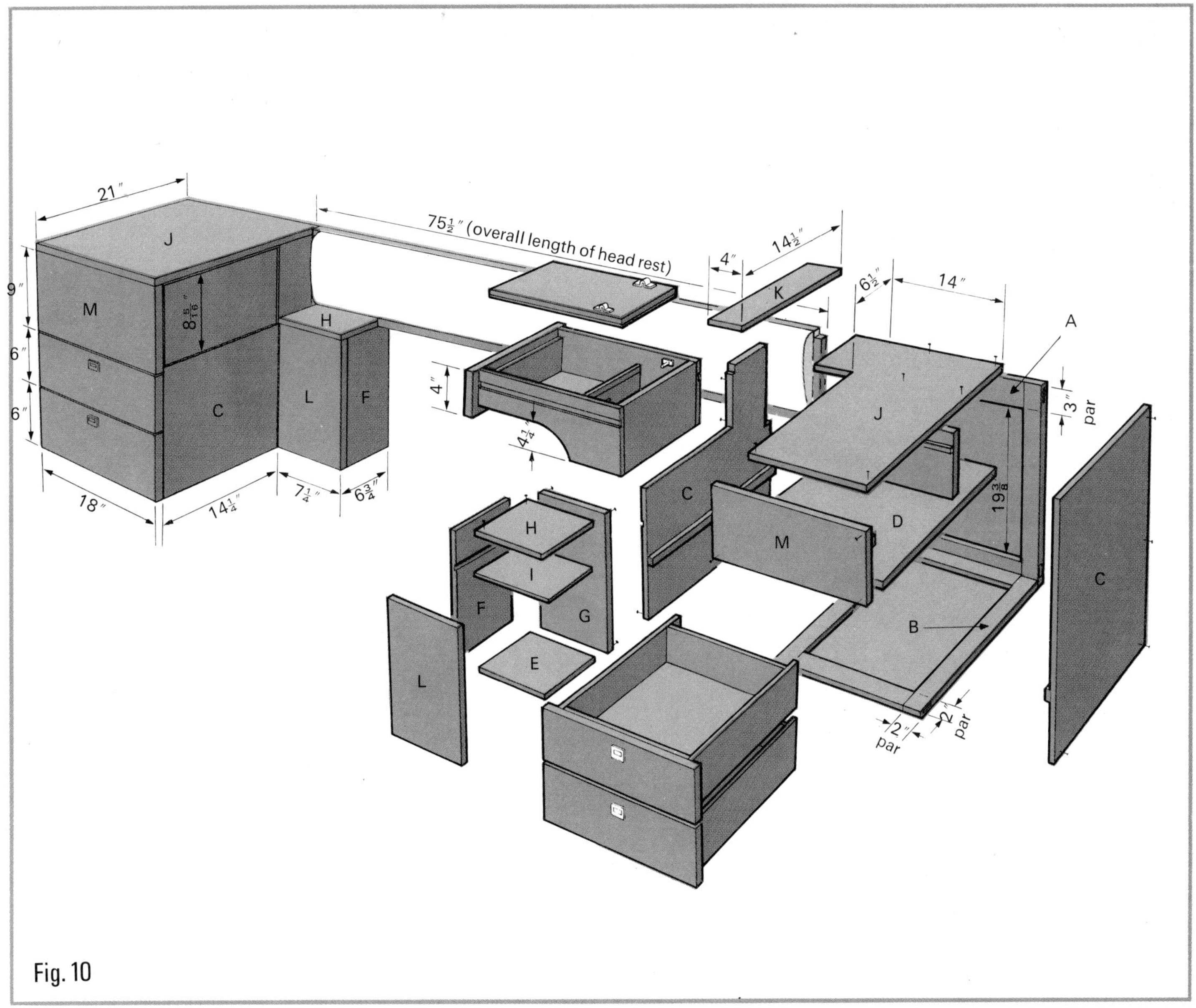

Fig. 10 (above). An exploded view of the entire bedhead unit. The side with the vanity drawer is on the right.

board. This is made from two long strips, one of chipboard and one of ¼in. ply (see Fig. 7). The ¼in. ply strip has its edges built up with scrap wood pinned into place from the rear and shaped with a rasp to a rounded contour. The pvc sheeting is wrapped over the plastic foam (which should be folded in three to make it the right width) and round the back of the ply strip to make a long padded roll. The sheeting is then stapled into place on the back of the strip, and the whole roll is screwed together with countersunk screws passing through the chipboard into the built-up sides of the ply from the rear.

Installation of the unit

This completes the assembly of the unit. It must now be fastened securely to the wall, and for this purpose some hardwood fixing battens must be made up. These are made of two strips of wood screwed together to the wall in a horizontal position so that the top one projects above the bottom one. The top strip acts as a lip that hooks over the rear frame and holds the unit up (see Fig. 9).

The battens must be very firmly fixed to the wall or there will be a danger of the unit falling off.

On a masonry wall, each batten should be fastened by at least three 4in. long No. 10 screws passed straight through both pieces of wood into a 2in. fibre plug let into the wall. The use of round-headed screws with washers under the head is recommended, to spread the load on the batten.

In a timber-frame wall, the studs are generally 16in. apart—but the battens are only just over 12in. long. The solution is to remove the plaster or plasterboard between the nearest pair of studs and insert a nogging ('bridge' piece) between them. A piece of 4in. by 2in. or 100mm x 50mm timber is sufficiently strong, but it must be anchored firmly to the studs with angle brackets and screws. After the plaster has been made good across the nogging, the batten should be fastened in place with 3in. No. 10 screws, putting washers under the heads as before.

To find the right place for the mounting battens, the following procedure is recommended: Place the units on the floor under the desired position and against the wall. Make sure they are the right distance apart by slotting the headboard between them. Take out the main drawers.

Put your hand through the hole where the drawers have been taken out and mark the inside measurements of the rear frame on the wall. Then take the units away and project the marks up the wall to the desired height.

Screw one set of battens to the wall and hang one cabinet on them. Check that it is level. Slot the headboard into the cabinet side and check it for level. At the far end, rule three short pencil marks to indicate the height and length of the headboard. This will help you locate the other battens correctly.

Provided the mounting battens are securely fixed to the wall, the unit should be quite strong enough to cope with someone putting his weight on it to lift himself from the bed. It should even stand up to someone sitting on it, provided he does not bounce up and down. If the wall is weak, the unit can be supported by screwing a leg on to each side under the front.

INDEX

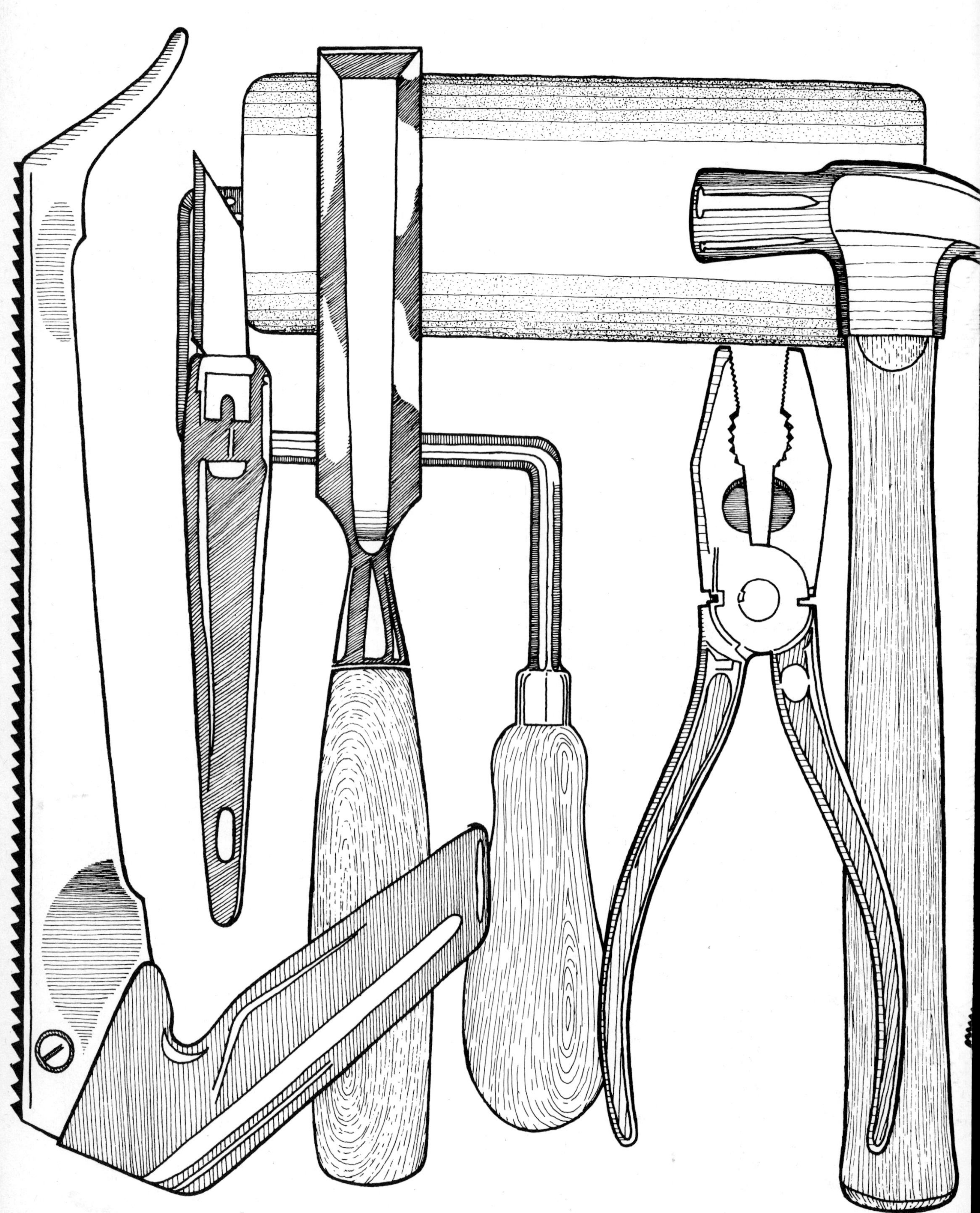